covertaction
the roots of terrorism

D0011486

William H. Schaap and **Ellen Ray** were co-founders of *CovertAction Quarterly*, the authoritative magazine which has been a multiple award-winner of Project Censored prizes for its decades of groundbreaking investigative reporting.

William Schaap is a New York attorney, who has worked with the Center for Constitutional Rights, and has testified as an expert witness on the CIA and intelligence matters in congressional and UN hearings, as well as federal, state and foreign courts.

Ellen Ray is an independent documentary filmmaker and was a consultant for Oliver Stone's "JFK." She is the co-author of *The CIA in Africa* and a two-time winner of the Project Censored Award.

covertaction

the roots of terrorism

Edited and with Introductions by
Ellen Ray and William H. Schaap

Produced by the Institute for Media Analysis, Inc.

Ocean Press
Melbourne ▪ New York
www.oceanbooks.com.au

The full texts of all *CovertAction* articles published in full or excerpted in this book will be available on the Institute for Media Analysis web site archives, www.covertaction.org. The full text of all articles published in *CovertAction Information Bulletin/CovertAction Quarterly* from 1978 through 2000, as well as all articles published by IMA in *Lies Of Our Times* from 1990 to 1995 will also be available on the web site archives.

Some articles have been slightly abridged from their original versions published in *CovertAction* magazine.

The editors wish to acknowledge the assistance of Joanna Schaap in preparing the material for publication and of Pilar Aguilera and Greg Ng in its production. Indexed by Bill Koehnlein.

PUBLISHED BY OCEAN PRESS

Australia: GPO Box 3279, Melbourne, Victoria 3001, Australia
Fax: (61-3) 9329 5040 Tel: (61-3) 9326 4280
E-mail: info@oceanbooks.com.au

USA: PO Box 1186, Old Chelsea Station, New York, NY 10113-1186, USA
Tel: (718) 246-4160

OCEAN PRESS DISTRIBUTORS:

United States and Canada: *Consortium Book Sales and Distribution*
Tel: 1-800-283-3572   www.cbsd.com
Britain and Europe: *Global Book Marketing*
E-mail: orders@globalbookmarketing.co.uk
Australia and New Zealand: *Palgrave Macmillan*
E-mail: customer.service@macmillan.com.au
Cuba and Latin America: *Ocean Press*
E-mail: oceanhav@enet.cu

www.oceanbooks.com.au

Contents

Introduction

As we write this, the world is only days away from Gulf War II and precipitously close to World War III. The administration of President George W. Bush and its corporate allies in the defense and oil industries are hell-bent on taking over the almost inconceivably vast resources of Iraq. Plans to recolonize that country have been publicly declared. Indeed, the hawks are thirsty to move on with "regime change" in Iran, Syria and Cuba. A major confrontation with North Korea appears likely, how major remains to be seen. The strong opposition of millions of people around the world is brushed aside, as is the condemnation of long-time allies.

The practical, economic forces driving this resurgent imperialism — in essence unmitigated greed — are not alone enough to explain current conditions. There are more metaphysical forces at play, undercurrents of the U.S. psyche as old as the nation itself. One such theme is U.S. exceptionalism, the notion that the United States is somehow unique, somehow beyond any need for international consensus, somehow entitled to do whatever it wants. Since the collapse of the Soviet Union, Washington has pursued a policy of unilateral, worldwide military conquest, attacking and destabilizing weak "rogue" states in the name of democracy.

This sea change in international relations has virtually destroyed hundreds of years of slowly evolving concepts of international law. The promise of the United Nations, of collective action, is moribund, if not already dead. When the United States saw UN approval for "force projection" as unlikely, it went with lesser approval, like NATO. When NATO approval was not forthcoming, it attacked with a "coalition" of allies. And when that appeared to have no chance, the president warned publicly that the United States does not need anyone's permission to do what it thinks is necessary, even if that means war, war on a large scale.

As former CIA Director Robert Gates noted prophetically in 1998, "a more militant approach toward terrorism would, in virtually all cases, require us to act violently and alone. No other power will join us on a crusade against terrorism." And this arrogant disregard for consensual international democracy was not a Republican Party monopoly; the liberal William J. Clinton led the attack on Yugoslavia, bypassing the UN, and he chuckled appreciatively when Boris Yeltsin shredded the Russian constitution and bombed his own parliament.

Another element driving this unilateralism is a form of religious funda-mentalism endemic to the United States from its earliest days, the messianic notion that the United States represents God's chosen people, God's chosen system of government, God's chosen way of life: triumphalism. In one poll, 46 percent of the people of the United States — including the president — described themselves as "evangelical" or "born-again Christians," an astonishing figure. Many of them and most of their shepherds, do not believe we should merely offer our God-given way of life to the other peoples of the world; we should foist our brand of democracy upon them whether they like it or not and by military conquest if necessary, appropriating their resources as God intended. A world composed of hundreds of U.S. protectorates. A hundred and fifty years ago, it was the "manifest destiny" of the United States to take over North America (and to wipe out its original inhabitants in the process). Today, it is as manifest that we must take over the world. God has chosen the United States to cleanse the world and George W. Bush to lead that battle.

As much of the material in this book makes clear, the strongest (and often the only) ally of this new U.S. triumphalism has been the government of the State of Israel. While many of Bush's key administration figures are indeed self-professed Zionists, many others are deeply fundamentalist Christians. Any detailed analysis of the complicated philosophical underpinnings of this alliance is beyond the scope of this book, though touched upon throughout. Yet many of the critics whose writings we have published come from a Jewish heritage, like Noam Chomsky, the son of a rabbi, and the late Israel Shahak, a Holocaust survivor, who bravely held a mirror to the Nazis' treatment of the Jews and saw reflected the Israeli treatment of the Palestinians. Because of the role of Israel as handmaiden to God's U.S. anointed, we have tried throughout to highlight the distinction between anti-Zionism and anti-Semitism. It is a distinction that is deliberately blurred in the media, for obvious purposes. It is one, however, that is necessary to an understanding of today's events.

The influence of the Israel-firsters cannot be gainsaid. It was the Jonathan Institute, described below in our introduction to *The New Red Scare*, that first promoted the notion of pre-emptive and punitive strikes. As this became U.S. doctrine, it served as an ex post facto justification for Israeli policies already in place. And it was the Jonathan Institute that provided the framework for the anti-UN sentiment that has consumed Washington.

The impetus for this collection is two-fold. Much of the world's turmoil is in response to the upsurge in U.S. imperialism, increasingly unchecked for decades. No one can truly analyze the dramatic rise in terrorism without conceding that it is largely reactive, largely driven by one brutal ploy after another by the Western powers, almost exclusively the United States. Not just invasions and wars, not just the removal of leaders distrusted by the West, not just the subversion of international institutions — but also the rape of the planet's environment, the dumping of dangerous products on the unwary of the world, and the callous disregard for the proliferation of disease and malnutrition everywhere.

Further, we believe that the ability of people around the world to attempt to withstand this juggernaut requires a sense of recent history that is often lacking, in large part due to the vise grip of imperialist, corporate media on what is reported, on what the people are told, on what they are taught.

For more than 20 years, *CovertAction* magazine reported on the relatively secret machinations of imperialism. When we began publication, few U.S. citizens even knew what the CIA was, much less what it did and had done — in stark contrast to its victims around the world. Today, much of what was done in secret in the past is done openly and one can barely imagine what continues under cover.

At the same time, our collective memory remains shockingly short-term. We believe that an understanding of events of the 1980s and 1990s is crucial to an understanding of events in the 21st century, partly because the current U.S. Administration is riddled with the aging major players of that period. We have tried to select articles from that period with critical relevance to today. It has been difficult, in the sense that events during the preparation of this book have overtaken us.

The introduction to each section of this book is designed to highlight the connections between the articles and the situation today. In some cases, the connections are by analogy; in some they are simply the continuation of unfinished or interrupted game plans. In many cases, indeed, the main players are identical. The opening section presents, somewhat eclectically, an overview, some guides to understanding the rest of the book. It moves from covert action to war to nuclear war. Ramsey Clark describes the corrosive effect on a democracy of covert operations, a guiding theme of our publications. Philip Agee presents a compelling early analysis of the future of covert and military actions, describing Paul Wolfowitz's 1992 Defense Planning Guidance, written on the heels of the Soviet demise and promoting an overarching goal for the United States: the prevention of the rise of another superpower, by any means necessary and the concomitant control of all the world's essential resources. In addition, as Agee notes, it was the first clear statement of the need for the United States to be able to act unilaterally. The paper was withdrawn in the face of protests, but reborn and reimplemented, when George W. Bush took power. It explains what the current and impending wars are all about. In "NATO and Beyond" we describe the new imperial U.S. military policies, visible after the war on Yugoslavia.

As in Israel, they will come home to civilians; no one seriously denies that Gulf War II will engender more terrorism here, not less. And, to maintain the apocalyptic sense needed to understand the vast changes in world power politics, we present Larry Jones's look at "Evangelicals for Nuclear War."

Dissent is not, as the warlords would have it, immoral; it is essential. As Albert Einstein noted, "warlike aims and activities [corrupt] the mentality of man; intelligent, objective and humane thinking is suspected and persecuted as unpatriotic." If the articles in this book provide some assistance to the arguments of the dissenters, it will have served its purpose.

Ellen Ray and William H. Schaap
March 8, 2003, International Women's Day

I. War Without End

The Corruption of Covert Actions

Ramsey Clark

Nothing is more destructive of democracy or peace and freedom through the rule of law than secret criminal acts by government. The fact, or appearance, of covert action by government agents or their surrogates rots the core of love and respect that is the foundation of any free democratic society. Every true citizen of any nation wants to be able to love her country and still love justice. Corrupt covert actions make this impossible. They are the principal source of the possibility that a contemporary U.S. poet would conceive of the lines penned by William Meredith more than three decades ago:

> Language includes some noises which,
> first heard,
> Cleave us between belief and disbelief.
> The word America is such a word.

Despite common knowledge that the U.S. Government is engaged continually in dangerous covert actions, some that can alter the futures of whole societies, most people cling desperately to the faith that their government is different and better than others, that it would engage in criminal, or ignoble, acts only under the greatest provocation, or direst necessity and then only for a greater good. They do not want information that suggests otherwise and question the patriotism of anyone who raises unwanted questions.

Our covert government's past is modest prologue to its new powers of concealment, deception and deadly secret violent actions. Too often the government is supported by a controlled, or willingly duped, mass media, by collaborating or infiltrated international governmental organizations and by key officials in vast transnational corporations.

The new evil empires, terrorism, Islam, barely surviving socialist and would-be socialist states, economic competitors, uncooperative leaders of defenseless nations and most of all the masses of impoverished people, overwhelmingly people of color, are the inspiration for new campaigns by the U.S. Government to search and Tomahawk (alas poor Tecumseh), to shoot first and ask questions later, to exploit, to demonize and destroy.

The CIA is rapidly expanding its manpower for covert operations against these newfound enemies. The National Security apparatus, with major new overseas involvement by the FBI, is creating an enormous new antiterrorism industry exceeding in growth rate all other government activities. U.S. covert actions and coverups are carried out against our own citizens within the United States with impunity.

The United States is not nearly so concerned that its acts be kept secret from their intended victims as it is that the people of the United States not know of them. The Cambodians knew they were being bombed. So did the Libyans. The long suffering Iraqis know every secret the U.S. Government conceals from the people of the United States and every lie it tells them. Except for surprise attacks, it is primarily from U.S. citizens that the U.S. Government must keep the true nature and real purpose of so many of its domestic and foreign acts secret while it manufactures fear and falsehood to manipulate the U.S. public. The reasons for and effects of government covert acts and cultivated fear, with the hatred it creates, must remain secret for the U.S. to be able to send missiles against unknown people, deprive whole nations of food and medicine and arrest, detain and deport legal residents from the United States on secret allegations, without creating domestic outrage.

As never before, it is imperative that the people of the United States care about and know what their government is doing in their name. That we be demanding of government, skeptical, critical, even a little paranoid, because not to suspect the unthinkable has been made a dangerous naiveté by a government that does unthinkable things and believes it knows best. We must challenge controlling power in America that seeks to pacify the people by bread and circuses and relies on violence, deception and secrecy to advance its grand plans for the concentration of wealth and power in the hands of the few.

(1998)

Tracking Covert Actions into the Future

Philip Agee

Once and Future Covert Operations

The current U.S. defense plan, at $1.5 trillion for the next five years, suggests that the money will be there for covert interventions. The Bush plan, largely accepted by both houses of Congress, calls for a mere three percent reduction in defense spending under projections made before the dissolution of the Soviet Union. According to Robert Gates, Director of Central Intelligence, reductions in the intelligence community budget — hidden in the overall defense budget but generally believed to be in excess of $31 billion — will begin at only 2.5 percent.[1] Meanwhile plans under discussion in Congress for reorganizing the whole intelligence community would maintain the capability and legality, under U.S. law at least, of covert operations.[2]

As the Defense Department, the CIA and other intelligence agencies have had to articulate new justifications for their budgets now that the Soviet menace is gone. In collection and analysis, announced targets include: arms control agreements; economic matters; the spread of nuclear, chemical and biological weapons; terrorism; the drug trade; Islamic fundamentalism; and regional, ethnic and national disputes. Generally they argued: With the breakup of the Soviet Union, the world is far less stable, less predictable and even more dangerous than before.

More suggestive of future intelligence operations was the 1992 series of leaks of highly classified Pentagon documents on military planning.

The first, in February, was a 70-page study projecting U.S. military requirements over the next 10 years. The report outlined seven possible scenarios which U.S. forces would have to be prepared to face and, presumably, would require those $1.5 trillion for the first five years:[3]

- war with Iraq
- war with North Korea
- simultaneous wars with both Iraq and North Korea
- a war to defend a Baltic state from a resurgent and expansionist Russia
- war to defend the lives of U.S. citizens threatened by instability in the Philippines
- war to defend the Panamanian Government and the canal against "narcoterrorists"
- the emergence of an anti-U.S. global "adversarial rival" or an "aggressive expansionist international coalition."

The following month the *New York Times* published excerpts from another classified Pentagon document revealing the latest military policy to which the war scenarios were linked. This 46-page document, known formally as "Defense Planning Guidance — 1994-99" was, according to the *Times*, the product of deliberations among President Bush, the National Security Council and the Pentagon. Its importance in prolonging U.S. militarism and the war economy into the 21st century could equal NSC-68's role in beginning the Cold War arms race in 1950.[4]

The goal of world hegemony expressed in the 1992 document should be as alarming to current U.S. friends such as Japan and NATO allies as to adversaries. "Our strategy must now refocus on precluding the emergence of any future global competitor... Our first objective is to prevent the emergence of a new rival, either on the territory of the former Soviet Union or elsewhere..."

Notably lacking was any mention of collective settlement of disputes through the United Nations, although future multilateral actions through coalitions, as in the Gulf War, were not ruled out. And in order to prevent acquisition of nuclear weapons by potential adversaries, the United States asserted the need to be ready for unilateral military action.

As for Washington's friends, both Japan and Western Europe would be locked into security arrangements dominated by the United States. Without mentioning countries, the United States "must account sufficiently for the interests of the advanced industrial nations to discourage them from challenging our leadership or seeking to overturn the established political and economic order... [W]e must maintain the mechanisms for deterring potential competitors from even aspiring to a larger regional or global role."

The document went on to suggest how to prevent Europe, with Germany in the lead, from becoming an independent regional arbiter in its own territory. "Therefore it is of fundamental importance to preserve NATO as the primary channel for U.S. influence... We seek to prevent the emergence of European-only security arrangements which would undermine NATO, particularly the alliance's integrated command structure... a substantial U.S. presence in Europe is vital..."

Publication of the globo-bully unipolar plan for the New World Order caused the diplomatic blowback one would expect, an unwanted new debate in Congress and wide criticism in the media. To no one's surprise, two months later a secret rewrite of the plan leaked again to the media — this time no doubt intended to quell the uproar from the earlier plan. Gone was the potential threat from allies and the projected global unilateralism.[5]

The first goal of U.S. defense planning in the rewrite was deterrence of attack, followed by strengthening alliances and preventing "any hostile power from dominating a region critical to our interests and also thereby to strengthen the barriers against the reemergence of a global threat to the interests of the United States and our allies." Cooperation was now the theme, although the rewrite also reserved the U.S. right to unilateral military intervention. In addition, the original seven war scenarios remained the basis for budget requests.

None of the three documents was published in full and the *New York Times* refused to share copies. Nevertheless, three observations can be made on the commentaries and excerpts that came out in the leaks. First, the rewrite did not preclude or renounce any of the ideas contained in the previous version. Second, the budget of $1.5 trillion and the base force of 1.6 million remain. Third, the purpose of the rewrite was doubtless to assuage critics and allies, while the true goal remains U.S. world hegemony.

Covert Ops Head East

Keeping in mind that covert operations, as well as overt diplomacy, are supposed to prevent war or the need to use military force — including the seven scenarios — consider how this would be done. To keep Russia from resurging, expanding and again rivaling the United States — like the sci-fi "blob" — that country must remain hopelessly indebted and dependent on imports of basic necessities. Aid must be calibrated to keep Russia stable without allowing the economy to "take off" on its own steam. For these purposes the usual instruments will suffice: the International Monetary Fund, the World Bank and the General Agreement on Tariffs and Trade. Russia's military industries must be dismantled or converted to alternative production and the country locked into security arrangements, perhaps eventually in NATO. Western experts, especially from the United States, must penetrate its economic and political decision-making and its most advanced research in science and technology. No one political party should become dominant and, where possible, Western parties should establish close working relations with Russian parties. Ultra-nationalists must be discredited and shackled along with unreconstructed remnants of the old regime. The media should be filled with Western and Western-style programming, including consumerism, infotainment for news and healthy doses of anticommunist and pro-free market propaganda. The same would hold for the other countries of the former Soviet Union.

The whole area is like Germany and Italy after World War II, wide open for a double whammy from the CIA and its new sidekick, the National Endowment for Democracy — and all the Western "private" organizations they use. As with European fascists and the scant de-nazification that occurred, the new Russia can be built on communists-turned-liberals or social democrats, or even, why not, conservatives and Christian Democrats. As after World War II[6] the usual suspects can be targeted, neutralized, or co-opted: political parties, military and security services, trade unions, women's organizations, youth and students, business, professional and cultural societies and, probably most important, the media.

Pure fantasy? Just imagine. If Carl Bernstein's long report in *Time*[7] on the 1980s operations of the CIA, NED, Vatican and their vast network to undo communism in Eastern Europe had any truth, and I believe it did, then can anyone imagine that, with their feet already through the door, they wouldn't follow up their success? The beneficiaries of this and other 1980s operations are now the key to transforming former Soviet bloc countries into traditional Third World-style markets and sources of raw materials and cheap labor. The CIA-NED team can be crucial in exercising political influence and in forming the permanent structures to assure that U.S. transnationals get their hot hands, in the race against Germany, on the resource-richest land mass on the globe.

Keeping the Government on War Footing

How to avoid another war with Iraq? United Nations sanctions and reparations payments can keep Iraq weak for a long time, while Saddam's continuation in power avoids the possibly even worse alternatives. Meanwhile covert operations can be useful for planning a cooperative, post-Saddam Iraq. Until then, we can expect cultivation of contacts within the Ba'ath movement, support for exile groups, clandestine radio and television broadcasts, joint efforts with "moderate" Arab governments and allies and occasional destabilization, like flooding the country with counterfeit currency. The Bush Administration, according to the *New York*

Times, is seeking $40 million for these covert operations in 1993, a nearly three-fold increase over 1992.[8]

How to avoid another war with North Korea? Keep South Korea strong as a deterrent and a U.S. troop presence to trigger military intervention should hostilities break out. Make certain that reunification talks lead toward the German solution, i.e., absorption of North Korea by the South. Use propaganda and cross-border contacts to foment dissidence in North Korea while conditioning any benefits on relaxation of internal controls, especially of the media. Repeat the CIA-NED strategy in Eastern Europe whenever an opening occurs. As for the Philippines, absent agrarian and other significant reforms, U.S. military intervention could be a last resort should the New Peoples' Army achieve enough momentum to create significant destabilization or even victory. For the time being, continue the CIA-Pentagon "low-intensity" methods already under way. *If* unsuccessful and stalemate continues, consider a negotiated settlement as in El Salvador and rely on CIA-NED electoral intervention to exclude the National Democratic Front from power.

The projected scenario of defending the Panama Canal from "narcoterrorists" is ironic, given the drug connections of the people that Operation Just Cause put into power. And why "narcoterrorists" would threaten U.S. access to the canal is difficult to imagine. If reports are true that drug trafficking and money laundering in Panama now exceed the Noriega era, the dealers ought to be quite happy with things as they are. With Noriega out of the way, the CIA-NED duet can take care of the local political scene, preventing resurgence of nationalism and *Torrijismo* while assuring retention of U.S. bases and control of the canal.

The same could be said of the electoral processes of any Third World country. CIA-NED preparations are no doubt already under way for defeating obvious coming electoral threats: the FMLN in El Salvador in 1994, the Workers' Party of Brazil in 1994 and the Sandinistas in Nicaragua in 1996 — to mention only three examples in Latin America. The goal is to exclude from power the likes of Jean-Bertrand Aristide, whose 1990 election in Haiti was a severe and unusual embarrassment for the system.

Many other scenarios for overt and covert intervention come to mind. The Shining Path in Peru is particularly worrisome for CIA-Pentagon planners in "regional and national" conflict management. So far, it seems, the standard "low intensity" methods have not been notably successful, nor has Peruvian Government and military cooperation been ideal. In a region where nearly half the population now lives under the official poverty line, a victory by this guerrilla force would reverberate like nothing since the Sandinista revolution in 1979. Collective action, including military intervention through the Organization of American States, might be possible in the case of Peru. Also possible is the whole range of covert and semi-covert interventions practiced against Cuba for many years and in Nicaragua, Afghanistan, Angola, Mozambique, Cambodia and elsewhere around the globe.

The Continuity of Oppression

One could go on, but the point is made. Worldwide opportunities and needs for covert operations will remain as long as stability, control and hegemony form the cornerstone of a U.S. policy that permits no rotten apples or bad examples. And the Pentagon budget is not the only indicator of continuity. In late 1991, Congress passed the National Security Education Act providing $150 million in "start-up" money for development and expansion of university programs in area and language studies and for scholarships, including foreign studies, for the next generation of national security state bureaucrats. Notable is the fact that this program is not to be administered by the Department of Education but by the Pentagon, the CIA and other security agencies.[9] Alternatives to continuing militarism, abroad and social decay at home exist, as any reader of the alternative press knows quite well. The House Black Caucus/Progressive Caucus budget, providing for 50 percent reduction in military spending over four years, got a full day's debate last March on the House floor and won 77 votes, far more than Bush's budget — stirring no mainstream reporting, non-news as it had to be. Steps toward formation of new political parties, the green movement and community organizing are also encouraging.[10]

Yet militarism and world domination continue to be the main national priority, with covert operations playing an *integral* role. Everyone knows that as long as this continues, there will be no solutions to domestic troubles and the United States will continue to decline while growing more separate and unequal.

(1992)

NATO and Beyond

Ellen Ray and William H. Schaap

Secretary of State Madeleine Albright referred to the August 1998 missile assaults against Sudan and Afghanistan (allegedly in retaliation for the U.S. embassy bombings in Africa two weeks earlier) as "unfortunately, the war of the future."[1] In one sense, she was lamenting the likelihood of various Islamic forces retaliating against U.S. civilian targets.

There is, as Albright understands, another side to these wars, more than guided missiles launched from a thousand miles away, with no danger to U.S. troops. U.S. military strategy calls for "the use of over-whelming force to minimize U.S. casualties."[2] But it is not that simple. Former CIA Director Robert Gates was more precise: "[O]ur people and our government must accept another reality: as potential official U.S. targets are 'hardened,' terrorists will simply turn to non-official targets — businesses, schools, tourists and so on. We can perhaps channel the threat away from the U.S. Government, but not away from Americans."[3] What grand scheme, then, is in place, that may bring these "unfortunate" wars back home, against civilians?

Recent U.S. strategy, to implement the administration's self-appointed role as global policeman, is now defined by its evolving military uni-lateralism, at home and abroad.

The Pathology of a Single Superpower

With the end of the Cold War and the dissolution of the Soviet Union, the United States at last realized its objective to be the world's only super-power. Though Washington — and Wall Street — had always been possessed of a rapacious ambition to control the world's economy (what "globalization" is all about), there is now the conviction in many quarters that it is developing the military capability to do so. The acting Secretary of the Air Force, F. Whitten Peters, described the development as "learning a new kind of military operations [sic] in a new world."[4]

It is unrealistic simply to wipe out every non-compliant government; and a few are too powerful for such a strategy. So the United States had devised a more comprehensive plan and now, after some 20 years, is approaching its millennial end game.

One critical element has been a redefinition of the "enemy," in order to disguise greed as a dispassionate desire to spread Western "democracy." Its complement has been the development of a military strategy for employing that definition to globalize U.S. power.

The New Enemy

It is commonplace to say that terrorism has replaced communism as the new enemy of Western democracy. But this replacement has been selectively applied, geared to the goals of U.S. global hegemony. Washington's characterization of a foreign government can change radically when little or nothing has changed in that country. The Clinton Administration's most recent pledge of more billions for defense came as the Pentagon upgraded North Korea, Iran and Iraq, which they call "rogue" states, as no longer "distant" threats of possible nuclear missile attacks, an official position they had held only a few weeks before.[5]

Of course, when this happens, it ought to raise eyebrows among the citizenry. That it doesn't is often blamed on the average U.S citizen's notoriously short political memory, but it is really due to the remarkable ability of the media to accept new policies, new "enemies," new "threats," without ever acknowledging their prior, unquestioning acceptance of the old ones.[6]

Enemies can become friends overnight, too. Recent events in Kosovo demonstrate how quickly and how hypocritically the U.S. Government recharacterizes a situation when it suits their needs. The Kosovo Liberation Army was branded a "terrorist organization" in early 1998, but by mid-year U.S. officials, including Richard Holbrooke, were meeting with its leaders, while claiming they were not in favor of Kosovan secession and the resulting inevitability of a "Greater Albania." Holbrooke was uncharacteristically frank: "I think the Serbs should get out of here."[7]

Ironically, after the CIA financed, armed and trained Islamic "friends" in Afghanistan, President Clinton now believes that the threat they pose may justify creating a new military command at home to fight terrorism. As we go to press, he is weighing Pentagon advice to establish a commander-in-chief for the defense of the continental United States, a first in peace time.

Weapons of Mass Destruction and NATO

The government and its media spin artists have incited Western fears by tarring enemy states like Iraq with the brush of "weapons of mass destruction" so repeatedly that the acronym WMD is now current jargon. Part of the "new vision" for NATO, discussed below, is to focus on WMD as a justification for military strikes anywhere, either as deterrence or as "pre-emptive retaliation." The campaign around WMD is described as "a microcosm for the new NATO and for its larger debates and dilemmas."[8] None of the analyses, however, point out that the United States is the only nation that has used all of these weapons — chemical, biological and nuclear.

The United States has employed biological weapons for 200 years, from smallpox in the blankets of Native Americans to spreading plagues in Cuba; from chemical weapons like mustard gas to cripple and kill in World War I to Agent Orange to defoliate Vietnam — and to create a generation of deformed children. It is the only nation that has dropped nuclear bombs and one that now makes, uses, and sells depleted uranium weapons.

The chemical weapons charges levied against Iraq are fraught with irony. When Iraq was at war with Iran, and the United States considered Iran the greater enemy (a view that changed under Israeli pressure), it was facilitating the sale of chemical weapons to Iraq.[9]

The weapons inspectors in Iraq claimed that their inventories of "unaccounted for" WMDs came from boxes of secret Iraqi documents discovered "hidden on a chicken farm near Baghdad,"[10] but there were easier ways to have compiled such inventories — like reviewing the CIA's reports of the secret arms deals it brokered in the 1980s.

Taking Control

For the United States, the United Nations has been a double-edged sword. Because of its Security Council veto, it can frustrate actions it opposes, but cannot always force actions it wishes.

Thus the United States has fostered — and funded — UN tribunals to punish alleged war crimes in Bosnia and in Rwanda, but would never allow such extraterritorial tribunals to investigate crimes against humanity in Indonesia, for example, or in any of its other client states. For this reason, the United States refuses to ratify the proposed International Criminal Court and opposes the trial of Augusto Pinochet in Spain.[11]

Where geographically possible, the military planners have turned increasingly to the North Atlantic Treaty Organization, which Secretary of State Madeleine Albright described as "our institution of choice."[12] NATO is not "hostage" to UN resolutions, one "strategic analyst" said.[13] A U.S. "official" explained that the UN "figures in this as far as possible," but that the new definition of NATO is meant to include the possibility of action without UN mandate.[14]

A *Times* editorial warned against "transforming the alliance into a global strike force against threats to U.S. and European interests."[15] But Secretary Albright reaffirmed that the shift is from collective defense of the NATO members' territory to "the broader concept of the defense of our common interests."[16] This means, in practical terms, the United States forcing the NATO imprimatur on military interventions in the internal affairs of sovereign states that are not members of the alliance.[17]

The UNSCOM Scam

U.S. abuse of the UN's mandate became apparent in the UNSCOM Scam. For some time, United Nations Special Commission inspectors in Iraq had attempted to gain access to President Hussein's homes and similar sites on the unlikely excuse that they could be CBW laboratories or storehouses. The media continually berated Saddam Hussein when he claimed that espionage was involved. Nonetheless, it came as a surprise to some to learn in January that U.S. spies had been operating against Iraq under cover as UNSCOM inspectors. To add insult to injury, Iraq had been forced to pay for the inspectors from its "oil for food" program income.[18]

UNSCOM was always beholden to the United States. From 1991 to 1997, UNSCOM had no UN budget, "but existed on handouts, especially from Washington,"[19] like the Hague Tribunal on Yugoslavia. He who pays the piper calls the tune.

Acting Alone

The United States has increasingly preferred NATO to the UN to avoid having its militaristic adventures vetoed. But with some disagreements within NATO as well, the Pentagon has taken to acting alone, or with a compliant ally. The August [1998] attacks on Sudan and Afghanistan were examples of totally unilateral military action by the United States. The recent bombing of Iraq, a joint U.S./U.K. operation, was taken without consulting either the UN or NATO. As one reporter noted, "the global coalition arrayed against [Saddam Hussein] in the Gulf War has been badly frayed. The United States and Britain are its only steadfast members."[20]

The arrogance of such an action (compounded by the repeated failure of its rationale, the removal of Saddam Hussein, and by the UNSCOM scandal), has generated considerable anger around the world, albeit mostly by people and governments that can do little or nothing about it but voice a "growing resentment."[21]

However, some of that resentment has clout. Russia, China and India have all voiced concerns and the recent air strikes may have prompted Russian Prime Minister Yevgeny Primakov's informal proposal for a strategic alliance between the three nations. While visiting India to discuss the initiative at the time of the attacks, he said, "We are very negative about the use of force bypassing the Security Council."[22] France and Canada also withdrew support. To the consternation of the Americans, France has formally ended its support for the embargo on Iraq, forcing a re-examination of sanctions and the tightly, restricted "oil for food" program.[23]

The "Parallel NATO"

Notwithstanding resentment and opposition, Washington is forging ahead with complex, ambitious and risky plans, if not to supplant, at least to rival NATO, whenever it balks at U.S. cowboy operations. The program is already well entrenched in Eastern Europe, where the Pentagon has bilateral military programs in 13 countries. Plans to expand into the Caucasus and former Soviet Asia are in the works.[24]

The result "is an informal alliance that parallels NATO, but is more acutely reliant on its U.S. benefactor."[25] Another consequence of this operation is that "the Pentagon is eclipsing the State Department as the most visible agent of U.S. foreign policy."[26]

Funding for some of the programs has an Orwellian flair. The U.S. European Command in Stuttgart runs a program called the Joint Contact Team Program, which was, according to the *Washington Post*, "initially paid for from a discretionary fund held by the chairman of the joint Chiefs of Staff. To work within congressional prohibitions of training foreign troops, the visits by U.S. military experts are called 'exchanges' and the experts are called 'contact teams' rather than trainers."[27]

One of the convenient side effects of the operation is the astonishing expansion of U.S. arms sales to the region. Eastern Europe "has become the largest recipient of U.S.-funded military equipment transfers after the Middle East." Some Eastern Europeans are justifiably concerned about "whether the United States is fuelling a regional arms race."[28]

Another sobering aspect of the Pentagon's preeminence is its growing collaboration with the Central Intelligence Agency. "Ever since the Persian Gulf War, when military commanders and CIA officials became convinced of the need for closer co-ordination between their services, planning for covert missions has been conducted jointly."[29]

The Consequences

Perhaps we act alone because we have to act alone. Former CIA Director

Robert Gates hinted about future wars when he wrote:

> Another unacknowledged and unpleasant reality is that a more militant approach toward terrorism would, in virtually all cases, require us to act violently and alone. No other power will join us on a crusade against terrorism."[30]

But, the terrorists having been created, the crusade goes on.

(1999)

Evangelicals for Nuclear War

Larry Jones

The "end of the world" has been an element of Christian mythology since before Christ's death. Most contemporary mainline churches in the United States and elsewhere have long since moderated this heavenly expectation, concentrating instead on the daily lives of believers. But the "end time" idea has retained all its fascination and power in a variety of U.S. Protestant churches, primarily evangelical and fundamentalist in outlook. In the "Scopes Monkey Trial" of 1925 fundamentalism was made a national laughingstock by defense counsel Clarence Darrow's eloquence and *Baltimore Sun* reporter H.L. Mencken's whiplash sarcasm.

By 1980, fundamentalist evangelicalism had made a stunning cultural comeback. The Moral Majority's claims about its contribution to the Reagan-Bush presidential victory were overblown but based on demographic facts. Once in office, Reagan himself spoke casually of nuclear Armageddon as possible because "it's in the Bible..." The close of the second millennium, or 1,000 years, since the first coming is certain to provoke an outpouring of end time expectation for the second coming of Christ. The reactions engendered by the Gulf War may offer a prelude of things to come.

Well before August 1990, many U.S. evangelical leaders were declaring the 1990s a "decade of destiny" or "the last decade." The war sparked a temporary upsurge in these millennial expectations. The ferment fits a pattern common in the post-World War II period; revivals followed the founding of Israel in 1948, the "Six-Day War" of 1967 and Israel's 40th birthday in 1988.

Propheteering Today

During the last week in January, apocalyptic tracts and images in-corporating Iraq and Saddam Hussein were prominently on display at the 1991 National Religious Broadcasters (NRB) Convention in Washington, D.C. Apocalyptic writers with books in print had quickly recycled old work, updating it for the new war. This annual trade show of religious broadcasting, less than two weeks after the U.S. attack on Iraq, hosted more than 200 evangelical organizations marketing their products and services in a huge exhibition hall.

Religious entrepreneurs displayed sweatshirts emblazoned: "Get Ready for the Big One; Jesus is Coming." A couple in fatigues hawked copies of the 91st Psalm bound in desert camouflage titled: "The Ultimate Shield." Plastic "Old Glory" lapel pins and stickers that read "Support Our Troops," both distributed free by exhibitors, were worn with pride.

The convention showcased the U.S. evangelical response to the Gulf crisis. Many of the broadcasters in attendance were convinced that the war was the prelude to Armageddon; some thought the "tribulation period" had already begun; others expected imminent "rapture"; the pru-dent cautiously avoided speculation.

The published materials on sale fleshed out the reaction of evangelical leaders and thus offered a preview of how the larger evangelical community would probably understand the war. For many evangelical writers, Iraq became the instantaneous equivalent of biblical Babylon — not the Babylon of history, but the Babylon of Daniel and the Apocalypse — a new cipher in their end-of-the-world calculus. Among the titles on display were: *I Predict the World in 1991; Armageddon, Oil and the Middle East; Toward a New World Order; The Countdown to Armageddon; The Mid-East Wars — Who Will Win?; Storm in the Desert: Prophetic Significance of the Crisis in the Gulf;* and *Islam, Israel and the Last Days.*

The New Focus of Evil in the World

As if to please, Saddam Hussein had conveniently identified himself with Nebuchadnezzar. His propaganda fit nicely with the evangelical obligation to interpret current events within the framework of biblical prophecy. As the new "Nebuchadnezzar," Saddam earned himself, virtually overnight, a starring role in evangelical expectations for the "Last Days."

In *The Rise of Babylon,*[1] Charles H. Dyer wrote:

> God declares that he will destroy Babylon when he "will punish the world for its evil, the wicked for their sins" (Isaiah 13:11). From shortly after the time of the flood, Babylon has symbolized humanity's rebellion against God. When God destroys Babylon, he will destroy all of the evil in the world.[2]

Similar imagery and language were broadcast widely over evangelical networks during the war. Member organizations of the NRB control 90 percent of all religious broadcasting in the United States and some 80 percent of religious broadcasting worldwide.[3] Within a few months, evil Iraqi Babylon became a part of United States, and perhaps worldwide, evangelical culture. Although Iraq cast as evil Babylon fell neatly into the evangelical end-time melodrama, the United States stubbornly continued to resist a biblical role. The absence of any explicit reference to the United States in Isaiah, Daniel, or other prophetic books has long troubled patriotic evangelicals, but has posed no major obstacles for their singularly circular logic. Pat Robertson, in *The Secret Kingdom*,[4] suggested a possible reference in Ezekiel 38:13, which mentions the traders of Tarchish.

Dyer's response to the dilemma shows plodding determination: "But the United States is a major world power – how could it not play a major role in the last days?" How indeed? Dyer offers several possible explanations, one of which is that because of the "rapture," which will whisk away "28 million U.S. believers," the United States will suffer a sudden and total moral and geopolitical collapse, thereby rendering it irrelevant to the writers of biblical prophecy. While all his explanations suffer the ignominy of acknowledging the decline of U.S. power, directly contradicting the official view, they balance the believers' disappointment with the consolation fantasy of a "rapture," sparing evangelicals from the most unpleasant earthly realities.

One wonders whether the overwhelming U.S. victory may have provoked a considerable confusion of emotions among evangelicals, since patriotism and prophecy – both of fundamental importance – stand in near total contradiction. But the contradiction was not universal: although before Saddam took center stage the United States was often cast as Babylon, sunk in the satanic bogs of a vile secular humanism, in the current crisis some writers seemed to equate the United States with a wrathful Jehovah come to dispense divine retribution to the evil Babylon.

Prophecy prepared believers for an extremely violent Gulf War. A video called "Saddam Hussein, The Persian Gulf and The End Times," produced in the fall of 1990 before the war began, predicted chemical and nuclear warfare and the final destruction of Iraq.

Bible verses about "Babylon" were cited as well as many more news clips about Saddam Hussein and Iraq. The lecturer, a mechanical engineer named Dr. Rob Lindsted, said he believed that the Bible predicted the destruction of "Babylon," by which he meant the annihilation of Iraq. The rather dull but bloody-minded presentation ended with the promise of rapture and a final altar call to anyone who had not yet "received Christ" during this "great time of excitement."

Evangelicals quickly became the chief religious apologists for the war against Iraq. Other Christian churches, Catholic and Protestant, refused to justify and support the war. Tel-evangelist and 1988 Republican presidential hopeful Pat Robertson was already calling for air strikes against Iraq in August 1990. Robertson has visited the White House to consult with President Bush several times since the Iraqi invasion. Billy Graham stayed the night at the White House, praying with the commander-in-chief as the bombs began falling in Baghdad.

Welcoming Nuclear War

Evangelical apocalyptic literature after World War II has shown a casual disregard for the world. The earth is viewed as disposable, its destruction imminent. Apocalyptic writers seem to relish wars and environmental catastrophes as signs from God. Such a hostile attitude toward the world has clearly had political consequences. Following the agenda of U.S. political elites, this hostility has usually focused on one or two, or even a list, of official enemies. Communism, as a vast international (and supernatural) conspiracy, has served as the chief enemy of God in the post-war era.

The typical apocalyptic scenario often includes a nuclear war, triggered by a crisis in the Middle East. Nuclear war becomes the mechanism for resolving the conflict (between the believer and the world) at the heart of this end-time drama. It is also a possible mechanism for fulfilling prophecies of world destruction in the Apocalypse of John. Looked at this way, evangelical ideology can be understood as a religious response to nuclear weapons. As in the title of Jerry Falwell's 1983 tape set and pamphlet, *Nuclear War and the Second Coming of Jesus Christ*,[5] the two events had become, Falwell wrote, "intimately intertwined." For Swaggart, prophecies of the apocalypse were also difficult to distinguish from contemporary politics. One of Swaggart's end of the world pamphlets was entitled *When God Fights Russia*.[6]

For believers, even the terrifying cloud of nuclear destruction has a silver lining: the Second Coming of Christ and the Millennial Kingdom. Belief in the rapture provides a magical escape from nuclear war, the cleansing fire needed to free the neighborhood of unrepentant backsliders, sinners and unbelievers. Popular dispensationalism thus retained its 19th century structure but took on a new, distinctly sinister emotional content after the World War II.

Evangelical apocalyptic ideology embraces nuclear weapons as a potential source of salvation. Any guilt or remorse from U.S. use of nuclear weapons was projected on to the enemy (the evil Japanese Empire, "Communism," and in 1991 "Babylon"). Nuclear weapons were seen as a reasonable response to the satanic intentions of official enemies. Demonization justified the construction of huge nuclear arsenals. Huge arsenals made war seem inevitable. And the looming threat of war counted as yet another sign of the End Times.

Evangelicals were the first to call for the use of nuclear weapons against Iraq. Representative Dan Burton (R-Ind.), a graduate of the Cincinnati Bible Seminary, urged that tactical nuclear weapons be used to destroy the Iraqi Army in Kuwait. Cal Thomas, a Washington-based journalist who once worked for Jerry Falwell and the Moral Majority, echoed the congressman's call for nuclear war in syndicated newspaper articles and on television talk shows. For evangelical opinion leaders, the utter destruction of Iraq seemed not only likely but desirable because it could be construed as a fulfillment of prophecy and a godly act.[7]

Evangelicalism and fundamentalism constitute the fastest growing segment of the U.S. religious community and have for some time. The ideology they promote, while limited in its appeal, vigorously disseminates one of the most virulent and implacable strains of U.S. militarism and xenophobia. Their "biblical" messages have injected an element of extreme irrationality into U.S. political discourse and it would be shortsighted to discount the utility of these messages for those who are wielding real power.

(1991)

II. From Cuba to Afghanistan

Instructive Examples

Introduction
Ellen Ray and William H. Schaap

The United States is the only country in the world where the terrorist attacks on September 11, 2001, are not viewed as a consequence of U.S. policy. It is true that proximity distorts perspective; but it is remarkable that, with some exceptions, the reporting and analysis of what happened was almost entirely without historical reference. Yet the record shows that the al-Qaeda network would not have been as extensive as it is and might even not have existed at all, had the United States not sponsored Islamic extremism in Afghanistan.

This is commonly understood outside the United States. No serious analyst, of course, suggests the victims were responsible, or that the hijackers of September 11 were not guilty of a crime. Yet in official and media circles in the United States, almost no memory evidently exists of the policies of just a few years ago, in the Reagan and first Bush administrations, that promoted radical, fundamentalist Islamic "holy warriors" as "freedom fighters" against the Soviet Union. Yet these, or their younger brothers, are the very people who are the core of the al-Qaeda network and its supporters.

In U.S. terms, the memory lapse is understandable. Once the U.S.-sponsored Islamic extremists had forced the Soviet Army out of Afghanistan in the late 1980s, the United States turned its back on them and on the country they were about to take over. In doing so, they neglected the possibility that the extremists might think their holy war was not over. In fact, they thought it was only beginning. They had an agenda for Afghanistan, for the rest of the Islamic world and for the "Crusaders," whom they viewed as Islam's enemies. The most important Crusader nation was and remains, the United States. Though this was understood by the CIA and other national security officials familiar with the Afghan situation, no one thought U.S. citizens needed to know.

As long as the Soviet Army was fighting in Afghanistan to support the Najibullah Government, U.S. intelligence operations, through their surrogate Pakistani services, created tribal "holy" warriors to unite under one fundamentalist, anti-Soviet banner. By using and later deserting, the people of this poor, remote country, the CIA operations ensured that Afghanistan would be ravaged by extreme fundamentalist movements, notably the fanatics the world came to know as the Taliban.

To the United States, these were mere details. When the Soviets gave up in 1989, U.S. policy makers concluded the job was done and lost all interest. As Afghanistan descended into pure anarchy, with Najibullah and his government massacred in 1992, the United States averted its gaze while first tribal extremists, then the Northern Alliance and finally the Taliban regime wreaked further havoc on the population.

To be sure, there were a few grumblings when news emerged of how the Taliban treated women and a few eyebrows were raised in the Western media when Taliban zealots destroyed the priceless Buddhist Colossi of Afghanistan. But throughout the 1990s, voices were heard repeatedly in the Arab and Muslim world warning of the monster that had been created by U.S. intelligence in Afghanistan. The United States rejected any responsibility when the holy warriors turned on other Islamic societies, notably in Algeria and Pakistan, for being too "secular" and vowing to "reform" them as they were reforming Afghanistan. Tens of thousands of people were killed in the Islamic world in the 1990s by these extremists, to the almost complete indifference of the U.S. Government and media. The truest reflection of the U.S. attitude was uttered by Zbignew Brzezinski, when he observed: "What is most important to the history of the world? The Taliban or the collapse of the Soviet empire? Some stirred-up Muslims or the liberation of Central Europe and the end of the Cold War?"

During the Cold War, Pakistan's military regime, under General Zia ul-Haq, was embraced by the United States for its anti-Soviet zeal (as was Anastasio Somoza's Nicaragua, Augusto Pinochet's Chile, Suharto's Indonesia, Mobutu's Zaire and many other allies of convenience), which, if nothing else, proves that the United States has no permanent friends, only permanent interests. Two thousand years before Machiavelli, an Asian philosopher observed that the exercise of morality and the exercise of statecraft are separate arts.

Zia's active support for the overthrow of the socialist, pro-Soviet

Government in Afghanistan was the quid pro quo for unstinting U.S. backing of his own despotic military dictatorship (to the tune of $4 billion, under Reagan, not long after Zia had rejected a $400 million offer from Carter). Pakistan became the home base for an unholy transnational *jihad*, what Zbignew Brzezinski called the "Muslim Holy War against Communism." Indeed, Brzezinski admitted recently that it was covert U.S. involvement in numerous attempts to overthrow the government of Afghanistan that caused the Soviet intervention in late 1979, not the other way around. "The U.S. secret operation," he said, "was an excellent idea. It had the effect of drawing the Soviets into the Afghan trap."

From early in the Reagan years, CIA Director William Casey met regularly with Zia, and covert assistance to his government ballooned. The CIA and Pakistan's ISI ran one after another Afghan operation, independently and jointly. The *mujahideen* never had it so good. Guerrilla training schools, dubbed "CIA U," churned out 20,000 fighters a year.

When the Taliban government was finally ensconced, it was largely due to the nurturing they received in training camps, bases, schools and other institutions established in Pakistan, with guidance from Pakistani intelligence and funding, directly and indirectly, from the United States and another client regime, Saudi Arabia. These institutions are still thriving. They have become part of Pakistani society. They are out of favor now that the dictatorial Pakistani regime is enlisted in the U.S. war on terror and, officially, Pervez Musharraf is "clamping down" on them. The U.S. public is not told that Musharraf supported these *jihadists* with U.S. approval — indeed that the *jihadists* themselves received the approval of officials, from Brzezinski on.

The United States, in other words, supported the Pakistan-Taliban alliance as long as it was convenient. And notwithstanding Musharraf's understanding of how his bread is buttered, military-political alliances of this kind cannot always be turned on and off like lights. Indeed, during the first weeks of the "war against terrorism" in Afghanistan, U.S. special forces turned a blind eye while Pakistan "evacuated" to safety from their entrapment in Kunduz hundreds of al-Qaeda and Taliban fighters, along with its own military officers and intelligence agents. The *New York Times*, the *New Yorker* and other media briefly exposed the airlift operation as approved by the White House. But U.S. officials debunked the reports and little more was heard of it or of the massacre of those left behind. A documentary film on U.S. war crimes in Afghanistan shocked Europeans in the Summer of 2002, with its evidence of the torture and murder of Taliban prisoners, but there were virtually no repercussions in the United States. Ironically, today the United States is attempting to institutionalize these crimes against humanity, with the administration providing the CIA with a "hit list" of assassination targets.

And the fact is that, nearly two years after the U.S. "liberation," Afghanistan is no more safe or secure or democratic than it had been. The United States controls a tiny area around Kabul and its forces are attacked almost every day.

In a prescient 1998 article, "*Jihad* International, Inc.," the late Pakistani scholar and activist, Eqbal Ahmad, reviewed the destabilizing conditions in Pakistan and Afghanistan in light of Islamic history, detailing the conversion, during recent decades, of an essentially secular struggle against colonialism into rabid religious fundamentalism. "As the chickens of *jihad* once nurtured by imperialism and the state come home to roost," he noted, "Afghanistan threatens to become a metaphor for the future."

It is a metaphor in more ways than one. The Islamic fundamentalism sponsored by the United States to promote its strategic interests (in a comparable way, Israel aided Hamas to weaken the PLO) is closely associated with the phenomenon of international terrorism, which lately has replaced communism as the embodiment of the "Threat," that metaphysical force the United States requires to define its foreign policy. But the U.S. definition of terrorism is profoundly distorted.

While the attention of the United States is newly focused on fundamentalism, it has refocused as well on another, closely related, phenomenon: terrorism. For some 20 years before September 11, Western corporate media toiled diligently to transform the "Enemy" from communism to terrorism — a very selective definition of terrorism that was being implanted in the collective consciousness of its audience. As Edward S. Herman notes, terrorism historically was defined as a mode of government control over its subjects; yet there has been precious little consideration of Western-sponsored state terrorism — of what Noam Chomsky and Edward Herman have dubbed "wholesale" terrorism. The media only publicize "retail" terrorism, the actions of relatively powerless "rogue states" and small organizations, or even individuals. In its time, the ANC in South Africa was deemed terrorist, not the vicious apartheid regime. The PLO was "terrorist", never the brutal policies of the Israeli Government. The Nicaraguan Sandinistas were "terrorists", not the bloody Somoza dictatorship. Carlos the Jackal is a "terrorist", not Ariel Sharon. The West's stranglehold on global media has, in large part, maintained this artificial distinction, even as the attacks on the World Trade Center and Pentagon caused so many people to ask, "Why?" This dichotomy, however, cannot explain satisfactorily the attack on the United States in September 2001. Who — or rather, what — policies created the violent international environment in which such an attack became justifiable and necessary?

George W. Bush, brushing aside the question, responded, almost without challenge, "If you're not for us, you're for terrorism." It might have been more accurate to say, "If you are not against whoever we call a terrorist on the day we define him as such, you're for terrorism."

Herman, a leading analyst of Western political doublespeak, examines this phenomenon in its largest context in "Power and the Semantics of Terrorism." International law recognizes that terrorism in time of war is not the same thing as terrorism in time of peace. It is still terrorism, however, and this must be understood if we are to understand why we are at variance with most of the world in the way we perceive the causes — and the aftermath — of September 11. If terrorism is the targeting of innocent civilians to instill fear and achieve political aims, he asks, what was Hiroshima? What were South Africa's armed attacks on the front-line states? What were the U.S.-supported policies of Chile and Indonesia? And what, indeed, are the policies of Israel, overwhelmingly funded by U.S. military aid? Herman outlines some of the rules that, unexpressed, permeate Western debate. Even ignoring statistics — the vast numbers of victims of wholesale state terrorism in contrast to the handful of victims of "rogue" terrorism — in the current climate it is still practically treason to suggest any moral equivalency at all, let alone to classify the actions of the powerless as self-defense. Palestinians only "attack"; Israelis only "retaliate." What the United States does is only "counterterror." The hypocrisy of the U.S. Government in this realm is equaled only by its brazenness. It should come as no surprise, however, that the U.S. public, mystified by years of such double standards, is confused and anxious.

In a short piece concluding this section, "Why Do They Hate Us?" Herman illustrates the depth of this hypocrisy by turning one example on its head to demonstrate the simplicity of the answer to his question.

Jihad International, Inc.

Eqbal Ahmad

The violence of Islamism has roused anxious concern throughout the world, especially the Muslim world. In the United States, the media and policy makers wage a campaign to demonize Muslims and Islam as a threat to Western interests and civilization itself. This politically motivated propaganda has been aided by the Islamic resistance to Israel's occupation of Lebanon, the West Bank, Gaza and Golan, along with such incidents as the plot to blow up New York's World Trade Center. The anti-Islam bias of media and policy makers is revealed in their double standard: They condone Israel's U.S.-aided violence – conducted on an enormous scale – while denouncing Arab resistance to it. They condemn "Islamic fundamentalism" but ignore the historic role the West played in spawning the violence of the groups and individuals they now label and denounce as terrorist. And after the West promoted the violent ideological enterprise that served its short-term interests, it largely withdrew, leaving the native peoples to pay the heaviest price.

The propaganda in the West suggests that violence and holy war are inherent in Islam. The reality is that as a worldwide movement *Jihad* International, Inc. is a recent phenomenon. It is a modern, multinational conglomerate founded not so much by fanatic *mullahs* in Teheran as it is sponsored by governments including the United States and its allies Pakistan and Saudi Arabia. It was the 1979-91 U.S.-sponsored anti-communist crusade in Afghanistan that revitalized the notion of *jihad* as the armed struggle of believers. Israel's invasions and occupation of Lebanon, the West Bank, Gaza and Golan continue to invest it with moral meaning and give it added impetus.

Never before in this century had *jihad* as violence assumed so pronounced an "Islamic" and international character. Nearly all the Muslim struggles of the 20th century were secular. The Ottomans fought their last wars on essentially secular terms — in defense of a tottering empire and, at least in the Middle East, against predominantly Muslim foes. The Egyptian national movement — from the rise of Sa'ad Zaghlul to the demise of Gamal Abdel Nasser — remained secular and explicitly Arab and Egyptian. This non-theological character was equally true of the Iraqi, Syrian, Palestinian and Lebanese national struggles. The Turks attained their liberation under the banner of intemperate secularism. Iranian nationalists fought and forged a Belgium-like constitution in 1906. In India, Muslim nationalism — opposed by an overwhelming majority of Indian *Ulema* (Muslim theologians) — defined the demand for and achievement of Pakistan. All these movements resonated among other Muslim peoples who were similarly engaged in anticolonial struggles, but none had an explicit pan-Islamic context.

Jihad — a noun meaning struggle, from the Arabic root verb *jhd* "to strive" — was a favored term among Muslims in their struggle for liberation from colonial rule. Its meaning was expansive and often secular. When my brother was expelled from school after raising the nationalist flag, for example, he was welcomed in our village as a *mujahid* — one who struggles, one who engages in *jihad*. In the Maghrib, Algerian nationalist cadres who warred against France for seven grueling years were called *mujahideen*. Their newspaper *El-Moudjahid* was edited for a time by Franz Fanon, a non-Muslim and their struggle was led by a secular organization — *Front du Liberation National* (FLN). In Tunisia, the national struggle was headed by Habib Bourguiba, a diehard Cartesian secularist who nevertheless enjoyed the title of Mujahidul-Akbar. And although the word *jihad* did occasionally appear as a mobilizing cry of the 1979 Iranian revolution, it was the cry of *Enghelab*-revolution — that sounded the uprising against the Shah. After seizing power, Iran's revolutionary government adopted *Jihad-I-Sazandegi* — *jihad* for construction — as its mobilizing call. Without significant exception during the 20th century, *jihad* was used in a national, secular and political context until, that is, the advent of the anti-Soviet war in Afghanistan.

Reagan's Holy War

Then, for the first time in this century the standard bearers of a Muslim people's struggle for liberation were Islamic parties committed to the violent overthrow of "godless communism" and dedicated to the establishment of an "Islamic state" in Afghanistan. Theirs was a *jihad* in the classical, strictly theological sense of the word. Ironically, they had the kind of support no other liberation movement had ever enjoyed: that of the Western powers. Washington and its allies supplied the *mujahideen* with an estimated $10 billion in arms and aid. They also invested in this *jihad* the legitimacy of their enormous power and the luster of their media-made glory. President Ronald Reagan treated them as glorious freedom fighters. Similarly, the United States and European media played up the war in Afghanistan as the greatest story of the 1980s. Foreign correspondents combed the Hindu Kush for stories of "Mooj" heroism. Competition for *jihad* narrative was so great that in one instance a major network, CBS, bought film of a staged battle between Islamism and Communism. As testament to the great importance and authority that Western media carry in the Third World, its Afghanistan war coverage made an enormous impact, especially on Muslim youth.

Within a year of the Soviet intervention, Afghanistan's struggle was on its way to becoming a pan-Islamic *jihad*. Hundreds, eventually thousands, of young Muslims, from as far apart as Algeria and the Philippines, Sudan and Sinkiang, traveled to Peshawar and Torkham, for military training. Under the strict guidance of various Islamic parties, they tasted the *jihad*-in-the-path-of-God and grew ideologically ripe.

Washington and its vaunted intelligence agency saw in this process a Cold War opportunity to pit militant Islam against communism. Had the Soviet Union not collapsed unexpectedly, it is likely that the United States would still be benefitting from this historic mobilization of *jihad*.

As the Afghan war raged, many knew of the violent pan-Islamic character it was assuming — with U.S. sponsorship. But no country — not Algeria, not Egypt — protested the participation of its nationals; all watched casually, then looked the other way. Pakistan, which served as a CIA conduit of U.S.-supplied arms, was hospitable to a fault. In 1986, for example, Egyptian intelligence had an effective presence in the Pakistani border town of Peshawar and excellent information on the demography of *jihad*. But it could not interfere with the agenda set by Washington, which was, after all, an ally and benefactor. It was only after the United States had cashed in its investments in Afghanistan and all hell broke loose in Algeria and Egypt, that demands for extradition started to reach Pakistan from Algiers and Cairo. But whom can Pakistanis request to rid its country of the thousands of armed zealots their own government has nurtured and continues to nurture?

Transnationalization of *Jihad*

Not since the crusades in the Middle Ages has *jihad* crossed cultural, ethnic and territorial boundaries with such vigor. Except for a brief emergence in the 19th century, pan-Islamism survived only as the abstract agenda of a microscopic minority of Muslim intellectuals and as an influence on the works of some modern writers and poets including Mohammed Iqbal.

The generalized sentiment of Muslim affinity on which pan-Islamism relied was real nevertheless and from time to time manifested itself in people's expressions of solidarity with co-religionists in Palestine, Bosnia, etc. Still, the national struggles of Muslim peoples remained national and pan-Islamism endured only as an inchoate sentiment of solidarity.

Until Afghanistan. With that war, pan-Islamism grew on a significant scale as a financial, cultural, political and military phenomenon with a worldwide network of exchange and collaboration. Myriad institutions — *madaaris*, Islamic universities, training camps and conference centers — arose in Pakistan and other places. Sensing its enormous opportunity, traders in guns and drugs became linked to the phenomenon, creating an informal but extraordinary cartel of vested interests in guns, gold and god.

Transnational involvement in the *jihad* not only reinforced links among Islamic groupings, but also militarized the conventional religious parties: Pakistan's *Jamaat-I-Islami* is an example. Until its involvement in Afghanistan, it was a conventional party, cadre-based, intellectually oriented and prone to debate and agitation rather than armed militancy. It now commands perhaps the largest number of armed and battle-hardened veterans outside of Pakistan's army and rangers. In 1948-49, its chief ideologue, Maulana Abul Ala Maududi, had rejected, on theological grounds, the notion of *jihad* in Kashmir. Today, his party openly boasts of its militant involvement there. In recent years, other conventional Islamic parties — the *Jamiat-e-Ulama-l-Islam* (JUI) and *Jamiat-e-Ulama-e-Pakistan* — have also been militarizing, thanks to their linkages with the Taliban; thanks also to their involvement in Kashmir. In addition, other armed sectarian groupings — the *Sipahe Sahaba, Lashkare Jhangvi, Harakatul Ansar, Sipahe Mohammed, Lashkare Tayba, Anjumane Sarfaroshane Islam* — have emerged to menace society no less than the state. They are all sectarian formations, apparently a far cry from Islamism as expounded by the older religious parties such as the *Jamaat-I-Islami* and JUI. Yet the fact remains that their antecedents lie with these parties and they draw sustenance from the neighboring wars, which are cast in Islamic terms. In effect, while Washington and the media blamed Iran as the source of organized Muslim rage, armed Islamic radicalism was actually nurtured in Zia ul-Haq's Pakistan with U.S. funding and CIA help.

Divisions in the Ranks

The birth of *Jihad* International coincided with another development that has had a particularly unwholesome effect on Pakistan. Following the prolonged hostage crisis during which Iranian radicals held U.S. diplomats captive in Teheran, a contest began between two versions of political Islam: the radical approach was supported by Iran; the conservative by Saudi Arabia and, until 1988, by Iraq.

While Washington was involved in this development, its logic was essentially regional. Iran's revolutionary Islamists were quite uncompromising in opposing the United States as an imperial power and in their rejection of monarchy as an un-Islamic form of government. As a pro-U.S. conservative kingdom, Saudi Arabia felt threatened by Iran. Riyadh was quick to counter Iran's proselytizing zeal and found support in such Gulf sheikhdoms as Kuwait. With the start of the Iran-Iraq war in 1980, Saddam Hussein's secular government joined in the theocratically cast campaign against Iran. Islamic organizations all over the Muslim world became beholden to one or the other side of this divide.

In countries with mixed *Sunni-Shi'a* population such as Lebanon, Pakistan and Afghanistan, this development had the greatest impact as sectarian groups and individuals found new incentive to arouse old hatreds. Although the Americans, Saudis and Iraqis may have promoted their brand of conservative Islam only to counter Iran's growing appeal, their anti-Iran campaign was easily translated into anti-*Shi'a* sentiments and actions. The *Sipahe Sahaba*, a die-hard anti-Iran, anti-*Shi'a* terrorist group in Pakistan, is one such result. It was funded first by the Saudis and then by Iraq. The terror and counterterror that followed have involved murders of Iranian diplomats and trainees, U.S. technicians, ordinary people in mosques and most recently, in a cemetery. Battles for souls often degenerate into a hankering after body counts. As the chickens of *jihad* once nurtured by imperialism and the state come home to roost, Afghanistan threatens to become a metaphor for the future.

Pakistan: Islamism's Front-line State

In Pakistan, as in Algeria and Egypt, a virtual civil war is raging between the differing hues of Islamists and the secular authoritarian government. Among these countries, Pakistan is distinguished in several ways: It was the original staging ground of *jihad* as an international movement. Unlike Algeria and Egypt, votes for Islamic parties in the last four Pakistani elections since 1988 have declined. Also unlike Algeria and Egypt, where *Sunni* majorities predominate, Pakistan is a multi-denominational country where about a quarter of the population is non-*Sunni*.

Furthermore, even Pakistan's *Sunni* are divided by theological disputes (notably between the *Barelvis* and *Deopbandis*) that have tended to turn violent. With *Sunni* against *Shi'a*, *Sunni* against Christians and *Ahmedis* and killings across the *Barelvi-Deobandi* divide, the potential for devastating violence is enormous.

Pakistan's position is also unique in that it is Islamism's "front-line state." The war in Afghanistan continues and, in numerous ways, impacts on Pakistan's internal developments. Finally, Pakistan's is an ideologically ambiguous polity; here, political paeans to Islam have served as the compensatory mechanism for the ruling elite's corruption, consumerism and kowtowing to the West. As a consequence, the fervent Islamist minority keeps an ideological grip on the morally insecure and ill-formed power elite. It is this phenomenon that explains the continued political clout of the extremist religious minority even as it has been all but repudiated by the electorate.

Pakistan is a prime example of the mayhem and official failure to address it. From the 1995 bombing of the Egyptian embassy in Islamabad to the recent massacre in Lahore's Mominpura Cemetery, this country is strewn with innocent victims of Islamist extremism. Yet, these tragedies have barely caused any reflection in Pakistan and other nations whose policies sowed the seeds of the so-called "Islamic terror."

(1998)

Power and the Semantics of Terrorism

Edward S. Herman

For the average citizen of the West, the idea of the United States as a sponsor of international terrorism — let alone the *dominant* sponsor[1] — would appear utterly incomprehensible. After all, one reads daily that the United States is leading the charge against something it calls "terrorism," and it regularly assails its allies for dragging their feet in responding to terrorism. On the other hand, the U.S. Government has organized a mercenary army to attack Nicaragua and even provided it with a printed manual of recommended acts of sabotage and murder, which has been implemented by the proxy army, at the cost of well over a thousand Nicaraguan civilian lives. The U.S. Government has given unstinting support to the apartheid government of South Africa, which has invaded and organized its own mercenary armies, to subvert a string of front-line states, again at the cost of many thousands of civilian lives.[2] The Western media, however, never refers to the United States or South Africa as "terrorist states," even though both of them have killed vastly greater numbers than Qaddafi or the Red Brigades.[3]

The reason for the Western misperception is that the powerful define terrorism and the Western media, loyally follows the agenda of their own leaders. The powerful naturally define terrorism to exclude their own acts and those of their friends and clients.

"If I don't like it, call it terrorism."

The current administration in Washington has found it possible arbitrarily to designate any group or country which it opposes as "terrorist," and this will be transmitted to the public by the mass media without serious criticism or laughter. In his speech before the American Bar Association on July 8, 1985, President Reagan named five states as engaging in serious state terrorism — North Korea, Libya, Iran, Cuba and Nicaragua. The Soviet Union was presumably omitted because of the upcoming summit meeting. The media reported that Syria had been spared as "a gesture of gratitude" to President Assad for his role in negotiating the release of 39 U.S. hostages in Lebanon.[4] The press failed to discuss the fact that South Africa and Guatemala (among others) were omitted, that Nicaragua does not murder its own citizens as South Africa and Guatemala have done on a large scale and that Nicaragua has not invaded other countries or organized subversive forces to destabilize other countries, as South Africa has done in many places and as the United States does quite openly to Nicaragua itself. The ludicrousness and hypocrisy of the United States calling Nicaragua a terrorist state was entirely unnoticed and without effect on the objective reporting by the U.S. press. With a compliant mass media, especially in the United States but also among its clients, terror is what the powerful U.S. Government declares to be terror. As it is now using the concept with audacious and arbitrary abandon, it is employing the "If I don't like it, call it terrorism" definition of terrorism.

Exclusion of State Terrorism: Retail Versus Wholesale Terror

In its semantic manipulation of terrorism and related words, a number of devices are used by the United States and its intellectual spokespersons to differentiate friends and self from "terrorists." Perhaps the most important is to confine the use of the word to nonstate actors and actions; i.e., to define terrorism as the use of violence to oppose governments.[5] This departs from standard and traditional usage, according to which terrorism is a mode of governing as well as of opposing governments by means of intimidation.[6]

By excluding governments, South Africa, Guatemala and Israel are removed from the category of terrorist, while the African National Congress (ANC), rebel groups in Guatemala and the PLO are automatically eligible. This is grotesque in terms of both numbers of victims and forms of violence employed by state and nonstate intimidators,[7] but it is extremely convenient in terms of Western priorities and interests. The governments protected by this word usage are allies, clients and self; the groups automatically made "terrorists" oppose these clients and Western defense of the status quo.[8]

To focus more sharply on the absurdity of this definitional system, I use the concepts of "retail" and "wholesale" terror: Dissident individuals and groups kill on a retail basis (that is, on a small scale, with limited technological resources to kill and with small numbers of victims); states kill wholesale.

Terrorism Versus "Retaliation"

A second important device allowing "terrorist" to be applied only to the enemy is distinguishing between terrorism and "retaliation," and simply asserting that we and our friends only "retaliate" to somebody else's "terrorism." In a sequence of violence, it is often very difficult to determine where the process began and thus the distinction between terror and retaliation is often arbitrary and depends on the ability of one side to establish its claim by sheer power. Thus, when Israel bombed Tunis, killing 20 Tunisian bystanders as well as many more Palestinians, the Reagan Administration and the West accepted this as "retaliation," even though the action at Larnaca that allegedly elicited the Tunis attack was explicitly stated by its perpetrators to have been a retaliatory act against Mossad agents involved in Israeli hijackings of ships. A note found on the body of one of the Rome terrorists speaks of vengeance for the Israeli-sponsored massacres of Palestinians at Sabra and Shatila, but this was not taken seriously in the West as making the Rome attacks merely "retaliation" for a prior terrorism.[9] As Israel is a client state of the United States, the West allows Israel to kill always in "retaliation," never as terrorism, whereas the PLO and other Palestinian groups are never allowed to be retaliating; they only engage in terrorism.[10]

Terrorists as Indiscriminate Killers

Terrorists are also sometimes distinguished from nonterrorist perpetrators of violence by an alleged randomness or indiscriminateness in their attacks. This is presumably less moral than non-random killing and the claim is used to lend an aura of evil to terrorists and benignness to the other (frequently state) killers. Well-targeted killing, however, is not evidently more decent than random killing, unless the targeted victims are thought to be deserving of their fate. If redheads, or school teachers were targeted, would this be morally superior to random killing? If, however, the targeted victims are alleged to be communists or PLO officials, in the West this may give the requisite moral aura. Frequently, of course, the targeted victims are not the only casualties, as in Tunis, but the claim of having gone after a "legitimate" target helps justify the casualties that are allegedly unintended.

As a question of fact, however, nonstate terrorists such as the Baader-Meinhof gang and PLO, or SWAPO in Namibia, or the NLF in Vietnam, have not been more prone to indiscriminate killing than state terrorists. Most nonstate dissident acts of violence are carefully targeted at some symbol of abuse and in the case of the NLF in South Vietnam, nonselective violence was punishable as alienating the popular base sought by NLF strategy. Where dissidents take hostages, of course, the victims are often random, but neither the number of such cases nor the ensuing casualties have been large. [11]

On the other hand, state terror also presents a mixed picture of targeted and indiscriminate killing. State terrorists in Latin America have deliberately sought out political activists and leaders and cadres of organized groups, but where the targeted groups are large and diverse and the term "cadres" is defined broadly (e.g., active union members), the policies are reasonably described as indiscriminate. Furthermore, state terror is often very "generous" in attacking civilians at large where these are seen as a virtual enemy population. McClintock points out that "in the case of a mass-based insurgency, seconded by the vast majority of the population, the perception of the 'innocent civilian' becomes obscured." He contends that in Guatemala and El Salvador in the mid-1980s and in the last years of Somoza in Nicaragua, the tactics of state terror "have taken on an almost random, mass-oriented form."[12] The point applies to the U.S. assault on Indochina. The essence of U.S. policy in Indochina was the massive use of firepower in the countryside, based on minimal targeting information. Civilian deaths were seen as having the merits of reducing an enemy population, forcing an exodus into the cities, arousing intense fear and occasionally even killing an enemy soldier. In the U.S. mass media, B-52 raids were generally reported to be directed at "enemy base camps," parroting the language of Pentagon press releases. This was partly true, in that the villages attacked did house a population supportive of the indigenous rebels. Clearly, however, bombing addressed to an entire rural population is reasonably described as indiscriminate. This is reflected in the staggering casualty rates that were imposed on the defenseless peasant populations.

These policies have been brought to El Salvador where the United States is now carrying out, mainly but not entirely by a proxy army and air force, a Vietnam-style anti-people's war in the countryside.[13] Casualty levels are huge, but the Western media have turned their attention to "terrorism." The same points apply to Israeli bombing raids during the 1982 invasion of Lebanon and those currently being carried out against *Shi'ite* villages in Southern Lebanon with heavy firepower directed at heavily populated civilian areas and therefore involving essentially random killing. Again, the West is not aroused and does not talk about going to the "source" of these killings; they are not "terrorism."

Terrorists as Manipulators of the Media

Another basis on which Western terrorism experts attempt to confine attention to individual and small group actions rather than the more massive state violence is by focusing on the alleged manipulation of the media by terrorists. Terrorism may even be defined by the use of violence in conjunction with a search for media publicity.[14] Some retail terrorist activities are designed to attract attention to grievances and the terrorists count on the media giving publicity to their hijackings and taking of hostages. State terrorists, by contrast, do not rely on the media in their own processes of intimidation, because their capacity for violence is sufficiently great to have the desired effects without deliberate enlistment of publicity. In fact, the problem for state terrorists is keeping the media quiet, so that violence can be carried out without undue public reaction.

As dissident terrorists seek publicity, while state terrorists shun it as interfering with their freedom to kill, it is obvious that a focus on the "theater of terror" automatically serves an apologetic function. It also allows conservatives to berate the media for "encouraging terrorism" by giving the terrorists a great deal of publicity. This involves a double deception. One is the implication that the media treat dissident terrorists sympathetically. While the media occasionally do convey some of the grievances of the terrorists and allow them to appear in a human light, media coverage of terrorist events is still heavily dominated by official views and by a focus on the fate of the victims. In the aftermath of the actions these emphases and recrimination against the terrorists are overwhelming.

The second deception is more serious. The analysts of "terror theater" fail to see the important role that publicity about dissident terror plays in sanctioning state terrorism. It was not a coincidence that the great increase in Western attention to "terrorism" has accompanied the Reagan arms buildup, placement of missiles in Western Europe and more aggressive attacks by the United States and its surrogates against Nicaraguans, Lebanese, Angolans and Salvadoran rebels. Reagan's explicit shift in emphasis from "human rights" to "terrorism" was virtual acknowledgment of support for state terrorists and simultaneous diversion of attention to lesser terrorists.[15] The great attention now given to the "theater of terror" doesn't help the retail terrorists;[16] it strengthens the claims of those who only "retaliate" to the terror of others. The Reagan Administration's manipulation of the Libyan threat, from the mythical "hit squads" of 1981 to the deliberately provoked encounters off the Libyan coast and recent direct attacks, have been designed to shift attention from the assault on Central America, the Palestinians and assorted other Arab groups and the front-line states of South Africa and to mobilize Western populations for aggressive adventures abroad. The "theater of terror" is managed from Washington to serve its perceived interests.

My Terror as "Counterterror"

Another frequently encountered concept in Western terrorism semantics is "counterterrorism." As the United States and its clients, like South Africa, El Salvador and Guatemala, do not (by definition) engage in terrorism, their attacks on their enemies require alternative words. One, as we have seen, is retaliation. But retaliation implies a response to an immediately preceding act. We need a word that allows a more continuous assault on the bases and populations of "terrorists." The gap has been filled by the concept of "counterterror." For us and our allies, immediate violent responses are retaliation; longer term attacks are counterterror. Thus, South Africa's systematic assaults on its neighbors to induce them to refuse sanctuary to the ANC and SWAPO — "terrorists" in Western semantics and political language[17] — are counterterrorism. Similarly, the massacres of peasants carried out by the Guatemalan state to root out any opposition (i.e., "terrorists") is counterterror.[18] In short, what in Western terrorism semantics is called "counterterror" is in reality a dressed up form of state (wholesale) terror.

"International Terrorism" and its Supporters

A final semantic adjustment is needed so that the Western establishment can tar certain disfavored states with the terrorist brush. This is done with the aid of the concept of an "international terrorist," who either kills across national borders or kills with the support of a foreign power. In Western terrorism semantics, a state whose agents cross a border to kill is not engaging in "international terrorism," nor is aiding a state that employs systematic violence supporting international terrorism. Thus, if the United States aids Pinochet and Botha, this is not supporting international terrorism. On the other hand, aid to the ANC, or any other group opposing government is automatically aid to international terrorists. This is enormously helpful to Botha, Pinochet and Reagan. On this system of definitions, also, aid by Nicaragua to the rebels of El Salvador makes the rebels international terrorists and the Nicaraguan Government a "terrorist state." Attacks on both are "counterterrorism." On the other hand, U.S. aid to the Salvadoran Government is exempt from any such labeling, even though it was massive killing by the U.S.-sponsored regimes in El Salvador that literally forced a guerrilla movement into existence in the early 1980s.[19] As the West is generally trying to bolster up existing regimes against threats from below, a definitional system that renders all rebels and liberation movements terrorists by virtue of receiving aid, while not doing the same for aid to a government they are trying to unseat, is extremely convenient.

A problem arises, of course, where the West itself supports rebel movements and alleged "freedom fighters," as in the case of the

Nicaraguan Contras and Savimbi in Angola. If the United States organizes and supports the Contras and South Africa (and the United States) do the same for Savimbi in Angola, strict adherence to the West's own skewed definition makes the United States and South Africa "terrorist states." How is this handled? The answer is, once again, power defines terrorism: what we and our allies do cannot be terrorism. Any incompatible definitions — even our own — must be temporarily abandoned and special exceptions made.[20]

The System of Terrorism Semantics

To summarize the Western definitional system and its consequences: If the Soviet Union gives aid to the PLO, it is supporting terrorism and is a terrorist state, because the PLO uses force to oppose Israel. That intimidation is terrorism. If the United States gives aid to Israel, which invades Lebanon, imposes collective punishment on West Bank Arabs and bombs Tunis and assorted other PLO "havens," this is not supporting terrorism because Israel only "retaliates" or engages in "counterterrorism," as does the United States. If the United States aids the Salvadoran Government as it slaughters several thousand civilians a year, this is not support of terrorism because a state killing and torturing its own citizens is excluded from the Western definition. Also, if some of the people being slaughtered are rebelling, they are "terrorists" and the allied government is slaughtering as "counterterrorism" (as in Guatemala). If the United States organizes and aids the Contras and supports South Africa as the latter invades its neighbors and organizes subversive armies across its borders, this is not terrorism either because the victims are aiding "terrorists" (and we and our allies are again "countering" terror), or by a special exemption to the especially virtuous — who also happen to own the most guns and the biggest cash balance.

(1986)

Why Do They Hate Us?

Edward S. Herman

Imagine this scenario: A major U.S. newspaper publishes an extensive interview with long-time Cuban refugee terrorist Luis Posada Carriles, in which Posada claims that his terrorist acts against Cuba over the past several decades have been funded by the Cuban American National Foundation (CANF), located in Miami. Posada, trained by the CIA for the Bay of Pigs invasion, asserts that he retains very good relations with U.S. officials, who look the other way as he organizes his terrorist operations. The paper describes several recent assassination attempts against Castro organized by Posada and several weeks after the interview, the paper reports that a further assassination attempt by Posada had fallen through because of resentment by his collaborators at his "confession."

As a result of the interview and based on other information on terrorist sites in Miami, the Cuban Government carries out secret bombing raids on Miami, knocking out the CANF building and damaging other sites, with only a modest number of "collateral" casualties. The Cubans claim the right of self-defense under Article 51 of the UN Charter, noting the ongoing activities of Posada and his own admission that the United States tolerates, if it does not encourage his terrorist activities. President Clinton, Secretary of State Albright and Defense Secretary Cohen, after considering the Cuban claims, acknowledge their justice and U.S. guilt and say that the United States will not retaliate but will instead clean out the terrorist sites.

Pretty far-fetched, isn't it? We would be outraged and Cuba would be immediately bombed in retaliation. And in fact Cuba would never attack Miami, because it would expect such retaliation. But in terms of the logic of their case for bombing Miami, it is exactly that of the United States in bombing Afghanistan and the Sudan and possibly more compelling because the terrorist attacks emanating from Miami have been going on for several decades.

The difference is that, as a superpower, we have taken upon ourselves the right to exercise force and to ignore legal processes, that seem grotesque when applied by others. This superior right is so ingrained that the public doesn't see the gross double standard involved and doesn't see that it is self-serving. The media causes the public to think that our behavior abroad is disinterested and generous. This applies to other matters. For example, we claim to be boycotting Cuba in the interest of "democracy," and even passed a "Cuban Democracy Act." But there is no "Saudi Democracy Act," and for 32 years we were closely allied with the Suharto dictatorship in Indonesia. Suharto was referred to by a Clinton Administration official in 1995 as "our kind of guy." What has driven us in these cases has hardly been generosity or a devotion to democracy; it has been the importance of oil and the access to and favorable climate for investment provided by the dictators. In both Saudi Arabia and Indonesia our policies have put us into an antagonistic relationship to popular and democratic forces in those countries.

Nevertheless, the media here do not focus on this double standard and our de facto support of convenient tyrants (for many years, even decades, including Mobutu, Marcos, the Somoza family, the Duvaliers and Trujillo).

Our double standards and opportunism go farther. In the deeply troubled Middle East, the United States not only protects the Saudi and other family dictatorships, it imposed the dictatorship of the Shah on Iran by a U.S.-organized coup in 1953 and in the 1980s it actively supported Saddam Hussein, even helping him obtain and use "weapons of mass destruction," as he fought Iran and attacked his own Kurds. The discovery that he was a bad man by invading Kuwait in 1990 and the subsequent war and extended boycott imposed on Iraq in the 1990s, may strike others as hypocritical and opportunistic. Similarly, the fact that the United States allows Israel alone to maintain a nuclear arsenal and protects each and every one of its incursions into Lebanon and steady dispossession of Palestinian homes, land and water, arouses immense anger in the Middle East.

The people of the United States are largely protected from understanding why large numbers hate us by politicians and pundits who demonize our enemies, stress the positives — and we do do decent things and support democracies, when not in conflict with business demands — and refuse to admit the elements of self-interest, opportunism and double standards in our actions, that are so obvious to many people abroad.

(1988)

The New Red Scare

Introduction
Ellen Ray and William H. Schaap

The term "blowback," though probably still unfamiliar to most people in the United States, has been used in the U.S. strategic-policy think tanks for years as an equivalent of the more down-home "chickens coming home to roost." Blowback is the result of a covert policy that may serve its purpose in the short run, but then goes awry and creates new problems for its architects at home.

No one doubts the Soviet war in Afghanistan was a catastrophe for the Afghan people, vastly increasing the destructiveness of a civil war (or more accurately, overlapping tribal conflicts) that had been endemic to the country since the downfall of the monarchy in 1973. The United States, working through Pakistani intelligence services, chose to become involved by funneling millions of dollars in assorted aid and military equipment to the most extreme fundamentalist Afghan organizations' militias. The most notorious of these were the Taliban. By the time the United States woke up to the consequences of this operation, a fundamentalist-terrorist state had taken the place of the Soviet-backed regime in Kabul and young men from across the Islamic world were launching *jihads* or joining ones already in progress on four continents: in North Africa, notably in Algeria; in South Asia; in Afghanistan itself; and on the Pakistan-India border (chiefly in Kashmir); in East Asia, in Indonesia and the Philippines and in Europe itself; and in the former Yugoslavia. The *jihadists* trained, in some cases directly, to fight against "godless communism" and hailed by the Reagan and Bush Administrations as "freedom fighters," were, as it were, on a roll. When the roll hit the World Trade Center, the former freedom fighters suddenly were transformed into terrorists and the states harboring them into "terrorist states." They were given a stark warning: turn yourselves into adjuncts of U.S. law-enforcement or be prepared to be bombed back into the stone age.

This was more than a little confusing to the U.S. public, which during the 1990s had been persuaded by its leaders that international problems were a thing of the past and, basically, there were no problems more than fluctuations in the price of stocks. But throughout the 1990s, the ex-freedom fighters who had defeated the Soviet Army in Afghanistan were not thinking about stocks. They were terrorizing the Afghan people. They were massacring Algerian villagers, as well as anyone suspected of "secular" leanings. They took part in wars in Bosnia and Kosovo.

The Taliban was hardly the first terrorist organization trained and funded by the United States. Terrorism as an instrument of state policy, though loudly condemned by the Bush Administration since September 11, 2001, has been a U.S. staple since the height of the Cold War. During its entire 43 years of existence, the revolutionary government of Cuba has been the target of U.S. intelligence-sponsored and -financed terrorism. Bombings, assassinations, economic strangulation and even biological warfare, have been used by the United States in its vengeful war against Fidel Castro. The first articles that follow, "Cuban Exile Terrorists on Rampage", and "New Spate of Terrorism", lay bare the Cuban exile terrorist network, a network still active and now comfortably ensconced in the George W. Bush Administration. Many of the figures closely related to terrorist operations in Latin America are back, advising the Bush Administration. Otto Reich, a compatriot of arch-terrorists Orlando Bosch and Luis Posada as head of Reagan's Office of Public Diplomacy in the 1980s, is Bush's Undersecretary of State for Western Hemisphere Affairs. Eliot Abrams, cynically pardoned by George H.W. Bush after his Iran-Contra conviction, is now on the National Security Council. John Poindexter, also indicted for Iran-Contra crimes, was appointed to the Pentagon's well-publicized but embarrassingly short-lived Total Information Awareness Office (for more on this, see "Iran-Contra and the Israel Lobby", in Section III below). John Negroponte, ambassador to Honduras during the worst periods of the U.S.-sponsored dirty wars against El Salvador and Nicaragua, is now ambassador to the United Nations.

Moreover, it would be a mistake to imagine that George W. Bush declared war on terrorism on September 11. Rather he "re-declared" a war that Ronald Reagan had first created and financed during a time in the mid-1980s Noam Chomsky calls "the years of death." While Jimmy Carter had used "human rights" as a focus for imposing U.S. hegemony, Ronald Reagan replaced that doctrine with his own war against "international terrorism." Within days of his inauguration, Secretary of State Alexander Haig announced that "international terrorism will take the place of human rights [as] our concern, because it is the ultimate... abuse of human rights." This fundamental shift in policy was due in large part to the influence of a shadowy Israeli-American organization, the Jonathan Institute, founded in 1979 by Benjamin Netanyahu, the future Israeli prime minister, whose brother Jonathan was killed in the commando raid on Uganda's Entebbe airport in 1976.

The Jonathan Institute became the emblematic think tank of Israeli and U.S. officials, from then Prime Minister Menachem Begin to the soon-to-be cabinet secretaries Caspar Weinberger, George Shultz and Jeane Kirkpatrick, as well as vice-presidential candidate George H.W. Bush, whose common themes, that the "war against terrorism" must take pride of place in both countries' foreign policies and that the "West" was engaged in a war to the death with "international terrorism."

The National Security state was giving way to the Counterterrorist state, with a catalogue of strategies that would come fully into the open when the September 11 attack made it possible for U.S. officials to speak without ambiguity — though with a generous degree of double standards for themselves — about their notions of appropriate response.

After the demise of the Soviet Union, the strategic equation changed only in its new definition of the Enemy. The acceptable policies of the Counterterrorist state were defined. A strong case can be made that the Jonathan Institute was established to insure not just the defeat of the Democrats in 1980, but the election of a Republican pledged to the international strategies of the Institute: Since international terrorism is the greatest threat in the world (and since international communism, led by the Soviet Union, was behind all of it — a major, no-holds-barred anti-terrorist offensive is needed; collective punishment is a necessity; civilian casualties are unavoidable collateral damage; nothing, including nuclear or chemical-biological warfare, can be ruled out. The provocative underlying message promoted was: We must not wait to be attacked, but must institute "preemptive retaliation," a formula already expressed in early meetings of the Jonathan Institute.

These themes — the backbone of Israeli policy against the Palestinians and the rationale for its continued occupation of their territory — soon became a part of the Reagan Doctrine. The precursor of the U.S.A. Patriot Act of 2002 can be found in Reagan's 1984 National Security Decision directive (NSDD) 138, authorizing paramilitary and military antiterrorist squads as well as preemptive retaliation. As one Defense Department official put it, if all else fails, "raids can be mounted to prevent an attack by killing the would-be terrorists." The directive is described in "Editorial on

NSDD 138," below. A host of programs were initiated, primarily through the Pentagon and the CIA. They are outlined in "Pentagon Moves on Terrorism." Years later, many of the NSDDs that had remained secret were declassified and they were described by Christopher Simpson in "The Uses of Counterterrorism." In particular, he underscored the vast powers granted to the then Vice-President George Bush, a former Director of Central Intelligence, who relied on these doctrines in his own presidency and bequeathed them to his son. Finally, we reprint a seminal article by Noam Chomsky, "Libya in U.S. Demonology," which demonstrates the mechanisms by which U.S. propaganda can focus national debate on small-scale, retail terrorism, to the exclusion of wholesale terrorism, such as that practiced by the United States and its allies in Libya, Guatemala, El Salvador, Israel, Nicaragua, Grenada and elsewhere. While Reagan appealed to the threat of the Evil Empire and George W. Bush appeals to the threat of Islamic Fundamentalism, the propaganda mechanisms are the same.

Cuban Exile Terrorists on Rampage

Editorial

"Fidel Castro will speak at the opening session of the United Nations...
There are those pledged not to let him leave the United States alive.
Frankly his presence in New York is an affront to thousands of Cuban
exiles who ought not passively accept it, no matter how much sacrifice
is necessary, no matter how many may have to fall, no matter how
many may be blown up."

Ultima Hora, September 9, 1979.

This chilling and provocative public call for terrorism in the gossip column
of a Cuban exile newspaper is only the latest outrage perpetrated by a
small but deadly group, created and nurtured by the CIA over the past 20
years and now, according to some, berserk and beyond the control of its
former masters.

For two decades, Cuban exile extremists have been at or near the center
of nearly every sensational terrorist action in the Western Hemisphere
and several in Europe and Africa as well. Police sources believe that the
elite of this group number less than 100, spread out within the exile
communities in New York, New Jersey, Miami and Puerto Rico. But they
are men who have known each other for 20 years, they are very hard to
infiltrate and with only a single exception they have with impunity
bombed, maimed and killed on four continents.

Their latest campaign — blatant threats on the life of Fidel Castro who
is scheduled to visit the United States sometime in October, coupled with
leaflets calling for demonstrations at and around the United Nations — is
a logical outgrowth of their hatred for the government of their homeland,
a hatred inflamed and fostered over the years by the CIA.

Throughout the 1960s and well into the 1970s, this Cuban exile network worked for the CIA and its associates not only in innumerable raids against Cuba, most notably the Bay of Pigs fiasco, but as mercenaries in the Congo and in Vietnam, as the foot soldiers of Watergate and as hired guns for the DINA of Chile and other such secret services — all of them at one time or another creations and pawns of the CIA.

But even the CIA and the FBI are beginning to realize that they have created a Frankenstein monster. The U.S. Government, quick to condemn terrorism abroad, is hosting one of the most vicious terrorist organizations on earth. The foot soldiers are dangerous, professional criminals, hit men and drug dealers. They threaten not only Cuba, which is in fact quite secure, but also the vast majority of the Cuban community in the United States, who want no part of them, as well as U.S. and foreign citizens who may have business with Cuba.

From the early 1960s these terrorists perfected their skills under Agency tutelage — the use and handling of explosives, demolition and bomb construction, and, through the Agency's and their own Mafia connections, the arts of kidnapping and assassination. They have assassinated diplomats in Washington, Argentina, Italy and elsewhere. They have blown a Cubana airliner out of the skies in Barbados, killing everyone aboard. And in recent months they have launched a frontal attack against any contact with Cuba. They have bombed the Cuban United Nations Mission in New York and the Cuban Interests Section in Washington; they have bombed travel agencies for the same reason; they have bombed newspapers for sympathetic statements about Cuba; they have even bombed a pharmacy in New Jersey to protest the shipment of medicine to Cuba.

Their only real mistake was the brazen belief that they could kill with impunity in Washington — traditionally a safe haven for diplomats. The September 1976 murder of Chilean diplomat Orlando Letelier and his associate Ronni Moffitt in downtown Washington forced the Justice Department to move with some vigor against this network. The Cuban terrorists had demonstrated that the U.S. Government no longer had any control over the monster it had created. Four underlings were caught and convicted; the U.S.-born organizer who planted the explosives, whose ties to the CIA were well established, got off with a few years' imprisonment.

Except for the Letelier-Moffitt investigation, however, there has been little movement against this network. Weapons and drugs charges are routinely dismissed or only perfunctorily prosecuted. Perhaps, like so many of the people involved in Watergate, many of the leaders of this network know too much. Yet it would seem that too much is at stake for the United States. These terrorists are a threat to many diplomats at the United Nations and in Washington. They add fuel to the arguments of those who want the UN to move from violence-torn New York City and the United States in general.

The authorities have not moved against this network, even though more and more is known about them. Their line has become more public — and more frenzied — with the commencement late last year of a dialogue between the Cuban exile community and the government of Cuba. Despite the condemnation of this dialogue by the terrorists, it has resulted in the release of more than 3,000 prisoners, the granting of exit visas to all of them and many others and blanket permission to Cubans outside the country to return to visit their relatives. The terrorists have been brutal; at a rally recently in Miami, one of the leaders of the Bay of Pigs Veterans openly threatened thousands of people in the audience. "We're not going to kill you people who visit Cuba," he said, "we're just going to make life painful for you."

In a recent article in *New York Magazine,* free-lance investigative reporter Jeff Stein has taken a close look at the terrorists, particularly the northern New Jersey community. On a side street in Union City, New Jersey, is found the public headquarters of the Cuban Nationalist Movement, a group with such illustrious alumni as Guillermo Novo Sampol, who, in 1964 fired a bazooka from Queens, New York, across the East River to the United Nations and through a window when Che Guevara was visiting. Members of the organization have been linked to major drug dealing and to almost all unsolved Cuban terrorist actions over the past several years. Although credit for most of those actions has been claimed by two groups, Omega 7 and Commando Zero, authorities are quite certain that both are merely different names for the Cuban Nationalist Movement. Indeed, Stein documents the overlapping identities quite well and quotes both federal and local officials who agree.

With all this information at hand, why have the authorities not moved more forcefully? Is it really true that with so many long-standing contacts in the Cuban exile community the government cannot infiltrate these bands of terrorists? How can they chat publicly in their newspapers and leaflets about trying to kill Fidel Castro when he visits the UN? If it were any other group, if it were the Pope, or President Carter who was being so threatened, do we seriously think that arrests would not be immediately forthcoming?

At the Sixth Summit of Non-Aligned Nations, Fidel Castro said: "It is all too well known, and has been admitted officially in the United States, that the authorities of that country spent years organizing and methodically plotting to assassinate the leaders of the Cuban Revolution, using the most sophisticated means of conspiracy and crime. In spite of the fact that these deeds were investigated and publicized by the U.S. Senate, the U.S.

Government has not deigned to give any kind of apology for those vituperative and uncivilized actions."

Perhaps the U.S. Government has ceased its attempts to assassinate the leaders of the Cuban Revolution; they have not stopped those who publicly announce they are continuing that campaign. Since the U.S. Government, most notably the CIA, organized and trained those people, one would think that its obligation to capture and destroy the Frankenstein monster is clear. It should not be left to the angry village mob.

(1979)

New Spate of Terrorism: Key Leaders Unleashed

William H. Schaap

For years, the rhetoric of the Western press has confused the public's image of terrorism. Virtually all progressive revolutionaries are referred to as "terrorists," while right-wing reactionaries are usually called "freedom fighters" or "rebels." Historically, when terrorism has applied to liberation struggles — notably the Irish Revolution of 1916-21 and the Algerian Revolution of 1957-61 — it has been in the context of a colonized people fighting the colonial settlers and occupiers.

In recent times, however, nearly all the terrorism in the world has been coming from the right, from some of the most reactionary forces in existence. Yet the effect of decades of linguistic manipulation has been to create the impression that terrorism is a weapon of the left and to obscure the real role that terrorism plays in rightist political movements. This confusion is most serious now, because of a series of events that indicates a massive increase in the use of terrorism by reactionaries, coupled with the inability of the Western powers to stem this tide, at best — or outright complicity with it, at worst.

The Antiterrorist Campaign

Some review of the posturing by the U.S. Government is in order. In March 1978, the then newly-appointed Director of the FBI, William Webster, announced with considerable fanfare the intensification of the FBI's anti-terrorism training programs. His concern, though, was not so much for innocent people as for political and commercial leaders, given the kidnappings that were occurring in Europe at the time. Only a month later the *New York Times* reported that despite Webster's assurances, the United States was woefully unprepared to deal with terrorism. Terrorism, an "operational specialist" was quoted as saying, "is like the weather. Everybody talks about it, but nobody does anything about it." But, in fact, such efforts as were mounted dealt almost exclusively with potential left-wing terrorism, indeed almost only with events such as kidnappings and takeovers of buildings. Right-wing murders and bombings were not even mentioned.

The Cuban Exiles

Yet, during this time and continuing to the present, the most visible, the most vocal, the most active terrorists in the United States have been a small group of Cuban exiles, based primarily in southern Florida and in New Jersey, operating under several names and generally well known to local authorities. This group originally was dedicated to the overthrow of the Cuban Government and concentrated its efforts in hundreds of attacks against Cuba and Cuban-related offices and personnel around the world. They were all involved in the Bay of Pigs fiasco. They were all trained, supplied and encouraged by the CIA.

During the 1960s, most of the group's efforts were directly related to their unending war against Cuba, but during the 1970s they expanded their horizons. In the words of investigative journalist Joe Trento of the *Wilmington News-Journal*, "they contracted themselves out as a hit team to provide at least two intelligence services with an assassination capability." Trento is referring to Chile's DINA and South Africa's BOSS. The group, centered around Orlando Bosch, is implicated in the killing of exiled Chilean General Carlos Prats and his wife in 1974; the attempted assassination of exiled Chilean politician Bernardo Leighton and his wife in 1975; the murder of Orlando Letelier and Ronni Moffitt in 1976; and the murder of South African economist Robert Smit and his wife in 1977.

According to a compilation of each incident attributed to this group in the October 19, 1980, *Granma,* they included, in addition to the foregoing, 85 bombings, one bazooka attack (for which Bosch served four years in prison in the United States), several shootings, four unsuccessful murder attempts and two other murders in 1979, those of Carlos Muñiz Varela, a member of the Antonio Maceo Brigade in Puerto Rico and of Eulalio J. Negrín, a Cuban living in New Jersey, who supported the dialogue between the Cuban exile community and the Cuban Government. (*New Times* magazine, on October 29, 1976, attributed "150 bombings and some 50 murders in the last two years" to Bosch, but no list was provided.)

U.S. Inaction

What is most amazing about this avalanche of terrorism is that the U.S. authorities, local, state and federal, have done virtually nothing to stop it. The conviction of the Letelier hit men was virtually the only retribution and that has been overturned. A Cuban activist living in Boston was recently quoted by *In These Times*: "The government allows the right-wing Cubans to operate with impunity. That's a fact. The government organized them, trained them and armed them years ago. Now the government has the responsibility to disarm them."

The influence of these terrorist groups is so great that they took over the processing of Cuban emigrants in Key West this spring. At a processing center staffed by 45 Marines, there were 500 "volunteers" from Brigade 2506 — the Bay of Pigs veterans. These terrorists — sometimes known as CORU (the Commandos of United Revolutionary Organizations), sometimes CNM (Cuban Nationalist Movement), sometimes Omega 7, sometimes Alpha 66, but always virtually the same group of people — must be taken seriously. Even the old-timers, particularly the Cuban Patriotic Junta, led by Tony Varona, a Cuban Government official in the 1930s and 1940s, announced in Florida October 3 that "more than 200 Cuban exile groups" were commencing a "united effort to overthrow Fidel Castro." He was accompanied by members of Omega 7, Alpha 66 and Brigade 2506.

How the members of these groups, who regularly phone newspapers and claim credit for dozens of bombings, shootings and killings, can not only walk the streets, but appear at press conferences and thumb their noses at the authorities remains a mystery. At the time of the García assassination in New York City, the Cuban Ambassador to the United States, Raul Roa Kouri, stated that the FBI knew the identities of the members of Omega 7. According to the *New York Times*, the reply of an FBI agent "who has been investigating the terrorist group for five years" was hardly reassuring: "Knowing and proving are two different things." At least that FBI agent admitted to knowing who the Omega 7 people are. The irrepressible Herbert Hetu, the CIA's press spokesman, was less honest: "It's a wild accusation," he said. "I cannot comment on something like that."

Perfidy in Venezuela

Incredible as the supposed impotence of the FBI may be, the government of Venezuela did them one better. They have thrown out murder charges against Orlando Bosch and three accomplices who had repeatedly confessed to the Cubana airliner sabotage.

The scenario was not complicated. During September 1976, Orlando

Bosch, in Caracas, Venezuela, under a false passport, conspired with three Venezuelan terrorists — veterans of a number of Bosch-planned ventures — to bomb a Cubana plane. The night of October 5, 1976, two of them, Freddy Lugo and Hernán Ricardo, left Caracas for Port of Spain, Trinidad. The third Venezuelan, Luis Posada, remained in Caracas with Bosch. The next morning, Lugo and Ricardo took the first leg of the Cubana flight, from Trinidad to Barbados, under assumed names. They planted two bombs on the plane while they were on it, one near the front and one at the rear, in the toilet. When the plane landed in Barbados, Lugo and Ricardo disembarked and took a plane back to Trinidad. Shortly thereafter, the Cubana plane took off, on its final leg to Havana. On board were 57 Cubans, 11 Guyanese and five North Koreans. Minutes after takeoff, the bombs exploded. Despite heroic efforts on the part of the pilot and copilot, the plane crashed into the sea within sight of Barbados, to which it was trying to return. Everyone aboard was killed.

The next morning, Lugo and Ricardo were arrested in Trinidad. Ricardo confessed to the Trinidadian authorities, implicating Lugo, Posada and Bosch. Lugo, in his statement, purported not to be involved in the plot, but admitted that Ricardo told him about the bombing. Both were returned to Venezuela and, along with Bosch and Posada, the four were held for trial.

The Venezuelan president at the time, Carlos Andres Pérez, determined, based on the information made available to him, that there was sufficient information to charge and detain the four. The decision was also put to a Venezuelan magistrate, who had to determine if there were sufficient jurisdictional evidence to hold the suspects. The magistrate, Judge Delia Estaba Moreno, agreed that there was sufficient evidence to hold them.

Four years went by, as various pretrial maneuvers were attempted by the defendants. In the interim, President Carlos Andres Pérez was replaced by Luis Herrera Campins and a Social Christian administration. On September 26, 1980, as the trial was to commence, the prosecutor announced to the court that the government had determined that there was insufficient evidence to proceed with the mass murder charges and asked that they be dropped, to which the court agreed.

The worldwide reaction to this obvious flip-flop was quick in coming. Protests were sent to the Venezuelan Government from many countries and scores of organizations. The Cuban Government, whose relations with the Herrera Campins Government were not good to begin with, recalled all of its diplomats from Caracas and Fidel Castro denounced the action in a speech distributed at the UN.

Former President Carlos Andres Pérez also spoke out. He said that, based on information made available to him both as president and as chief magistrate, he has "the moral conviction that those being tried were in fact guilty."

The Venezuelan military tribunal which threw out the murder charges found Bosch and Ricardo guilty of possession of false identification papers, for which they were sentenced to four and a half months in prison. However, since they are credited with time served in pretrial confinement, all four would walk out of jail as soon as the trial court decision is ratified by the military review court. That action was to have taken place within two weeks of the decision, but the court announced that it was extending the deadline by nearly two months. No reason was given, though it may be due to the world outcry against the action and the criticism which the Venezuelan Government was receiving from all quarters. It remains to be seen whether the decision will be reversed, though. If it is not, four of the most vicious and remorseless killers on earth will be walking the streets in a matter of weeks.

The Letelier-Moffitt Assassins

Bosch and his cellmates are not the only terrorists being let out. On September 15, the District of Columbia Court of Appeals reversed the convictions of Guillermo Novo, his brother Ignacio Novo and Alvin Ross. Guillermo Novo and Ross had been found guilty of the murders of Orlando Letelier and Ronni Moffitt and Ignacio Novo had been convicted of lying to a grand jury about the killings and failing to report certain information to authorities. They were convicted primarily on the testimony of Michael Vernon Townley, who had planned and helped execute the bombing and who had been returned from Chile, pleaded guilty and testified against the others in exchange for leniency. Townley was given such favorable treatment, it is understood, because of the vast personal knowledge he had of CIA operations, including its involvement with the Chilean fascists, information that never surfaced in court. In fact, he was sentenced to three-and-a-half to 10 years for the double murders and will shortly be eligible for parole. Townley was a DINA operative who worked with the notorious Chilean terrorist group Patria y Libertad during the overthrow of Allende. He testified in great detail about how he had recruited the two Cuban exiles, Novo and Ross, for the operation and himself planted the bomb in the wheel housing of Letelier's car.

Less than two weeks later, Ignacio Novo was released on $25,000 bail; no bail decision for the other two has yet been made. The government announced that it would seek a review of the appeals court panel decision from the full court; failing that, it would petition the Supreme Court to review the decision; and, if the Supreme Court declined, it would retry the men.

The legal reasons for the reversals of the convictions were not entirely unexpected and appeared to be the result of prosecutorial overzealousness. The government, unable to force the Chilean Government to extradite to the United States the real mastermind of the Letelier killing, former DINA head Juan Contreras Sepúlveda and having already given Michael Townley the deal of a lifetime, decided to go all out against the three "footsoldiers" at the bottom of the totem pole. In addition to Townley's testimony, the government secured further confessions by planting informers as cellmates of the defendants while they were awaiting trial. In between the trial and the appeal decision, however, the Supreme Court ruled that such tactics violated a prisoner's constitutional rights and that such testimony was inadmissible. With regard to Ignacio Novo, the court ruled that it was improper and unfair to put him on trial for such relatively minor offenses with two people who were on trial for a double murder. In fact, there seems no reason for the prosecutors to have insisted on trying Ignacio Novo with the others and there was probably no need for the use of the testimony of the cellmates, although of course they had no reason to know that the Supreme Court was going to denounce such a practice.

In any event, of the eight terrorists in jail — the only people charged after hundreds of bombings, shootings and murders — one is out on bail already, two more may be out on bail shortly, one will be out on parole in a few months and four more will be released in Venezuela in a matter of weeks. All of them, especially Orlando Bosch, the mastermind, have vowed consistently to continue their murderous careers.

The Killing of Felix García

Felix García Rodríguez, the protocol officer at the Cuban Mission to the United States, had been active in the student movement in Havana prior to the Cuban Revolution, twice arrested in anti-Batista demonstrations. He served as a combat militiaman after the revolution and became a journalist. After some time with the Cultural Department of the Foreign Affairs Ministry and attending the School of Diplomatic Law, he became, in 1977, an attaché at the UN Mission. He was described by a colleague to the *New York Times* as the "most widely known and the most widely liked" person at the Mission. On September 11, 1980, he became the first diplomat in the history of the United States to be murdered on the streets of New York City. Omega 7 claimed credit for the murder and said that Raul Roa, the ambassador, would be "next." The group had bombed the Cuban Mission last December and unsuccessfully attempted to assassinate Roa in March. To date, not a single person has been charged with any involvement in any of the scores of attacks on Cuban offices and personnel. Nor does any action seem likely.

Ironically, all of this is occurring at a time when the Cuban Government is attempting to be conciliatory to the U.S. Government, despite the blockade, the SR-71 overflights and the occupation of Guantánamo. The Cubans returned to the United States airplane hijackers for the first time and released all U.S. citizens in their jails. According to a recent *New York Times* report, the Cuban Coast Guard and the U.S. Coast Guard have been working together in the apprehension of drug smugglers in the Caribbean.

Conclusion

When the United States talks about antiterrorist measures, it refers almost exclusively to protection from kidnapping attempts of corporate executives, embassy personnel and other government officials. It creates the impression that all terrorism comes from the left. Yet the evidence is mounting that there are several widespread terrorist networks active in the United States, all from the extreme right. Paramilitary groups like the Klan are openly training and drilling. The Omega 7 gang openly boasts of its accomplishments and sends representatives to Florida political meetings. Brigade 2506 is actually a potent factor in Florida politics. Hit squads roam the States and even contract out for overseas work. Not only is no one being apprehended, but those who were are getting out.

The U.S. Government admits that it knows who most of these people are. That they cannot obtain an arrest, much less a conviction is incredible.

(1980)

Editorial on NSDD 138

In 1984 it is appropriate to anticipate the latest newspeak of the Reagan Administration. The most significant buzzword today is "terrorism," which term has effectively replaced "communist" or "subversive" in the jargon of the guardians of national security. After six years of building a national consciousness attuned to the issue of terrorism, however aberrantly defined through repetition of the word, the administration is playing the final cards in its hand.

On April 3, President Reagan secretly issued National Security Decision Directive 138 outlining new policies in the administration's fight against "terrorism." Details of the secret Directive were first exposed in the April 15 *Los Angeles Times*, although indications of its existence could be gleaned from the April 4 *Washington Post* report of a speech by Secretary of State George P. Shultz to the Trilateral Commission the night before. Shultz stressed the need for "preemptive actions" to stop "state-supported terrorism," and called for a "bold response" to a problem he saw exemplified by the bomb attack that killed 241 U.S. Marines at Beirut airport last October. (Predictably, he saw no need to mention the 2,000 Nicaraguans killed by the CIA's Contras or the more than 30,000 Salvadorans killed by the military dictatorship the U.S. arms and trains.) At the moment Shultz was telling his audience about the serious questions raised in a democracy responding to terrorism, he was fully cognizant that his boss had preempted public debate on the subject by unilaterally signing NSDD 138 earlier that day. The cynicism of this administration knows no bounds.

NSDD 138

Even sketchy details of the new Directive, as described in the *L.A. Times*, were chilling. It approves of preemptive strikes against terrorists as well as reprisal raids. Both concepts, of course, are highly illegal — nearly incomprehensible — in the realm of domestic law enforcement. The document also approves of the creation of FBI and CIA paramilitary squads for antiterrorism actions and the Defense Intelligence Agency is authorized for the first time in its history to use intelligence agents. A Joint Special Operations Agency has been created under the Joint Chiefs of Staff to coordinate military counterterrorist units in each service. Although the Directive stops short of authorizing assassinations (purportedly banned in 1981 by Executive Order 12333), it does authorize preemptive and retaliatory strikes which could kill not only their targets, but innocent bystanders as well. The Directive contains a "dubious morality," one "senior administration official" conceded.

The entire thrust of the document's discussion of "state-sponsored terrorism" deals only with Warsaw Pact and other socialist nations. And state-sponsored terrorism, Shultz made clear in his speech, is "a contemporary weapon directed at America's interests, America's values and America's allies." There is never any consideration of even the possibility that U.S. allies might be the perpetrators of state-sponsored terrorism. The bottom line was exposed by a Defense Department official who confirmed that if all else fails, "raids can be mounted to prevent an attack by killing the would-be terrorists." As the *L.A. Times* noted, "The most significant aspect of the administration's new tactics has been acceptance of the concept that violent preemption of a terror attack is legitimate."

On April 26 the administration dropped the other shoe; four bills were sent to Congress "to help detect and prosecute people involved in international terrorism." The proposed legislation is staggering. The Secretary of State alone is authorized to designate any country or group as "terrorist," a determination which could not then be challenged in the courts. Ten-year prison terms are prescribed for anyone who provides "any logistical, mechanical, maintenance, or similar support services" to a designated terrorist government, faction, or group. The implications, especially for the dozens of well-known and completely lawful internationalist support groups in the United States, are tremendous. Groups that send medical supplies to El Salvador or powdered milk to Nicaragua, for example, could and would be criminalized by the stroke of a pen. As the *New York Times* pointed out, this administration has frequently referred to the governments of Nicaragua, Cuba and many others, as "terrorist."

Who Really Sponsors Terrorism?

The most widespread state terrorism in the world today is that of the United

States' client regimes against their own people and their neighbors. In El Salvador, Guatemala and Honduras the populations of those countries and of Nicaragua are being tortured and killed by the thousands with U.S.-made weapons in the hands of U.S.-trained military and paramilitary personnel. In many cases, as we are slowly discovering, the personnel are North American as well. Revelations regarding the bombing and mining of Nicaraguan ports, the reconnaissance flights over El Salvador and Nicaragua and the resupply missions for the Contras, discussed in this issue, show the presence of U.S. operatives on the front lines. We have also learned that U.S. soldiers have participated in sabotage raids over the Honduran border deep into Nicaraguan territory. If this is not state-sponsored terrorism, what is?

The U.S. Government has chosen to define terrorism in its own way, but its definition is Orwellian doublethink. In the same vein, the government's repetition of a theme eventually finds its way to the front pages of the nation's newspapers as fact. A case in point is the disinformation spread by the conservative and extreme right-wing media regarding alleged drug trafficking by Cuba. Now the government has coined the word "narcoterrorism," attached the label to Cuba without a single iota of proof and the story has been accepted *in toto* by the *Wall Street Journal* (April 30).

If it is true, as a current poll indicates, that a majority of people in the United States fear the president is getting the country into a Central American war, then this insight has been gained in spite of the major media, not because of them.

(1984)

Pentagon Moves on Terrorism

Ellen Ray and William H. Schaap

To understand the increasingly confusing public debate over "terrorism," it is essential to acknowledge the ideological semanticism inherent in defining the term, particularly within the Reagan Administration. In its 1980 report on the subject, the CIA defined terrorism as "the threat or use of violence for political purposes by individuals or groups, whether acting for, or in opposition to, established governmental authority, when such actions are intended to shock or intimidate a target group wider than the immediate victims." A more precise definition was put forward recently by former CIA Director William Colby in a *New York Times* Op Ed piece (July 8, 1984). His ensuing discussion of terrorism, however, suggested that he did not comprehend his own meaning.

Colby noted that terrorism "is a tactic of indiscriminate violence used against innocent bystanders for political effect — and it must be distinguished from the selective use of violence against the symbols and institutions of a contested power, which is unfortunately a norm of international life." This is an accurate statement as far as it goes, although, as international law professor Alfred P. Rubin noted in a letter to the editor of the *New York Times* responding to Colby (July 11, 1984), it would be clearer to define terrorism as "acts committed in time of peace that, if committed by a soldier in time of war, would be war crimes."

Colby demonstrates an utter failure to grasp his own definition. He says the distinction is necessary "to distinguish 'your' terrorist from 'my' freedom-fighter or to differentiate aid to terrorists from covert support of friendly forces like the Nicaraguan Contras, or counterrevolutionary fighters. Aid to friendly guerrilla forces, from the U.S. colonists to the Afghans today, is a regular part of the international contest, whereas the indiscriminate use of violence can be denounced on a solid moral basis."

In a burst of unmitigated hypocrisy, Colby glosses over the most important issue: Suppose the "friendly forces" one aids are using indiscriminate violence as a part of their struggle? Columnist Carl T. Rowan focused on the discrepancy in the Chicago *Sun-Times* (April 30, 1984): "In the eyes of officials and citizens of a given country, a 'terrorist' is someone who is killing friends, but the murderer of political enemies is labeled a 'rebel' or a 'freedom fighter.'" Rowan's remarks were made in the context of examining the deeply ingrained double standard which infects virtually all the establishment media in this country. The bombing of the Marine barracks in Beirut and the shooting at passersby from the Libyan Embassy in London received massive coverage in the United States. But, Rowan notes, two days after the London incident, UNITA guerrillas, supported overtly by South Africa and covertly by the United States, drove a car bomb into a government building in Huambo, Angola, killing 20 Cubans and 10 Angolans. The massacre was unreported for three days and then was given barely an inch or two in the U.S. press. A more recent example is the Reagan Administration's vituperative condemnation of the alleged Libyan mining of the Red Sea contrasted with the same administration's contorted justifications for its own CIA mining of the harbors of Nicaragua.

Terrorism as War

The administration has compounded public misunderstanding by describing "international terrorism" as a war being waged against the U.S. In addition to advancing the totally unwarranted assumption that all (or even most) terrorists are on the "enemy" side, it also confuses conventional warfare with war crimes. The administration, Brian Michael Jenkins of RAND Corporation noted in *Newsday* (May 6, 1984), "has shown a tendency to define terrorism in extremely broad terms, encompassing within the term both suicide drivers in Lebanon and Marxist guerrillas in El Salvador. But if the United States treats terrorism as a component of its global contest with the Soviet Union, or of its involvement in regional conflicts in the Middle East or Central America, it risks alienating allies who might be willing to cooperate in combating terrorism but who differ with U.S. policy and methods for dealing with Marxist guerrillas, or who, for political or economic reasons, are reluctant to participate in America's battles."

In fact, when the Western nations met in London in early June [1984] to discuss "international terrorism," President Reagan and Prime Minister Thatcher suffered a setback in their plan for the conference to condemn the Soviet Union as the source of terrorism. They also failed to get agreement on establishing coordinated policies for exchanging intelligence and technical information, passing unified legislation on dealing with terrorism, or expelling large numbers of diplomats thought to be involved in terrorism.

State and Mercenary Terrorism

Indeed, right-wing ideologues have begun to speak of terrorism as if it is identical with leftist guerrilla warfare and liberation movements in general. In reality, however, the two most significant types of terrorism — state terrorism and mercenary terrorism — are in the vast majority of instances supported, or at least condoned, by the U.S. Government.

State terrorism — government by the imposition of terrorism upon its own people — is the norm for many present and past U.S. allies, although their excesses are excused as merely "moderately authoritarian" by Reagan Administration officials. Chile under Pinochet, Haiti under the Duvaliers, Paraguay under Stroessner and Guatemala, Uruguay and El Salvador under all of their recent regimes are the most obvious examples in our hemisphere. It is also the rule in South Korea, Zaire, the Philippines, South Africa (with respect to the nonwhite majority), Turkey and elsewhere.

Mercenary terrorism is a less obvious phenomenon, but one which bears the U.S. stamp. "Soldiers of fortune" everywhere commit atrocities against populations struggling to liberate themselves from the yoke of imperialism.

Because of the administration's carefully orchestrated publicity campaign — devised by the intelligence complex and its media friends — public hoopla about terrorism fingers the Soviet Union as its source, followed closely by Cuba, Libya and Bulgaria. It is interesting that little mention is made of two unassailable facts: First, within the United States there has been a considerable decline in what the FBI calls "domestic terrorist" incidents and they were never plentiful in the first place. And, second, the major "terrorist" attacks which have taken place internationally, particularly in Lebanon and elsewhere in the Middle East, have actually been nationalist and even religious in nature, not terrorist. Both Palestine and parts of Lebanon have been occupied by Israel and the warfare being waged against that occupation and its U.S. supporters is just that, war. We call the other side terrorists simply because they are the other side. How can anyone call the U.S. Marines innocent bystanders? U.S. aid to and support for Israel and its annexationist policies cannot be taken as innocent, nor can the military enforcers of that policy be viewed as bystanders.

Moreover, as the war escalates in the Middle East and the U.S. role deepens, it is inevitable that attacks on U.S. targets will proliferate. A look at the Middle East escalation bears this out. In the 1960s U.S. ambassadors and other officials were targeted, in the 1970s there were demonstrations and occupations of embassies and in the 1980s the attacks have involved massive armed actions against embassies, missions and military installations.

In his first press conference, on January 28, 1981, Secretary of State Alexander Haig said that "international terrorism will take the place of human rights [as] our concern, because it is the ultimate... abuse of human rights." This became, in a way, a self-fulfilling prophesy.

The Israeli Model

All of these developments, including the truck bombs, can be seen as developments which parallel U.S. support for Israeli policies. This year the Reagan Administration is considering emergency aid of at least $1 billion on top of $2.6 billion already approved by Congress for the new "unity" government of Prime Minister Shimon Peres. Far more than half of that aid is earmarked for military use.

Additionally, the Reagan Administration is fashioning its policies — in military training, in criminal law and even in constitutional theory — on Israeli models. There is simply no comprehension by the U.S. Government of the fact that adopting Israel's "ten eyes for an eye" rhetoric and military policy will assure the United States's future as a legitimate target of the national aspirations of the victims of Israeli aggression.

This is not a hypothetical point. The Reagan Administration, embarrassed and frustrated by the bombing of the Marine barracks in October 1983, not only used the Grenada invasion as a scapegoat for our "lost honor," but also ordered the battleship *New Jersey* to fire into Druse villages, tolerating, in the words of conservative terrorism expert Robert Kupperman, "killing hundreds of people who had nothing to do with the bombings." (*USA Today*, April 20, 1984.) Kupperman was not commenting on the morality of this retaliation, only noting how much simpler it would have been to allow the direct assassination of people thought to be involved in such bombings, "preemptive retaliation," for which the administration has since announced its wholehearted support. The London conference also discussed preemptive retaliation, but according to the *Washington Post* (June 10, 1984) these "Western democracies" produced no resolution on it because "the issue is considered too sensitive for public discussion."

"Proactive" Measures

The "latest buzzword in security circles," *Time* Magazine called it (April 30, 1984). Proactive, the opposite of reactive, is how the administration wants to respond to terrorists. Instead of waiting for them to commit a terrorist act, they should be attacked and if necessary killed, before they have a chance to commit the act. The practice of such a theory ought to require omniscience, but that does not seem to bother U.S. officials. As one told Robert Toth of the *Los Angeles Times* (April 15, 1984). "If we knew the whereabouts of Carlos, I'd recommend to the president that we go after him. I'd worry later about what we'd call it" if Carlos were killed in the process. This is from a representative of the same intelligence officialdom which loudly and repeatedly pays lip service to the regulation that prohibits assassination.

CIA Director Casey was rather blunt in his adoption of a strong retaliatory stance. In a *U.S. News & World Report* interview in April he said:

> "There's a question of deterring terrorism by sending the message that if the terrorists attack there will be retaliation. The Israelis, for example, send the message: 'If we're hit from your territory, that's your responsibility and we're going to kick you in the teeth somehow.' I think you will see more of that — retaliation against facilities connected with the country sponsoring the terrorists, or retaliation that just hurts the interests of countries which sponsor terrorism."

Developments in the United States

The use by the Reagan Administration of an amorphous public fear of terrorism to justify its increasingly repressive government has grown in leaps and bounds. For the last four years a succession of laws, regulations, Executive Orders and administrative actions, involving particularly the Pentagon and the CIA, have been put in place.

The Intelligence Support Activity

The first serious development commenced even before the new administration took office. In late 1980, in the wake of the abortive hostage rescue attempt in Iran, the U.S. Army established the super-secret Intelligence Support Activity (ISA). According to the *New York Times* (June 8, 1984), the ISA was formed "without the knowledge of the Secretary of Defense, the Director of Central Intelligence or Congress."

This group was to collect intelligence for "special operations" — a synonym for covert actions — and soon developed the capability to conduct them. According to the *Times,* the ISA then "became involved in supporting CIA covert activities in Central America, including aid to Nicaraguan rebels."

The Joint Special Operations Command

Around the same time that the ISA was created the Pentagon established the Joint Special Operations Command at Fort Bragg, ostensibly to coordinate counterterrorist activities. It has, according to the same *Times* article, "a core force of elite troops" to supplement Special Forces personnel. It also reportedly has "a separate budget for the development and procurement of special assault weapons." These special units have been providing "both equipment and personnel to the CIA for its covert operations in Central America." The command is headed by Brig. Gen. Richard A. Scholtes.

In 1982 there were also significant developments in arms transfers. The Special Defense Acquisition Fund was created to stockpile arms and equipment for quicker transfers to Third World allies. In fact, the United States now supplies about 40 percent of the Third World's arms, to the tune of $9.5 billion in 1983. *(Washington Post,* June 10, 1984.)

Executive Order 12333

In December 1981, President Reagan signed Executive Order 12333 on foreign intelligence gathering. This continued the trend toward increasing CIA power and White House support. In particular, it authorized the infiltration, manipulation and disruption of domestic organizations by the FBI and the CIA even in the absence of any evidence of wrongdoing. It also authorized the broad use of warrantless electronic and other surveillance, taking the position that constitutional warrant requirements did not apply whenever the government said it was acting for intelligence gathering purposes rather than for law enforcement purposes.

Subsequent to the promulgation of E.O. 12333, the CIA established antiterrorist attack teams and the Pentagon created a counterterrorism strike force, reportedly of about 100 to 150 personnel *(Philadelphia Inquirer,* April 22, 1984). Coordination between these two operations seems likely in view of a secret memorandum reportedly prepared by Defense Secretary Caspar Weinberger for President Reagan some time in 1983.

The Secret Weinberger Memorandum

The memorandum informs the president of a pledge by the Pentagon, to "provide a wide range of logistical support and manpower to assist CIA covert operations in Central America, including support of Nicaraguan rebels" *(New York Times,* June 8, 1984).

Apparently both the House and the Senate intelligence committees investigated whether the function of this memorandum was to circumvent congressional restrictions on spending levels for covert operations in Central America. However, the "surprise" expressed over the discovery that the planes used by the Civilian-Military Assistance mission in Nicaragua had been given by the Pentagon to the CIA and by the CIA to CMA suggests that no such investigations had been completed — or if they had, that the results were ignored.

By late 1983 it had become apparent that the CIA had upgraded its war against "terrorism" to a new level, emphasizing the infiltration and penetration of suspect groups. But, as the *Philadelphia Inquirer* pointed out, the problems raised by infiltration "may skirt the edges of the law and raise new controversies for the frequently embattled CIA." It is a logical enough argument from their point of view that to obtain the best information about an organization one must infiltrate it, but left unspoken is what the CIA must do to infiltrate such a group. An infiltrator participates, to establish his or her bona fides. Thus to learn about terrorism, the CIA will be participating in — and in some instances instigating — terrorism, a role in which the CIA has excelled in the past.

A "long-time intelligence specialist" confided to James McCartney of the *Philadelphia Inquirer* (April 22, 1984), "Some of our people may have to be a part of low-level assassinations and we will have to keep their mouths shut to protect their cover." Low-level assassinations, whatever they are, are not all they may have in mind. A congressional source told McCartney that Cuban President Fidel Castro, "once a specific target of CIA assassination attempts, may again be a potential target, this time of non-Americans but possibly with the unspoken acquiescence of the CIA."

Command Centers

For 12 years the coordination of CIA counterterrorist activities has been the purview of the Global Issues Staff, responsible for intelligence collection and analyses and for related covert operations.

The army formed the First Special Operations Command in 1982 to coordinate Special Forces activities and the Air Force created a similar unit, the 23rd Air Force, in 1983. Then, in January of 1984, the Pentagon established its own unit for coordination of "special forces operations and war plans against terrorists." This unit, the Joint Special Operations Agency, is headed by Marine Corps Maj. Gen. Wesley H. Rice. According to the Defense Department, there is a "shortfall... in doctrinal development" for guerrilla wars, a problem this Agency is "moving to correct." *(Washington Post,* June 10, 1984.) This Agency also reportedly manages a top secret commando unit with personnel from all four services. General Rice is not looking for publicity, either. He offended the members and staff of the House Intelligence Committee when he told a subcommittee in April that he did not view his organization "as an agency of interest to the intelligence oversight committee."

The 1984 Offensive

The first half of 1984 saw major offensives in both the legislative and the executive arenas. In Congress, a package of incredible antiterrorism laws was introduced by Senators Denton and Thurmond, at the request of the White House. The two most significant bills create the offense of terrorism and the offense of assisting terrorist governments, factions, or groups. The only thing clear about these proposed laws is that they would be used selectively, against supporters of the administration's enemies, not against the backers of its friends.

Conclusion

It is not only because of the administration's blatant double standards that we should worry about the sanctimonious campaign against terrorism; it is not simply that they disapprove of terrorism in Lebanon but approve of it in Nicaragua. It is also that they do not understand — or if they do, they are decidedly disingenuous — the causes and meaning of what they call terrorism, either historically or contemporarily. As history Professor Thomas Goldstein put it in a letter to the *New York Times* (June 17, 1984), "Modern terrorism... is the modern individual's rejection, under desperate provocation, of physically intolerable infringements of his rights... What keeps our present world in turmoil... is that during the last century the West has spread its gospel of individual self-assertion clear around the globe."

(1984)

The Uses of "Counterterrorism"

Christopher Simpson

During the Reagan years, George Bush used "crisis management" and "counterterrorism" as vehicles for running key parts of the clandestine side of the U.S. Government.

Bush proved especially adept at plausible denial. Some measure of his skill in avoiding responsibility can be taken from the fact that even after the Iran-Contra affair blew the Reagan Administration apart, Bush went on to become the "foreign policy president," while CIA Director William Casey, by then conveniently dead, took most of the blame for a number of covert foreign policy debacles that Bush had set in motion.

The trail of National Security Decision Directives (NSDDs) left by the Reagan Administration begins to tell the story. True, much remains classified and still more was never committed to paper in the first place. Even so, the main picture is clear: As vice-president, George Bush was at the center of secret wars, political murders and America's convoluted oil politics in the Middle East.

The Reagan-era National Security Council (NSC) used NSDDs to formulate high-level policy on political and military matters. The directives ranged from presidential orders for testing nuclear weapons to negotiating strategies for U.S. representatives at various international summits.

Reagan and the NSC also used NSDDs to settle conflicts among security agencies over bureaucratic turf and lines of command. It is through that prism that we see the first glimmers of Vice-President Bush's role in clandestine operations during the 1980s.

NSDD 3. Crisis Management (Confidential, Sanitized Version), December 14, 1981

When the Reagan Administration began, Secretary of State Alexander Haig tried to write a large crisis management role for himself into draft presidential orders. Bush and NSC Adviser Richard Allen blocked the maneuver.

After Reagan was wounded in an assassination attempt in early 1981, Bush engineered NSC approval for an interagency crisis management committee that reported to him. The working assumption was that Reagan would leave the difficult decisions to Bush and the NSC, which would assume de facto presidential powers during a crisis, including the authority to wage war or to declare martial law.

Haig, who was on the NSC, later wrote that he first learned of the vice-president's move from a newspaper report.[1]

The Crisis Management Group was the first of a series of names for a senior deputies' committee through which the vice-president handled crisis management, covert operations and particularly sensitive foreign policy initiatives. Later names for substantially the same committee included the Special Situations Group, Crisis Pre-Planning Group, Planning and Coordinating Group and the Policy Review Group.

NSDD 30. Managing Terrorist Incidents, April 10, 1982

During the Reagan-Bush years, "terrorism" was a label that could be applied to tactics of almost any opposition group who would not play by White House rules. By taking on administrative responsibility for dealing with terrorism, Bush extended his administrative turf to include almost every aspect of clandestine security policy.

NSDD 138. Preemptive Strikes Against Suspected Terrorists, (Declassified Fragment, Classification Level of Original Text Not Disclosed), possible date April 3, 1984

On March 16, 1984, Islamic guerrillas kidnapped William Buckley, CIA chief of station in Beirut. One result was presidential authorization of NSDD 138, a de facto U.S. declaration of war against Islamic guerrilla groups in the Middle East and Northern Africa.

The still-classified portions of the directive authorized establishing secret FBI and CIA paramilitary squads and use of existing Pentagon military units such as the Green Berets and Navy SEALs for conducting what amounted to guerrilla war against guerrillas.[2] It authorized sabotage, killing (though not "assassination"), preemptive and retaliatory raids, deception and a significantly expanded intelligence collection program aimed at suspected radicals and people regarded as sympathizers.

("Assassination," in CIA parlance, referred to the murder of heads of state and was barred by a presidential order first issued during the Ford Administration. Killing suspected guerrillas and lower-level state officials, in contrast, was regarded as "preemptive self-defense.") The order placed special stress on campaigns against Iran, Libya, Syria, Cuba, Nicaragua, North Korea and the Soviet Union.

The NSC has thus far released only a one-page "extract" of sentences from this original order. Other portions of the directive, however, were made public in the form of a Presidential Message to Congress and associated statements to the media.

U.S. Policy on the Iran-Iraq War, May–June 1984, Use of U.S. Military to Keep the Strait of Hormuz Open to Oil Tanker Traffice, May–June 1984

An unnamed "senior [Reagan] Administration official" revealed the existence of these presidential directives to the *Washington Post* during a 1987 interview, when they were cited as the basis for the administration's decision to protect Kuwaiti oil tankers passing through the Strait of Hormuz during the Iran-Iraq war.

The United States "tilted" toward Iraq in its war with Iran. It prepared contingency plans for aiding Iraq and other Persian Gulf states in a confrontation with Iran or uprising by domestic Islamic militants.[3] In a broader sense, the two directives set the stage for the Bush Administration's transfer of military equipment and satellite intelligence to Iraq prior to its invasion of Kuwait.

Legal Protections for Clandestine Killing Teams, November 13, 1984

Shortly after President Reagan's landslide reelection victory, CIA Director William Casey met with the president in the White House to convince him to authorize intelligence findings and a directive to implement the antiguerrilla campaign outlined in NSDD 138. Casey's draft NSDD was designed to provide legal guarantees to U.S. field officers and foreign strike teams that would protect them from punishment for activities that would otherwise violate U.S. law or the Executive Order that nominally bars U.S. agencies from participating in assassinations. White House officials later called this new directive "a license to kill" and a "go anywhere, do anything" authority to combat guerrillas viewed as hostile to the United States.[4]

The directive indicated that actions taken "in good faith" by U.S. agents conducting authorized antiguerrilla operations "must be and are deemed" lawful. The ambiguous wording insisted on legal acts, yet paradoxically "deemed" antiterrorist acts to be legal in advance. The first "preemptive self-defense" teams were to be created in Lebanon, then expand into other countries with an initial budget of about $1 million.

The accompanying intelligence findings approved CIA and U.S. military programs to recruit and train clandestine death squads in about a dozen countries, including Lebanon and Honduras. In at least one case, a U.S.-sponsored Lebanese Christian militia killing squad undertook what was later described as an "unauthorized" bombing aimed at an Islamic fundamentalist religious leader linked to the bombing of the U.S. Marine barracks in Beirut. On March 8, 1985, the Lebanese killing team bombed the apartment building of Islamic fundamentalist Mohammed Hussein Fadlallah, killing 80 and wounding 256, many of whom were schoolchildren from a nearby academy. Fadlallah was not injured. After considerable publicity, White House officials told the *Washington Post* that the NSC had approved creation of the Lebanese team, but that the bombing was unauthorized. The CIA was said to have "rescinded" the project after the bombing.[5]

NSDD 159. Management of U.S. Covert Operations, (Top Secret/ Veil Sensitive), January 18, 1985

The Reagan Administration's commitment to significantly expand covert operations had been clear since before the 1980 election. How such operations were actually to be managed from day to day, however, was considerably less certain. The management problem became particularly knotty owing to legal requirements to notify congressional intelligence oversight committees of covert operations, on the one hand and the tacitly accepted presidential mandate to deceive those same committees concerning sensitive operations such as the Contra war in Nicaragua, on the other.

The solution attempted in NSDD 159 was to establish a small coordinating committee headed by Vice-President George Bush through which all information concerning U.S. covert operations was to be funneled. The order also established a category of top secret information known as Veil, to be used exclusively for managing records pertaining to covert operations.[6] The system was designed to keep circulation of written records to an absolute minimum while at the same time ensuring that the vice-president retained the ability to coordinate U.S. covert operations with the administration's overt diplomacy and propaganda.

Only eight copies of NSDD 159 were created. The existence of the vice-president's committee was itself highly classified. The directive became public as a result of the criminal prosecutions of Oliver North, John Poindexter and others involved in the Iran-Contra affair.

U.S. Strategy For Iran After Khomeini, June 1985 (Not Officially Adopted, Top Secret) and Covert Action Finding Regarding Iran, (Top Secret), January 17, 1986

This draft NSDD, drawn up primarily by NSC staffer Howard Teicher, illustrated the political splits within the Reagan NSC that eventually gave rise to the Iran-Contra crisis.

According to the Tower Commission report, Teicher synthesized this draft order from a Special National Intelligence Estimate on Iran and a CIA study of potential covert operations against the Khomeini Government. The draft authorized "the supply of Western military hardware" to Iran and other measures, according to its cover memo.[7]

George Shultz and Caspar Weinberger disapproved, however, killing the draft order. Nevertheless, George Bush, William Casey and key members of the appropriately named Crisis Pre-Planning Group continued to support the initiative and secretly implemented it over the next two years.[8]

In January 1986, NSC staffer Oliver North drew up a formal Covert Action Finding for President Reagan. It authorized the CIA and NSC staff to proceed with the controversial effort to transfer U.S. weapons to Iranian "moderates" in exchange for their cooperation in freeing U.S. hostages in Lebanon. In effect, the finding implemented the program that had been outlined in the rejected NSDD, but without the approval of Shultz, Weinberger and congressional intelligence committees. The handwriting at the bottom includes Reagan's initials and a note by security adviser Poindexter indicating that the "President was verbally briefed from this paper. VP [Vice-President Bush], Don Regan [presidential chief of staff] and Don Forties [Poindexter's deputy and focal point for covert operations on Bush's Planning and Coordinating Group]" were present.[9] In later testimony, President Reagan insisted that he had not understood the content of the North/Poindexter Finding memo at the time he approved it.

NSDD 179. Task Force on Combating Terrorism, (Confidential), July 20, 1985

In June 1985, Islamic fundamentalist guerrillas hijacked TWA Flight 847, took more than 150 hostages and began a highly publicized, 17-day series of negotiations with U.S. officials. Despite a public commitment from President Reagan that "America will never make concessions to terrorists," the confrontation ended with an agreement by the United States and Israel to release hundreds of Lebanese *Shi'ite* prisoners in exchange for the TWA passengers.[10]

The existing U.S. policy of preemptive strikes against suspected terrorists (NSDD 138) had not been properly implemented because of sluggish bureaucracies in the United States and indecision among U.S. allies, at least as Reagan, Shultz, Casey and other prominent officials saw things.

This directive again appointed Bush to serve as the administration's coordinator for all major decisions concerning "terrorism," and to develop strategy and tactics for "preemptive or retaliatory actions to combat terrorism" that could garner international support.[11] This order was classified "Confidential," indicating that it was designed for circulation throughout the government.

NSDD 207. National Program for Combating Terrorism, (Top Secret), January 20, 1986

This nine-page directive was the "comprehensive presidential statement of U.S. counterterrorism policy" in effect during both the Reagan and Bush administrations, according to an NSC deposition filed in U.S. District Court.[12] It formalized the recommendations of Vice-President Bush's Task Force on Combating Terrorism (NSDD 179). Washington's announced policy, both in public forums and in classified orders such as this one, was that the U.S. Government would make "no concessions [to guerrillas]... pay no ransoms, nor permit release of prisoners or agree to other conditions that could serve to encourage additional terrorism."

In fact, of course, President Reagan, Vice-President Bush and others had already engineered a series of concessions to secure release of hostages in what would come to be called the Iran-Contra affair.

From the standpoint of broad policy, this directive covered much of the same ground as NSDD 138, signed the previous April. In addition to the "no concessions" pledge, the U.S. Government asserted that it would "take measures to protect our citizens" (preemptive action); "make every legal effort to... prosecute terrorists" (later acknowledged to include seizure of foreign nationals abroad for prosecution in the United States); pay substantial rewards for information concerning guerrilla activity;[13] and ensure that states that support anti-U.S. guerrillas "will not be allowed to do so without consequence."

NSDD 207's innovation lay in its new administrative measures to implement the broad policies. It created an Antiterrorism Assistance Program within the government, ordered new restrictions on the Freedom of Information Act and renewed efforts to pass new emergency powers legislation developed by the Federal Emergency Management Agency (FEM), which would authorize declaration of martial law in the United States during "emergencies" announced by the president.

The directive authorized creation of a "proposed organization" within the U.S. Government specializing in antiguerrilla intelligence gathering, paramilitary operations and rescue techniques. The existence, budget, tactics, leaders and personnel of the group were intended to remain classified.[14] Other measures included: authorization of an FBI and Immigration and Naturalization Service campaign to review the immigration status of political suspects in the United States; preparation of legal arguments designed to justify various U.S. responses to guerrillas, including use of deadly force and unilateral military operations abroad; and creation of specialized tactics, equipment and squads of trained paramilitary operatives useful for striking at guerrilla targets.

NSDD. Psychological Warfare Against Libya, (Classified, No Text Available), August 14, 1986

On August 6, 1986, senior State Department and CIA political officers drew up orders for a clandestine campaign to encourage a "coup or assassination attempt" against Libyan leader Muammar Qaddafi. Bush, Shultz, Casey and Poindexter supported the plan in NSC meetings, contending that even if a coup attempt failed, the resulting confusion would sow mistrust within Libya and keep Qaddafi off balance. The president signed the order on August 14.[15]

The campaign had at least three main parts. First, the United States used previously scheduled, joint U.S.-Egyptian military exercises to position warships off the Libyan coast. Second, the CIA, NSC and State Department meanwhile spread rumors through the media that a new U.S. "confrontation" with Libya was imminent, perhaps involving attacks on the seacoast and along the contested Libya-Chad border to the south. The CIA, meanwhile, stepped up covert operations designed to encourage Libyan exiles and dissidents in the military to strike against Qaddafi, while the NSC dispatched U.S. Ambassador Vernon Walters to Europe and Japan on a mission that was to be described in intentional leaks to the press as an effort to drum up international support for the coming "confrontation."

Although the covert operations among Libyan exiles were real enough, the NSC sought to spur a coup against Qaddafi, not invade the country. The CIA and NSC systematically leaked false information to sympathetic reporters abroad and in the United States, claiming among other things that the Libyan leader had become sexually impotent and was "off his rocker." Much of the disinformation was reported as fact by television, major newspapers and even supermarket tabloids.[16]

The psychological warfare campaign dramatically self-destructed about a month later. On October 2, the *Washington Post* reported many of the details of the NSC effort against Qaddafi, including the false stories planted in the *Wall Street Journal* and *New York Times*. The resulting loss of media support was to cost the administration dearly a few months later when new information surfaced about U.S. covert operations in Nicaragua and arms trade with Iran.

NSDD 286. Administration of U.S. Clandestine Operations In the Wake of Iran-Contra Revelations, (Sanitized Version — Original Classificatoin Not Disclosed), Late October-Early November 1987

This directive, together with NSDD 266 and NSDD 276, sketched out the purported reforms in NSC procedure for management of clandestine operations adopted in the wake of the Iran-Contra and Libyan debacles and the growing realization that President Reagan had become mentally incapacitated. The declassified version of the new procedures required somewhat more rigorous documentation of presidential approval of "special activities" (covert operations) and barred the NSC staff from the "conduct" (but not the management) of special activities.

Beyond that, though, there was little change in the management or the content of U.S. clandestine operations. Some experts contended that NSDD 286 effectively weakened congressional oversight of U.S. covert operations by opening a new loophole that exempted special activities from existing reporting requirements during unspecified "extraordinary circumstances."

NSDD 26. U.S. Policy Toward Iraq and the Persian Gulf Region, (Sanitized Version, Original Classification Not Disclosed), October 2 1989

And so the cycle began again. This directive authorized the U.S. Government to offer political, economic and intelligence incentives to Iraqi leader Saddam Hussein to encourage Iraqi cooperation with the U.S. strategic goal of maintaining control of Persian Gulf oil. President Bush's order encouraged U.S. companies to "participate in the reconstruction of the Iraqi economy" following Iraq's protracted war with Iran and approved U.S. training of the Iraqi "defense establishment... on a case by case basis."

The new president's NSDD precipitated a series of policy decisions concerning U.S. aid to Iraq that became highly controversial in the wake of the Iraqi invasion of Kuwait in August 1990. Under NSDD 26 and earlier U.S. NSDDs concerning Iraq, the State Department ensured $1 billion in agriculture credits for Iraq, some of which was diverted into arms purchases; Bush signed a waiver permitting Export-Import Bank loan guarantees for the country despite official censure of Iraq's human rights record; the CIA provided unusually detailed military intelligence to Iraq that its security agencies put to use in a genocidal campaign against Iraq's Kurdish minority group; the Pentagon began efforts to upgrade U.S.-Iraqi military relations; and U.S. export control agencies permitted sale of advanced missile technologies to Iraqi customers, among other measures. U.S. financial relations with Iraq and CIA operations in the country also became entangled in the complex Bank of Credit and Commerce International (BOCCI) banking scandal.[17] Most of these activities were highly secret at the time, as was the existence of the NSC 26 order that provided the policy framework for those decisions.

During later debates, Bush's first NSC Adviser Brent Scowcroft, contended that the Bush Administration "did not 'coddle' Saddam," as it had been accused of doing by congressional Democrats. "There was broad bipartisan consensus behind the open U.S. policy of providing political and economic support to Iraq during the later stages of its war with Iran... Congress debated and approved Operation Earnest Will (protection for Kuwaiti oil tankers in the Gulf). Congressional intelligence committees reviewed and concurred with our activities in the region."

Partisan politics concerning U.S. policy on Iraq had become "sheer McCarthyism," Scowcroft said and an "attempt to transform a legitimate policy debate into a criminal conspiracy."[18]

(1996)

Libya in U.S. Demonology

Noam Chomsky

St. Augustine tells the story of a pirate captured by Alexander the Great, who asked him "How he dares molest the sea." "How dare you molest the whole world?" the pirate replied. "Because I do it with a little ship only, I am called a thief; you, doing it with a great navy, are called an Emperor."

The pirate's answer was "elegant and excellent," St. Augustine relates. It captures with some accuracy the current relations between the United States and Libya, a minor actor on the stage of international terrorism.

More generally, St. Augustine's tale reaches to the heart of the cynical frenzy over "international terrorism" currently being orchestrated as a cover for Western violence and illuminates the meaning of the concept in contemporary Western usage. The term "terrorism" came into use at the end of the 18th century, primarily to designate violent acts of governments intended to ensure popular submission. That concept, plainly, is of little benefit to the practitioners of state terrorism, who, holding power, are in a position to control the system of thought and expression. The original sense has therefore been abandoned and the term "terrorism" has come to be applied mainly to retail terrorism by individuals or groups.[1] Whereas the term was once applied to Emperors who molest their own subjects and the world, now it is restricted to thieves who molest the powerful.

Extricating ourselves from the system of indoctrination, we will use the term "terrorism" to refer to the threat or use of violence to intimidate or coerce (generally for political ends), whether it is the wholesale terrorism of the Emperor or the retail terrorism of the thief.

In the true sense of the term, Libya is a terrorist state: the latest Amnesty International Report lists the killings, through 1985, of 14 Libyan citizens by this terrorist state, four abroad, the major acts of terrorism plausibly attributed to Libya. In the course of the hysteria orchestrated to serve other ends, all sorts of charges have been made, but the record confirms the April 1986 statement of a senior U.S. intelligence official that "what happened a few weeks ago is that Qaddafi, who previously had used his people primarily to assassinate Libyan dissidents, made a clear decision to target Americans."[2] Qaddafi's alleged decision followed the Gulf of Sidra incident, when a U.S. air and naval armada sank Libyan vessels with many killed and is entirely legitimate, indeed much belated, under the cynical doctrines professed by the U.S. executive, as we shall see directly.

Amnesty International reports that Libya's terrorist killings began in early 1980, at the time when Jimmy Carter launched the terrorist war in El Salvador with José Napoleón Duarte serving as a cover to ensure that arms would flow to the killers. While Libya was killing 14 of its own citizens, along with a handful of others, the U.S. client regime of El Salvador killed some 50,000 of its citizens in the course of what Bishop Rivera y Damas, who succeeded the assassinated Archbishop Romero, described in October 1980 as "a war of extermination and genocide against a defenseless civilian population." The security forces who perform these necessary chores were hailed by Duarte, a few weeks later, for their "valiant service alongside the people against subversion" while he conceded that "the masses were with the guerrillas" when this exercise began under the Carter-Duarte alliance. Duarte expressed this praise for the mass murderers as he was sworn in as president of the junta in an effort to lend it legitimacy and ensure the flow of arms after the murder of four U.S. churchwomen, generally regarded here as improper, though such partisans of terror and torture as Jeane Kirkpatrick and Alexander Haig offered justifications even for this act.

The slaughter in El Salvador is not mere state terrorism on a massive scale, but international terrorism, given the organization, supply, training and direct participation by the ruler of the hemisphere. The same is true of the massacre of some 70,000 Guatemalans in the same years, when U.S. arms to the murderers flowed at close to the normal level contrary to what is commonly alleged, though it was necessary to call in U.S. proxies, the neo-Nazi Argentine generals and Israel, to implement the slaughter more efficiently and to construct an arms pipeline involving Belgium and other collaborators, under the illegal direction of the Pentagon and the CIA. Meanwhile Reagan and his associates extolled the killers and torturers for their human rights improvements and "total dedication to democracy." "The striking feature of Libyan atrocities," two observers note in reviewing the Amnesty International study of state terror, "is that they are the only ones whose numbers are sufficiently limited that the individual cases can be enumerated," in striking contrast to Argentina, Indonesia, or the Central American states where the Emperor molests the world.[3]

U.S. international terrorism in El Salvador is hailed as a magnificent achievement across the mainstream political spectrum in the United States because it laid the basis for what is called "democracy" in Western parlance: namely, the rule of elite groups serving the needs of the Global Enforcer with the public occasionally mobilized to ratify elite decisions. In El Salvador, the United States organized what Herman and Brodhead call "demonstration elections" to pacify the home front, carried out in an atmosphere of "terror and despair, macabre rumor and grisly reality," in the words of the observers of the British Parliamentary Human Rights Group.[4] The U.S. press lauded this demonstration of our passionate commitment to democracy, as *Pravda* does under similar circumstances. Guatemala is also considered a success, for similar reasons. When half the population is marched to the polls after it has been properly traumatized by U.S.-backed violence, enlightened U.S. humanists are overjoyed at this renewed demonstration of our love for democracy, untroubled by the rise in death squad killings after the elections (including at least 94 deaths and 35 disappearances in the weeks following President Marco Vinicio Cerezo Arevalo's January inauguration), the open recognition by the newly elected president that he can do nothing given the roots of actual power in the military and the oligarchy and that the civilian government represents merely "the managers of bankruptcy and misery,"[5] and the fact that the reaction in the United States helps convert the elections into a means for the United States to participate more fully in state terror and repression, as in El Salvador. In fact, elections in U.S. terror states are often a disaster for the domestic population, for this essential reason. These two examples, of course, represent only a small part of the U.S. role in international terrorism during the 1980s and the grisly record goes back many years.

In short, Libya is indeed a terrorist state, but in the world of international terrorism, it is hardly even a bit player.

"Their Side" Is Terrorist

The pirate's maxim explains the useful concept of "international terrorism" only in part. It is necessary to add a second feature: An act of terrorism enters the canon only if it is committed by "their side," not ours. Consider, for example, the public relations campaign about "international terrorism" launched in early 1981 by the Reagan Administration. The major text was Claire Sterling's *The Terror Network*, which offered an ingenious proof that international terrorism is a "Soviet-inspired" instrument "aimed at the destabilization of Western democratic society." The proof is that the major terrorist actions are confined to the Western democratic states and are not "directed against the Soviet Union or any of its satellites or client states." This profound insight much impressed other terrorologists, notably, Walter Laqueur, who wrote that Sterling had provided "ample evidence" that terrorism occurs "almost exclusively in democratic or relatively democratic countries."[6]

The Sterling thesis is true, in fact true by definition, given the way the term "terrorism" is employed by the Emperor and his loyal coterie. Since only acts committed by "their side" count as terrorism, it follows that Sterling is necessarily correct, whatever the facts. In the real world, the story is quite different. The major victims of international terrorism[7] in the several decades prior to the Sterling-Laqueur pronouncements were Cuba and the Palestinians, but none of this counts, by definition. When Israel bombs Palestinian refugee camps killing many civilians — often without even a pretense of "reprisal" — or sends its troops into Lebanese villages in "counterterror" operations where they murder and destroy, or hijacks ships and places thousands of hostages in prison camps under horrifying conditions, this is not "terrorism"; in fact, the rare voices of protest are thunderously condemned by loyal Party Liners for their "anti-Semitism" and "double standard," demonstrated by their failure to join the chorus of praise for "a country that cares for human life" (Washington Post), whose "high moral purpose" (Time) is the object of never-ending awe and acclaim, a country which, according to its U.S. claque, "is held to a higher law, as interpreted for it by journalists" (Walter Goodman).[8]

Similarly, it is not terrorism when paramilitary forces operating from U.S. bases and trained by the CIA bombard Cuban hotels, sink fishing boats and attack Russian ships in Cuban harbors, poison crops and livestock, attempt to assassinate Castro and so on, in missions that were running almost weekly at their peak.[9] These and innumerable similar actions on the part of the Emperor and his clients are not the subject of conferences and learned tomes, or of anguished commentary and diatribes in the media and journals of opinion.

Not only is "terrorism" defined for ideological serviceability, but standards of evidence are also conveniently set so as to achieve the Emperor's goals. To demonstrate Libya's role as a state terrorist, the flimsiest evidence, or none at all, will suffice. The headline of a New York Times editorial justifying the terrorist attack that killed some 100 people in Libya reads "To Save the Next Natasha Simpson," referring to the 11-year-old U.S. girl who was one of the victims of the terrorist attacks in the Rome and Vienna air terminals, on December 27, 1985; these victims entitle us to bomb Libyan cities "to discourage state-supported terrorism," the editors solemnly inform us. It is only a minor defect that no evidence has been presented to implicate Libya in these actions. The Italian and Austrian governments stated that the terrorists were trained in Syrian-controlled areas of Lebanon and had come via Damascus, a conclusion reiterated by Israeli Defense Minister Rabin. Four months later, in response to U.S. claims about Libyan involvement in the Vienna attack, the Austrian Minister of Interior stated that "there is not the slightest evidence to implicate Libya," again citing Syria as the connection and adding that Washington had never presented the evidence of Libyan complicity it had promised to provide to the Austrian authorities. He also added the correct but — in the U.S. — inexpressible comment that the problem of Lebanese-based terrorism lies largely in the failure to solve the Palestine problem, which has led desperate people to turn to violence, exactly the result intended by U.S.-Israeli terrorism, a matter to which we will return.[10]

If an individual implicated in a terrorist act once paid a visit to Libya, or is alleged to have received training or funds from Libya in the past, that suffices for condemnation of Qaddafi as a "mad dog" who must be eradicated. The same standards would implicate the CIA in the murderous exploits of Cuban exiles, among numerous others. Keeping just to 1985, one of the suspects in the bombing of the Air India jumbo jet near Ireland that was the year's worst terrorist act, killing 329 people, was trained in an anticommunist school for mercenaries in Alabama. The terrorist action that cost the most lives in the Middle East was a car-bombing in Beirut in March that killed 80 people and wounded 200, carried out by a Lebanese intelligence unit trained and supported by the CIA — in an effort to kill a *Shi'ite* leader who was believed to have been involved in "terrorist attacks against U.S. installations" in Beirut; the term "terrorism" is commonly used by foreign armies in reference to actions against them by the local population which, as in this case, plausibly see them as an occupying force attempting to impose a detested political settlement.[11] By the standards of evidence used in the case of Libya, the United States is the world's leading terrorist power, even if we exclude the wholesale terrorism ruled ineligible by the propaganda system by the means already described.

What the president calls "the evil scourge of terrorism" (in the specific Western sense) was placed in the central focus of attention by the Reagan Administration as it came into office in 1981. The reasons were transparent, though inexpressible within the doctrinal system. The administration was committed to three related policies, all achieved with some success: (1) transfer of resources from the poor to the rich; (2) a massive increase in the state sector of the economy in the traditional American way, through the Pentagon system — a device to force the public to invest in high technology industry by means of the state-guaranteed market for the production of high technology waste (armaments) and thus to contribute to the general program of public subsidy, private profit, called "free enterprise"; and (3) a substantial increase in the U.S. role in intervention, subversion and international terrorism (in the true sense of the expression). Such policies cannot be presented to the public in the terms in which they are intended. They can be implemented only if the general population is properly frightened by monsters against whom we must defend ourselves.

The standard device is an appeal to the threat of Reagan's "Evil Empire," what President Kennedy called "the monolithic and ruthless conspiracy" bent on world conquest, as he launched a rather similar program.[12] But confrontation with the Evil Empire can be a dangerous affair, so it is preferable to do battle with safer enemies designated as the Evil Empire's proxies, a choice that conforms well to the third plank in the Reagan agenda, pursued for quite independent reasons: to ensure "stability" and "order" in our global domains. The "international terrorism" of properly chosen pirates, or of enemies such as Nicaragua or Salvadoran peasants who dare to defend themselves from our terrorist attack, is a far preferable target and with an efficiently functioning propaganda system it can be exploited to induce a proper sense of fear and mobilization among the domestic population.

Qaddafi as Scapegoat

Libya fit the need perfectly. Qaddafi is easy to hate and Libya is weak and defenseless, so that martial flourishes and, when needed, murder of Libyans can be conducted with impunity. The glorious military victory in Grenada, a culmination of the extreme hostility and aggressiveness of the Carter-Reagan administrations after the Bishop Government threatened to consider the needs of the poor population, served similar ends. The point is readily perceived abroad. U.S. journalist Donald Neff, writing in a British publication about the March 1986 Gulf of Sidra incident, comments that "this was less of a Rambo-style operation than a demonstration of the bully on the block picking a fight. It was typical of Reagan. In his five years in office, he has repeatedly got away with lording it over little guys. He did this time too."[13] It is an interesting fact about U.S. culture that this regular show of cowardice and two-bit thuggery seems to strike a responsive chord.

The public relations specialists of the Reagan Administration understood the utility of the Libyan enemy and wasted little time in confronting this dangerous foe. Libya was at once designated as a prime agent of the Soviet-inspired "terror network," and in July 1981, a CIA plan to overthrow and possibly kill Qaddafi with a paramilitary campaign of terror within Libya was leaked to the press.[14]

We might note parenthetically that by U.S. standards, this plan authorized Qaddafi to carry out acts of terror against U.S. targets in "self-defense against future attack," the words of White House spokesman Larry Speakes presenting the official justification for the bombing of Tripoli and Benghazi. The same justification was reiterated at the United Nations by Vernon Walters and Herbert Okun. The administration even had the gall to argue that this right, which not even Hitler claimed and which, if proclaimed by other violent states, would tear to shreds what little remains of global order and international law, is in accord with the United Nations Charter; no form of legal sophistry can bridge that gap, but Reagan's pronouncement was duly acclaimed by Anthony Lewis for its reliance "on a legal argument that violence against the perpetrators of repeated violence is justified as an act of self-defense." The reason why the United States justified the attack "on the basis of pre-empting an attack, which could be seen as a form of self-defense, [rather] than as a retaliatory action" was explained by a State Department official, who noted that the UN Charter expressly forbids the use of force except in self-defense — in fact, self-defense against armed attack, until the UN acts after a formal request by the country that regards itself as the victim of a sudden and over-whelming armed attack.[15]

In August 1981, the anti-Qaddafi message "was reinforced by the trap laid for Libya in the Gulf of Sidra," a trap "elaborately planned on the U.S. side" with the intent of a confrontation in which Libyan jets could be shot down, as they were, Edward Haley observes in his bitterly anti-Qaddafi study of U.S. relations with Libya. One specific purpose, Haley plausibly argues, was to "exploit the 'Libyan menace' in order to win support for steps [the administration] wished to take in pursuit of Secretary Haig's 'strategic consensus' against the Soviet Union and as an element in the arrangements necessary for the creation of a Rapid Deployment Force," targeted primarily at the Middle East. In November, the administration concocted a ludicrous tale about Libyan hit men roaming the streets of Washington to assassinate our Leader, eliciting feverish media comm-entary along with some limited skepticism. When questioned about the plot, Reagan stated: "We have the evidence and [Qaddafi] knows it."[16] The story faded away when its purpose was served and the press was sufficiently disciplined so as not to report the exposure in the British press that the "assassins" on the official U.S. list, leaked in England, were prominent members of the (passionately anti-Libyan) Lebanese Amal, including Nabih Berri and the elderly religious leader of the Shi'ite community.[17]

Other tales included a Libyan threat to invade the Sudan across 600 miles of desert (with the Egyptian and U.S. air forces helpless to impede this outrage) and a plot to overthrow the government of the Sudan in

February 1983 — conveniently discovered at a moment when the administration's reactionary constituency was charging it with insufficient militancy — a plot so subtle that Sudanese and Egyptian intelligence knew nothing about it, as U.S. reporters who took the trouble to go to Khartoum to investigate quickly discovered. The United States responded to the fabricated plot with an elaborate show of force, enabling Secretary of State Shultz, who had been denounced as too faint-hearted, to strike heroic poses on television while announcing that Qaddafi "is back in his box where he belongs" because Reagan acted "quickly and decisively" against this threat to world order. Again, the episode was forgotten when its purpose had been served. There have been a series of similar examples. The media has generally played its appointed role, with only occasional demurrers.[18]

The events of March-April 1986 fit the familiar pattern to perfection. The Gulf of Sidra operation in March was plainly timed to stir up jingoist hysteria just prior to the crucial Senate vote on Contra aid, coinciding with a fabricated Nicaraguan "invasion" of Honduras as Nicaragua exercised its legal right of hot pursuit to expel from its territory U.S. proxy forces dispatched by their master from their Honduras bases to sow terror in Nicaragua prior to the Senate vote. The public relations campaign succeeded brilliantly as demonstrated by the enraged reaction of congressional doves and the media fairly generally and the Senate vote. The charade also permitted the administration to provide $20 million of military aid to Honduras which Honduras officially maintains that it did not request and which has no doubt been conveniently "lost" in the Contra camps, yet another method by which the lawless band in Washington evades the weak congressional restrictions on their thuggery.[19] The Libyan provocation, too, was a success, enabling U.S. forces to sink several Libyan boats, killing more than 50 Libyans and, it was hoped, to incite Qaddafi to acts of terror against U.S. citizens, as was subsequently claimed.

While the U.S. forces were successful in killing many Libyans, they were singularly unable to rescue survivors. The task was apparently not impossible, since 16 survivors of the U.S. attack were rescued from a lifeboat by a Spanish oil tanker.[20]

The official purpose of the U.S. military operation was to establish the right of passage in the Gulf of Sidra. Perfect nonsense, since dispatch of a naval flotilla was hardly the necessary or appropriate means to achieve this end; in fact, under international law, a public declaration or the commencement of court proceedings would have sufficed. Since there was plainly no urgency, it was possible to resort to legal means to establish the right of innocent passage. But a violent terrorist state will naturally observe different priorities.

The U.S. position is dubious on narrower grounds. The press

continually speaks of "the law of the sea," but Libya shot at U.S. planes, not U.S. ships and "the law of the air" barely exists. States make various claims in this regard. The United States, for example, claims a 200-mile Air Defense Identification Zone within which it has the right to exercise "self-defense" against intruding aircraft judged to be hostile. There is no doubt that U.S. aircraft were well within 200 miles of Libyan territory — 40 miles, the Pentagon claims — and that they were hostile, so that by U.S. standards, Libya was within its rights to intercept them. The point was noted by the conservative legal scholar Alfred Rubin of the Fletcher School at Tufts University, who commented that "by sending in aircraft we went beyond what we were clearly authorized to do under the Law of the Sea" in "an unnecessary provocation."[21] But for a gangster state, such matters are irrelevant and the exercise was a success, domestically at least.

The extent of the provocation in the Gulf of Sidra was made clear by Pentagon spokesman Robert Sims, who "said that U.S. policy is to shoot at any Libyan boat that enters international waters in the Gulf of Sidra for as long as the U.S. naval exercise in that region continues — no matter how far away the boat might be from U.S. ships." "Given the 'hostile intent' displayed by Libya when it tried to shoot down U.S. warplanes," Sims stated, any Libyan military vessel is "a threat to our forces."[22] In short, the United States maintains the right of "self-defense" against any Libyan vessel that approaches its naval armada off the Libyan coast, but Libya does not have a right of self-defense in airspace comparable to that claimed by the United States.

There is more to the story. David Blundy interviewed British engineers in Tripoli who were repairing the Soviet-installed radar system. One, who says he was monitoring the incident throughout on the radar screens (which, contrary to Pentagon claims, were not rendered inoperative), reports that he saw U.S. warplanes cross not only into the 12 miles of Libyan territorial waters, but over Libyan land as well. "'I watched the planes fly approximately eight miles into Libyan air space,' he said. 'I don't think the Libyans had any choice but to hit back. In my opinion they were reluctant to do so'." The engineer added that "American warplanes made their approach using a normal civil airline traffic route and followed in the wake of a Libyan airliner, so that its radar blip would mask them on the Libyan radar screen."[23]

No hint of this information appeared in the national press, to my knowledge, apart from a typically excellent report by Alexander Cockburn, playing his usual role of personal antidote to media subservience and distortion. Blundy's article was not mysteriously missed by the U.S. press. It was cited by Joseph Lelyveld of the *New York Times,* but with its crucial content entirely omitted.[24]

One likely consequence of the Gulf of Sidra operation was to elicit acts of Libyan terrorism in retaliation. These would then have the effect of inducing a state of terror in the United States and, with some luck, in Europe as well, setting the stage for the next escalation. The bombing of the La Belle discotheque in West Berlin on April 5 [1986], with one American and one Turk killed, was immediately blamed on Libya and was then used as the pretext for the April 14 bombing of Tripoli and Benghazi, with about 100 Libyans killed, neatly timed the day before the expected House vote on Contra aid. In case the audience missed the point, Reagan's speech writers made it explicit. Addressing the American Business Conference on April 15, he said: "And I would remind the House voting this week that this arch-terrorist has sent $400 million and an arsenal of weapons and advisers into Nicaragua to bring his war home to the United States. He has bragged that he is helping the Nicaraguans because they fight America on its own ground."[25] The idea that the "mad dog" is bringing his war home to the United States by providing arms to people the United States is attacking with its terrorist proxy army was a nice touch, which passed without notable comment, but the public relations operation did not, for once, succeed in steamrollering Congress, though the bombing of Libya did inflame chauvinist passions. This consequence was largely attributable, perhaps, to the rampant anti-Arab racism in the United States and the absence of any sane reaction to earlier episodes of manufactured hysteria over Qaddafi's real and alleged crimes.

The April 14 attack was the first bombing in history staged for prime time television. As the subsequently published record shows, the bombing raids were carefully timed so that they would begin precisely at 7:00 p.m. Eastern Standard Time — as they did; that is, precisely at the moment when all three national television channels broadcast their national news, which was of course preempted as agitated anchor men switched to Tripoli for direct eyewitness reports of the exciting events. As soon as the raids ended, the White House had Larry Speakes address a press conference, followed by other dignitaries, ensuring total domination of the propaganda system during the crucial early hours.

Difficult Questions

One might argue that the administration took a gamble in this transparent public relations operation, since journalists might have asked some difficult questions, but the White House was justly confident that nothing untoward would occur and its faith in the servility of the media proved to be warranted.

Questions could have been raised, surely. To mention only the most obvious one, Speakes stated that the United States knew on April 4 that the East Berlin Libyan "People's Bureau" had informed Tripoli that an attack would take place in Berlin the following day and that it then informed Tripoli that the La Belle discotheque bombing had taken place, as planned. Thus the United States knew on April 4-5 — with certainty, the White House alleged — that Libya was directly responsible for the disco bombing. One might have asked, then, why the reports of U.S. and West German investigations from April 5 to the moment of the attack consistently stated that there were at most suspicions of Libyan involvement. In fact, every journalist listening to the administration story had in his or her hands — unless we assume the most astonishing incompetence on the part of the news rooms — a report from Berlin which came across the wires at 6:28 p.m. EST, a half-hour before the bombing, stating that "the Allied military command [in West Berlin] reported no developments in the investigation of the disco bombing" and that "U.S. and West German officials have said Libya — possibly through its embassy in Communist-ruled East Berlin — is *suspected* of involvement in the bombing of the La Belle nightclub" (my emphasis).[26] Some journalist might have asked, then, how it is that just prior to the attack, the United States and West Germany still had at most suspicions of Libyan involvement — as throughout the preceding period — while on April 4-5, 10 days earlier, they had certain knowledge of it. But no embarrassing questions were asked then, nor have they been since and the relevant facts have been largely suppressed.

Reagan stated on the evening of April 14 that "our evidence is direct, it is precise, it is irrefutable" — just as "We have the evidence and [Qaddafi] knows it" in the case of the Libyan hit men, not to speak of the Sandinista involvement in drug-peddling, their announcement of a "revolution without frontiers," the support of Helmut Kohl and Bettino Craxi for the Libyan attack (angrily denied by "shocked" officials in Germany and Italy),[27] and numerous other fabrications of an administration that has broken the usual records for deceit, but continues "to commit any crime, to lie, to cheat" — in the words of the titular leadership, referring to his Stalinist models — to achieve its ends, confident that the occasional exposure in the small print, well after the fact, will not prevent the constant stream of lies from setting the terms of debate and leaving the appropriate impressions firmly implanted, exactly as it does.

Beyond the borders, discipline does not reign. In Germany, a week after Washington had stated its certain knowledge 10 days earlier of Libyan responsibility for the disco bombing, *Der Spiegel* reported that the famed telephone intercepts apparently do not exist and that West Berlin intelligence has only suspicions about Libyan involvement, also suspecting "rival groups of drug dealers" among other possibilities, including neo-

Nazi groups. Washington's war is "a means of politics," "insofar as the enemy is as small as Grenada and Libya — and the adversary is as ideal a scoundrel as Qaddafi," and no European leader should have any illusions that Europe's concerns or interests will be considered if the United States decides to escalate international violence, even to the level of a final World War, editor Rudolf Augstein adds.[28] In an interview on April 28 with a reporter for the U.S. Army journal *Stars and Stripes,* Manfred Ganschow, chief of the Berlin Staatschutz and head of the 100-man team investigating the disco bombing, stated that "I have no more evidence that Libya was connected to the bombing than I had when you first called me two days after the act. Which is none." He agreed that it was "a highly political case" and hinted at considerable skepticism about what "the politicians" were saying and would say about it.[29] The U.S. press has concealed the doubts expressed by the Berlin investigators, but the careful reader will discern them in the reports of the continuing investigation, as suspects alleged to have Syrian and other connections are investigated.

For much of the world, the United States has become an object of considerable fear, as its "bizarre cowboy leader" engages in acts of "madness" in organizing a "band of cutthroats" to attack Nicaragua and playing mad bomber elsewhere, in the words of Canada's leading journal, generally restrained and quite pro-U.S. in tendency.[30] The Reagan Administration is playing on these fears. At the Tokyo Summit of the advanced industrial democracies in May, the Reagan Administration circulated a position paper in which it stated that one reason why Europe would be wise to line up in the U.S. crusade is "the need to do something so that the crazy Americans won't take matters into their own hands again." The threat succeeded in eliciting a statement against terrorism mentioning only Libya by name.[31]

The reaction to the bombing of Libya at home and abroad was sharply different. Expecting the worst, the 12-member European Economic Community called upon the United States to avoid "further escalation of military tension in the region with all the inherent dangers." A few hours later, U.S. warplanes struck, as West German Foreign Minister Hans-Dietrich Genscher was on his way to Washington to explain the EEC position. His spokesman stated that "We want to do everything we can to avoid a military escalation." The bombing aroused extensive protest throughout most of Europe, including large-scale demonstrations and evoked editorial condemnation in most of the world. Spain's major journal, the independent *El Pais,* condemned the raid, writing that "The military action of the United States is not only an offense against international law and a grave threat to peace in the Mediterranean, but a mockery of its European allies, who did not find motives for economic sanctions against

Libya in a meeting Monday, despite being previously and without success pressured to adopt sanctions." The conservative *South China Morning Post* in Hong Kong wrote that "President Reagan's cure for the 'mad dog of the Middle East' may prove more lethal than the disease," and his action "may also have lit the fuse to a wider conflagration" in the Middle East. In Mexico City, *El Universal* wrote that the United States "has no right to set itself up as the defender of world freedom," urging recourse to legal means through the United Nations. There were many similar reactions.

The U.S. press, in contrast, was overwhelmingly favorable. The *New York Times* wrote that "even the most scrupulous citizen can only approve and applaud the American attacks on Libya," describing this as a just sentence: "the United States has prosecuted [Qaddafi] carefully, proportionately — and justly." The evidence for Libyan responsibility for the disco bombing has been "now laid out clearly to the public"; "Then came the jury, the European governments to which the United States went out of its way to send emissaries to share evidence and urge concerted action against the Libyan leader." It is irrelevant, apparently, that the jury was hardly convinced by the evidence and issued a "judgment" calling on the executioner to refrain from any action.

Most governments also condemned the action, though not all. The government-controlled South African Broadcasting Corporation said the attack "underlines the commitment the leader of the Western world has made to taking positive action against terrorism"; the United States was justified in attacking Qaddafi, "whose name is virtually synonymous with international terrorism." In Israel, Prime Minister Shimon Peres stated that the U.S. action was clearly justified "in self-defense": "If the Libyan Government issues orders to murder U.S. soldiers in Beirut in cold blood, in the middle of the night, what do you expect the United States to do? Sing Hallelujah? Or take action in her defense?" The idea that the U.S. was acting in " self-defense" against an attack on her forces in Beirut two-and-a-half years earlier is an intriguing innovation, even putting aside the circumstances of that earlier act of "terrorism" against the military forces that much of the population saw as imposing the "New Order" that Israel had sought to establish: the rule of right-wing Christians and selected Muslim elites.[32]

In the United States, Senator Mark Hatfield denounced the U.S. bombing raid "on a nearly deserted Senate floor," and in a letter to the *Times*. Leaders of several major Christian denominations condemned the bombing, but Jewish leaders generally praised it, among them, Rabbi Alexander Schindler, president of the Union of American Hebrew Congregations, who "said the U.S. Government 'properly and vigorously responded' to the 'mindless terrorism' of Qaddafi. Harvard international affairs professor Joseph Nye said Reagan had to respond "to the smoking gun of that Berlin thing. What else do you do about state-supported terrorism?" — such as U.S.-supported terrorism in Central America, for example, where the "smoking gun" is considerably more in evidence. Eugene Rostow supported the bombing as part of a "more active defense against the process of Soviet expansion," a step that was "inevitable and overdue." The "forcible removal of the Qaddafi regime," he explained, "would be fully justified under the existing rules of international law," since he "has flagrantly and continually violated these rules." "That being the case, every state injured by Libya's actions has the right, alone or with others, to use whatever force is reasonably necessary to put an end to Libya's illegal behavior. Libya is in the legal position of the Barbary pirates." He urged NATO to "issue a declaration on the responsibility of states for illegal acts committed from their territory." *A fortiori*, then, NATO should condemn the Emperor, not just the pirate and states from Indochina to Central America to the Middle East, among others, should organize to use whatever force is necessary to attack the United States, Israel and other terrorist states.[33]

The U.S. bombing of Libya had nothing to do with "terrorism," even in the hypocritical Western sense of the word. In fact, it was clear enough that the Gulf of Sidra operation and the bombing of Libyan cities would if anything incite such retail terrorism, one major reason why the likely targets in Europe pleaded with the United States to refrain from such action.

This is hardly the first time that violent actions have been executed with the expectation that they would incite retail terrorism. Consider the U.S.-backed Israeli invasion of Lebanon in 1982, undertaken against the background of persistent U.S.-Israeli refusal to permit a peaceful settlement of the Arab-Israeli conflict.[34] After the Israeli-initiated exchange across the Israel-Lebanon border in June 1981 with some 450 Arabs and six Jews killed, the border was "quiet" in the racist terms of U.S. discourse, meaning that there was no PLO response to the many Israeli provocations (including bombing of civilian areas with many killed) undertaken in an effort to elicit a "terrorist act" that could be exploited to justify the planned invasion. Finally, Israel invaded on a pretext in June 1982, proceeding to destroy the civilian base of the PLO in Lebanon and demolish much of what remained of Lebanese society. The goal was to establish a "New Order" under Israeli domination, at least in Lebanon, and to secure Israel's integration of the occupied territories. It was clear at once that these acts could only have the effect of inspiring what the West calls "terrorism," and indeed, most terrorism, in the Western sense, has since originated in the ruins of Lebanon.

The real reason for the 1982 invasion was not the threat to the northern Galilee, as the sanitized history regularly offered to U.S. audiences pretends, but rather the opposite, as was plausibly explained by Israel's leading specialist on the Palestinians, Yehoshua Porath, shortly after the invasion was launched. The decision to invade, he suggests, "flowed from the very fact that the cease-fire had been observed." This was a "veritable catastrophe" for the Israeli Government, because it threatened the policy of evading a political settlement. "The government's hope," he continued, "is that the stricken PLO, lacking a logistic and territorial base, will return to its earlier terrorism; it will carry out bombings throughout the world, hijack airplanes and murder many Israelis," and thus "will lose part of the political legitimacy it has gained" and "undercut the danger" of negotiations with representative Palestinians, which would threaten the policy — shared by both major political groupings — of keeping effective control over the occupied territories.[35] The plausible assumption of the Israeli leadership was that those who shape public opinion in the United States — the only country that counts, now that Israel has chosen to become a mercenary state serving the interests of its provider — could be counted on to obliterate the actual history and portray the terrorist acts resulting from Israeli aggression and atrocities as random acts of violence ascribable to defects in Arab character and culture, if not racial deficiencies. Recent U.S. commentary on terrorism fulfills these natural expectations with some precision.

The basic points are understood well enough in Israel. Prime Minister Yitzchak Shamir stated over Israeli television that Israel went to war because there was "a terrible danger... Not so much a military one as a political one," prompting the fine Israeli satirist B. Michael to write that "the lame excuse of a military danger or a danger to the Galilee is dead." We "have removed the political danger" by striking first, in time; now, "Thank God, there is no one to talk to." Other Israeli commentators have made essentially the same point.

In short, the goals of the war were political, the occupied territories being a prime target. The tale about protecting the border from terrorism is agitprop, eagerly swallowed by the docile Western media. If Palestinian terrorism can be revived, so much the better. And if we can't pin the blame on Arafat, he can at least be stigmatized as "the founding father of contemporary Palestinian violence,"[36] so that his efforts at political settlement can be evaded. The attack on Libya may also inspire retail terrorism, which will serve to mobilize domestic and foreign opinion in support of U.S. plans at home and abroad. If U.S. citizens react, as they have, by general hysteria, including fear of traveling to Europe where visitors will be at least 100 times as safe as in any U.S. city, this too is a net benefit, for the same reasons.

U.S. Escalation Strategy

The real reasons for the U.S. attack on Libya have nothing to do with self-defense against "terrorist attacks" on U.S. forces in Beirut in October 1983, as Shimon Peres would have it, or any of the other actions attributed rightly or wrongly to Libya, or "self-defense against future attack" in accord with the astonishing doctrine proclaimed by the Reagan Administration to much domestic acclaim. Libya's terrorism is a minor irritant, but Qaddafi has stood in the way of U.S. plans in North Africa, the Middle East and elsewhere: supporting Polisario in Western Sahara and anti-U.S. groups in the Sudan, forging a union with Morocco, intervening in Chad,[37] and in general interfering with U.S. efforts to forge a "strategic consensus" in the region and to impose its will elsewhere. These are real crimes, which must be punished.

Furthermore, the Libyan attack had the purpose and the effect of preparing opinion at home and abroad for further acts of U.S. violence. The immediate response might be negative, but once absorbed, the level of expectation is heightened and the United States can proceed to further escalation.

There are two major areas where such escalation is likely. The first is Central America. While the U.S. proxy army has succeeded in its major task of "forcing [the Sandinistas] to divert scarce resources to the war and away from social programs," as explained in a rare moment of candor by administration officials,[38] it is unlikely that it can "cut out the cancer"; hence the threat of successful independent development in terms that might be meaningful to the suffering population of U.S. client states will remain. Domestic and international pressures prevent the United States from attacking directly, as the United States attacked South Vietnam in 1962 and later all of Indochina; and the more indirect means of terror, while largely successful in El Salvador, may be inadequate for Nicaragua. It would be natural, then, for the United States to move to an arena where it is more likely to prevail: international confrontation. The United States has succeeded in cowing most of its allies into refraining from offering any meaningful assistance to Nicaragua, thus largely achieving the intended goal of forcing them to rely on the Soviet bloc for survival. The recent congressional battle over $100 million of aid is basically a sideshow; a lawless administration will find ways of funding its terrorist army somehow, whatever Congress legislates. What is important is a more symbolic victory: congressional authorization for direct CIA involvement and escalation by other means. The obvious means are threats to Soviet and Cuban shipping. Nicaragua would not be able to respond, but the

Soviet Union and Cuba might. If they do, the U. S. propaganda system can be counted on to react with outrage over this new proof of communist aggression, allowing the administration to construct an international crisis in which, it may be assumed, the Soviet Union will back down, so that Nicaragua will be effectively blockaded. If they do not respond, the same result will be achieved. Of course, the world may go up in smoke, but that is a minor consideration in comparison with the need to excise the cancer. U.S. and European opinion must be prepared for these eventualities. The bombing of Libya turns the ratchet another notch.

The second area where world opinion must be prepared for eventual escalation is the Middle East. The United States has blocked political settlement of the Arab-Israeli conflict at least since 1971, when President Sadat of Egypt made his first proposal for a full peace treaty (offering nothing to the Palestinians and in almost precise accord with official U.S. policy as well as the international consensus). In the situation of military confrontation that results from U.S.-Israeli rejectionism, Israel cannot permit any combination of Arab states to approach its military power, since it will face the threat of destruction. The Camp David agreements succeeded in excluding the major Arab state, Egypt, from the conflict, thus allowing Israel to expand its steps towards integrating the occupied territories and to attack its northern neighbor. But Syria remains a growing threat and, sooner or later, Israel will have to act to eliminate it. There is substantial war talk in Israel today, generally alleging Syrian belligerency and threat, but concealing the Israeli intention — indeed, need, as long as a political settlement is averted — to strike to eliminate a possible military rival. The U.S. media follow along, as usual.

Meanwhile, the U.S. Government surely wants to leave its options open. It would make sense for an Israeli strike against Syria to be accompanied by U.S. bombing, the former presented as a "preemptive strike" in "self-defense against future attack," the latter packaged for Western consumption as "self-defense" against Syrian-inspired terrorism. The purpose of direct U.S. participation would be to warn the Soviet Union that a global war will result from any attempt on their part to support their Syrian ally. European and U.S. opinion must be prepared for such possible moves. The attack on Libya and the subsequent propaganda campaigns, help set the stage, leaving the United States more free to consider these options if they are later deemed necessary. Again, the likelihood of a nuclear war is not small, but the United States has shown repeatedly that it is prepared to face this danger to achieve its ends in the Middle East, as elsewhere.

(1986)

Setting the Stage: Afghanistan

Introduction
Ellen Ray and William H. Schaap

In 1998, Eqbal Ahmad could write about chickens coming home to roost; today it is almost treasonous to do so. Yet what we face now is but the bitter irony of "blowback" from U.S.-sponsored funding of the anti-Soviet *jihad* in Afghanistan. The United States, Arundhati Roy reminded us just after September 11, had been "financing a future war against itself." More tragically, she noted, this current war "is being fought to uphold the American Way of Life. It'll probably end up undermining it completely."

The actions of Afghanistan, of the Taliban, even of Osama bin Laden, have been seen on all sides as a metaphor for a global conflict, whether between Western civilization on the one hand and intolerant religious fundamentalism on the other, as the pundits would have us see it; or between rapacious global imperialism on the one hand and the yearnings of the exploited have-nots of the world on the other, as everyone not under the spell of television networks intuitively understands. But there is also a real, local, on-the-ground aspect to the last 30 years of conflict in Afghanistan, not all that different from the 19th century's battles over spheres of influence in the area between Russia, Germany and Britain. The compulsive Western urge to contain the Soviet Union was only one aspect. Oil and drugs are others. Trade routes, natural resources, markets, all figure into the equation. Billions have been spent and millions killed, not just over abstract principles, but over precious natural resources and how they are moved around the earth. It is extremely instructive to study the details of U.S. involvement in Afghanistan and such a study was made possible in a rather unique way.

After the takeover of the U.S. Embassy in Teheran in 1979, many secret documents relating to Afghanistan were discovered, and they appeared in the pamphlets of reprinted documents (often pieced together from shredder baskets) published in Iran and widely distributed around the world. They became known in the United States through the efforts of veteran journalist William Worthy; the set of pamphlets he carried back from Iran was confiscated when he arrived in the United States, but the duplicate set he had mailed to himself was duly delivered. These classified State Department and CIA cables up to October 1979 laid bare the development of the U.S. policy that led to incursion of Soviet troops two months later. Steven Galster analyzed those documents in "Destabilizing Afghanistan"; he shows how overall strategic U.S. policy is converted into funding, training, directing and propagandizing a proxy war. Funneling billions of dollars in covert aid is a logistical challenge, to say the least. But it is money that keeps a proxy war going. Another article by Galster, "The Afghan Pipeline", describes the intricacies of manipulating such covert funds. Most of it is converted into weapons and ammunition. Among other things, Galster elucidates the central — indeed the essential — role of Pakistan in this massive undertaking, charting a worldwide flow of ordinance into Karachi and Peshawar and thence to the Afghan rebels. He also explains the role of propaganda in such an operation, from the establishment of clandestine radio stations, to the building of the public perception that this was nothing but a war between communism and Islam, to the scuttling of peace negotiations. He demonstrates that the United States did not want any settlement until the Soviets had been sufficiently "bled." And, he amply proves, the "bleeders" were firmly in control of U.S. policy.

Tragically, the departure of the Soviets and the collapse of the Najibullah regime did not lead to an enlightened or peaceful or democratic Afghanistan, but to endless war.

Destabilizing Afghanistan

Steve Galster

The Soviet invasion of Afghanistan in December 1979 was regarded by the United States then, as it still is today, as a blatant, unprovoked act of Soviet aggression and "expansionism." As a secret intelligence report issued several days after the invasion put it, Moscow's "key motivation was to bring its long-standing strategic goals within reach. Control of Afghanistan would be a major step toward... domination of the Asian sub-continent."[1] For the past eight years the White House and Congress have continually invoked this view to justify their consistently increasing support for the Afghan covert aid program — a program that now dwarfs U.S. covert activities in Nicaragua, Angola, Kampuchea and the rest of the world combined. The Soviet withdrawal from Afghanistan is seen merely as a sign that the application of the Reagan Doctrine there has foiled the Soviets' "grand" strategy.

However, classified documents seized in Iran during the takeover of the U.S. Embassy, along with an abundance of declassified materials, reveal that the Soviet decision to invade did not stem from a thirst for expansionism; rather, it was a response to actions by the United States and its allies who, starting shortly after the April ("Saur") Revolution in 1978, tried to destabilize the new pro-Soviet regime in Kabul by covertly supporting the anti-Soviet Afghan resistance. The case of Afghanistan illustrates how U.S. covert action can be disastrously counterproductive.

The communist takeover in Afghanistan in April 1978 presented the United States with a policy dilemma summed up in a secret memo to Secretary of State Cyrus Vance at the time: "We need to take into account the mix of nationalism and communism in the new leadership and seek to avoid driving the regime into a closer embrace with the Soviet Union than it might wish. On the other hand, anti-regime elements in Afghanistan will be watching us carefully to see if we acquiesce in or accept the communist takeover."[2]

The memo also noted that "Pakistan, Iran, Saudi Arabia and others of our friends will see the situation clearly as a Soviet coup."[3] Thenceforth, a debate ensued within the Carter Administration as to how the United States should react to the situation in Afghanistan. Moderate elements, led by Vance, urged self-restraint in Afghanistan so as not to attract more Soviet attention there; hard-liners led by National Security Adviser Brzezinski warned the president that to stand back from Afghanistan, especially in light of the growing instability in Iran, would project the image to America's regional allies that the United States had written off the region as not essential to U.S. interests.

Not knowing which way to lean at first, the president compromised (perhaps by not deciding) by allowing Brzezinski to seek an alternative regional strategy while the State Department was to establish "correct" relations with the new Afghan regime (Democratic Republic of Afghanistan or DRA). Brzezinski took advantage of his strong supervisory role of the CIA and proceeded immediately to establish a covert support network for the resistance consisting of several anti-Soviet governments. Brzezinski maintained close supervision of these and other CIA activities through the NSC's Special Coordinating Committee (SCC).[4] In May, one month after the DRA came to power and 19 months before the Soviet invasion, Brzezinski met with Deng Xiaoping in China and reached an "understanding" on mutual security issues, including Afghanistan.[5] This "understanding" must have included Pakistan because the following month the first Afghan rebel camps were set up in Peshawar (soon to be staffed by Chinese military instructors).[6]

Initially Brzezinski and the CIA found it difficult to provide significant assistance to the guerrillas. Pakistan refused to allow too much outside support on its soil out of fear of Soviet retaliation, and the State Department, with the President's tacit approval, was still trying to pursue normal relations with the DRA. But Brzezinski pressed the issue with both the president and the State Department and by the end of March 1979 he had "prevailed."[7] Several weeks later, he notes in his memoirs, Brzezinski pushed a decision through the SCC to "be more sympathetic to those Afghans who were determined to preserve their country's independence."[8]

While deliberately opaque as to what this meant, it is clear when examining the surrounding evidence that the decision entailed stepping up assistance to the Afghan rebels in order to destabilize the DRA. Apparently, however, Brzezinski was able to do more than just convince State Department officials that the rising Soviet influence in Afghanistan threatened U.S. national security. He also got them to see that the Afghan situation presented a valuable political opportunity for the United States. As a State Department report later put it, "the overthrow of the DRA would show the rest of the world, particularly the Third World, that the Soviets' view of the socialist course of history as being inevitable is not accurate."[9]

Starting no later than April 1979, several weeks after Brzezinski's SCC decision, U.S. foreign service officers began to meet with Afghan rebel leaders on a periodic basis to determine their needs.[10] The rebels' most obvious problems were their lack of weapons and their inability to create a unified opposition. The obvious answer to both problems was more money and a sure supply of weapons. The rebels had already made one attempt at unifying in June 1978. However, because of the incongruous nature of the different factions, who were as used to fighting each other as much as they were the government, the coalition crumbled within six weeks.[11]

By May, after having directed several resistance leaders to potential donors for their cause, the State Department reported that China, Saudi Arabia, the United Arab Emirates and Iran had pledged their assistance.[12] Saudi Arabia offered the rebels several million dollars up front if they could quickly reforge an alliance.[13] The rebels used these and other funds to purchase weapons from the Pakistanis and the Chinese, whose supplies were close at hand. Also, pressure was applied to Pakistan to relax its restrictions on being a sanctuary and a supplier. CIA field reports show that Pakistani Director of Military Operations, Brigadier Mian Mohammad Afzal, was brought onto the CIA payroll to ensure Pakistani cooperation.[14] Afzal reported to the CIA in October that in a series of meetings between President Zia ul-Haq and Chinese officials plans were developed to ensure Pakistan's continued role as a sanctuary and to further supply the resistance with weapons from Pakistan's stock.[15] The CIA closely monitored subsequent transactions between resistance leaders and Pakistani military personnel in Peshawar.[16]

In addition to facilitating the funding by other countries, the CIA itself was almost certainly funding the resistance as early as August 1979. At this time, the U.S. Embassy in Kabul issued a secret report which concluded that "the United States' larger interests... would be served by the demise of the Taraki-Amin regime, despite whatever setbacks this might mean for future social and economic reforms in Afghanistan."[17] The State Department had obviously swept aside any inhibitions it may have had about deliberately destabilizing the DRA Weeks later, the CIA office in Los Angeles wired to Kabul a request from a CIA-paid Afghan to send money to an Afghan rebel account in Iran with the name of the bank and the account number included.[18] This cable also revealed that many Afghans had been undergoing "Douglas" espionage training in Washington to assist the CIA in Afghanistan.

The United States Pushes Ahead

On the propaganda front, the CIA was busy funding and orchestrating public demonstrations throughout South Asia and Europe to denounce the "Soviet puppet" regime in Kabul.[19] And deep inside Afghanistan, the CIA was helping Afghan expatriates set up a dissident radio station to broadcast anti-government messages throughout the country.[20]

The decision by the United States to ignore its original warning to "avoid driving the [Afghan] regime into a closer embrace with the Soviet Union" and to instead covertly aid the regime's opponents, is especially curious in light of two things. First, the United States was well aware that the resistance could never serve as a viable alternative to the DRA leadership. The rebel leaders themselves had confided to State Department officials in secret meetings in Pakistan that they likened a dissident provisional government to "putting five different animals in the same cage."[21] Second and more significant, while the United States was clandestinely supporting the military efforts of the resistance, U.S. officials in Afghanistan were discovering that the Soviets were making desperate attempts to bring about a political solution to the situation.

One month after Brzezinski's SCC decision, U.S. intelligence reports suggested that "the Soviets [were] already moving forward with plans to engineer replacement of the... Khalqi leadership."[22] Shortly thereafter, East German Ambassador Hermann Schwiesau told the U.S. Embassy in Kabul that the Soviets were hoping to replace the unpopular Amin with a broader-based government.[23] At about the same time, the U.S. Embassy reported that the Soviets were including a former Afghan royal minister in their "National Front" negotiations, implying that the Soviets were trying to forge, as they are today, a broad-based coalition government in Kabul that would be willing and able to respect their security interests (i.e., remaining outside a U.S. alliance), thus rendering a Soviet presence unnecessary.

Instead of concluding from these observations that the United States should refrain from intervening in Afghanistan in the midst of the Soviets' troubles there, hard-line U.S. officials saw the situation as an opportunity to stick it to the Soviets while they were vulnerable. Such an approach, it was believed, would not provoke Soviet intervention. The Soviets themselves had told U.S. officials that an invasion "might solve one problem but would create another."[24] The U.S. Embassy in Moscow strongly agreed with that assessment and doubted the Soviets would risk their other foreign policy priorities for a war in Afghanistan.[25]

But as hard as they both tried, neither the Soviets nor the resistance were able to unseat Amin. This and the growing instability in both Afghanistan and Iran were making the Americans and the Soviets very nervous about each other's intentions in the region. Seeing that the resistance alone could not protect America's regional interests from Soviet "aggression," the United States decided to cover all bases by courting President Amin. If the United States could lure Amin out of the Soviet sphere, it was thought, then the Soviets would be unable to use Afghanistan as a launching pad for invading Iran or Baluchistan.

Washington Courts Amin

The United States knew that Amin was becoming increasingly wary of the Soviets, especially after he deposed and assassinated Communist Party leader Nur Mohammad Taraki, the Soviets' favored choice for president, in September. So beginning in September 1979, Bruce Amstutz, the U.S. chargé d'affaires in Kabul, began to hold friendly meetings with Amin to show him that he need not worry about his unhappy Soviet allies as long as the United States maintained a strong presence in Afghanistan.[26] The strategy worked. On September 27 Amin made a special appeal to Amstutz for improved relations with the United States.[27] Two days later in New York, Afghan Foreign Minister Wali quietly expressed the same sentiments to State Department officials David Newsom and Harold Saunders.[28]

The Soviets became increasingly concerned about the war below their border and Amin's stubbornness and incompetence in dealing with it. Amidst the growing instability, it appeared to the Soviets that Amin was preparing to leave the Soviet orbit and approach the United States for help. They were probably right. On October 30, the U.S. Embassy in Kabul reported after having talked with Amin that he seemed extremely eager to improve U.S.-Afghan relations and was "painfully aware of the exiled leadership the Soviets [were] keeping on the shelf."[29] Suddenly realizing the potential consequences of their strategy, the U.S. officials quickly backed away from Amin. Abandoned, Amin then turned to Pakistan for help. In early December he sent "frantic messages" to President Zia asking for an immediate meeting, obviously making a last-ditch effort to escape the Soviet grasp.[30] Zia declined to go but planned to send his foreign minister, Agha Shahi, who was to have flown to Kabul on December 22, but was prevented from doing so by bad weather.[31]

When the Soviets invaded Afghanistan three days later, Congress immediately decided to fully back the Afghan rebels to oppose what President Carter called "the greatest threat to world peace since World War II." What Congress and other U.S. citizens failed to realize then, as they still do today, is that the United States was not only a victim of Soviet intervention in Afghanistan by covertly challenging Soviet influence there before the invasion — it was a cause as well.

(1988)

The Afghan Pipeline

Steve Galster

While revelations of Reagan's covert war in Nicaragua continue to dazzle the U.S. public, a far bigger and more complex covert program has gone relatively unnoticed in Afghanistan. After nearly nine years of covert involvement, the United States has poured over $2 billion [in fact, more than $10 billion, as later confirmed — eds.] into the Afghan war, far more than the total amount that has gone to Nicaragua, Angola and Kampuchea combined.[1] In fact, the estimated amount of money "lost" in the Afghan pipeline by the CIA's own estimates easily exceeds the total amount of U.S. support that has gone to the Contras.[2]

Congressmen who strongly opposed Contra aid have not only supported Reagan's covert war in Afghanistan but have teamed up with Reagan Doctrine advocates to expand the administration's program. Whereas the war in Nicaragua is now the "bad" war, Afghanistan has from the start been viewed as the "good" war and as the rebels call it, a "holy" war or *jihad*. Thus, with their broad base of support and their strategically placed war below the Soviet border, the Afghan rebels have earned the forefront position in President Reagan's global strategy of "rollback" and billions of dollars in CIA support.

Officially, the Reagan Administration's policy toward Afghanistan is to "seek the earliest possible negotiated political settlement there to effect the withdrawal of Soviet forces."[3] This policy, which is a continuation of that set up under Jimmy Carter, is ostensibly pursued along two tracks: covert aid and negotiations. Carter believed that a "modest" amount of secret military aid would enhance the prospects for a negotiated settlement.[4]

The Reagan Administration, on the other hand, has reasoned that the more aid the United States can provide to the rebels the better the chances are of bringing the Soviets to the negotiating table. Even with a Soviet withdrawal assured today, the administration has vowed to pursue this strategy of "peace through strength" by continuing its support of the rebels. However, a closer look at the administration's seven year secret war in Afghanistan reveals that it has been little interested in peace there. In fact, the evidence strongly suggests that U.S. policy has been to sabotage attempts at a negotiated settlement until the Soviets have been, in the view of some, "sufficiently bled."

The Policy and the Pipeline

In March 1981 CIA Director Casey proposed to President Reagan that the CIA upgrade and expand the Afghan covert aid pipeline.[5] Under Carter, the CIA had coordinated the Afghan weapons supply line with Pakistan, China, Saudi Arabia and Egypt. The United States and Saudi Arabia provided the funds, Egypt and China provided the weapons and Pakistan served as the conduit and sanctuary.[6] Initially the United States and Saudi Arabia provided about $30 million each to purchase Soviet-style weapons manufactured in Egypt and China.[7] Retired U.S. military officers contracted out by the CIA — along with Chinese and Pakistani officials — were on hand to the rebels.[8] But the secrecy of foreign involvement was the important element of the program. "The Afghan struggle (was) an 'Islamic' struggle," President Carter told his aides, "and U.S. assistance should not disturb that impression."[9]

Much has changed in the CIA's Afghan war under Reagan. Most of the same countries are still involved and the cultivation of the war's image as a fight between Islam and communism remains crucial to maintaining the rebels' broad support. But with the rapidly expanding political and financial support for the program, the U.S. Afghan policy and its covert aid pipeline have been significantly altered.

After Casey's proposal to expand the Afghan program in March 1981, the United States looked directly to Saudi Arabia for more assistance. With the promise that Reagan would get Congress to approve the sale of AWACS to them, the Saudis immediately doled out $15 million to the resistance, mainly through private bank accounts in Oman and Pakistan.[10] In October, when the United States delivered the first five AWACS to Saudi Arabia, King Fahd agreed to increase assistance to both the Afghan rebels and the Nicaraguan Contras.[11]

The role of Pakistan, which worried about its vulnerable position vis-a-vis the Soviets, was also enhanced. To allay President Zia's concerns and to ensure further Pakistani cooperation, the Reagan Administration secretly offered to station U.S. troops in Pakistan.[12] However, Zia stated that he preferred weapons to troops.[13] The next month, in September, the United States agreed to a six-year, $3.2 billion program of U.S. economic and military assistance.[14] It was also agreed that Pakistan would continue its coordinating role in weapons supply. This agreement, which is still in effect today, went as follows: once in Pakistan, whether at the port of Karachi or the Peshawar airport, the weapons would be handed over to the National Logistics Cell (NLC) of the Pakistani Interservice Intelligence Directorate (ISID), the equivalent of the CIA and FBI combined. CIA station officers in Karachi and Peshawar would examine the receipts for the weapons but would not even check the crates to see if they were accurate.[15] The NLC officials would then drive the weapons to either Quetta in the West or Peshawar in the East. Once there, the ISID, under CIA supervision, would distribute the arms to the seven rebel groups recognized by the Pakistani Government. These groups would then drive the weapons to either their arms depots along the border or the local arms bazaar where they could make a healthy profit selling their new AK-47s and RPG-7s to drug dealers and local tribesmen.[16]

In this early period the CIA looked largely to Egypt and China for supplies. Both countries handed over weapons from their own stocks while CIA-supervised factories outside Cairo turned out Soviet-style arms to add to the flow.[17] Hughes Aircraft Company was contracted out to upgrade some of Egypt's weapons, particularly the SAM-7 anti-aircraft guns.[18] The Egyptian arms stock was replenished with new U.S. weapons and China earned much-needed hard currency, in addition to fulfilling one of its own foreign policy goals of containing the Soviets.[19] A fair amount of the rebels' weapons were also captured from and sometimes even sold by Afghan Government troops.[20] Still, getting outside weapons to the rebels in Pakistan remained an important task. Eventually China made some use of the newly opened Karokaram highway and continued to load CIA-run planes and ships destined for Peshawar and Karachi.[21] Egyptian weapons continued to be flown directly to Pakistan but were sometimes landed in Oman, from where they were shipped to Karachi to avoid being traced.[22] The Reagan Administration was quite impressed with the rebels' surprising show of force during this first year. Members of the 208 Committee (the restricted inter-agency committee that handled covert operations) suddenly saw tremendous prospects in Afghanistan for gaining a global strategic edge on the Soviets. This elite group included Vincent Cannistraro, an ex-CIA official who served as White House head of covert operations; Morton Abramowitz, State Department head of intelligence; Bert Dunn, Chief of the CIA's Near East and South Asia Division; Oliver North and alternating members from the Defense

Department including Elie Krakowski, head of Regional Defense, and Richard Armitage.

These and other administration officials thought that by tying down and "bleeding" the Soviets in Afghanistan the United States could divert Soviet attention away from other Third World hot spots like Nicaragua and Angola, making room for the United States to maneuver. If the Afghan rebels could keep up their fight for several years (if not decades), the Soviets would eventually incur serious financial, military and political problems. Little danger was seen in the Soviets expanding their war out of frustration into Iran or Pakistan because of Iran's intransigence and Pakistan's beefed-up military, not to mention its mutual defense pact with the United States.[23] It began to appear, as one congressman put it, that "the United States [had] a real chance to make Afghanistan the Soviets' Vietnam."[24]

Sabotaging a Settlement

The only thing standing in the way of creating a morass for the Soviets in Afghanistan was the near-term prospect for peace. Although some U.S. officials have, since the beginning of the war, wanted to negotiate a Soviet withdrawal from Afghanistan, the evidence suggests that they were not very influential. Following the first formal UN-sponsored peace talks in the summer of 1982, UN mediator Diego Cordovez announced that the negotiating parties, Pakistan and the Afghan Government, had made important concessions and that he planned to present a broad outline of an agreement that fall.[25] However, just before Cordovez was to unveil his peace plan, President Reagan ordered the CIA to increase the quantity and quality of weapons to the rebels.[26] The "bleeders" had been at work. Several months later, in December, Yuri Andropov told President Zia at Leonid Brezhnev's funeral that the Soviet Union would leave Afghanistan "quickly" if Pakistan ceased its support of the resistance.[27] Subsequently the White House ordered the CIA to immediately provide the rebels with increased amounts of bazookas, mortars, grenade launchers, mines, recoilless rifles and shoulder-fired anti-aircraft guns.[28]

It appears that this trend of sabotaging peace negotiations as long as the resistance was willing and able to fight became the unofficial Afghan policy in the White House. Proof of this policy manifested itself in 1983 when an end to the Soviet occupation seemed as certain as it does today. In late April of that year, the negotiating parties gathered in Geneva to map out another plan for a Soviet withdrawal. To enhance the prospects for a settlement, the Soviets secretly told the Pakistani Government in late March that they would begin to withdraw by September if the Pakistanis ceased their support for the resistance.[29] The Pakistanis took the Soviet pledge seriously and several weeks later issued a directive to the rebels to move their headquarters from Peshawar and to disperse their groups.[30] The resistance alliance, which has been dominated by the radical fundamentalist factions, was furious. The withdrawal of Soviet troops was only one of their goals; the militant fundamentalists also intended to purge the country of everything that smacked of communism, including anyone who had served the government in any way. For them the war was far from over. These groups had even stated their intention to carry their *jihad* into the Soviet Union.[31]

Meanwhile UN officials Diego Cordovez and Javier Pérez de Cuellar shuttled to the Soviet Union and China where they received guarantees for a possible settlement.[32] By late April, the Pakistani and Afghan governments had "virtually settled" the simultaneous withdrawal of outside support which would begin in September.[33] But one week later, the White House for the first time leaked to the press the fact that it was covertly aiding the resistance and would continue to do so until the political aims of the resistance alliance were met.[34] Needless to say the talks came to a screeching halt.

Embarrassed, but still hopeful about salvaging a settlement that June, Pakistani Foreign Minister Yaqub Khan scurried to Washington in May to enlist the Reagan Administration's cooperation. Khan told Vice-President Bush and Secretary of State Shultz that the Soviets wanted to withdraw from Afghanistan but with minimal humiliation.[35] Bush and Shultz apparently convinced Khan that the United States was not interested in facilitating a graceful Soviet withdrawal. The following next month the UN-sponsored talks broke down immediately when Khan wanted to re-open discussion on clauses concerning noninterference.[36] Two weeks later Shultz visited Pakistan to reassure both the resistance and the Pakistani Government that the United States would not abandon them "in their fight against Soviet aggression."[37]

Congress and the *Jihad*

With Pakistan now cemented into the "bleeders" camp, the United States was well positioned to turn up the heat on the Soviets. Starting in 1984 and continuing to the present, the administration has received continual boosts to pursue this strategy from Congress. Congressman Charles Wilson, (Dem.-Cal.) a high-ranking member of the Defense Appropriations Committee who claims "we owe the Soviets one for Vietnam," visited President Zia in late 1983 to see what the United States could do to strengthen the rebels.[38]

In the spring of 1984 he and his colleagues summoned Deputy Director of Central Intelligence John McMahon to explain why the CIA wasn't doing more for the rebels. McMahon, who was neither interested in providing the rebels with sophisticated weaponry nor in expanding the already large paramilitary operation below the Soviet border, claimed that the rebels were being adequately supplied.[39] The congressmen, realizing that they had allies in the State Department (Abramowitz), the White House (Cannistraro) and the Defense Department (Krakowski and Armitage) and that CIA Director Casey was supportive of their cause, proceeded to draft legislation that would force high-level bureaucrats like McMahon to cooperate in expanding the Afghan program.

In the fall of 1984 Congress passed a resolution calling for "effective" aid for the Afghan rebels and immediately doubled the administration's request for aid.[40] To handle the growing amount of funds, the CIA established a joint bank account with the Saudis in Switzerland. The Saudis promised to match the U.S. funds dollar-for-dollar and both governments began by pledging $250 million each.[41] The CIA began to upgrade the quality of weapons for the rebels. In January 1985 it purchased 40 Oerlikon anti-aircraft guns from the Swiss firm Oerlikon-Buhrle at a cost of $50 million.[42] Also, many of the Chinese weapons destined for the rebels were being upgraded. Some were sent to Egypt while many were flown to a CIA weapons plant somewhere in the midwestern United States.[43] In addition, a New Jersey company was contracted to make explosives for the rebels.[44]

As the CIA upgraded the covert pipeline, the Soviets again began to hint that they wanted out of Afghanistan. In March 1985, new Soviet leader Mikhail Gorbachev told Pakistani President Zia at Konstantine Chernenko's funeral that the war could end as soon as Pakistan ceased its support of the rebels.[45] But in keeping with U.S. policy, President Reagan several weeks later signed National Security Decision Directive 166 calling for efforts to drive Soviet forces from Afghanistan "by all means available."[46] One of the "bleeders," Morton Abramowitz, succeeded in inserting language into the directive calling for an expansion of the program every year.[47]

Thus, with $250 million in newly appropriated funds, the CIA's mission was clearer than ever. The only problem was finding the weapons to spend all the new money on. Neither the Chinese nor the Egyptians could fill the increasing requests. So to quickly expend a large portion of the new money and to satisfy the constant demand for better anti-aircraft guns, the CIA in late 1985 purchased 300 British-made Blowpipe missiles from Short Brothers Company in Belfast, Northern Ireland.[48] Since Britain has had no official policy to militarily support the rebels, the weapons were sold to a third country who then handed them over to the CIA for a profit.[49]

But the rebels were still in need of more AK-47 rifles and SAM-7s, among other types of unsophisticated weaponry. The problem was finding another supplier. Someone suggested Poland and judging by documents from the Iran-Contra hearings it was probably the ever-present John Singlaub. Through the GeoMilitech Corporation, Singlaub and his associate Barbara Studley had arranged to get Polish weapons to the Contras. And Studley had proposed a plan to DCI Casey in December 1985 for GeoMilitech to facilitate the supply of weapons to the rebels.[50] By early 1986 weapons were being purchased in Poland and quietly shipped out of the northwest port of Stettin.[51] To handle the increasing flow of weapons into Pakistan, the Pakistani Government built a new network of roads from Peshawar and Quetta to the small border towns that act as arms depots.[52] To transfer the weapons from these towns over the border into Pakistan, the Afghans initially had to rent mules and trucks. In order to cover the rebels' transportation expenses the CIA counterfeited and provided to the rebels millions of dollars worth of Afghan currency.[53]

Leaks In The Pipeline

As the pipeline was expanded it began to spring big leaks. Problems with the pipeline had existed from the beginning, but by 1985 they were becoming more obvious. Twenty-nine of the 40 Oerlikon anti-aircraft guns the CIA had purchased in Switzerland at over $1 million a piece never made it to Afghanistan.[54] Somewhere along the line these and many other weapons were put to other uses by either the Afghans, the Pakistanis or the CIA itself.

A significant amount of the leaking was (as it still is) coming from within Pakistan, where corrupt government and rebel officials had suddenly become quite rich. Pakistani General Akhtar Abdul Rahman, head of the ISID up to 1987 and his successor, General Hamid Gul, are suspected to have been prime benefactors of the pipeline. They and their subordinates within the NLC could easily have made a fortune off CIA supplies.

Since the genesis of the pipeline, the NLC has had the sole responsibility of transporting newly arrived weapons from Karachi to Quetta and Peshawar (weapons that come by plane, especially those that are U.S. or British-made, are flown directly to these cities).[55] NLC trucks have special passes that allow them to travel unharassed by customs or police officials on their several hundred mile-drive.[56] Along the way it is very easy for the NLC officials to exchange the new weapons and other supplies for old ones from the government's stock.

Widespread corruption also exists among the rebel leaders but has gone practically unnoticed in the United States thanks to CIA propaganda. The same kinds of things that tarnished the Contras' image, such as killing civilians, drug smuggling and embezzlement are practiced by many

Afghan rebels. Taking no prisoners, assassinating suspected government collaborators, destroying government-built schools and hospitals, killing "unpious" civilians are just a few of the inhumane acts they have carried out. But the picture we receive of the rebels in the United States is of an uncorrupt, popular group of freedom-loving people who aspire toward a democratic society.

The CIA and the State Department have worked hard to project this image. In 1984 Walter Raymond, on loan to the NSC from the CIA, "suggested" to Senator Humphrey (Rep.-N.H.) that Congress finance a media project for the rebels that would shed favorable light on the rebels' side of the war.[57]

Humphrey easily got Congress to approve the new "Afghan Media Project" which was handed over to the United States Information Agency (USIA) and Boston University. At Boston University the project was headed up by a man named Joachim Maitre, an East German defector who had close connections with International Business Communications and the Gulf and Caribbean Foundation (both of which served important roles in illegally raising funds for the Nicaraguan Contras). He also had worked closely with Oliver North to make TV commercials attacking congressmen who had opposed aid to the Contras.[58] Maitre escaped criticism for his Contra connections and proceeded to train Afghan rebels to report on and film the war.[59] Since it is illegal for the USIA to disseminate information in the United States, the Afghan Media Project's films and reports were to be sold only to foreign news agencies. However, U.S. journalists who have a quick story to write or don't want to enter Afghanistan have often found the rebels' information too tempting to pass up. CBS, the station that has covered the Afghan war the most and in a very pro-rebel light, may have been one guilty party. CBS used footage provided by the rebels claiming that it was taken by its cameraman, Mike Hoover.[60]

Corruption surrounding the CIA's Afghan program has begun to surface during the last several years. For example, the fact that the rebels have been harvesting a large amount of opium was brought to light by the *New York Times* in 1986.[61] And DEA officials have privately admitted recently that the shipment of CIA weapons into Pakistan has allowed the trade in heroin — three tons of which reaches the United States every year — to flourish as never before.[62] One DEA official noted that virtually no heroin was refined in Pakistan before 1979, but "now Pakistan produces and transships more heroin than the rest of the world combined."[63] Neither U.S. nor Pakistani drug enforcement officials are any match for these heavily armed drug dealers.

In spite of these problems, from 1986 to the present, the CIA has expanded the pipeline to handle over $1 billion in new monies. As part of this package the CIA is sending the rebels highly sophisticated U.S.-made weaponry. Ironically, the CIA — particularly its former Deputy Director John McMahon — originally opposed this idea and insisted on continuing the supply of average Soviet-styled weapons.[64] But by March 1986 the impasse was broken. On March 4, McMahon resigned from the CIA; one week later UN negotiator Diego Cordovez announced that he had "all the elements of a comprehensive settlement of the Afghan problem."[65] With McMahon gone and the prospects for peace again on the horizon, members of the 208 Committee, with the president's approval, decided immediately to send the rebels several hundred of the world's most sophisticated anti-aircraft gun, the U.S.-made Stinger.[66]

Although the Stingers are delivered more carefully than other weapons (they are flown on U.S. airplanes through Germany en route to Pakistan), once in Pakistan they can easily fall into dangerous hands. Initially the Stingers were safeguarded by keeping them from the rebels. Although the media began in April 1986 to report on the rebels' immediate successes with the Stingers, the rebels hadn't even touched one yet. Ethnic Pushtuns in the Pakistani Special Forces, disguised as rebels, were the ones firing the Stingers then and many probably still are today.[67] Meanwhile, a group of "ex-Army specialists" hired by the CIA were training the rebels to use the new weapon.[68]

Once the rebels were adequately trained, the politics of the pipeline began to come into play. The ISID distributed a disproportionate amount of the Stingers to the more radical fundamentalist groups.[69] ISID has skewed the distribution of weapons to favor the fundamentalists all along, but it took the Stinger issue to highlight this fact. These are the groups that were responsible for selling nearly a dozen Stingers to Iranian Revolutionary Guards in July 1987 and who are stockpiling their weapons to continue their *jihad* if and when the U.S. cuts off its supply.[70] The CIA was aware of the Iran connection two months before it was revealed and before Congress approved sending more Stingers.[71] It is also aware now that by arming these same groups, the United States is setting the scene for a major post-withdrawal bloodbath.

But today President Reagan is flaunting the covert operation in Afghanistan as the prize of the Reagan Doctrine. The Soviets are finally negotiating in "good faith," he claims, because U.S. aid allowed the "freedom fighters" to keep up their fight. Although the war has had its costs, the benefit of driving the Soviets out will make them worth it. The costs of intentionally prolonging the Afghan war have been a flourishing drug trade, an estimated one million dead and the provisions for a bloody

Islamic revolution. Unfortunately, in light of the administration's hardening stance in the current negotiations, we must wonder whether the "bleeders" are really ready to end it now.

(1988)

III. Terrorist Wars
in the
Middle East

Israeli-U.S. Terror

Introduction
Ellen Ray and William H. Schaap

For more than 35 years, the violent and bitter history of the Palestinian-Israeli conflicts have centered around a history of collaboration between U.S. and Israeli military and intelligence services and their coincidence of interests. Israeli covert operations have backed up U.S. clandestine schemes, especially in the Middle East, but also in Central America, southern Africa and elsewhere in a global conquest in which U.S. domination has reached its apex under George W. Bush.

Ever since the discovery of vast, almost unimaginable oil reserves in the region, the overriding strategic objective of the United States in the Middle East has been access to and eventual control over that resource. And since its 1967 victory in the six-day war, when Israel established itself as the regional military superpower capable of aiding in this primary U.S. objective, massive U.S. foreign aid and subsidized weapons of war have ensured an Israeli-U.S. alliance with mutually expansionist agendas. Both want unfettered access to Arab oil and more.

The second U.S. imperative is its strategic partnership with Israel, a function of the power of the pro-Israel lobby in the United States, exemplified by the ability of the American-Israel Political Action Committee to influence congressional and even presidential elections. And the White House, State Department and Pentagon are riddled with insiders with dual loyalties, the belief that U.S. and Israeli interests are and should be, identical.

The quid pro quo for Israel, an extension of this objective, Is the relative free play given to its own designs in the Middle East as a military force and an ever-expanding Zionist state.

The United States has given Israel virtually every sophisticated weapon system it has to offer, more than $18 billion in the last decade, with more than $2 billion in military aid slated for the next fiscal year (2003-4). As a further reward for cooperation in covert activities around the globe, the U.S. remained silent, if not actually assisted, Israel's development and testing of its own nuclear weapons.

Just how cooperative the Israelis have been and how some U.S. power brokers view its role in Washington's overall strategy was expressed by Senator Jesse Helms when he boasted in 1995 that "Israel is at least the equivalent of a U.S. aircraft carrier in the Middle East."

Although no significant policies of the Israeli Government could be implemented without the tacit concurrence of its U.S. benefactor, when it suits Washington's rapacious oil policies, arrangements of convenience with Israel's enemies were not precluded in the past. The United States (and Britain) supplied chemical and other weapons to Iraq during the Iraq-Iran war, while covertly working with Israel to supply Iran.

And Israel has also conducted its own military intelligence operations against U.S. targets, such as the seemingly inexplicable Israeli bombing of the *U.S.S. Liberty* during the 1967 war, a deliberate act apparently to prevent the U.S. communications ship from monitoring, perhaps disrupting its invasion and occupation of the Golan Heights. And, of course, each nation spies on the other; while Jonathan Pollard was caught and jailed, both countries have active operatives, collaborators and media assets in each other's territory.

But no matter which regime may be in power in either country, both Israeli and U.S. campaigns plot the elimination of any viable, sovereign, Palestinian state. Together, their machinations of incremental negotiations followed by betrayal, assassination and invasion have imposed upon the Palestinians what Noam Chomsky called "a system of permanent neo-colonial dependency."

Brutal attacks on Palestinian civilians, collective punishment, obliteration of entire villages, mass forced expulsions, illegal settlement of occupied land including East Jerusalem, torture, terrorism, starvation and murder have been used by successive Israeli governments with U.S. approval. They have reached new heights under the Sharon Government, with the approval of the current Bush Administration. Indeed, the Israel lobby has been jubilant over the nearly identical policies of Sharon's Likud and Bush's Republicans, dominated as it is by Likudniks.

Universal military conscription of Israeli youth thrusts young draftees into endless confrontations with Palestinians in Israel and in the occupied territories, ensuring an existential racial hatred in deliberately provocative "strategies of tension" and expansion, all in the name of a "fragile" Israeli state security. This while Israel has one of the most powerful and best-equipped armed forces in the world, the only nuclear power in the region.

Sharon defended his unilateral military carnage as his country's "best path to security." What he described as antiterror tactics, including stepping up assassinations of Palestinian military and civilian leaders, led to the predictable increase in acts of terrorism against Israeli citizens themselves, most notably indiscriminate suicide bombings. While Sharon claimed he was "making every effort to prevent" escalation, his military actions suggested precisely the opposite: Each deadly suicide bombing that followed Israeli military assassinations became the justification for the next Israeli atrocity.

War crime charges leveled against Sharon are legion, from his demolishing of a Jordanian village in 1953, to his complicity in the Sabra and Shatila massacres in Lebanon in 1982, to his Central American adventures involving arms and drugs, to his multiple invasions and reoccupation of most of the West Bank and Gaza in 2002. The U.S. role in this mayhem cannot be overemphasized. U.S. F-16 fighter jets and Apache helicopter gun ships were employed daily. Washington vacillated as the military assault was consolidated, trying all the while to appease its Arab critics.

Sharon's deliberate and systematic rampage through every Palestinian town and village has been conducted with personal hatred and revenge, in furtherance of the Israeli Government's intention of destroying the Palestinian people's social and physical will for self-government. Jewish religious graffiti splashed on walls of occupied Palestinian Authority offices were stark evidence of domination, symbols of Israel's goal of killing, imprisoning, or transporting Palestinian militants and their families from their homeland.

Despite Israel's control through the CIA-approved, Oslo-directed Palestinian Authority, the PA was locked in an endless cycle of repression and corruption through enforced collaboration with security committees run by the CIA and Israeli intelligence against the Palestinian people. Sharon's campaign against its institutional infrastructure also included intentional killings of large numbers of Palestinian civilians through saturation bombings of refugee camps and villages and the homes of suspected terrorists (with no regard for the lives of innocent neighbors), aided by computerized targeting and the rounding up of thousands of Palestinian men and women and their families for planned expulsion.

The Palestinians themselves, dispersed and dispossessed and used as pawns by other Arab nations, have never been able to develop a united vision. There are Palestinian nationalists and socialists and there are Palestinian fundamentalists. The fostering of disunity and corruption within these factions — whether in the Occupied Territories or in exile — has been a major element in the U.S.-Israeli targeting of the Palestinian national struggle by covert manipulation of Palestinian exiles and groups. In what was hardly a coincidence, during the early 1980s, while the United States actively encouraged an Islamic "Holy War" in Afghanistan, the Israelis infiltrated and supported a burgeoning Islamic fundamentalist movement, later allowing Islamic charities, religious schools and training sites to flourish, as their well-financed graduates countered the growing influence of Palestinian nationalists.

The occupation army's control of land, travel, water, food and medicine intensified, even as Palestinians attempted to negotiate an ever-changing "peace process" with Israel. Orchestrated with the United States as a delaying tactic, this effectively prevented an independent Palestinian state. The Oslo accords achieved only greater Israeli control over the territories and the geometric expansion of armed, militant Zionist settlements entrenched in the West Bank and Gaza.

The plan for the gradual creation of an autonomous Palestine was transformed from a blueprint for a contiguous territory into a jigsaw puzzle divided by Jewish settlements, fortified access roads and innumerable security zones. The proposed map of Palestinian areas resembles the Bantustans of apartheid South Africa. Israeli tanks and troops poured into these tiny "cantons," bombing and killing civilians at will. And Bush's minimal support for such a state, conditioned upon "regime change" in the Palestinian Authority, may disappear altogether, as events suggest a Likud push towards a final ethnic cleansing.

At an estimated cost of well over $1 million per mile, Israel has begun construction of a "security fence" that will eventually stretch 225 miles, walling off Palestinians on the West Bank — from Israel, from each other and from Israeli Palestinians. While the implausible rationale is put forth that this wall will inhibit the infiltration of suicide bombers, in fact this physical separation will facilitate the long-standing "transfer policy," discussed below. The psychological and historical implications of such separation cannot be overemphasized. Many informed commentators, including some Israeli journalists, see these developments as inevitably leading to the forced expulsion of all Palestinians from all Israeli-occupied territory.

With this escalation in Israeli terrorism, the devastating retaliatory suicide bombings have turned a war against occupation soldiers and settlers into the targeting of civilians within Israel. And after September 11, Western fears of Islamic extremism conflated the fanaticism of organizations like the Taliban with the genuine national aspirations of the Palestinians. With the world focused first on George W. Bush's "war against terrorism" and then on his unilateral attack on Iraq, Sharon was free to launch a massive re-invasion of Palestinian-controlled territory. Now both Israel and the United States have brought the *jihad* of their own creation home to plague their own civilian populations.

The first *intifada* erupted in 1987 when Israeli expanding settlements in the occupied territories stripped Palestinians of more of their land, while Israeli and U.S. intelligence operations to weaken Palestinian unity intensified. "Preemptive retaliation" began with the Israeli assassination of Abu Jihad, the cofounder, with Yasser Arafat, of Fateh. In "Israeli State Terror", Professor Naseer Aruri briefly outlines some of the history of the Zionist movement and its terrorist methods, dispossessing Palestinians to found the modern Israeli state, culminating in the rebellion of the Palestinians against the inhumanity of the occupation. The spontaneous outpouring of rage against the occupation could not be stopped. Stone-throwing youths faced down Israeli tanks and guns, until the first U.S. bombs were dropped in Gulf War I.

In "Israel Shahak on the 'Transfer' Proposal", an interview with the late Professor Shahak, a Holocaust survivor and one of the most informed and passionate critics of Israeli state religion and politics, he analyzes the totalitarian implications of the long-planned "transfer policy," the forcible removal of all Palestinians from the occupied territories, a Zionist goal since Israel's birth.

In "Israel Wages Chemical Warfare With American Tear Gas", Louis Wolf researches an example of U.S. complicity in Israeli crimes, its providing of deadly CS gas to Israel for the indiscriminate use against civilians. Then, to give some examples of Israeli involvement on the international scene, in "Washington's Proxy: Israeli Arms in Central America", Clarence Lusane examines one of the lesser known aspects of the U.S.-Israeli partnership, Israel's support of the dirty United States war in Central America, showing how Ariel Sharon undertook such a role. And Jack Colhoun then describes the collaboration between Israel and the apartheid regime in South Africa.

Israeli State Terror

Naseer Aruri

In his personal diary, which was published against the wishes of the Israeli establishment, former Israeli Prime Minister Moshe Sharett reveals that Israeli military operations against Arab civilian populations were designed to terrorize them and create fear, tension and instability.[1] Sharett's documentation shows that Israel's territorial expansion (such as in the Suez in 1956) was facilitated by Israeli acts of provocation, which generated Arab hostility and created pretexts for intervention. For example, the attack by Israeli Army Unit 101 led by Ariel Sharon on the Palestinian village of Kibya in October 1953, causing numerous civilian casualties and destruction of homes, was condemned by Sharett. He writes, "[In the cabinet meeting] I condemned the Kibya affair that exposed us in front of the whole world as a gang of blood-suckers, capable of mass massacres regardless it seems, of whether their actions may lead to war."[2]

More recent accounts by Israeli writers show how earlier acts of terrorism provided a historical background to adoption of a policy of state terrorism by Israel.[3] Benny Morris's explanation of the Palestinian exodus in 1948, based on state, military and Zionist archives, refutes the official Israeli version that the Palestinians bear responsibility for their own expulsion. An earlier work by Irish journalist Erskine Childers demonstrated that, contrary to the official Israeli version, there were no Arab radio broadcasts ordering the Palestinians to leave.[4] And Israeli journalist Tom Segev reveals in his book how instrumental was Zionist terrorism in the creation of the Palestinian refugee problem. Sixteen months after 250 Arab civilians were massacred in the village of Deir Yassin (April 9, 1948) by the combined forces of ETZEL (known as Menachem Begin's Irgun) and LEHI (known as Yitzhak Shamir's Stern Gang) there was a debate in the Israeli set in which, according to Segev, a member of Begin's Herut Party had boasted: "Thanks to Deir Yassin, we won the war."[5]

Another account by Lenny Brenner[6] reveals that Israeli Prime Minister Shamir was a convert to the pro-Mussolini Betar (Zionist Brownshirts) in the late 1930s and that his Stern Gang had attempted to strike a deal with the Nazi regime in Germany in 1941 in which the establishment of a Jewish state in Palestine on a "totalitarian basis" would be bound by a treaty with the German Reich.

Shamir's commitment to right-wing causes and to terrorism was unmistakably revealed in an article he wrote in the LEHI journal *Hehazit* (The Front) in the summer of 1943. This excerpt stands in contrast to Shamir's constant moralizing and condemnation of what he calls "PLO terrorism:"

Neither Jewish ethics nor Jewish tradition can disqualify terrorism as a means of combat... [T]errorism is for us a part of the political battle being conducted under the present circumstances and it has a great part to play: speaking in a clear voice to the whole world, as well as to our wretched brethren outside this land, it proclaims our war against the occupier.[7]

Shamir's cabinet colleague Yitzhak Rabin who, as defense minister in charge of the occupied territories, proclaimed the policy of "might, force and blows" in January 1988 (which has so far resulted in an estimated 281 deaths, more than 50,000 injuries and 30,000 detentions) has also had a consistent record of terrorism for more than 40 years. As the deputy commander of Operation Dani, he, along with the late former Prime Minister David Ben-Gurion and the late former Deputy Prime Minister Yigal Allon, were responsible for the expulsion of between 50,000 and 70,000 people from the towns of Lydda and Ramleh in July 1948. The town of Ramleh had surrendered without a fight after the withdrawal of the Jordan Army but the inhabitants were rounded up, expelled and told never to come back. Benny Morris characterized that as the "biggest expulsion operation of the 1948 war." Rabin expressed empathy with "the great suffering inflicted upon" his men who caused the expulsion.

One of those expelled was a 13-year-old boy by the name of Khalil al-Wazir, later known as Abu Jihad. Yitzhak Rabin, who was responsible for that act as a member of the Zionist militia, was one of the inner cabinet decision-makers who decided, 40 years later, to assassinate al-Wazir far away from his home in Ramleh. The man who headed the inner cabinet, Yitzhak Shamir, told an inquirer who wanted to know who killed Abu Jihad, "I heard about it on the radio."

It was typical of the official response to the killing; claims of ignorance, broad hints that Abu Jihad's responsibility for the Palestinian uprising could only trigger that kind of response and the usual reference to a factional conflict within the Palestinian movement as being responsible for the assassination. In fact, the murder of Abu Jihad is the latest incident in a continuous pattern of Israeli assassinations of Palestinian leaders and intellectuals among whom are Karmal al-Adwan, Ghassan Kanafani, Kamal Nasser, Majid Abu Sharar, Abu Yurif and many others.

In a *New York Times* article summarizing the official Israeli interpretation of its own policies, Thomas Friedman maintains that Israel endeavors to "turn terror back on the terrorists." This strategy has gone through several different stages. For the period of 1948-56 the strategy was described as "counterterrorism through retaliation or negative feedback" and was employed against Egypt and Jordan to prevent border crossings by Palestinian refugees attempting, in the main, to check on the conditions of their former homes."[8] By 1972, Israel was striking against "the nerve centers and the perpetrators themselves" using letter bombs, exploding cars and telephones and quiet assassinations of Palestinian leaders and intellectuals on the back streets of Europe. Later acts of terrorism including the destruction of entire villages in Lebanon, raids on Beirut, Baghdad and Tunis have become typical of Israeli policy towards Arab nonacceptance of its regional hegemony. Such acts have rarely evoked U.S. condemnation. In fact the Reagan Administration characterized Israel's raid on the PLO headquarters in Tunis as an act of self-defense.

United States and Israel — A "Special" Relationship

Strategic cooperation between Israel and the United States was consummated between 1982 and 1988 and has dramatically elevated Israel's role in U.S. global strategic calculation. By 1983, the Reagan Administration had accepted the Israeli view that the Palestine question was not the principal cause of instability in the Middle East. Henceforth, it would not be allowed to interfere in the "special relationship" between a superpower and its strategic ally.

In the special relationship between the United States and Israel, the latter is considered a "unique strategic asset"[9]. In the crucial Middle East, Israel is viewed as the cornerstone of U.S. policy, which is perceived as a bulwark against the Soviet Union and radical revolutionary transformation. Outside the Middle East, Israel has emerged as the most important supplier of the technology of repression, antiguerrilla training and infrastructure to combat revolution, all euphemistically phrased "counterterrorism." Israel ranks as the fifth largest exporter of arms in the world, according to CIA estimates and it has become an essential component of the global counterinsurgency business. "Hit lists" used by the death squads in Guatemala have been computerized with Israeli assistance and the Uzi machine gun is the standard weapon of the death squads. The special relationship between the United States and Israel is a two-way street. Israel is the largest recipient of U.S. economic and military aid and in return Israel has much to offer the United States. The Reagan Administration has publicly declared that Israel's substantial experience and "success" in coping with terrorism should provide guidance for the United States. When George Shultz spoke at a New York synagogue in 1984 he said:

> No nation has more experience with terrorism than Israel and no nation has made a greater contribution to our understanding of the problem and the best way to confront it. By supporting organizations like the Jonathan Institute, named after the brave Israeli soldier who led and died at Entebbe, the Israeli people have raised international awareness of the global scope of the terrorist threat... [T]he rest of us would do well to follow Israel's example. [10]

The fact that the United States and Israel are so closely allied and use the same criteria for defining who are "terrorists" and who are not, necessarily makes the United States a dubious participant in mediating the Israeli-Palestinian conflict and brings into question the possible results of U.S.-sponsored negotiations with George Shultz behind the wheel.

When Secretary of State Shultz became the Reagan Administration's chief proponent of close strategic cooperation with Israel he went far beyond the initiatives of his predecessor Alexander Haig. Haig's framework for U.S. Middle East policy was the "consensus of strategic concerns," which would bring together a conservative constellation of regional powers that would include Israel. Shultz's framework, however, promoted Israel to the center of U.S. policy and assigned it a global role in addition to its regional duties on behalf of the status quo. Thus with Shultz in power, the United States conducted its Middle East policy on the basis of the "consensus of strategic concern" plus the special relationship with Israel.

With all the attention Shultz received on his five trips to the Middle East in the last six months and with the outcome never in question, it is important to ask: What were the real objectives behind the 'Shultz shuttles'?

Reagan's Commitment to Peace

U.S. involvement in the Middle East since the 1967 war reveals a number of precedents for unimplementable peace plans actually designed to justify U.S. obstruction of the global consensus and to contain Palestinian nationalism. An example was the Reagan plan of September 1, 1982, which denied sovereignty over the West Bank and Gaza to Israel and the Palestinians. Its territorial and confederal aspects evoked a swift yet predictable rejection from the Israeli cabinet.

The principal spur for the Reagan plan was the siege of Beirut, which tarnished Israel's image and at the same time provided a catalyst in the world community for linking PLO withdrawal to Palestinian statehood. To justify its virtual sole dissent from the international will, the Reagan Administration felt obliged to launch its own initiative based on "the Jordan option," which proved to be a nonoption.

More recently, Reagan has sent his premier ambassador of peace, George Shultz, to the Middle East to again make a public press for a settlement. However, knowing that Israel will not meet even the minimum requirements for a territorial settlement, what then does Mr. Shultz hope to accomplish in view of the fact that his initiative lacks any means of pressuring Israel?

The United States has three objectives:

> 1. The Shultz plan is an attempt to contain the Palestinian uprising and prevent its extension to U.S. allies and clients in the region. It is also designed to repair Israel's tarnished image in the United States.
> 2. The United States would like to set the terms before any other actor emerges with a plan for settlement. The Soviet Union, which has been trying to broaden its options in the region, is one such actor. The Arab states or the PLO are also possible sources of peace initiatives. The Shultz plan represents a reaffirmation of U.S. custodianship over the Middle East. It serves as a reminder that the area is U.S. turf and hence it is designed to elbow out or preempt any genuine proposals for a settlement.
> 3. The plan also attempts to bridge the gap between the requirements of public opinion and those of public policy in the United States. The United States has broken barriers for the first time in the Middle East. The public mood in this country has changed and the people seem ready for a political settlement. Yet Palestine has never been high on the official agenda. There is no sense in Washington that the Palestine question is urgent. Unless it becomes urgent, there will be no movement towards peace.

America's policy objectives in the region center on oil and containment of Soviet influence as well as containment of the natives. As long as Palestine does not interfere with these objectives, the administration feels no compulsion to initiate peace proposals. But given that the public mood has changed in this country, the Shultz plan offers the U.S. public a rejectable plan, which would absolve Washington of responsibility for the impasse.

The Reagan Administration clearly perceives the uprising as a political threat to its hegemony in the region and would like to check its potential for extension beyond the occupied territories into Arab countries ruled by conservative regimes. The administration is also concerned about Israel's repressive image — perhaps more than Israel itself — in the United States. Washington's strategic relationship with Israel must continue to have the blessings of U.S. public opinion.

Hence, Shultz's sudden awakening to the fact that the unresolved Palestine-Israel conflict is a threat to the status quo and his embarking upon a mission to save Israel in spite of itself. The erosion of U.S. public support for Reagan's policy towards Israel is seen as a dangerous strategic step backward and his administration is desperately trying to counter the bad publicity.

Shultz's endeavor turned out to be a series of diplomatic shuttles not only between Arab capitals and Israel but also between the two heads of the Israeli Government. His diplomacy seems to operate on the assumption that the crucial choices are between Likud's preference for functional autonomy (which keeps "Greater Israel" intact as the Palestinians in the West Bank and Gaza are enfranchised in the Jordanian state) and Labor's "territorial" autonomy, which is a diminutive version of the Jordan option. His diplomacy also assumes that the only choices are between Labor's cosmetic international conference and Likud's direct negotiations.

The fact that the Jordan option is dead, that the concept of a Palestinian-Jordanian delegation is unacceptable and that the Camp David formula is discredited throughout the Arab World seems to have escaped Mr. Shultz's attention. The outcome of Shultz's diplomacy has so far worked for the benefit of Israeli Prime Minister Yitzhak Shamir. Shamir's visit to the United States in March 1988, ostensibly to discuss peace with the Reagan Administration, enabled him to respond to U.S. critics of Israeli repression in the occupied territories, to raise funds in the U.S. Jewish community and to solidify and upgrade the U.S. strategic alliance. In his visit, Shamir repeated the Israeli position that the Palestinian uprising was not a demonstration of civil disobedience but a war waged "against Israelis, against the existence of the State of Israel"; hence, he declared the media coverage unfair and noncontextual.[11] This theme was dutifully repeated by prominent U.S. Jewish figures such as Morris Abram, chairman of the Council of Presidents of Major Jewish Organizations and New York Mayor Edward Koch, among others. Henry Kissinger, who had erected the principal barrier to a Palestinian-Israeli settlement back in 1974 and who was willing to bomb Vietnam back to the stone age, was already on record one week prior to Shamir's visit as saying, "Israel should bar the media... accept the short term criticism... and put down the insurrection as quickly as possible — overwhelmingly, brutally and rapidly."[12]

The recent dramatic ascendancy of the far right in the Israeli body politic and the rampant anti-Arab racism sweeping the country provide a fertile environment for the kind of state terrorism witnessed today on the West Bank and in Gaza.

The orientation of this rapidly growing group toward brute force and its contempt for debate is partly the cause for the sharp increase in repression against Palestinian civilians under occupation. Worse yet is the tendency of members of the political and religious establishment to encourage such acts of terrorism.[13] Given the close and special relationship between the United States and Israel, given that no prominent U.S. politician is willing to condemn Israel publicly for its repression of the Palestinians and given that the United States and Israel share the same understanding of what terrorism is, it seems likely that if peace is to come to the Middle East it will be in spite of what the United States and Israel do.

(1988)

Israel Shahak on
the "Transfer Proposal"

Ellen Ray

In February 1988, *CAIB* coeditor Ellen Ray and other members of a delegation of U.S. women visiting the West Bank and Gaza met with Hebrew University chemistry professor Israel Shahak, a leading opponent of Israeli Government policies. The following are excerpts of his talk to the delegation, dealing particularly with the "transfer policy." [During that visit, the delegation experienced first hand the tear gas described by Louis Wolf in the article that follows this one.]

I will begin from the Israeli Jewish angle by telling you what, in my opinion, are the reasons why the Palestinian rebellion broke out in December 1987. There are very deep and immediate reasons, which proceed from the changes in the Israeli Jewish society in the spring or summer of 1987, when Jewish chauvinism began to increase enormously and in a visible way. Out of many open manifestations I will mention two.

Pogroms

From June to August 1987, a period during which the occupied territories were quiet — completely quiet — there were a series of pogroms against Palestinians in Israel itself. By "pogroms" I mean exactly the common use of the word. In a given neighborhood, usually quite a big neighborhood, all of a sudden all the flats or houses or rooms rented by Arabs were vandalized and burned. The Arabs were beaten and expelled from the neighborhoods. I mean all Arabs — both from the Palestinian territories and Israeli Arabs. The police did not give any protection and the neighborhoods became free of Arabs. The Hebrew press at that time invented, or reinvented, using Hebrew characters, a German word, *Arabrein*, which means in German, "clean of Arabs," from the German word employed by the Nazis, *Judenrein*, "clean of Jews." They invented the expression in order to refer to what was happening — a process of Nazification.

The "Transfer Proposal"

The second deep manifestation was what we call the "transfer proposal." "Transfer," in the Israeli use of the word, refers to a proposal which has been current in Israel from July or August 1987 to expel all the Palestinians — I emphasize, *all* the Palestinians — from all occupied territories. Not from Israel, but from all occupied territories. By the way, I am not speaking about Kahane, as you will see; I am speaking about "respectable" members of Israeli society. Here the difference from Kahane comes out. This is not proposed for so-called reasons of security, but from so-called reasons of principle.

The one who proposed this plan is General Rahaban Zahevi, a very good friend of Defense Minister Rabin. Only last week he held a big symposium in Tel Aviv about this proposal which was attended by a former chief of military intelligence, General Shlomo Gazit. Also attending were the former chief of the Central Command of the West Bank, Uri Orr and many other distinguished figures from Israeli military intelligence, retired of course, and even from the literary establishment. Another person who publicly supported this idea last summer was Mr. Michael Dekel, Deputy Minister of Mr. Rabin. And Mr. Rabin, who could, under Israeli constitutional law, dismiss Mr. Dekel and simply ask that the Likud nominate another deputy, did not do it.

I want to emphasize, first of all, that from last summer, the idea of expulsion of all the Palestinians from all the occupied territories was supported by important people who are completely different from Kahane and completely different also from the settlers. Second, this transfer idea is always supported for reasons of principle, not for reasons of security. One reason, given both by Mr. Dekel and by General Gazit, is opposition to assimilation. If Palestinians remain in the occupied territories, then sooner or later there will be mixed marriages between Palestinians and Jews. And since they believe that mixed marriages are the greatest calamity for the Jewish people that can be imagined — a proposition which, I am afraid, is accepted by a good half of Israeli society — this can be a very strong argument. Try to imagine how a similar argument would have gone in Mississippi and Alabama 40 or 50 years ago.

The second important argument made by those people, who are much more serious in their political approach than either Kahane or the settlers, comes from the history of Zionism. They make many references to Ben-Gurion and to other leaders of a labor or socialist type of Zionism who supported expulsion. They point out that expulsion was not carried out only during time of war, but also during the time of absolute peace, such as the expulsion which was carried out by Ben-Gurion, from 1949 to 1957. For example, near Gaza there is a town now called Ashkelon which once was called Majdal and from this town all the Palestinians — 15,000 of them — were expelled by an agreement with Egypt in 1951, at a time of complete peace.

A visible transformation of about half of Israeli society took place in the summer of 1987, as anyone who has followed the Hebrew press — and any Palestinian — will tell you. The treatment of Palestinians — the humiliation, the daily oppressions, the suffering — everything that the Palestinians have to endure in the occupied territories and to some extent also in Israel, has been changing rapidly for the worse since that time. This is, in my opinion, the most important reason for the rebellion of Palestinians. Thirty or 40 percent of Israeli society, more among the young who are serving as soldiers in the occupied territories, are believing more and more that the Palestinians are going to be expelled — the transfer idea.

Death Squads

There is another factor, beyond the usual aspects of an occupation, which is still unknown outside Israel. But in Israel the use of death squads to murder Palestinians has been discussed in some of the Hebrew press. It was not employed in the occupied territories until about September or October 1987, when we had one very well-documented case in the Gaza Strip. According to the Israeli Hebrew press, three Palestinians were discovered dead, in a car. One of them was a Palestinian guerrilla who had escaped from prison. The two others were collaborators [Palestinians who work with or support the Israelis] — well-known, rich collaborators. One of them had established a branch of the Tel Aviv stock exchange in Gaza. The other was of a similar background. So you can understand that such people are neither guerrillas nor helpers of guerrillas.

Since the families were very rich they could employ very good lawyers — Palestinian lawyers from Israel. And by using such lawyers and with the help of a Hebrew weekly called *Koteret Rashit*, which is sensitive and courageous about corruption in the intelligence and security services, even if not so good about Palestinian national rights, the case was brought into the open. By now it is completely clear that the two businessmen were murdered simply because they were accidentally eyewitnesses to the murder of the guerrilla.

There was also a recent case in which Israeli television, against orders, photographed an Israeli Jewish civilian shooting straight into a crowd of Palestinians. But when it was discovered that the person was a member of the General Security Service, Shabak, there was not even the smallest judicial investigation. It was simply announced that he was reprimanded. And that was it.

It is well known that Israel is involved with death squads in countries like Guatemala and many others, so it is only natural that this matter would come home. I think there is no doubt that the employment of death squads, especially in the Gaza Strip, was one of the sparks which ignited the violence.

The Palestinian Boycott

There is another subject we should discuss, the Palestinian boycott of the Israeli economy. In the beginning the Israeli Government made light of the boycott and there were also severe limitations on reports relating to it. But as the situation develops, it is very clear that the boycott is seriously harming the Israeli economy.

First of all, if you read the U.S. press, you will hear that only seven percent of the workers in the Israeli economy are Palestinians from the territories. This is just a lie. The number is much greater. First of all, most of the Palestinians are self-employed, presenting themselves for work in what used to be called slave markets in the towns. Palestinians from the territories dominate some areas of the Israeli economy: construction, low-paying agriculture jobs like picking and several other things, like what we call the cleaning jobs.

In Tel Aviv, 40 to 50 percent of the workers employed in garbage removal have been absent now for six weeks, although this fact was only published this week. The city literally stinks, but it was not reported for several weeks that it stinks. In construction work there are great differences around the country, but for example, in the area around Beersheva in the Negev, 80 percent of the construction workers are Palestinians.

Next week Israel is going to import 5,000 workers from Romania. There are also negotiations to bring workers from Portugal, Thailand and the Philippines. I think that it all may be tied in to the transfer plan.

The History of Transfer

Two respected reporters in *Davar*, the paper of the labor organization Histadrut, wrote a two-page article (February 19, 1988) called "This is the History of Transfer." Because of censorship, I will have to describe it in full.

Most of the article is devoted to information which appeared for the first time in Israel in this paper. Apparently the Labor Party in 1967 had discussed on the highest government level the transfer of Palestinians for reasons of principle. In 1967, a few weeks after the Six Day War, the Minister of Finance of the Labor Party with the support of Minister of Foreign Affairs, Mr. Abba Eban, proposed that all the refugees be settled in Arab states, especially in Syria and Iraq. But because of the long discussion no decision could be taken for mass resettlement in that meeting. However, the spirit of the discussion was according to the ideas of the Deputy Prime Minister at the time, Mr. Yigal Allon, of the Labor Party, who proposed that the Palestinian refugees of the Gaza Strip be removed to Sinai and once there, that an attempt be made to force them to emigrate. Allon also complained that we are not doing enough to encourage emigration of Arabs out of this country.

The rest of the article discusses attempts actually made between 1967 and 1972 to encourage emigration of Palestinians to Paraguay, Uruguay and Brazil. In Paraguay — the country of Mengele and so many Nazis — the Israeli officers who were in charge of this plan cheated the Palestinians. They promised them that after going to Paraguay, money would be delivered to them there, to begin work. And then they did not pay the money. In 1970, some Palestinians who despaired entered the Israeli Embassy in Paraguay and tried to kill the ambassador, but only killed his secretary. The program was transferred to Uruguay and Brazil and continued up until 1972.

After describing this history at great length and emphasizing the role of the Israeli Labor Party, the article jumps to the transfer plan which I have described for you. There is great emphasis on the notion that it is the Palestinian uprising which is causing part of the Israeli establishment to support transfer. The last paragraph says and I must explain that the word "riot" is the official name in the Hebrew press for the Palestinian revolution:

The latest riots in the territories are causing polarization in Israeli public opinion and especially in the Israeli establishment. On one side, more and more people understand that they cannot escape the need to find a political solution which will free Israel from most of the territories. But on the other hand, in the opinion of those people who welcome the mass expulsion as the most efficient means now remaining in the hands of Israel after the ballot, the clubbings and beatings are not sufficient. What will happen between those two points of polarization we cannot yet predict.

The Future

Now, about the future. The question to be asked is not so much about the Israeli Government, but about the Israeli Jewish people. Even if there is enough pressure from the Palestinian people or from other, outside forces, we still are in great danger. Half the Israeli Jewish people are prepared to make a war, not only on Palestinians but on other states, in order to effect this transfer.

But there is also great hope. If the Palestinian people continue the uprising, a majority of the Israelis can be persuaded to withdraw from the territories. But, I must be clear, we are now no more than 15 percent of the people with this moral consideration. We might increase to 30 percent, but that is not enough. However, by making things unpleasant for our society, we could capture the majority. Then it would not be a question of an international conference; we would speak directly with representatives of the Palestinian people, just as we did with Sadat. That was not because Sadat came to Jerusalem but because of the war of 1973; because the Egyptian Army and the Egyptian society which supported the army had shown itself to be effective. If the Palestinian society continues to be as effective as it is now, they have a very great chance of achieving independence.

Now an international conference by itself is very unclear, because what the PLO and the majority of the world mean by the term "international conference" is completely different from what the Israeli Government, Mr. Peres and the government of the United States mean. Because of this, I am of the opinion that if anything real can be settled, it will not be by an international conference; it will be settled by negotiations between the elected and rightful representatives of the Palestinian people and the Israeli Government.

Let me make one other point. Palestinians, in general, did not correctly analyze why Israel withdrew from Lebanon. Israel withdrew from Lebanon not because of Sabra and Shatila and not because of the bombardment of Beirut. During the first half of 1983, Israel intended to remain in occupied Lebanon forever. It was already being called in Hebrew the North Bank. Israel left Lebanon because, from 1983 to 1985, 390 Israelis were killed, which was actually a bigger number than those killed in 1982 and because there was no end to it.

Under the rules of Israeli society an Israeli minister must always attend the funeral of a fallen soldier. In the year of 1985 it happened not once but many times, that when a Likud minister attended a funeral where the father of the dead soldier was also a Likud person, known to him, the father actually said, at the open grave, "I tell you, if you are a party supporter, let my son be the last." This is a very, very powerful form of immediate pressure when you have elections.

Conclusion

In my opinion, the Israeli Government, together with its military experts, is awfully stupid. Not just immoral, but also stupid. The Israeli Government will try in the coming months to break the spirit of the Palestinians and to restore them to what in their opinion is the normal situation of servility. Meaning that they obey orders; that they go back to picking up the garbage. But for the Palestinians from the territories, it has been a state of slavery. You cannot use any other expression to describe their daily life. This is why they prefer to starve and to suffer all the things you know they are suffering rather than to go back to a state of slavery.

The Israeli Government wants to reduce them to slavery again. I do not think they will succeed. It is only a prediction and I admit that we cannot always predict Israeli steps. Do not ask me what the Israeli Government will do. Accept that they will do horrible things; but they will not succeed.

(1988)

Israel Wages Chemical Warfare With American Tear Gas

Louis Wolf

In the first five months of the *intifada,* at least 50 Palestinians died from exposure to U.S.-made tear gas and more than 150 pregnant women suffered miscarriages or fetal deaths.[1] Thus it was a major victory when, on May 6, the company producing the gas — the California-based TransTechnology Corporation, through its Federal Laboratories, Inc. subsidiary in Saltsburg, Pennsylvania — decided to suspend its brisk sales to Israel.

The decision did not come easily. Internal company documents underscore the continuing urgency Israel attached to its need for the tear gas. On December 16, Israel placed a priority order, assigned Number 161414 by Federal, for Model 519 CS Rubber-Ball grenades, a 9.8-pound spherical rubber device that when thrown at its target spews out peppery CS smoke fumes as it bounces and rolls along the ground. The document entry reads: "Rush for Israel." Federal kept seven people working full-time on the order. By January 10, 1988, 35,000 grenades were completed, with most of them already shipped to Israel before Christmas.

Illustrative of the ubiquitous supply from Federal's Saltsburg plant to the Israeli military was that, on January 13, 1988, while on a congressional fact-finding visit to Israel, Rep. Mervyn Dymally (Dem.-Cal.) was given a spent Federal canister used that week and returned with it to the United States. On its shiny metal outer casing were the words: "Made in USA 123456789 Mfg 1988." Other U.S. delegations visiting the West Bank and Gaza since then also returned with the U.S.-made gas canisters.

A special viciousness has marked the behavior of Israeli forces deployed against the Palestinians. They have used expressly lethal weapons like Galil assault rifles and Uzi submachine guns and long fiberglass batons have been used repeatedly as "bonebreakers" in beatings (modified from the wooden batons which gave Israeli soldiers splinters). Federal tear gas grenades and canisters have been shot or thrown at crowds or individuals in streets and alleyways, into elementary school playgrounds and repeatedly inside of houses, hospitals, schools, stores and mosques, as well as dropped from helicopters into teeming refugee camps. It must be remembered that based on repeated public pronouncements by Israeli Prime Minister Yitzhak Shamir, Foreign Minister Shimon Peres, Defense Minister Yitzhak Rabin and West Bank military commander Maj. Gen. Amram Mitzna, individual soldiers are following their orders in these actions.[2]

The effects of Federal's patented pyrotechnics as they are employed by Israeli troops are profound and disturbing. A highly concentrated lachrymatory (tear-producing) agent dispensed in a finely pulverized, dust-like substance, the CS gas[3] initially attacks the eyeball and the lachrymal gland which produces tears and is the passage from the eye to the nose. An intense burning sensation renders it exceedingly difficult to open the eyes, compounding the pain and blinding the victim to what is happening.[4]

Children can die from one-fourth the toxic level fatal to adults, death following pneumonia and loss of consciousness. The tear gas has also killed elderly persons suffering from asthma or heart problems.[5]

In addition to its immediate effects, the food chain is contaminated weeks after the initial exposure. CS gas is known to break down into cyanide, particularly as food is cooked. Rice, flour, sugar and other staples in every place where tear gas has been used are all repositories of gas residues which do not disappear for long periods.

On April 4, 1988, after several weeks of being confronted by the media and Arab-U.S. organizations with detailed eyewitness accounts of how Israeli forces were using the gas, its effects on the Palestinian population and, according to a spokeswoman, "after a lot of pretty tough deliberations" among company executives, TransTechnology President Dan McBride wrote to Prime Minister Yitzhak Shamir. He referred to the many reports and inquiries and asked for an explanation. However, he also noted that, "Our company values our role in supplying tear gas products to your country... We look forward to continuing our long-standing business relationship with your military and police agencies." To that end, he offered "additional training information or assistance in training to you if you feel that this would be of benefit to your personnel." No explanation was forthcoming and, on May 6, TransTechnology announced that its sales of CS tear gas to Israel had been "concluded."

This decision was not made simply because of media reports, pressures from Arab-U.S. organizations, or an impressive public demonstration outside the Federal Laboratories factory April 16. In fact, Federal had several tear gas contracts with Israel, each of them renewable every month or so as supplies of the gas needed replenishing. By April, the last contract had been fulfilled, so it was an opportune time to make the suspension announcement.

TransTechnology chairman Arch Scurlock stressed that sales had been "concluded" rather than "terminated," leaving an option to resume sales in the immediate future if Israel were to agree to use the tear gas "properly."[6]

"The undisputed leading manufacturer and developer of chemical riot control weapons" is how the company describes itself in its manual. Federal sells tear gas to some 80 countries. Ironically, one of Federal's overseas competitors, an Israeli company called Israel Product Research Company, Ltd., which manufactures CS gas both for domestic use and for export, including to South Africa, vies with Federal for Third World business.

In the United States, Federal sells a wide range of tear gas products to local police departments primarily for use by the assorted "SWAT" teams that have blossomed in the last two decades, to state police in many states, to the military for "riot" contingencies and to the Bureau of Prisons for distribution to hundreds of penitentiaries and jails across the nation.

Tear Gas is Good Business

Since December, Federal has delivered to Israel 60,000 CS 560 long-range tear gas projectiles, 60,000 CS 400 tear gas grenades ("reworked" from Model 519) and 800 203A 37mm gas guns used to shoot the projectiles some 150 yards. These shipments, sent more or less weekly since December, were confirmed by the Pentagon. Their records give the estimated total price tag of these purchases as $1,693,800.

Significantly noteworthy is the way Israel pays for the tear gas. Israel and Egypt enjoy an unusual dispensation not found in any other U.S. military aid program. They are granted "credits" given in the form of loans under the Foreign Military Sales (FMS) program, administered by the Defense Security Assistance Agency. Pentagon spokesperson Lt. Col. Jim Jannette put it this way: "They [the Israelis] are given a bucket of money to spend and they can spend it however they see fit." In the case of Israel's tear gas purchases, the "credits" are generously being rolled over and "forgiven," which means free tear gas.

Federal's Parent

Just as Federal Laboratories is dependent upon the continuance of political unrest and repression both at home and abroad to sustain and increase its tear gas sales, Federal's parent, TransTechnology, is largely dependent on the U.S. war machine and the military thrust of the space program for its rate of growth. U.S. Government business has produced a very significant portion of the company's total revenues.[7] With operating revenues in 1987 of $212.3 million, the company's net profits were up 53 percent from 1986.

TransTechnology has three main production divisions. Its Aerospace-Defense sector is the busiest and most lucrative, with over one-half the company's more than 2,600 employees and production facilities in 11 states. Among the many military contracts it has won from the government are components for the following: MX Peacekeeper missile, Navy Tomahawk Cruise missile, Navy Harpoon Cruise missile, Navy Phoenix missile, Navy SeaLance missile, Navy A-6 Intruder aircraft, Navy F-14 Tomcat fighter plane, Navy Phalanx missile, Pershing 11 missile, Army Multiple-Launch rocket system, Patriot air-defense system, pyrotechnics for the Space Shuttle and pyrotechnics for military and commercial satellites.

Environmental Dangers

Federal's business grew steadily, from its founding in 1923, with a flurry of activity during World War II. In 1964, when the White House and Pentagon decided to use tear gas in Vietnam, Federal's production line buzzed once more. By mid-1965, they were making 3,000 pounds of CS a day.

When questions about the possible dangers of the gas were raised in March 1965, Defense Secretary Robert McNamara insisted that the effects of CS only last about "five to 10 minutes."[8] Yet as early as December 1964, farmers living near the Federal factory had been complaining about various ill effects due to tear gas fumes which occasionally wafted across the area. In fact, CS production was discontinued from April to December 1965.

In fact, the specter of long-term effects of CS on the body and on future generations, as well as on the environment, is just beginning to emerge in the scientific literature. CS and 17 other similar chemicals were recently tested for mutagenic content. It (and 13 other substances) showed "significant" mutagenic response.[9] Moreover, the National Toxicology Program, part of the National Institutes of Health, now has a contract with Battelle Laboratories in North Carolina to test CS gas for carcinogenic potential.

Conclusion

As clouds of Federal Laboratories' tear gas filled the air in the West Bank and Gaza, a worried Austrian Foreign Ministry official sent an urgent message to the embassy of Austria in Washington. With an embattled ex-Nazi, Kurt Waldheim, as president, Vienna was worried about "embarrassment" arising from rumors that neutral Austria was selling tear gas to Israel. A sigh of relief went out when it was learned that the manufacturer was in Saltsburg, Pennsylvania, not Salzburg, Austria. Austria was not implicated in this war crime.

(1988)

Washington's Proxy: Israeli Arms in Central America

Clarence Lusane

The war drums are beating in Central America and Israel is an important player. The State of Israel has emerged as a major and in some cases, principal supplier of arms, advisers and training to the repressive forces in the region. Long denounced for its military ties to South Africa, Chile and the Philippines, the Zionist regime has extended its role as surrogate for the United States to the front line of Central America. Although much of what is happening is held in strict secrecy, the vast extent of Israeli aid has begun to fray the cover under which Reagan Administration policy objectives circumvent congressional obstacles.

Stopping U.S. military aid to Central America also requires stopping U.S. military aid to Israel. By the end of the 1960s Israel had emerged as an arms exporter, but only since the Reagan Administration has it been able to reach its potential as a full junior partner to U.S. imperialism.

The Israeli Arms Industry

Fourteen percent of Israel's industrial labor force is employed in its arms industry. If the armed forces are included, the number rises to 25 percent. According to the latest CIA estimates, Israel is the fifth largest exporter of arms in the world, up from its seventh place ranking in 1980. Israel remains the largest supplier of arms to sub-Saharan Africa and Latin America.

In 1977, Israel's arms exports were valued at $285 million. Despite the loss of two reliable customers, Iran and Nicaragua, by 1981 military exports had risen to $1.3 billion. The Israeli-built Uzi submachine gun,,, is the shining star of Israeli weaponry. It is the choice of NATO and is used in at least 43 countries, including virtually all the nations of Latin America.

Since 1970, Israel's military budget has consumed more than 30 percent of its national budget. Limited domestic use has made the export of arms essential to its economic survival. Latin American money has become indispensable to the Israeli arms industry. Central America has become a goldmine for Israeli arms sales.

Honduras

After the Israeli-sanctioned massacres at Sabra and Shatila then Israeli Defense Minister Ariel Sharon and the Air Force Chief arrived in Honduras. In his 38-hour visit, Sharon and the Hondurans agreed that Israel would send Honduras 12 Kfir planes, radar equipment, light weapons and spare parts and 50 advisers. Military training was also proposed.

Less than six months later, Israel was sending weapons to Honduras: artillery pieces, mortar rounds, mines, hand grenades and ammunition. Most were to go to U.S.-backed counterrevolutionaries seeking to overthrow the Nicaraguan Government from bases in Honduras.

In the period of 1970-80, Honduras received the following weapons from Israel: 12 Dassault Super Mystere fighters; four Arava (STOL) transports; I Westwind reconnaissance plane; 14 RBY Mk armored cars; five fast patrol boats (unconfirmed); 106-mm mortars; and 106-mm rifles.

The estimated $25 million in weapons promised to Honduras by Sharon is a continuation of past practice. However, Honduras is now playing a new role in Central America, similar to the one Israel plays in the Middle East, strategically important to U.S. interests and goals in the region as a rear base for the contras attacking Nicaragua and as a training ground for Guatemalan and Salvadoran fascists. In addition to aid from the United States and Israel, Honduras has received military aid from Argentina and Chile allowing it to increase its armed forces six-fold since 1970 (from 5,000 to over 30,000). The Honduran Air Force is the most powerful in Central America.

U.S. officials have admitted that Israeli assistance is important in achieving Reagan Administration military and political goals. Worried about potential congressional locks on aid to the Nicaraguan contras, the administration's military aid to Honduras will go toward buying weapons from Israel which have themselves been produced with U.S. military aid.

By its own account, the United States has at least 300 military advisers, technicians and engineers in Honduras. The United States is spending $20 million to construct a modern airport at Comayagua to accommodate U.S. troop transports. Another four airstrips are being expanded to handle military jets.

It is the goal of the United States, with the critical assistance of Israel, to make Honduras the chief gendarme of Central America. There is one central objective in the U.S.-Honduras-Israel connection. If U.S. policy makers launch an all-out invasion of Nicaragua, it will duplicate the Israeli invasion of Lebanon, launched from Honduran soil.

El Salvador

Ronald Reagan pledged to draw the line against communism in El Salvador and any hesitation by the U.S. Congress to send military aid finds a willing substitute in Israeli aid. For example, in 1981 when the administration was scrambling to find more aid to send El Salvador, Israel agreed to "lend" the U.S. $21 million to give to El Salvador, money which came from previous U.S. aid to Israel. In other words, the United States took out a loan on its original funds, thereby violating the expressed will of Congress.

The United States has only recently become a major supplier of military aid to El Salvador. Through the 1970s, Israel was the biggest seller of weapons and aircraft to the country. The arsenal made up more than 80 percent of El Salvador's military imports, supplemented by an estimated 100 Israeli advisers, who, like their U.S. counterparts, are training the Salvadoran military in counterinsurgency strategy and tactics at a secret base near Tegucigalpa. In addition, Israeli pilots are believed to be flying Israeli-made aircraft against the guerrillas. The Gouga Magisters and Dassault Ouragans are actually outmoded French planes which have been overhauled by Israel Aircraft Industries Ltd. (IAI), fitted with motors manufactured by the U.S. company, Pratt & Whitney.

Israel has also set up advanced computer systems to gather and analyze intelligence about the citizenry. Similar to the Israeli-installed computers in Guatemala, the network in El Salvador also monitors changes in water and electricity consumption. All Israeli aid to El Salvador comes from U.S. military and economic aid to Israel. The fact is that to cut off U.S. aid to El Salvador also requires cutting or limiting aid to Israel.

Somoza's Nicaragua

After the killing of journalists by Somoza's National Guard in 1978, President Carter cut off all U.S. aid to Nicaragua. Israel picked up the slack and until just before the Sandinista victory, providing 98 percent of Somoza's arms. When questioned about selling arms to Somoza, Israeli Prime Minister Menachem Begin responded, "We have a debt of gratitude with Somoza." In 1948, the UN General Assembly recommended the partition of Palestine and the creation of a Jewish state. The new state of Israel needed weapons and had almost nowhere to turn. Israel struck a deal with Somoza. Somoza appointed Yehuda Arazi as a Nicaraguan ambassador to Europe where he could purchase weapons in the name of

Nicaragua. Eventually, all the weapons ended up in Israel. Arazi, it turned out, was a member of the Jewish underground's clandestine army organization, Haganah.

Guatemala

Since 1976, Israel has been the main provider of weapons, aircraft and training to Guatemala. In fact, between 1977 and 1981, after the U.S. cut off aid due to gross human rights violations, Israel was the only nation giving military aid to the regime.

Training of Guatemalan military strongmen by Israel has included education in the use of terror and interrogation techniques, modern intelligence methods and psychological warfare. Israeli advisers are the key link in Guatemalan counterinsurgency operations. From national planning to civilian rural cooperative programs to military maneuvers, Israel is centrally involved. Israeli advisers have trained many of the officers of Guatemala's police intelligence (G-2). The right wing openly calls for the "Palestinianization" of the rebelling Mayan Indians. Some of Israel's most advanced electronic and computer technologies have been installed in Guatemala. Hit lists used by the death squads have been computerized. Technologically sophisticated murder is coordinated by a Regional Telecommunications Center (RTC) built and managed by Israeli Army experts. The RTC is also linked to the U.S. Army's Southern Command at Fort Gulick in the Panama Canal Zone. The RTC is run by the generals from the fourth floor of the National Palace Annex.

The U.S. Agency for International Development has said that the RTC is Guatemala's principal presidential level security agency and works with a high level security network. It links the key officials of the National Police, Treasury Police, Detective Corps, Ministry of Government, the Presidential Palace and the Military Communications Center.

The Tel Aviv newspaper *Haolam Hazeh* and the London *Guardian* revealed in December 1982 that Israeli advisers work closely with Guatemala's G-2 police units in the use of interrogation and torture. Computerized death lists are a mainstay of government terror; by 1980, computers already listed 80 percent of the Guatemalan population.

In November 1981, the Israeli-sponsored Army Electronics and Transmission School was opened in Guatemala to teach computer and electronic monitoring of the Guatemalan people. Equipment at the school is capable of doing everything from checks on potential apartment renters to detecting changes in electricity consumption that might indicate that an illegal printing press is in operation.

[Editors' Note: Although not known at the time this was written, these activities were made possible by the notorious Promis software, pirated and modified by Israel. See Ari Ben-Menashe, *Profits of War: Inside the Secret U.S.-Israeli Arms Network* (New York: Sheridan Square Press, 1992), pp. 136-39.)]

Israel has also been helpful in developing Guatemala's major military-civilian program, to create Vietnam-style strategic hamlets. The means of implementing these counterinsurgency plans were couched in terms of establishing peasant cooperatives similar to the kibbutzim in Israel. Guatemalan and Israeli agricultural and military officials were exchanged.

Under the Ríos Montt regime, the Israeli model was put into full operation. In August 1982, a "Plan of Assistance to Conflict Areas" (PAAC) program was begun, reproducing many of the tactics applied by the Israelis on the West Bank, such as finding mayors willing to accommodate to the status quo.

Ríos Montt's strategic relations with Israel began before his March 23, 1982, coup. Tel Aviv newspapers reported that 300 Israeli advisers had helped to execute the takeover. On August 8, 1983, Rios Montt was overthrown in another military coup led by General Oscar Humberto Mejía Victores. Mejía, who was Defense Minister under Ríos Montt, is also a fierce anticommunist. While the precise U.S. role in this latest coup is unclear, it has been reported that some of the Israeli-trained officers that brought Ríos Montt to power also participated in his overthrow.

Costa Rica

Costa Rica's northern border has become an operational base for attacks by contras on Nicaragua. Former Sandinista turned traitor, Eden Pastora, leads a small army estimated at 5,000 from this border area.

At one point, Pastora claimed that he had to shut down his activities because he had run out of funds. He stated that because of his "anti-U.S." stance, he would not accept funds from the CIA. Within days he was fighting again, reportedly with an infusion of funds from Israel, as well as other countries. In fact, much of this was a propaganda charade, as Pastora has been receiving CIA aid all the time.

Although Costa Rica has no army, Israeli military trainers and arms are beginning to pour into the country. In 1982, President Luis Alberto Monge met with Menachem Begin in Washington. They discussed the possibility of Israeli military aid in building up Costa Rican security forces. The funds would come from Washington.

The United States has been pressuring Costa Rica to consolidate its security forces. This would include a 5,000-member Civil Guard, a 3,000 member Rural Guard, 1,700 prison guards, the 100-member National Security Agency and the Chilean-trained, 500-member Organization of Judicial Investigation. In 1983, the United States will have spent $150,000 to train 103 members of Costa Rica's security forces, three times the amount spent in 1982.

Israel has been chosen by AID to build a $10 million settlement project along the Nicaragua-Costa Rica border. The military squeeze that the contras are currently operating from Honduras and Costa Rica would obviously be enhanced should the U.S. Congress fund this proposal.

The U.S. Role

Has exposure of illegal arms transfers by Israel forced the United States to cut back on aid? Or has the fact that Israel has sent arms to countries which the U.S. Congress and others have designated as flagrant violators of basic human rights made the Reagan Administration voice any criticism of Israel? The answer to both questions is no.

The immense scale of continued U.S. military and economic aid to Israel is obscene. Israel remains the largest recipient of U.S. foreign aid. It receives about one-third of all U.S. foreign aid, which in the last 10 years has amounted to about $25 billion, or roughly $7 million a day. Since 1976 Israel has not spent a penny of its own for military imports. The average U.S. subsidy to Israel for military imports has been 129 percent of the actual cost of those imports.

Israel's Defense Minister, Moshe Arens, was in Washington in late July to discuss more military aid and the right to use U.S. aid to develop weapon systems that are currently only available in the United States The State Department and White House refused to comment on the results of the meeting, but an Israeli official said "this trip was one of the most successful trips ever made by an Israeli minister to Washington."

The above figures shed light on the important and central role that Israel plays in U.S. foreign policy goals. No amount of struggle against U.S. aid to repressive dictatorships and juntas will be complete, or even marginally successful, unless Israel is also taken to task.

(1984)

Israeli-South African Collaboration

Jack Colhoun

Over the last decade the world community has increasingly ostracized South Africa's white minority regime. Arms embargoes, economic sanctions, bans on the transfer of nuclear and other high technology have been applied to compel South Africa to dismantle its racist system of apartheid. But at the same time a triangular strategic partnership of Israel, South Africa and the United States has developed to cushion the apartheid state from the full force of these sanctions.

To understand the Israeli relationship with South Africa, it is useful to put it in the context of Israel's growing involvement in the Third World. Benjamin Beit-Hallahmi, a former professor at the University of Haifa who now teaches at Columbia University, writes, "Consider any Third World area that has been a trouble spot in the past 10 years and you will discover Israeli officers and weapons implicated in the conflict — supporting U.S. interests and helping what they call 'the defense of the West.'" Chile, El Salvador, Guatemala, Haiti, Honduras and Nicaragua under the Somoza dictatorship are examples.

"In South Africa," Beit-Hallahmi observes, "Israel is actively involved in defending what Washington sees as 'a strategic outpost' — with the complicity and encouragement of the United States. In this case, although the United States is committed to the survival of the South African regime, Washington feels that the overt support it can give to South Africa is severely limited by world opinion."[1]

But, Beit-Hallahmi notes, "Israel's role in South Africa is qualitatively different from its role elsewhere."[2] Israel's investments in South Africa, the burgeoning volume of trade between the two countries and their extensive sharing of high technology and military experience has resulted in a unique network of mutual support.

Extensive Trade

In *The Unnatural Alliance: Israel and South Africa,* James Adams points out, "While it is impossible to place an accurate figure on the true total volume [of trade between the two countries], it is probable that when all trade is taken into account, Israel may be South Africa's biggest trading partner."[3] Economic relations between the two countries are shrouded in secrecy, says Adams, an executive of the London *Sunday Times.*

According to International Monetary Fund statistics for 1983, South African exports to Israel totaled $142 million, while Israeli exports to South Africa amounted to $69 million.[4] But these numbers don't include Israel's secret arms trade with South Africa, or South Africa's export of raw diamonds to Israel.

"South Africa stands out as the single largest customer [of Israeli weapons]," Aaron Klieman, a political scientist at Tel Aviv University, concludes in his book *Israel's Global Reach: Arms Sales as Diplomacy.* "It is thought to have been the purchaser of 35 percent of all sold in the years 1970-79."[5] The Tel Aviv regime doesn't allow much information to reach the public about its weapons sales, especially those to South Africa, which are in defiance of the UN's 1963 and 1977 arms boycotts of the apartheid state.

"It is believed that Israel currently gets 50 percent of its diamonds from South Africa," Adams reveals. "South Africa currently exports in excess of $100 million of uncut gems to Israel each year and it has been a steady and lucrative market for both parties." The diamond polishing industry is a mainstay of the Israeli economy. Israel's foreign sales of polished diamonds in 1983 totaled $1 billion.[6]

Many Israeli companies have invested extensively in South Africa. Afitra and Koors, corporations owned by Israel's Histadrut labor federation, are big investors in South African commercial agriculture, high technology and power generation industries. Israeli investments are also concentrated in other critical sectors of the apartheid state's economy, such as communications, computers, advanced computer software and electronics.[7]

As writer Jane Hunter explains, "One of Israel's chief attractions, as far as South African industrialists are concerned, is its preferred status with the European Economic Community and the United States."[8] Under the 1984 U.S. Free Trade Agreement, all Israeli exports to the United States will eventually be duty free. "To take advantage of Israel's privileged trade status, South African companies have systematically established manufacturing facilities in Israel, most often joint ventures with Israeli firms. Raw or semifinished materials are shipped from South Africa to Israel where sufficient 'local content'... is added, a 'made in Israel' label is attached and the finished merchandise is shipped off to unsuspecting consumers abroad."[9] This practice of "springboarding" is made profitable by the slave wages paid to black South African workers.

The Military Alliance

A military alliance between the two countries evolved gradually in the 1960s as the UN adopted its first arms embargo against South Africa in 1963 and European suppliers of weapons to Israel stopped selling their wares to Israel after Israel's aggressive land grabs in the 1967 Arab-Israeli war. But the Israeli-South African military partnership intensified after South African Prime Minister Johannes Vorster visited Israel in 1976 and signed an agreement with the Tel Aviv regime setting up a Ministerial Joint Committee of the two nations' defense ministers. According to the agreement, "the exchange of Israeli arms and advice has three major areas: conventional arms trade, nuclear collaboration and counterinsurgency."[10]

Israel has exported sophisticated Kfir aircraft and rebuilt Mirage jet warplanes to South Africa. Israel has also supplied the apartheid state with Dabur coastal patrol boats, Reshef-class gunboats armed with Gabriel missiles, self-propelled 105 mm howitzers, antitank missiles, air-to-air missiles, assault rifles, radar bases and surveillance equipment."[11]

"Beyond outright sales, Israel has enabled South Africa to become almost completely self-sufficient in several types of weaponry and weapons systems," Hunter notes. "The two countries have set up a joint helicopter manufacturing project — Rotoflight of Capetown and Chemavir-Masok in Israel — which supplies the armed forces of both countries with Scorpion helicopters."[12] Without the Israeli-South African alliance, she concludes, Pretoria could not have broken the UN arms embargo.

Adams points out Pretoria's debt to Israel in its counterinsurgency wars against the black African front-line states surrounding it and its repression of South Africa's black majority. Much of the efficiency of the South African security services must be placed at the door of Israel," Adams writes, "for both army experts and specialists in counterintelligence operations and interrogation from Mossad [the Israeli central intelligence agency] have been based in South Africa in a permanent advisory capacity since 1976."[13]

Israel Aircraft Industries constructed an electrified fence between Angola and Namibia, which South Africa illegally occupies, to block the infiltration into Namibia of SWAPO guerrillas fighting to liberate their homeland. Antipersonnel mines made in Israel are planted by South Africa along the Angolan and Mozambican borders. An Israeli spy drone was shot down in 1983 flying over Mozambique.[14]

Israeli military officers helped South Africa plan its 1975 invasion of Angola. In 1981 Gen. Ariel Sharon, then Israeli Defense Minister, spent 10 days with South African troops in Namibia near the Angolan border.[15] The London *Financial Times* and the London *Observer* published reports of Israeli involvement in 1983-84 with Jonas Savimbi's UNITA guerrillas, the South African backed contras fighting against the MPLA government of Angola.[16]

Nuclear Cooperation

Israel and South Africa have also collaborated with regard to nuclear weapons technology since the mid-1960s. Adams states, "For South Africa, Israel had one primary advantage: a relatively advanced nuclear industry that had been working on uranium-enrichment techniques and on the design of a nuclear bomb. For the Israelis, South Africa possessed almost unlimited supplies of uranium that it might be persuaded to part with as part of a uranium-for-technology swap."[17]

Despite a curtain of secrecy, it appears that both Israel and South Africa have developed nuclear weapons and could not have done so without each other's help. Israeli nuclear scientists were frequently reported to have been in South Africa in 1977, the same year the apartheid state abruptly canceled what the CIA thought were preparations for an atomic weapons test in the Kalahari desert.[18]

Two years later, the CIA concluded, Israel and South Africa carried out a nuclear bomb test in the south Atlantic Ocean, although the Carter Administration and the regimes in Pretoria and Tel Aviv denied it. CBS News correspondent Dan Raviv reported in 1980 that Israel "had detonated an atomic bomb in a joint nuclear project in the south Atlantic," referring to the 1979 double flash in the south Atlantic, which is characteristic of an atomic explosion.[19]

Sophisticated weapons technology purchased by Israel from the United States also has been diverted to South Africa. Adams reveals how the Israelis helped the racist white-minority regime obtain the 155 mm howitzer, then the world's most advanced artillery piece. Israel bought the weapon from the U.S.-based Space Research Corp. (SRC) and used the big gun with great effectiveness in the 1973 Arab-Israeli war.[20]

After South African troops were repelled in their 1975 invasion of Angola by MPLA forces with superior artillery, Pretoria turned to Israel. Although the Israelis were willing to sell the 155 mm howitzer technology to South Africa, Tel Aviv didn't own the rights to the weapon. So the Israelis teamed up with some former CIA agents to fashion a clandestine deal. SRC in the end not only sold Pretoria the advanced weaponry but also trained South African technicians, who later reconstructed the howitzer.

"It is possible that another major weapons system — Israel's Lavi aircraft, which incorporates highly advanced U.S. technology and is largely dependent on U.S. financing — is now making its way to Pretoria," Hunter warns.[21] There have been numerous reports in the Israeli and international press that South Africa is covertly financing part of the Lavi project in return for a deal that would eventually allow the South Africans to build the Lavi under license in the apartheid state.

Hunter notes that the U.S. corporations may, under pressure from anti-apartheid campaigns, stop their operations in South Africa, but use their corporate subsidiaries in Israel to continue doing business with South Africa. "Motorola has recently won praise for its announcement that it will stop selling two-way radios to the South African police. However, its subsidiary, Motorola Israel, which produces military communications systems and distributes them in South Africa through Afitra, can offer Pretoria continued access to those radios," she writes.[22]

U.S. Encouragement

The Israeli-South African partnership evolved in part as a relationship between two nations faced increasingly with international isolation because of their destabilizing and oppressive policies in the Middle East and Southern Africa. But this relationship was also encouraged by the United States.

"[Secretary of State Henry] Kissinger in early 1975 secretly asked the Israeli Government to send troops to Angola in order to cooperate with the South African Army in fighting the Cuban-backed MPLA," the British magazine The Economist wrote. "They sent South Africa some military instructors specializing in antiguerrilla warfare plus equipment designed for the same purpose. In return, the Israelis took Kissinger's request as the green light for an Israeli-South African partnership."[23]

The next year the United States turned again to its covert partner in Tel Aviv. "British television (and subsequently the press as well) aired a report referring to the sale of U.S. helicopters to South Africa, in the middle of their notorious invasion of newly liberated Angola. It turns out Kissinger, with reason, expected the U.S. Congress would not confirm the sale of such equipment... so... an 'Israeli solution' was found for this problem by means of a fictitious sale effected by 'unknown Israeli companies,' and the 'copters were transferred to South Africa'," Hebrew University professor Israel Shahak writes.[24]

Jane Hunter sums up: "Israel has become an indispensable covert partner for the United States because this partnership isn't subject to congressional scrutiny or even public debate because of Israel's 'special relationship' with Washington." But, she concludes, "The question for progressive Americans should be simply whether we are doing all that we can to end apartheid. If we find, therefore, that the 'special relationship' between the United States and Israel spills over into South Africa, then issues like the level of U.S. aid to Israel, the role of U.S. firms in three-way trade and U.S. diplomatic attempts to cover up this involvement cannot be ignored."[25]

(1986)

Iran-Contra and the Israel Lobby

Introduction
Ellen Ray and William H. Schaap

> God appointed America to save the world in any way that suits America.
> God appointed Israel to be the nexus of America's Middle Eastern policy
> and anyone who wants to mess with that idea is a) Anti-Semitic, b)
> anti-American, c) with the enemy and d) a terrorist.
>
> — John LeCarré, London *Times*, January 15, 2003

Today, the U.S. Government and its goose-stepping corporate media tightly control the most powerful propaganda apparatus the world has ever seen. It is not, as portrayed by apologists in Congress and the press, a vague, general public relations operation, flacking for democracy and the American Way; it is a specific, sinister, often clandestine, tool, designed to bolster the imperial policies and military predilections of this administration.

The New World Order that George Bush senior heralded after the Soviet demise is now George Bush junior's legacy — his New Imperial Order to be imposed by any means necessary. Past failures must be redressed; Iran was not isolated internationally, as planned; Saddam Hussein was not overthrown. And Israel has not yet achieved its final solution to the Palestinian problem. All this must be redressed.

The roots of this current power grab go back to the last months of the Carter Administration in 1980. Reagan-Bush campaign hawks plotted feverishly against the possibility that the U.S. Embassy hostages held in Teheran might be released just before the November election — a devastating public relations coup for the incumbent, a so-called October Surprise. On the heels of the disastrously botched hostage rescue attempt, only the negotiated release of the hostages would have kept Carter's chances alive. Reagan's minions secretly negotiated with ranking advisers to Iranian leader Ayatollah Khomeini for a delay of any action until after the election, and their success left Jimmy Carter facing the polls with the Americans having languished in captivity for an entire year.

The campaign for world economic and political domination gathered momentum during the final years of the Cold War, including the decade-long Iran-Iraq War of the 1980s (in which the United States sold arms to both sides) and the "clandestine" wars against Nicaragua's Sandinista Government and the revolutionary movements in El Salvador, Guatemala, Angola, South Africa and elsewhere. What became known as the Iran-Contra scandal — clandestine U.S. arms sales to Iran, facilitated by Israeli intelligence guidance, with the huge profits used to fund the terrorist war of the contras against the revolutionary government of Nicaragua — was a major part of these operations. Both ends of the operation were ostensibly prohibited by U.S. law and the secret sales to Iraq were not even part of the publicly known equation.

The psychological operations, or "psyops" apparatus, institutionalized today, which have virtually eliminated public media debate while severely damaging civil and constitutional rights, began in earnest during the Reagan and Bush I administrations. And the forces shaping administration policies and consequently government propaganda, include familiar faces from those years: Dick Cheney, Donald Rumsfeld, Colin Powell, Richard Armitage, Eliot Abrams and Michael Ledeen, among many others.

During the Reagan years, the State Department ran an Office of Public Diplomacy, which was little more than a separate disinformation office. And it was riddled with Iran-Contra figures like Lt. Col. Oliver North and Adm. John Poindexter. With the "war on terrorism" as its justification, the current Bush Administration tried to establish a formal international disinformation agency, a shadowy Pentagon operation called the Office of Strategic Influence, directed to "conduct covert operations aimed at influencing public opinion and policymakers in friendly and neutral nations." Even the mainstream press found the open espousal of disinformation too much and Congress refused to fund the program. Of course, the secret operations continue, as they always have. Secretary of Defense Rumsfeld was unusually frank and openly cynical about it. After announcing that the exposure of their plans had forced the Pentagon to shut down this operation, he defiantly told reporters, "fine I'll give you the corpse..., you can have the name, but I'm gonna keep doing every single thing that needs to be done and I have."

More successfully, the Pentagon established the Total Information

Awareness Program, to collect and collate all available electronic information on U.S. citizens, compiling credit-card, travel, medical, school, banking and other data. Brought in to head this agency was Adm. John Poindexter, despite his conviction in Iran-Contra on five felony counts of lying to Congress (later overturned because he was deemed to have been granted immunity). This, too, was a bit much for the Congress and Poindexter's appointment was rejected.

The compelling international issues today, those which will shape the future, are most importantly the Middle and Far East — Israel, Iraq, China, North Korea. Preeminent is Israel, for it is the Israel lobby (sometimes called the Israel firsters), broadly defined, which is setting the entire, immediate, agenda. Traditional lobbying of Congress is still dominated by the American-Israel Political Action Committee, but its power base today is the Pentagon's Defense Policy Board, chaired by Richard Perle, a Reagan Defense Department veteran. Perle was a cofounder of the Jewish Institute for National Security Affairs (JINSA), which maintains that there is no difference between Israel's national security interests and America's. It calls for "regime change" not just in Iraq, but in Iran, Syria, Saudi Arabia and the Palestinian Authority. "Total war," JINSA cofounder and pundit Michael Ledeen (another Iran-Contra figure) calls it. Two other JINSA board members are on the policy board, Adm. David Jeremiah and former CIA Director James Woolsey.

Before 1980, the Israel lobby functioned mostly on the fringe, through independently funded, extremely conservative organizations like the Committee on the Present Danger, JINSA, the Center for Security Policy, the Project for a New Century and the American-Israel Political Action Committee. Some were based at mainstream academic institutions. Some were closely tied to religious organizations, ironically both Zionist and fundamentalist Christian.

They asserted that the defense of Israel and the consequent and necessary control of the Middle East rests solely on the virtually un-questioning support of Israel's every policy — including the settlements in the occupied territories, collective punishment, preemptive strikes and the ultimate "transfer" of all Palestinians out of what once was Palestine — and that such support should be the fundamental pillars of U.S. foreign policy. Their justifications were as diverse as their constituents, but all saw Israel as the proxy guarantor of U.S. domination over the Middle East and its oil and water resources, perfectly designed to keep Arab nationalist aspirations at bay and in disarray. Christian fundamentalists viewed Israel as the key battleground for the Second Coming, Armageddon, the Day of Judgment.

The Israel lobby flourished during Ronald Reagan's presidency, but was somewhat less influential during the first Bush Administration, which tried to put the brakes on Israeli settlements in the West Bank. George W. Bush, on the contrary, is toeing the Sharon-Likud line, another "man of peace."

One of the most powerful pro-Israel flacks is Paul Wolfowitz, the Deputy Secretary of Defense. Wolfowitz has been in the Pentagon and the State Department since the early 1970s, except for the Clinton years. He was ambassador to Indonesia during some of the worst years of the Suharto dictatorship and worked hard during the 2000 presidential campaign to keep the Reagan-Bush support for Suharto out of the debate. It was Wolfowitz who authored the 1992 "Defense Policy Guidance," which has been reborn as Bush II's "National Security Strategy." Though not formally affiliated with the Israel lobby organizations, Wolfowitz is known not only as a super-hawk, but also as a profound supporter of right-wing Israeli positions. In a speech to the Pro-Israel rally in Washington in April 2002, he concluded, "May God bless America, may God bless Israel."

Also part of this group is Douglas Feith, Under Secretary of Defense for Policy. Feith is on JINSA's board of advisers and is the most vocal proponent of another fundamental tenet of the Israel lobby (and others), that any and all arms limitation treaties are anathema. Feith was in charge of oversight of the short-lived Office of Strategic Influence.

Another key figure is John Bolton, Under Secretary of State for Arms Control and International Security. He is truly the fox in charge of the chicken coop; he was instrumental in Washington's decision to withdraw from the Anti-Ballistic Missile Treaty. He led the U.S. attack on the International Criminal Court. Bolton was vice-president of the American Enterprise Institute and on the boards of the avowedly racist Manhattan Institute and the New American Century. He is a long-time advocate of diplomatic recognition of Taiwan, scoffing at the notion China would respond with force. Together with Ariel Sharon, he endorsed the game plan that, after Iraq, the United States and Israel must deal militarily with Iran and Syria. Of Bolton, Jesse Helms said, "[he] is the kind of a man with whom I would want to stand at Armageddon.

Eliot Abrams, one of the most vicious of the Iran-Contra gang, has been appointed senior director for Near East and North African affairs on the National Security Council.

And Michael Ledeen, for all practical purposes an Israeli fifth columnist, is a longtime propagandist for the cabal, a Fellow of the American Enterprise Institute, who, as Fred Landis's article that follows shows, was deeply involved in the Iran-Contra crimes. Ledeen is one of the most vocal proponents of "total war," calling for the overthrow of Iraq, Iran, Syria and even Saudia Arabia, as well as the removal of Yasser Arafat.

Perhaps the Israel lobby's greatest asset has been its ability to stifle criticism of its views by conflating opposition to the murderous policies of the Sharon Government of Israel with anti-Semitism, including a shameful denigration of the horror of the Holocaust, constantly equating Middle Eastern regimes with Hitler's. Donald Rumsfeld, a staunch supporter of this group, has referred to "the so-called occupied territories," and demonized French and German opposition to his Iraq war plans by slyly referring to the "Old Europe," a reference to Nazism and collaboration. Only as this agenda became open and blatant with the United States on the brink of war and threats of possible preemptive nuclear attacks emanating from the Pentagon, were some voices in the mainstream media speaking out with trepidation against the unbridled power of these hawks and the outrageous fallacies of their arguments .

Control over the limits of debate in the media has been vicious, with swift retaliation against any attempted breach in the wall surrounding Israeli righteousness. This goes well beyond the long-standing linguistic tricks, whereby, for example, Palestinians only "attack," and Israelis only "retaliate," whereby a Palestinian child who throws a rock at an Israeli tank is a terrorist, while an Israeli soldier who bulldozes the home of the mother of a suspected terrorist, killing her in the process, is an antiterrorist.

The first two articles in this section, Fred Landis's "Disinformationgate", and our "Deltagate?" describe some of the psyops machinations of the Reagan-Bush years and suggest that, even before the possibility of an October Surprise was eliminated, Jimmy Carter's chances of reelection were deliberately crippled by the foredoomed hostage rescue effort.

The other articles, Jane Hunter's "Out of the Loop", Anthony L. Kimery's "What Vice-President Bush Knew and Why He Knew It", and Karen Branan's "Inside Track to Power", give a broad-brush picture of the corruption and machinations of the Reagan-Bush years and detail how, during the Iran-Contra activities, then Vice-President Bush, while insisting he was "out of the loop," was not just deeply involved in the Iran-Contra affair, but was virtually coordinating it, a role enhanced by his long years of involvement with the CIA.

Disinformationgate

Fred Landis

If Contragate is the new Watergate, then Lt. Col. Oliver North is G. Gordon
Liddy and Michael Ledeen is E. Howard Hunt. One thing that unites these
two characters is an almost infantile fascination with psychological
propaganda operations — "psyops."

The North-Ledeen Team

North and Ledeen have worked together in a number of operations in
recent years, very different, but all, one way or another, involving psyops
or disinformation. In 1983, North was involved in the Grenada invasion.[1]
The media were excluded and U.S. Army psyops took over the local press
and radio. The mainstream U.S. media got a bizarre white paper authored
by Michael Ledeen, purportedly based upon the three tons of documentation the U.S. invaders seized.

That same year Ledeen and North participated in a National Security
Council planning group that led to the creation of the State Department's
Office of Public Diplomacy. North fed the office CIA and DIA material on
Nicaragua, grist for its propaganda mill, while Ledeen and others churned
it out.

In 1984, North masterminded an attempted drug trade sting against
Nicaragua. North's colleague, "retired" Gen. Richard V. Secord, purchased
a C-123K cargo plane from Southern Air Transport. It was outfitted with
hidden cameras and turned over to DEA agent Barry Adler Seal. Seal then
force landed at a military airfield in Nicaragua, where he got photos of a
Nicaraguan official, Federico Vaughn, investigating. That photo then
became the basis of much disinformation on a supposed Borge-Castro
narcotics trafficking ring.[2] President Reagan used the photo on television,

stating, with utterly no evidence or justification, that a box in the picture was filled with drugs. Like a bad penny, the same plane returned to Nicaragua in October 1986, carrying Eugene Hasenfus.

After the 1984 congressional elections, North helped plan a series of sonic booms over Nicaragua, in an attempt to rattle the Sandinistas. Ledeen then orchestrated a rumor campaign among the Washington press corps that the invasion of Grenada had just been a preamble to the invasion of Nicaragua.

In the 1986 congressional elections, North assisted in the political campaigns of Senators Paula Hawkins (Rep.-Fla.) and Jeremiah Denton (Rep.-Ala.). They lost. But interestingly, Denton's Subcommittee on Security and Terrorism and Hawkins's Subcommittee on Children, Family, Drugs and Alcohol were both favorite platforms for Ledeen to spread his media hoaxes.

Ledeen and Contragate

Ledeen's role in Iran-a-scam and Contragate begins with his secret missions to Israel. But it is unclear who was urging whom to do what. According to leaked portions of a Senate Intelligence Committee report, the sale of arms to Iran was planned and implemented by the Israeli intelligence service, Mossad. Each time that the United States rejected further participation in the Israeli plan, some Mossad agent was urgently dispatched to the United States to put their plan back on track. Throughout the leaked Senate report, there are references to "the Israeli plan." And the text of a memo by Lt. Col. Oliver North titled "Covert Action Finding Regarding Iran" reads: "Prime Minister Peres of Israel secretly dispatched his special adviser on terrorism (Amiram Nir) with instructions to propose a plan by which Israel, with limited assistance from the United States, can create conditions..."

But instead of trying to shift the blame to Israel, the White House sought to delete all references to the Israeli role from the Senate report and the media accounts followed suit.

Naturally, the *New York Times* placed the initiative with the National Security Council: President Reagan contended that the program had its inception in mid-1985 when McFarlane sent a U.S. consultant, Michael Ledeen, to Israel.[3]

The Israeli press depicted Ledeen as an U.S. agent who got Israel invoked as a broker in a deal between the United States and Iran. Defense Minister and former Director General of Foreign Affairs David Kimche told the *Los Angeles Times* that the purpose of his July 1985 visit to Washington was to confirm Ledeen's bona fides. However, there were a number of glaring problems with the Israeli cover story. Kimche had already met with McFarlane in January 1985 to urge arms sales to Iran.[4]

He had been pushing for this policy since 1981.

And Ledeen was hardly a stranger to Israeli officials. In fact, the ludicrous part of the Israeli cover story is the allegation that Kimche, who lived in New York for five years in the 1960s as chief of Mossad's Western Hemisphere operations division, had to travel to Washington to establish Ledeen's bona fides. David Kimche and Amiram Nir spent their professional lives in the Mossad, an agency not unknown to Ledeen.

Ledeen and Israel

Michael Ledeen was a founder of the Jewish Institute for National Security Affairs and was a major participant in the 1979 and 1984 Jonathan Institute conferences on terrorism.[5] Both institutes have substantial ties to Mossad. Indeed

Ledeen is the missing link of covert operations by Mossad in the United States during the Reagan Administration.

The most visible trail left by Mossad is the disinformation activities of Ledeen and friends. Michael Ledeen, Robert Moss and Claire Sterling were all speakers at the 1979 Jerusalem conference of the Jonathan Institute, a meeting which many Israeli intelligence agents attended. The speakers bemoaned the fall of Somoza and the Shah; Moss blasted the KGB;[6] Ledeen pointed out that even the KGB would not have succeeded if it were not for their mole (unnamed) in the Carter Administration. Ledeen and his co-disinformationists always raise the specter of a KGB role in Iran and Nicaragua, primarily to justify more U.S. covert action. Indeed one of the themes at the Jerusalem Conference was that Carter had destroyed the CIA.

Israel's Worries

Governments like South Korea, Taiwan, Turkey and especially Israel, simply cannot survive without continued U.S. military and economic assistance. The loss of Iran and Nicaragua under the Carter Administration led them to a certain concern about the reliability of the United States. Israel decided it would have to play a more aggressive role in U.S. domestic politics in order to guarantee an unwavering partner. The propaganda themes spread during the Jerusalem conference were aimed at the 1980 U.S. elections, to discredit Carter, support conservatives and present Israel as the U.S.'s most reliable ally in the face of terrorist and Soviet threats. The vehicle was disinformation.

The Golden Age of Disinformation

At no other time in U.S. history, not even during World War II, have so many millions of U.S. citizens been led to believe such hysterical hoaxes.

The Reagan era will go down in history as the golden age of disinformation. And if you follow the paper trail of verifiable disinformation spread the last six years within the United States, the Israelis are first, the CIA a poor second and the KGB dead last as a source of disinformation spread in the United States.

Disinformation became one of the buzzwords of the Reagan Administration. It covered every piece of news they didn't like, including statements by Democrats. Meanwhile the CIA spread disinformation about Libya, Iran, Grenada and Nicaragua. Hours before the Grenada invasion, Admiral Poindexter told reporters an invasion was out of the question. Later he wrote his famous memo outlining a policy of disinformation aimed at Libya. President Reagan accused Sandinista leaders of being dope dealers. As part of McFarlane's cover story for U.S. involvement in Iran, he repeated disinformation about a massive buildup of Soviet strength on the Iranian border.

Disinformation is intrinsically of interest to journalists because someone is polluting the information stream. What is not generally realized is that disinformation is always coordinated with other covert operations. Often a specific disinformation theme is deception and cover for other activities by the originator. Michael Ledeen has been involved in the dissemination of a number of disinformation stories which provide sufficient data to test this proposition.

Before popping up in the middle of the Iran-Contra scandal, Ledeen had built up a reputation concocting or spreading major disinformation themes, among them:

- The notion that the CIA was destroyed under Carter;
- That there was a KGB mole in the Carter Administration;
- That the loss of Iran and Nicaragua was the work of the mole;
- That the Soviet Union is behind an International Terror Network;
- That it tried to kill the Pope;
- That the Libyans tried to kill President Reagan;
- That the Iranians tried to kill President Reagan; and
- That Fidel Castro and Tomás Borge are major narcotics dealers.

These fake stories, spread with the conspicuous help of Israel, had the surface appearance of being solely right-wing U.S. propaganda. In fact, Israel was actively covering its penetration of the U.S. foreign policy establishment. Indeed, the first four hoaxes were the Mossad Party platform for the 1980 U.S. elections. To sell its expertise in the area of combating terrorism and to get the attention of credulous U.S. conservatives, Israel fostered a Soviet angle. It tried to curry favor with the CIA and to discredit further the existing liberal U.S. foreign policy establishment by launching a witch-hunt against nonexistent moles.

Mossad cannot stand détente, between Iraq and Iran or between the United States and the Soviet Union. It is to the advantage of Israeli intelligence to promote the notion that the Soviet Union tried to kill the Pope and that it is behind all acts of international terrorism.

While everyone else was amused by the preposterous story of a Libyan "hit squad" out to kill the president, a story which originated with Israeli intelligence,[7] Reagan had concrete bunkers built to surround the White House and heavily armed Marines in fatigues on the roof. If you are an intelligence agent and you want to get the attention of some world leader, tell him you have uncovered a terrorist plot to kill him. The CIA had been employing this trick in the Third World for years; why should we be surprised that Mossad pulled it on Reagan?

Arms Deals

The Israeli media are focusing on Ledeen, describing him as an U.S. agent, not because he really helped organize the plan, but to divert attention from David Kimche and Amiram Nir. On one level, the Iran-Contra scandal is merely a giant footnote in the story of Israeli intelligence operations in support of arms sales.[8]

According to the *New York Times*, hundreds of retired Israeli Army officers, ex-agents of Israel's secret service, the Mossad and private arms merchants are circling the globe trying to put together arms deals. The *Washington Post* put the number of such Mossad agents and arms dealers at "between 700-860."

The Iranian arms deal that Oliver North and Michael Ledeen were involved in is similar in nature to two previous cases where criminal charges were brought: those of Israeli General Abram Bar-Am in New York and Paul Cutter in Orlando, Florida. In fact these two cases shed new light on the clear pattern of Israeli involvement behind all these so-called "Iran arms cases."

The Israeli role in the New York case is straightforward, even though the sums are staggering: $2.5 billion worth of weapons to Iran, including an entire brigade of tanks. The cast of characters is familiar: Adnan Khashoggi, his attorney, Ghorbanifar, McFarlane, etc. The other case is less well known.

When Michael Ledeen founded the Jewish Institute for National Security Affairs, Paul Cutter became a director. He had been the editor of *Military Science and Technology*. After the invasion of Lebanon, when Ariel Sharon was getting some bad press in the United States, Cutter's magazine was full of articles by Sharon and friends, along with puff pieces extolling Israel.

Cutter became director of a new company, European Defense Associates, with offices in Paris, London, Washington and Tel Aviv. It sold arms captured by Israel in Lebanon to U.S. allies and later, U.S. weapons stockpiled in Europe to Iran. He set up a new magazine, *Defense Systems Review,* where he shared the masthead with Brig. Gen. Meier Ben Neftali and Shoshana Bryen. Shoshana Bryen was identified as executive director of the Jewish Institute for National Security Affairs, while Ben Neftali was assigned to the United States as head of the Israeli Procurement Mission.

Cutter was caught in an FBI sting in Orlando, for conspiracy to sell arms to Iran and of the six defendants was the only one sent to jail. Cutter might be forgiven a certain amount of bitterness, sitting in his jail cell in Arizona watching Ledeen on ABC's "Nightline" and Israeli arms dealers living in palatial estates.

Israeli Penetration

Even granted constant Israeli pressure, the question remains why the Reagan Administration collaborated in a deal in which it stood to gain very little. The answer lies in a combination of Israel propaganda and covert Israeli penetration of the U.S. foreign policy establishment.

Preceding the 1980 elections, Israel had already built up a significant influence in the Committee for the Free World, the Committee on the Present Danger, the National Strategy Information Center and the Center for Strategic and International Studies. These organizations went on to staff the Reagan transition teams for the CIA, NSC, Pentagon and State; and members later took over top positions in these foreign-policy-making bodies.

Michael Ledeen was brought to the CSIS by David Abshire and Walter Laqueur. Laqueur is part of the Israel lobby at CSIS, together with Yonah Alexander and Edward Luttwak. Ledeen was transmogrified from a petty propagandist into a national security expert through his post at CSIS. When Reagan took office, Ledeen was one of over 30 CSIS staffers to join the new administration.

People outside Washington do not realize the extent to which U.S. foreign policy is initiated by the staffs of congressional committees and the staffs of the Directors of the CIA or NSC. This is the case even in normal times. Under Reagan, foreign policy sank all the way to the basement.

Why Did They Do It?

It is not part of any White House cover-up to portray Reagan as detached and uninformed, or even senile. The locus of Iran policy really was the White House basement. And if Reagan did not know everything the NSC was up to in his basement, the public knew nothing at all. It was fed a diet of secrecy, deception and disinformation.

There is a connection between disinformation and covert action, between deception and political intrigue. While Kimche, Nir, Ledeen and North were acting behind closed doors, what the public got was disinformation.

Who Is the Mole?

Ledeen is the kind of person who thinks that the shortest distance between two points is a tunnel. As befits an individual obsessed with moles, Ledeen has spent a great deal of time in Washington and Tel Aviv tunnels. The Iran-Contra story is fairly complex, but journalists are missing the real story: Michael Ledeen is the mole.

(1987)

Deltagate?

Ellen Ray and William H. Schaap

One of the main reasons soft-spoken Jimmy Carter lost his 1980 bid for reelection was his disastrous attempt to get tough with Iran — the Desert One hostage "rescue" fiasco. Ironically, tough-talking Ronald Reagan is currently embroiled in the Iran-Contra scandal as a result of his equally bungled effort to sell Iran weapons in return for the release of hostages.

Marine Lieutenant Colonel Oliver North was involved in both escapades and one organization, the Delta Force, has played a key role throughout the entire period. But while Oliver North's every move, every decision and every memo is scrutinized by the world's press and a raft of congressional committees, no one is looking very closely at the Delta Force. Despite an unmitigated record of failures, the Delta Force enjoys a totally undeserved reputation as the heroic front line of America's escalating war against world terrorism. A best-selling (if less than accurate) book and a gung-ho (equally fictitious) Chuck Norris movie haven't hurt.

What is the Delta Force?

As recently as early 1986, the Pentagon refused to acknowledge publicly the very existence of the Delta Force,[1] despite the fact that its founder and first commanding officer, Colonel Charlie A. Beckwith, had published his autobiography, *Delta Force*, in 1983. Statistics about personnel, budget and capabilities are still hard to come by, but events of the last two years have thrust the Delta Force into the news. Careful investigation reveals many details about the super secret unit and its place in the grand strategy of antiterrorism, a strategy which had become an obsession of the Reagan Administration — at least until the Iran-Contra revelations exposed its hypocritical façade.

The Delta Force was organized in 1977 to provide a unit more specialized than the Army's Special Forces (Green Berets) and the Navy's SEAL commandos. It was not intended for counterinsurgency operations, such as Vietnam War, but for counterterrorist, commando raids. Its motto is "Speed, Surprise, Success," and its men are trained to use some rather exotic weapons, such as "flash-bang" devices to temporarily stun and blind terrorists. They are issued sub-machine guns with silencers and night scopes, learn how to pick locks and blow doors with plastique and fly in black helicopters with infrared sensors for night flights. Delta Force has about 100 "operators," selected from throughout the military, the cream of the crop.[2] However, as we shall see, they have had few chances to use their unique arsenal and on the rare occasions Delta Force teams saw combat, they have been singularly unsuccessful.

Ironically, it was the failure of the Delta Force in Iran in 1980 which led to the creation of a confusing jumble of units, commandos and agencies all struggling, sometimes at cross purposes, in the Reagan Administration's "war against terrorism." Reagan's strategists believed from the outset that this war should be carried out by beefed-up, elite, secret commando units, extending the military's concept of Special Forces from counterinsurgency to counterterrorism. The Delta Force became a part of that structure.[3]

Of course, in order to defend its support of the *mujahideen* fighting Afghanistan and the Contras fighting Nicaragua, while at the same time denouncing the Palestine Liberation Organization fighting Israel and the Farabundo Martí Liberation Front fighting in El Salvador, the administration had to engage in some fancy semantic trickery. Terrorism was defined in terms of aggressive, indiscriminate acts of violence, but America's friends never attacked, they only retaliated against legitimate targets.

The Big Flop

Although it was organized in 1977, the Delta Force did not see action until the night of April 24, 1980, when Charlie Beckwith led an ill-prepared team with faulty equipment on an impossible hostage rescue mission. The mission, personally approved by a frustrated President Carter, was dubbed Operation Eagle Claw. Four Air Force C-130s were to fly a team of more than 100 men to Desert One, where they would transfer to eight Navy helicopters coming in on a different route. The helicopters would refuel and take the commandos to Desert Two, 50 miles from Teheran. From there they would travel by truck into downtown Teheran, where the 53 U.S. Embassy personnel had been held hostage for half a year, raid the embassy, free the hostages and make their exit.

The plan fell apart at Desert One. One of the helicopters never made it;

two that did, clogged with desert sand. One crashed into a C-130. Without enough helicopters to transport the full team, Beckwith decided to beat a hasty retreat. He left eight men dead (killed in the crash) and three helicopters filled with classified documents which fell into Iranian hands and compromised the cover of a number of CIA agents — many of whom had recently arrived in Teheran to arrange for the trucks.

One of the men waiting at Desert Two until word of the fiasco was transmitted was Oliver North.[4] Soon after his return to Washington, he reportedly began work on a second rescue plan, Operation Honey Bear, with Major General Richard Secord, who had previously served as U.S. military liaison in Teheran. But by the time the plan was fully drafted, Reagan was president and the hostages were home. Six years later, Secord, now retired, was to be deeply involved in the Iran-Contra scandal, master of Swiss bank accounts, arms dealer extraordinare.

North's role in Desert One has never been forgotten by the Iranians, even as they negotiated for U.S. arms in 1985 and 1986. Last November, in a speech discussing the clandestine visit of former National Security Adviser Robert McFarlane to Teheran the previous May, Speaker of the Parliament Hashemi Rafsanjani noted that the man who "designed and conducted" the ill-fated raid accompanied McFarlane.[5] Of course, Rafsanjani's evident displeasure did not prevent the Iranians from accepting 20 planeloads of weapons in the wake of McFarlane's visit.

Was Carter Sandbagged?

A number of commentators have concluded, with considerable evidence, that Beckwith's mission was doomed before it began.[6] That conclusion has led to the intriguing notion that the rescue operation was deliberately intended to damage Jimmy Carter's already plummeting popularity, with an eye to the upcoming elections. Some support for this hypothesis comes from the belief that the coordinator at the time of overall ISA operations (of which Delta Force was a part) was General John Vessey, Jr., who had been one of the two high ranking public critics of Carter's 1979 plan to withdraw some U.S. troops from South Korea. The other, Vessey's colleague, Major General John K. Singlaub, was fired by Carter and went on to prominence as the head of the extreme right-wing World Anti-communist League and a major conduit for funding the Contras with private and hidden government money. Vessey remained in the military and was later appointed by President Reagan to the post of Chairman of the Joint Chiefs of Staff.

(1987)

Out of the Loop: The VP's Office — Cover for Iran-Contra

Jane Hunter

Throughout George Bush's presidential campaign and well into the first year of his presidency, polls consistently showed that a majority of the U.S. public did not believe Bush was telling the truth about his role in the Iran-Contra affair. Of course, they were right — he wasn't.

Bush's plea of ignorance of the arms sales to Iran, that "I was out of the loop," was widely repeated and always certain to get a laugh. However, we should not forget that in reality, George Bush attended all but one of the important White House meetings on the subject. (The one he missed conflicted with the December 7, 1985 Army-Navy football game.)

Secretary of State Shultz testified before the Iran-Contra committee that, at a key January 6, 1986, meeting about the "finding" authorizing arms sales to Iran, Bush had not supported Shultz's own vehement opposition to the plan. This undercut Bush's assertion that he had had "reservations" about trading arms for hostages but just didn't think it was proper to reveal the counsel he had given President Reagan on the subject.[1]

The Harari Network

One of the most compelling revelations came in 1988 and related to the connection between [Bush's national security adviser] Donald Gregg and the so-called "Harari network." The Harari network consisted of Israelis, Panamanians and U.S. citizens set up by the Reagan Administration and the government of Israel in 1982 to run a secret aid program for the Contras.

Its namesake was Mike Harari, a longtime Mossad official, who since around 1979 has served as Israel's agent in Panama.[2] Still reliably reported to be a senior intelligence operative,[3] Harari supervises Gen. Manuel Antonio Noriega's security arrangements and is credited with helping the general withstand a coup sponsored by the Reagan Administration in 1988. Harari also acts as a financial adviser and business partner to Noriega.[4] Following the October 1988 coup attempt, Harari reportedly took over the day-to-day supervision of Panama's military intelligence.[5] The existence of the Harari network became publicly known in April 1988, during testimony before the Subcommittee on Narcotics, Terrorism and International Operations of the Senate Foreign Relations Committee, which was looking into the connections between the war against Nicaragua and drug trafficking. It is, however, possible that the congressional Iran-Contra investigators knew all about this organization but, because the committee made a decision not to examine anything prior to 1984, it easily avoided exposing it.

In April 1988 José Blandon, a former intelligence aide to Gen. Noriega told the narcotics subcommittee, headed by Sen. John Kerry (Dem.-Mass.), that the Harari network had brought Eastern Bloc arms to Central America for the Nicaraguan Contras and had smuggled cocaine from Colombia to the United States via Panama. Blandon testified that on occasion, the aircraft and Costa Rican airstrips the Harari network used for arms deliveries to the Contras also carried narcotics shipments north to the United States.[6]

Three days after Blandon testified, ABC News interviewed a U.S. pilot, who said he had helped purchase and deliver the Harari network's arms and had also flown drugs from Colombia to Panama. Using the pseudonym "Harry," the pilot said he had regarded Israel as his primary employer and the United States as his secondary employer.[7]

A short time later, Richard Brenneke, who was also involved in the Harari network, went public. Brenneke is an Oregon businessman who claims to have worked for both the Mossad and the CIA. Brenneke said he was recruited to work with the Harari network by Pesakh Ben-Or, the Mossad station chief in Guatemala. When he asked if the operation was approved by the United States, Brenneke claims that Ben-Or gave him Donald Gregg's phone number in Washington, D.C., to call to verify that it was. He said that when he called Gregg on November 3, 1983, Gregg told him that he should "by all means cooperate."[8]

ABC News reported that Israel had provided $20 million start-up capital for the Harari network and was later reimbursed from U.S. covert operations funds. Brenneke claimed that the funding, aircraft and occasionally pilots for the Harari network and its counterpart in Honduras, dubbed the "Arms Supermarket," were supplied by the Medellin Cartel.[9] According to United Press International, the Arms Supermarket consisted of three warehouses in San Pedro Sula, Honduras, which were filled with Eastern Bloc arms. Brenneke stated that it was established "at the request of the Reagan Administration" and "initiated jointly by operatives of the Israeli Mossad, senior Honduran military officers now under investigation for drug trafficking and CIA-connected arms dealers."[10]

Brenneke, however, claims the supermarket was a separate operation from the Harari network. This was because Pesakh Ben-Or did not get along with Mario Del Amico and Ron Martin, the CIA arms dealers connected to the supermarket.[11]

In a May 1988 article about the Arms Supermarket, *Newsweek* said it had possession of a 1986 report prepared for Oliver North by an arms dealer "warning bluntly that disclosure of 'covert black money' flowing into Honduras to fund military projects 'could damage Vice-President Bush.'"[12]

Both Brenneke and ABC News identified Félix Rodríguez, the former CIA official who managed secret Contra supply operations from Ilopango Air Base in El Salvador, as the Harari network's U.S. contact in Central America.[13]

Brenneke said that in 1985, after becoming disenchanted with the drug smuggling element of the operation, he called Gregg to warn him about the Harari network's connection to the Medellin Cartel. Brenneke claims that Gregg told him "You do what you were assigned to do. Don't question the decisions of your betters."[14]

Making Brenneke's allegations about Gregg more plausible are classified documents, which, according to Steven Emerson, author of *Secret Warriors*, "show that the National Security Council had assumed a new operational role as early as 1982, with Gregg serving in a key role as a pivotal player in the NSC 'offline' links to the CIA."[15]

"By early 1983," wrote Emerson, "officials of the NSC and the vice-president's staff assumed authority over Central America policy having wrested control over it from the State Department."[16] Gregg was a lifelong CIA officer before going to work as a member of the NSC staff between 1979 and 1981, after which he became Bush's national security adviser.

Just Say No To Quid Pro Quo

After Bush was safely ensconced in the presidency it was revealed that in March 1985 he had served as an emissary to Honduras, as part of a Reagan Administration effort to keep that government cooperating with its illicit support of the Contras. Bush was sent a copy of a February 19, 1985 memorandum from National Security Adviser Robert McFarlane to

President Reagan, in which McFarlane advised accelerating the flow of economic and military aid to Honduras as "incentives for them to persist in aiding the freedom fighters."[17] A second memo by McFarlane, dated the same day, suggested sending an emissary to then Honduran President Roberto Suazo Cordoba to privately offer this quid pro quo. Another memo which gave details of this proposal was written by North to McFarlane the following day and had a notation by John Poindexter saying, "We want VP to also discuss this matter with Suazo."[18]

The memos were two of six documents that were released during North's trial but which the congressional committees investigating the Iran-Contra affair never received. Rep. Lee Hamilton (Dem.-Ind.), who chaired the House side of the joint Iran-Contra committee, said the missing documents were "about as clear a statement of quid pro quo as you'll ever see in a government document" and did not discount the possibility that they would be cause to reopen the Iran-Contra investigation.[19]

Not surprisingly, when the Senate intelligence committee did investigate the matter of the withheld documents, they concluded there was "no evidence to suggest" that the documents "had been deliberately and systematically withheld by the White House, or persons within the White House, from the congressional investigating committees."[20]

President Bush denied discussing a quid pro quo with Suazo and he refused to respond to the stories while North's trial was underway. Michael G. Kozak, acting Assistant Secretary of State for Inter-American Affairs, told Congress that from his review of the documents, the plan to have Bush carry the message to Honduras had been killed.[21] He said he had a secret cable proving that Bush never explicitly linked Contra aid and assistance to Honduras. However, the Council on Hemispheric Affairs pointed out that the cable, written by then Ambassador John Negroponte — himself a main Iran-Contra player — would have been routinely sanitized (in this case, probably by Donald Gregg) before it was consigned to the permanent files.[22]

None of this back and forth even touched on a paragraph contained in a document submitted in Oliver North's trial. Referred to as an official admission of facts, the document summarized classified material North was not permitted to introduce. The government agreed, for the purposes of the trial, that the 107 assertions contained in its 42 pages, were true.

The 79th stipulation recounts preparations for a Bush mission to Honduras:

> In mid-January 1986, the State Department prepared a memorandum for Donald Gregg (the vice-president's national security adviser) for Vice-President Bush's meeting with President [José] Azcona. According

to DoS [Department of State], one purpose of the meeting was to encourage continued Honduran support for the Contras. The memorandum alerted Gregg that Azcona would insist on receiving clear economic and social benefits from its cooperation with the United States. Admiral Poindexter would meet privately with President Azcona to seek a commitment of support for the Contras by Honduras. DoS suggested that Vice-President Bush inform President Azcona that a strong and active Contra army was essential to maintain pressure on the Sandinistas and that the United States Government's intention to support the contras was clear and firm.[23]

Gregg's Reward

Donald Gregg's reward for his loyalty to George Bush, as well as for his role in running the Nicaraguan contras, was to be nominated as ambassador to South Korea. According to Sen. Alan Cranston (Dem.-Calif.), Gregg's diplomatic nomination came after "key members" of the Senate Intelligence Committee blocked a move to appoint him to a "top CIA post." Gregg claimed that he lost out on the CIA job when discreet inquiries had revealed that his nomination to a top CIA post would embroil the Agency in questions over his role in the Iran-Contra affair.[24]

The confirmation hearings that stretched over May and June 1989 were a test of strength, with the committee destined from the start to be the loser. Speaking — under oath — in an indifferent monotone, Gregg baited Alan Cranston, chairman of the Foreign Relations Subcommittee on East Asian and Pacific Affairs and his principal interrogator, with outrageous answers. For example, after denying that in 1985 he met with Oliver North and Col. James Steele — then the chief U.S. military adviser in El Salvador — to discuss the Contra operation, Gregg coolly absorbed the news that Steele had confirmed the meeting.[25]

An indignant Cranston charged: "Your career training in establishing secrecy and deniability for covert operations and your decades-old friendship with Félix Rodríguez apparently led you to believe that you could serve the national interest by sponsoring a freelance operation out of the Vice-President's office."[26]

Copters not Contras

The greatest moment of absurdity (and outright lying) came when Gregg offered what he called a "speculative explanation" for a reference to a mention of "resupply of the Contras" in a May 1, 1986, memo, prepared for a meeting between Bush and Rodríguez. It was "possible," Gregg said, that it "was a garbled reference to resupply of copters instead of resupply of Contras." Later, Gregg remarked to reporters, "I don't know how it went over, but it was the best I could do."[27]

Cranston failed to question Gregg on a key point. Steven Emerson reported that he had seen a March 1983 memo prepared by Gregg which accompanied a plan to organize a "search-and-destroy air team." The plan was drafted by Félix Rodríguez and contained a map which "strongly suggested that targets inside Nicaragua would be attacked." Emerson said these "still classified" documents bore the handwritten approval of then National Security Adviser William Clark.[28]

Cranston repeatedly tried to crack Gregg's facade and Gregg continued to deny any connection to the Contras or ever having discussed the mercenaries with Bush. He didn't even back away from his earlier statement that Bush had learned of the secret resupply network from an interview Gregg gave the *New York Times* in December 1986.

At his trial Oliver North testified that "I was put in touch with Mr. Rodríguez by Mr. Gregg of the Vice-President's office"[29] and that Gregg knew about the arms shipments. During his confirmation hearing Gregg said North's statements were "just not true."[30]

Hopeless as all of this was, Cranston's interrogation hovered around the fundamental question. Recalling Bush's statement in October 1986 that Félix Rodríguez was not working for the U.S. Government and Gregg's own knowledge that Rodríguez had received help from the U.S. military in El Salvador, Cranston asked Gregg, "Did you inform Bush of those facts so he could make calculated misleading statements, or did you keep him in the dark so he could make misleading statements?"

Gregg evaded the question, contending that Rodríguez was not being paid a government salary but was living off his CIA pension. He also insisted that Bush "made no misleading statements."[31] During the hearings, Cranston had accused Gregg of using Rodríguez's work with the Salvadoran Government as "a cover story," to which Gregg replied that Cranston was providing "a rather full-blown example of a conspiracy theory." [32]

That Donald Gregg had blithely lied under oath was apparent to everyone. Even one of his Republican supporters on the committee, Sen. Richard Lugar (Rep.-Ind.), said that some of Gregg's testimony "certainly strains belief." [33]

Ultimately it was power that overrode perceptions, not to mention truth. The senators did not really want to challenge Bush, whose popularity was soaring. Just to get the administration to release relevant documents it had been withholding, Cranston had to promise to schedule a vote on Gregg.[34]

Three Democrats on the Foreign Relations Committee joined all the Republicans, in voting to report the nomination favorably to the full Senate.

One of the Democrats, Terry Sanford of North Carolina, confirmed Cranston's explanation of his vote — that he was afraid "the path would lead to Bush." "If Gregg was lying," said Sanford, "he was lying to protect the president, which is different from lying to protect himself."[35]

(1990)

What Vice-President Bush Knew and Why He Knew It

Anthony L. Kimery

"What is striking about George Bush's role as vice-president is that he was much more than has ever been suspected. [In the Iran-Contra operation, he]... actually helped execute the dirty-tricks schemes that hijacked Congress's prerogatives in the 1980s," wrote Frank Snepp and Jonathan Marshall.[1] Bush was in the big middle of the Reagan Administration's covert operations; not just as a yes man to Reagan, but as an ardent supporter of and facilitator for, the CIA and the covert operations crowd at Langley and the Old Executive Office Building.[2] That involvement buttresses emerging evidence that Bush has been connected to the clandestine services for nearly four decades.[3]

From his early days at Yale in the 1940s, when he was a member of the Agency-linked Skull and Bones Society, to his career as a moderately successful Texas businessman in the 1950s and early 1960s, to his stint as a political player in the 1960s and 1970s, Bush has been unofficially linked to the CIA in one way or another. In 1976, when Bush became head of the Agency, the connection came into the open and stayed unusually close through his term as vice-president. Bush orchestrated CIA covert activities employed by the Reagan Administration to achieve its foreign policy objectives — the same ones Bush had a heavy hand in designing.[4]

In 1981, when CIA Director William Casey first laid out his plan to launch a secret war against the Sandinista Government, Bush eagerly supported the scheme. And for good reason: It was drafted by his longtime friend, CIA career officer Donald Gregg, who was the Agency's man on the National Security Council (NSC) and who arranged for an expansion of Bush's role in the planning and approval of covert operations.[5] Shortly after Casey's plan was adopted by the White House, Bush appointed Gregg his national security adviser. Resigning from the Agency in 1979 to sever the official link, Gregg began in 1981 to manage the Contra supply effort that Oliver North was running from the NSC.[6] By this time, Bush was a member of the NSC, the National Security Planning Group, the Task Force on Combating Terrorism and chair of the White House Special Situations Group.

From then on, Bush attended nearly every key meeting concerning Iran-Contra, signed off on early deliveries of arms to the Contras, helped organize a resupply bridge to Contra bases in Honduras, sent members of his staff into the field to write progress reports and helped stage-manage the Israelis' central role in arming the Contras and brokering the initial arms sales to Iran.[7]

Given his hands-on approach, institutional centrality and personal involvement, Bush's contention that he was out of "the loop" is elementally ludicrous. In a recently surfaced 1987 memo, then Secretary of State George Shultz and then Secretary of Defense Caspar Weinberger expressed incredulity at Bush's assertion that he was unaware that the two cabinet members had opposed the Iran arms sales to fund the contras. "He [Bush] was on the other side [of the debate]. It's on the record," the memo noted recording Shultz's anger. "Why did he say that."[8]

A key link was Donald Gregg, Bush's national security adviser. Gregg oversaw the operation through his trusted friend Félix Rodríguez, a Cuban-American career CIA operative who first linked up with the Agency during its war against Fidel Castro.[9] According to some accounts, Gregg specifically pitched the idea of putting Rodríguez in charge on the ground in Central America, to which Bush replied: "This sounds like a good idea. See if you can arrange it."[10]

Since Rodríguez reported to Gregg and met on several occasions with Bush,[11] it is not surprising that Bush's office was one of the first places notified when, on October 5, 1986, Nicaraguan soldiers shot down a cargo plane trying to drop weapons to the Contras.[12] Onboard were ex-CIA operatives working for the White House, including Eugene Hasenfus, the sole survivor of the shoot-down. Orchestrated denials, particularly by Bush's office and frenetic high-level "spin controls" began immediately. Until forced to recant by the weight of incontrovertible evidence, the White House stonewalled. "There is no government connection with that plane at all," Reagan declared;[13] the aircraft was part of a private Contra supply operation, Shultz and Assistant Secretary Eliot Abrams claimed.[14]

Indictments and More Lies

The extent and nature of that protection involved an elaborate fabric of both legal lies to the public and illegal lies to the Congress. This screen served to distance Vice-President Bush from the mess — until Tuesday, July 9, 1991. That morning, the first of many indictments against former CIA officials was handed down by Independent Counsel Lawrence Walsh who was conducting what would become a five-and-a-half year investigation.

It was then that Alan D. Fiers, chief of the CIA's Central America Task Force (1984-88), pleaded guilty to lying to Congress when he testified that "we do not know" whose airplane was shot down or "who was behind the flights."[15] Fiers told Congress that the CIA, like Bush, had been out of the loop. Significantly, Fiers stated he was ordered to lie by Clair George, his superior at the Agency. He also admitted knowing that George planned to lie in his testimony to Congress. When Fiers presented George with a suggested opening statement explaining the Hasenfus flight as an unfortunate aberration from the legal "humanitarian" aid flights, George rejected admitting any administration connection to the downed flight. "No," testified Fiers quoting George's response, "I [George] don't want that... It puts the spotlight on the White House, Ollie North or the administration... I don't want to be the *first* person to do that," a weeping Fiers testified in George's trial. (Emphasis added.)[16] Nearly a year earlier, Fiers had testified that George had told him "this was a State [Department]-White House operation."[17]

This high-level coverup is important not only because it hid facts, but because it disguised the trail that might — had the truth been impossible for congressional investigators to dismiss — have led to George Bush.

Following the Trail to Bush

That trail is dotted with the intersecting footprints of Donald Gregg, Félix Rodríguez, a.k.a. Max Gomez, G. Phillip Hughes (the vice-president's deputy national security adviser) and George Bush. From 1984 to 1986, Fiers dealt directly with Gregg, notably in matters concerning Rodríguez — a key manager of the Contra operation. Fiers's testimony strongly contradicts Gregg's claim that he did not know what North was up to.[18] The connection between Bush and Rodríguez is less intimate, but also long-standing. Having earned Bush's loyalty somewhere along the line, perhaps during the Agency's anti-Castro exploits, Rodríguez met with the vice-president several times at the White House and received his blessing for the anticommunist quest.[19] In a January 6, 1986, entry in his personal notebook, Oliver North reported that Fiers had expressed concern that "Felix [was] talking too much about VP connection..."

Rodríguez's part in the Contra supply operation was truly an explosive matter that the CIA and the White House were particularly intent on keeping secret. As Fiers's former legislative and legal adviser Louis Dupart has testified, the CIA hid Rodríguez's role in resupplying the contras. The CIA even continued to conceal what it knew about Rodríguez after Fiers and George acknowledged to Congress that Max Gomez and Félix Rodríguez were one and the same.[20] Meanwhile, Bush and Gregg have stonewalled all along, maintaining their ignorance of North's network until it was publicly acknowledged by Attorney General Edwin Meese in November 1986.

In fact, the vice-president knew precisely what was going on with the Contras. His office was the central command post and he, Gregg and Hughes were deeply involved.[21] Fiers has testified that he met with Gregg to discuss Rodríguez's charges that the resupply network was raking off considerable profits.[22] A nearly identical charge had been made by another Contra supply operative, former Air Force Col. Richard B. Gadd, in sworn testimony on behalf of a damage lawsuit brought by Eugene Hasenfus. Gadd stated that Robert Dutton, another key participant in the supply operation who worked closely with Richard Secord, told him in 1986 that Bush had discussed supply problems with Rodriguez, including selling "cheap parts or inadequate ammunition" to the Contras.[23] Included in Dutton's testimony before the House Select Committee to Investigate Covert Arms Transactions with Iran, were NSC memos containing Rodríguez's alias.[24]

Throughout 1985 and 1986, Hughes also met with North and his name turns up in the North notebooks as early as July 1984. Hughes was also involved in a 1985 incident in which Bush put an allegedly CIA-tied Contra supporter in touch with North.[25]

George and Twetten Fudge the Truth

In his summer 1992 mistrial for nine felony counts of lying and obstructing congressional and grand jury investigations, George charged the Senate investigators with "hypocrisy." And there is some truth to his claim that it was "an open secret in Washington," and a well-documented truism in the left media, that the resupply effort was an official (albeit covert), illegal U.S. operation.

Rodríguez's role, for example, was well understood. George, however, stonewalled the Senate Foreign Relations Committee by denying the centrality of the CIA connection — through Rodríguez — to the White House operation in Central America. His lawyers presented scores of cables identifying Rodríguez — including several that had arrived at the CIA headquarters just days before the hearing — and exposing George's and Fiers's lies to the committee. Even George's CIA briefing book, prepared for his Senate testimony by Fiers, contained two pages on Rodríguez and incorporated information from a CIA cable that came the night before he appeared in front of the lawmakers. The denial nevertheless served to placate the nervous congresspeople.

Six years after the Senate Foreign Relations Committee hearing, Sen. John Kerry (Dem.-Mass.) testified at George's trial and accused George of lying to the committee. At the time, Kerry said, all that was known was that Hasenfus was claiming to work for the CIA and that "Max Gomez" was in charge. If the CIA had come clean about Rodríguez and his connection to Bush, Kerry told the jury, "you would have had a totally different attitude in the Congress" toward the $100 million Contra aid package then being debated. The bill was passed by Senate and House conferees the same day George testified.

Fiers and George aren't the only ones implicated in not being truthful with Congress. Thomas Twetten, 31-year CIA veteran, appointed by Bush in 1990, is still CIA Deputy Director for Operations. During Iran-Contra, he was chief of the Near East Division and handled the Agency's end of financing and logistics for the arms transfers to Iran.[26] Despite having been North's case officer at the CIA from 1985 to 1986, Twetten swore to Congress that he knew nothing about the diversion of profits from arms sales in Iran to the Contras. This claim was repeated by his boss, Clair George. Twetten, who is also under investigation by Walsh,[27] testified that although the circumstances of the arms sales were unusual, his suspicions were not roused. Despite the gaping disparity between what the Iranians were charged for certain weapons and the CIA's cost, "It never occurred to me," Twetten said, "that North was raking it off [for the Contras]. That was beyond the pale."[28]

More important than what Twetten knew about the diversion of profits to the Contras is what he knew about and whether he helped conceal the Bush-linked arms shipments to Iran prior to the initial officially acknowledged delivery. Intelligence provided by a high-level Iranian in Teheran (recruited by FBI counterintelligence to report on illegal arms shipments to Iran), clearly shows that arms were arriving in early September 1985,[29] two months before the CIA acknowledged involvement. At that time, the FBI began to receive accurate intelligence from its Iranian agent on U.S. arms shipments to Iran.[30]

In 1985, when the Iranian began reporting that the arms were being flown into Teheran on U.S. registered aircraft, his FBI handler was bewildered. He turned for an explanation to his CIA liaison, a ranking officer in the Iranian branch of Twetten's operations division. Twetten told the CIA officer that it was "a White House operation," exactly what Fiers testified he had been told by George. The Agency man was ordered to tell his FBI counterpart not to report the Iranian's information to anyone in the FBI. "In other words, I was being told to cover it up," the ex-CIA officer says. Allegedly, Twetten gave the order to suppress the affair and alter all related memos prepared by the CIA liaison.[31]

Quid Pro Quo Foreign Policy

Elaborately covered tracks, webs of plausible deniability, false trails and sturdy facades of misinformation are endemic hazards of efforts to disentangle CIA connections and operations. The ultimately futile stalling effort to distance Bush from the loop and the carefully orchestrated campaign to downplay his Agency connections are in themselves revealing.

The weak links, however, show increasing strain. In November 1989, yet another CIA official, CIA Costa Rica Station Chief Joseph Fernandez, a.k.a. Tomás Castillo, was indicted by Iran-Contra Independent Counsel Walsh for lying to the CIA inspector general and the Tower Commission about his role in the CIA's illegal arms conduit to the Contras. Fernandez was intimately involved in the White House's Contra operation and dealt directly with Rodríguez in Rodríguez's capacity as its manager on the ground. Rodríguez also dealt with North. George knew all about Fernandez's dealings with the White House and apparently went to great lengths to protect them.[32]

After a federal judge ruled that the Fernandez defense could use top secret CIA records, the Justice Department, at the urging of the White House and especially the CIA, invoked, for the first time, the decade-old Classified Information Procedures Act (CIPA).[33] Under CIPA, the U.S. attorney general — then Richard Thornburgh — is the final arbiter of what classified information can be disclosed at trial. After the Reagan appointee blocked release of the secret material, the court dismissed all charges against Fernandez, ruling that he could not fairly defend himself without it.[34]

Privately, CIA sources and aides to Walsh said the White House blockade had nothing to do with the Agency's claim that the information could cause "serious damage to the national security."[35] Rather, the administration feared embarrassing new disclosures that, if backtracked, would lead though Gregg and Rodríguez to Bush, revealing the vice-president's and the CIA's illegally organized effort to keep the Contras in arms.[36] "It was Bush that was being protected," said an ex-CIA officer, "not national security."[37]

Oliver North's indictment provoked another attempt to block

information potentially damaging to Bush. As his droning trial neared its end in April 1989, the young Marine's attorneys presented surprise documents. They indicated that Bush's participation in Iran-Contra had constituted an impeachable offense — the violation of the Boland Amendment prohibiting indirect aid to the Contras. More than just a smoking gun, these once "top secret" documents seemed to offer conclusive proof of a crime — the first in the whole sordid scandal which appeared to catch Bush red-handed. The documents showed that the vice-president participated in an illegal White House-sanctioned extortion scheme: In exchange for becoming a staging ground for the Contra war, Honduras got U.S. military aid and more than $4 million in CIA assistance. And the Oval Office crisis management group — led by Bush — had hatched the deal. It was the vice-president's responsibility to brief Reagan, while North served as liaison to the rest of the intelligence community.[38]

As in many other cases, the denials of illegal activity were eventually eroded by the revelation of lies. At first, the Honduras deal was completely denied. When the documents surfaced the administration fell back on plan B. It admitted discussions had taken place, but denied that the scheme was ever implemented. The plan, said acting Assistant Secretary of State for Inter-American Affairs Michael Kozak, who participated in the discussions, was simply another one of North's foolish ideas killed by the State Department. It could "wind up compromising us," Shultz expanded.[39] For the most part, Congress and the press not only accepted the denial, but also the Bush White House's assurance that no documents were deliberately concealed. One disgruntled House Foreign Affairs Committee investigator protested: "This thing has been swept under the carpet."[40]

And there it lies, along with the large, ominous lump of Bush's lies and cover-ups. Bush's direct involvement with and close proximity to these documented covert operations while Reagan's vice-president provoke legitimate concerns about the growing evidence that he has been a loyal secret member of the intelligence establishment for nearly 40 years. Inevitably, more people will trip over the mess under the carpet. The significant question is: Will they point at George Bush as they fall?

(1992)

Vice-President Bush:
Inside Track to Power

Karen Branan

Bush's pale image — as a traditional vice-president who attended foreign funerals — served him well. Behind this bland facade, the former head of the CIA was a hands-on vice-president. He actively headed a powerful, little-known institution which was key in shaping U.S. policy. While others around him were called to testify in the Iran-Contra scandal and some were tried and indicted, Bush walked easily into the White House on a pathway of unchallenged denials. "I was not aware of and I oppose any diversion of funds, any ransom payments, or any circumvention of the will of Congress," he said.[1]

"The evidence that was before the [Iran-Contra] Committee," wrote Maine Senators George Mitchell and William Cohen, "gave no indication that the vice-president was aware of the diversion of funds."[2]

Most efforts to link Bush to the Iran-Contra affair failed because they focused on Bush as adviser to the president ("What did he tell Reagan?"). They ignored this particular vice-president's unique and central position within the National Security Council and, in particular, his relationship to Adm. John Poindexter, Lt. Col. Oliver North and the cabal of special operations officers who carried out the activities that became known as Iran-Contra. Unlike many of the others, Bush never testified under oath and therefore remained invulnerable to perjury and cover-up charges.

Given Bush's institutional role, that omission, his own denials and the whitewash investigations are incredible. Bush was not only one of four statutory members of the National Security Council where foreign policy was formulated; he chaired a little-known back channel called the Crisis Management System.

In November 1984 Robert McFarlane, then National Security Adviser, explained the two-track system at the NSC. First there was Track 1, called SIG/IG (Senior Interagency/Interagency Group), providing for careful study and thoughtful debate. Then there was Track 2, the Crisis Management System, strongly resembling an intelligence unit.

Track 2 had two major elements: the Special Situations Group (SSG), chaired by George Bush; and the Crisis Pre-Planning Group (CPPG), led by the Deputy Assistant to the President for National Security Affairs. The CPPG provided "to the SSG, recommended security, cover and media plans that will enhance the likelihood of successful execution."[3]

"The principal difference between the Crisis Management System and the SIG/IG system," wrote McFarlane, "... is that the former is controlled more directly by the White House for reasons of policy responsiveness. While the SIG/IG system is able to ensure that policy proposals receive thorough study and analysis before coming to the president for decision, the system is *too slow moving* to be used for crisis management." [Emphasis added.][4]

Their failure to look at Track 2 could explain why Congress's Iran-Contra Report found the August 6, 1985, draft finding signed by Reagan authorizing arms sales to Iran "unusual in that it has been drafted without inter-agency participation." In his autobiography, *Looking Forward,* Bush agreed: "The NSC advisory apparatus was there, but it wasn't used. Instead, it was bypassed..."[5] He failed to note that it was detoured straight into the Crisis Management System — which he chaired.

The official $4.6 million NSC budget was supplemented by another $25 million from the Pentagon and intelligence agencies. Much of that went to an entity within Bush's back channel, the Crisis Management Center, staffed by a platoon of military special operations officers active in Iran and Contra operations.

The Crisis Management channel spun off numerous subgroups, task forces, compartments and bureaucratic boxes. Most Iran-Contra players, large and small, such as William Casey, Dewey Clarridge, Donald Gregg, Oliver North, John Poindexter and Terrell Arnold, participated in one or more of these subgroups. According to depositions taken by Congress, there were boxes marked Contra, hostage and Iran, but often these boxes broke open and spilled into one another. Key, of course, is the fact that all the boxes were inside a big one marked Crisis Management and that was Track 2, presided over by George Bush.

(1992)

The Bush Family: Oiligarchy and the Emirs

Introduction

Ellen Ray and William H. Schaap

When the U.S. economy falters, conventional wisdom calls for war preparations, or, better yet, war. Thus there are peculiar ramifications to the scandal over massive corporate malfeasance that broke early in the George W. Bush Administration, hard on the heels of his fraudulent 2000 election. At present, the U.S. economy is in a shambles — not from September 11, but because of corporate greed, publicly revealed corporate greed, on a scale never exposed before. There was thus overwhelming hypocrisy in the call by Bush for stricter business ethics, even as he demanded of Congress massive tax breaks for the mega-corporations and the super-rich.

The president, his father, his uncle and all his brothers have been neck-deep for decades in the corruption he now pretends to find so shocking. When the economy was booming in the Bush I years, there was scant interest that the president's son, George W., sold a chunk of shares in his oil exploration company, Harken Energy, just before their price plummeted, or that he violated SEC filing regulations. Nor did anyone notice that his original purchase into the company was funded by Middle Eastern financiers anxious to curry favor with his father.

Except for George W., nearly everyone who invested in Harken took a bath. The Harvard Management, the largest endowment in the world, invested deeply in the president's son's company and ultimately took a staggering $200 million loss. (Harvard recouped some of the loss through the insider-trading machinations of the Harvard Institute for International Development in Russia, but are facing federal charges for that.) Harken was connected with both the notorious Bank of Commerce and Credit International and Saudi financiers tied to the Bin Laden family and funding Osama and other terrorists in Afghanistan.

Many key figures of the Reagan and Bush I administrations made huge profits not from any business acumen but from their political and military connections, sought after by corrupt Middle Eastern potentates, with assistance from shameful and unethical lawyers, banks and accountants.

Vice-President Dick Cheney, having prosecuted Bush senior's Iraq and Panama wars as Secretary of Defense, spent most of the inter-Bush years as CEO of Halliburton, Inc., which reaped huge profits from defense contracts, including rebuilding the oil fields in Iraq that Cheney's Defense Department had demolished. Halliburton is now accused only of "accounting irregularities" (some $100 million) during Cheney's tenure and continues to benefit from billions of dollars in contracts relating to the current president's "war on terrorism", including contracts to build the prisons in Guantánamo that house Taliban and al-Qaeda captives.

The now bankrupt Enron Corporation was linked intimately with the Bush crowd; disgraced former CEO Ken Lay was Bush I's energy adviser and a major congressional investigation should examine the extent to which Lay and other energy industry leaders influenced Bush II's energy policies. But the investigation has been stalled by the White House's refusal to divulge the records of its meetings with Enron lobbyists. And while Halliburton was rebuilding the oil fields in Iraq, Enron was doing the same in Kuwait, under a contract negotiated for them by Bush I's Secretary of State, James Baker. The details of Cheney's secret meetings with Enron executives to shape this administration's energy policies are still unknown and are likely to remain so. Public service builds an acute sense of deferred gratification. As the scandal faded from public memory, Joseph Kelliher, a former aide to Vice-President Cheney and the Enron-Administration go-between, was appointed head of the Federal Energy Regulatory Commission. The fox is not just in the chicken coop, he is in charge of it.

Even now, as some of the past wheeling and dealing is rehashed in the press, the truly far-reaching and long-standing implications are only superficially questioned. The extensive involvement of Bin Laden family money in Harken is glossed over. Little is said of that family's powerful position in the Carlyle Group — a massive investment conglomerate whose top officers include former President Bush, former Secretary of Defense (and former Deputy Director of the CIA) Frank Carlucci (now chairman of the company), former British Prime Minister John Major and former Secretary of State James Baker. Secretary of Defense Donald Rumsfeld, Carlucci's college classmate and friend, has awarded Carlyle some giant and very questionable military contracts. For example, Carlyle made over $200 million in one day shortly after September 11, selling shares in a giant defense contractor just as congressional support for greatly increased defense spending peaked.

The common thread — notwithstanding the lion's share of media attention given in the 1980s to the support of the Nicaraguan contras — is and always has been the control of oil. Middle Eastern oil in particular and world energy supplies in general.

The "war against terrorism" and the jockeying for oil are intertwined, the former providing cover for the latter. Before September 11, Washington's overarching thirst for oil had to be disguised. During the Iran-Contra congressional hearings much of the press coverage was spun to highlight Oliver North's escapades with the Nicaraguan counter-revolutionaries, not his role as an arms dealer in Iran and Iraq, whose oil was not in the U.S. grip. (As a former CIA Director, then vice-president George H.W. Bush was in effect his handler, the director of these operations; it is not surprising the current President Bush has blocked the release of critical Reagan presidential papers.)

The United States has five percent of the world's population, but consumes 25 percent of its oil, half from overseas, a share that is growing. Access to and control of Middle Eastern oil and gas reserves is a fundamental tenet of U.S. foreign policy. But in the current frenzy of antiterrorism, it is seldom acknowledged by the corporate media that the primary targets of Washington's wrath, its "Axis of Evil" — Iran and Iraq — are major oil producers. Afghanistan, also an integral part of the oil picture, is a prime potential location for Western-controlled Transcaucasian pipelines, as well as a source of untapped reserves. The sometimes unfathomable targets of carpet bombing there probably helped these endeavors.

Jack Colhoun's seminal article, "The Family that Preys Together", describes in considerable detail the corporate misdeeds of the Bush clan — George II, his father George I, his uncle Prescott Jr. and his brothers Jeb and Neil. As early as 1992, the misdeeds at Harken and elsewhere were public knowledge.

The current administration's domestic oil policies are equally shameless; while Bush tried, unsuccessfully, to open a vast wildlife refuge in Alaska to drilling and supported offshore oil leases in California, he committed hundreds of millions of U.S. taxpayers' dollars to buy out offshore leases in Florida, ostensibly to protect its beaches and wetlands, but really to boost his brother Jeb's chances in his successful race for reelection as governor.

The enormity of this heritage, embodied in the president of the most powerful country in the world, is frighteningly predictable. But it also throws considerable light and necessary exposure on the policies of the U.S. Government, not just then, but now.

The Family That Preys Together

Jack Colhoun

George Jr.'s BCCI Connection

"This is an incredible deal, unbelievable for this small company," energy analyst Charles Strain told *Forbes* magazine, describing the oil production sharing agreement the Harken Energy Corporation signed in January 1990 with Bahrain.[1]

Under the terms of the deal, Harken was given the exclusive right to explore for gas and oil off the shores of the Gulf island nation. If gas or oil were found in waters near two of the world's largest gas and oil fields, Harken would have exclusive marketing and transportation rights for the energy resources. Truly an "incredible deal" for a company that had never drilled an offshore well.

Strain failed to point out, however, the one fact that puts the Harken deal in focus: George W. Bush, the eldest son of George and Barbara Bush of 1600 Pennsylvania Avenue, Washington, D.C., is a member of Harken's board of directors, a consultant and a stockholder in the Texas-based company. In light of this connection, the deal makes more sense.

The involvement of Junior — George Walker Bush's childhood nickname — with Harken is a walking conflict of interest. His relationship to President Bush, rather than any business acumen, made him a valuable asset for Harken, the Republican Party benefactors, Middle East oil sheikhs and covert operators who played a part in Harken's Bahrain deal. In fact, Junior's track record as an oilman is pretty dismal. He began his career in Midland, Texas, in the mid-1970s when he founded Arbusto Energy, Inc. When oil prices dropped in the early 1980s, Arbusto fell upon hard times. Junior was only rescued from business failure when his company was purchased by Spectrum 7 Energy Corporation, a small oil firm owned by William DeWitt and Mercer Reynolds. As part of the September 1984 deal, Bush became Spectrum 7's president and was given a 13.6 percent share in the company's stock. Oil prices stayed low and within two years, Spectrum 7 was in trouble.[2]

In the six months before Spectrum 7 was acquired by Harken in 1986, it had lost $400,000. In the buy out deal, George "Jr." and his partners were given more than $2 million worth of Harken stock for the 180-well operation. Made a director and hired as a "consultant" to Harken, Junior received another $600,000 of Harken stock and has been paid between $42,000 and $120,000 a year since 1986.[3]

Junior's value to Harken soon became apparent when the company needed an infusion of cash in the spring of 1987. Junior and other Harken officials met with Jackson Stephens, head of Stephens, Inc., a large investment bank in Little Rock, Arkansas (Stephens made a $100,000 contribution to the Reagan-Bush campaign in 1980 and gave another $100,000 to the Bush dinner committee in 1990.)[4]

In 1987, Stephens made arrangements with Union Bank of Switzerland (UBS) to provide $25 million to Harken in return for a stock interest in Harken. As part of the Stephens-brokered deal, Sheikh Abdullah Bakhsh, a Saudi real estate tycoon and financier, joined Harken's board as a major investor.[5] Stephens, UBS and Bakhsh each have ties to the scandal-ridden Bank of Credit and Commerce International (BCCI).

It was Stephens who suggested in the late 1970s that BCCI purchase what became First American Bankshares in Washington, D.C. BCCI later acquired First American's predecessor, Financial General Bankshares. At the time of the Harken investment, UBS was a joint-venture partner with BCCI in a bank in Geneva, Switzerland. Bakhsh has been an investment partner in Saudi Arabia with Gaith Pharoan, identified by the U.S. Federal Reserve Board as a "front man" for BCCI's secret acquisitions of U.S. banks.[6]

Stephens, Inc. played a role in the Harken deal with Bahrain as well. Former Stephens bankers David and Mike Edwards contacted Michael Ameen, the former chief of Mobil Oil's Middle East operations, when Bahrain broke off 1989 talks with Amoco for a gas and oil exploration contract. The Edwardses recommended Harken for the job and urged Ameen to get in touch with Bahrain, which he did.[7]

"In the midst of Harken's talks with Bahrain, Ameen — simultaneously working as a State Department consultant — briefed the incoming U.S. ambassador in Bahrain, Charles Hostler," the *Wall Street Journal* noted, adding that Hostler, a San Diego real estate investor, was a $100,000 contributor to the Republican Party. Hostler claimed he never discussed Harken with the Bahrainis.[8]

Harken lacked sufficient financing to explore off the coast of Bahrain so it brought in Bass Enterprises Production Company of Fort Worth, Texas, as a partner. The Bass family contributed more than $200,000 to the Republican Party in the late 1980s and early 1990s.[9]

On June 22, 1990, George Jr. sold two-thirds of his Harken stock for $848,560 — a cool 200 percent profit. The move was well timed. One week after Junior sold his stock, Harken announced a $23.2 million loss in quarterly earnings and Harken stock dropped sharply, losing 60 percent of its value over the next six months. On August 2, 1990, Iraqi troops moved into Kuwait and 541,000 U.S. forces were deployed to the Gulf.[10]

"There is substantial evidence to suggest that Bush knew Harken was in dire straits in the weeks before he sold the $848,560 of Harken stock," asserted *U.S. News & World Report.* The magazine noted Harken appointed Junior to a "fairness committee" to study possible economic restructuring of the company. Junior worked closely with financial advisers from Smith Barney, Harris Upham & Company, who concluded "only drastic action could save Harken."[11]

George Jr. also violated Securities and Exchange Commission (SEC) regulations which require "insider" stock deals to be reported promptly, in Bush's case by July 10, 1990. He didn't file the stock sale with the SEC until the first week of March 1991.[12]

Meanwhile, a cloak-and-dagger aura surrounds Junior's business dealings. James Bath, a Texas entrepreneur who invested $50,000 in Arbusto Energy, may be a business cutout for the CIA. Bath also acted as an investment "adviser" to Saudi Arabian oil sheikhs, linked to the outlaw BCCI, which also has ties to the CIA.[13]

Bill White, a former Bath partner, claims that Bath has "national security" connections. White, a United States Naval Academy graduate and former fighter pilot, charges that Bath developed a network of off-shore companies to camouflage the movement of money and aircraft between Texas and the Middle East, especially Saudi Arabia.[14]

Alan Quasha, a Harken director and former chair of the company, is the son of attorney William Quasha, who defended figures in the Nugan Hand Bank scandal in Australia. Closed in 1980, Nugan Hand was not only tied to drug-money laundering and U.S. intelligence and military circles, but also to the CIA's covert backing for a "constitutional coup" in Australia that caused the fall of Prime Minister Gough Whitlam.[15]

The Harken deal with Bahrain raises another troubling question: Did the Bahrainis and the BCCI-linked Saudi oil sheikhs use the production sharing agreement with Harken to curry favor with the Bush Administration and influence U.S. policy in the Middle East?

Talat Othman's sudden rise to prominence in Bush Administration foreign policy circles is a case in point. Othman, who sits on the Harken board as Sheikh Bakhsh's representative, didn't have access to President Bush before Harken's Bahrain agreement.

"But since August 1990, the Palestinian-born Chicago investor has attended three White House meetings with President Bush to discuss Middle East policy," the *Wall Street Journal* pointed out. "His name was added by the White House to a select list of 15 Arab-Americans chosen to meet with President Bush, [then White House Chief of Staff John] Sununu and National Security Adviser Brent Scowcroft in the White House two days after Iraq's August 1990 invasion of Kuwait."[16]

Prescott's Big Asian Adventure

Prescott Bush, Jr., the president's older brother, also has a knack for nailing down "incredible deal[s]." Prescott took advantage of his brother's first presidential visit abroad in February 1989 to schedule a business trip to the same countries — China, Japan and South Korea.[17]

Prescott arrived in Tokyo on February 14, 1989, 10 days before President Bush's stop in Japan, to drum up business for Prescott Bush Resources Ltd., a real estate and development consulting company. Prescott said he was dealing with four Japanese companies wanting to do business in the United States.

From Japan, Prescott went to China, where he had a joint partnership with Akoi Corporation to develop an $18 million golf course and resort near Shanghai. Prescott had introduced the Tokyo-based Akoi to Chinese officials in 1988. With a 30 percent stake in the project, Prescott used his China connections to pave the way for capital-rich Akoi. Akoi had run into business obstacles in China because of lingering Chinese resentment over Japan's brutal occupation of China in the 1930s and 1940s.[18]

Some of Prescott's most controversial business deals have been with Asset Management International Financing & Settlement Ltd., a Wall Street investment firm which has been in bankruptcy proceedings since fall 1991. Prescott was hired by Asset Management, which paid him a $250,000 fee for consulting in its joint venture with China to set up its internal communications network. Asset Management enlisted Prescott's services soon after President Bush imposed economic sanctions in June 1989 in response to Beijing's brutal crackdown on antigovernment demonstrators in Tiananmen Square.[19]

Under the sanctions, United States export licenses were suspended for

$300 million worth of Hughes Aircraft satellites, a key component of Asset Management's joint venture with the Chinese Government. The satellites would beam television programming to broadcasters in China and provide telecommunications links for the country's far-flung provinces. In November 1989, Congress passed additional sanctions specifically barring the export of U.S. satellites to China unless the president found the sale "in the national interest."[20]

On December 19, 1989, President Bush lifted the sanctions that blocked the satellite deal, citing "the national interest." Two months earlier, the Bush Administration had granted Hughes Aircraft "preliminary licenses" to exchange data with Chinese officials to ensure that the satellites met the technical specifications of the Long March rockets which would launch them into space.[21]

Meanwhile, Prescott was hard at work in the summer of 1989 as middleman in the takeover of Asset Management by West Tsusho, a Tokyo-based investment firm linked to one of Japan's biggest mob syndicates. Prescott, as head of Prescott Bush & Co., received a $250,000 "finder's fee" from West Tsusho when the deal was closed and was promised an annual retainer of $250,000 over the next three years as a "consultant." Asset Management, however, went bankrupt in March 1991. In May 1992, West Tsusho filed a $2.5 million lawsuit against Prescott claiming that he reneged on his promise to protect the mob-linked firm's $5 million investment in Asset Management.[22]

According to Japanese police, West Tsusho is controlled by the Inagawakai branch of the *Yakuza*, the Japanese equivalent of the Mafia crime syndicate. By the mid-1980s, the *Yakuza* were buying up real estate and investments in Japan and overseas to launder their ill-gotten profits from drug sales, prostitution, gambling and extortion. *Yakuza's* annual income is estimated at $10 billion.[23]

Like George Jr., Prescott combined business with secret operations. He offered his services to the covert operations of the Reagan-Bush campaign in 1980 and later to the Reagan Administration.

A September 3, 1980, letter from Prescott to James Baker indicates Prescott was part of the Reagan-Bush campaign's secret surveillance of the Carter Administration's efforts to obtain release of U.S. hostages held in Iran. Prior to inauguration, the Reagan-Bush campaign recruited retired military and intelligence officers to monitor activities of the CIA, the Defense Department, the National Security Council, the State Department and the White House. This operation later became known as the "October Surprise."[24]

"Herb Cohen — the guy that offered help on the Iranian hostage situation — called me yesterday afternoon," Prescott wrote in a letter designated "PRIVATE AND CONFIDENTIAL." "Herb has a couple of reliable sources on the National Security Council, about whom the [Carter] Administration does not know, who can keep him posted on developments."

Prescott continued, "He cannot come out now and say that Carter is going to do something on Iran in October because he said everything is a contingency plan that is loose and fluid from day to day... Herb says, however, that if he and others in the administration who really care about the country and cannot stand to see Carter playing politics with the hostages, see Carter making a move to politicize the release of the hostages, he and they will come out at that time and expose him."

Prescott's covert associations continued while his younger brother was vice-president. He appears to have aided the Reagan Administration's clandestine support of the Nicaraguan Contras. In the 1980s, he served on the advisory board of Americares; the U.S.-based relief organization with ties to prominent right-wing Republicans and the intelligence community.[25] Bush's other son, Marvin, also helped the family's pet charity and accompanied a flight of medical supplies to Nicaragua three days after Chamorro's inauguration.

An undisclosed amount of the $680,000 in Americares aid to Honduras was delivered to Nicaraguan Miskito Indian guerrillas. Based in Honduras, they were aligned with the CIA-funded Contras, according to Roberto Alejos, a Guatemalan sugar and coffee grower who coordinated the Americares project in Honduras. In 1960, Alejos had permitted the CIA to use his plantations to train right-wing Cubans in preparation for the Bay of Pigs invasion of Cuba.

In 1985 and 1986, after Congress cut off U.S. aid to the Contras, Americares donated more than $100,000 worth of newsprint to the pro-Contra newspaper La Prensa in Managua. Americares supplied $291,383 in food and medicine and $5,750 in cash to Mario Calero, New Orleans-based quartermaster and arms purchaser for the Contras and brother of Contra leader Adolfo Calero. In this same period, groups associated with Lt. Col. Oliver North's off-the-shelf Contra arms network provided covert support for La Prensa.[26]

Jeb: Liaison to Anti-Castro Right

George Herbert Walker Bush's second eldest son, John Ellis or Jeb, was also linked to clandestine schemes in support of the Contras. Soon after congressional prohibition in late 1984, Jeb helped put a right-wing Guatemalan politician, Dr. Mario Castejón, in touch with Oliver North. Jeb acted as the Reagan Administration's unofficial link with the Contras and Nicaraguan exiles in Miami.

Jeb was contacted in February 1985 by a friend of Castejón, who gave him a letter from Castejón to be passed on to then Vice-President Bush. In his letter, Castejón, a pediatrician and later an unsuccessful National Conservative Party presidential candidate, requested a meeting with George Bush to discuss a proposed medical aid project for the Contras. Jeb forwarded the letter to his father. In a March 3, 1985, letter, Vice-President Bush expressed interest in Castejón's proposal to create an international medical brigade.

"I might suggest, if you are willing, that you consider meeting with Lt. Colonel Oliver North of the President's National Security Council Staff at a time that would be convenient for you," Bush wrote. "My staff has been in contact with Lt. Col. North concerning your projects and I know that he would be most happy to see you. You may feel free to make arrangements to see Lt. Colonel North, if you wish, by corresponding directly with him at the White House or by contacting Philip Hughes of my staff."[27]

Castejón later met with North in the White House, where he also saw President Ronald Reagan. When Castejón returned to Washington for a second visit, he was introduced to members of North's secret Contra support network, including retired Maj. Gen. John Singlaub and Contra leader Adolfo Calero. Castejón also met with a group of doctors working with Rob Owen, North's liaison with the Contras.

"He [Castejón] was offering us a pipeline into Guatemala," said Henry Whaley, a former arms dealer who said he was asked by his intelligence community connections to help Castejón. Whaley was optimistic about opening a new shipping route to the Contras through Guatemala. "If you can move Band-Aids," he reportedly said, "you can move bullets."[28]

With Castejón, Whaley prepared a proposal to the State Department for the purchase of medical supplies for the contras from the Department's newly established Nicaraguan Humanitarian Assistance Office. The document included requests for mobile field hospitals and light aircraft to evacuate wounded Contra guerrillas. Congress approved $27 million in "humanitarian" aid to the contras in 1985.

The Castejón proposal was hand-delivered to TGS International Limited in the Virginia suburbs of Washington. Whaley said he sent the report to TGS so it would be "quietly" forwarded to the CIA. TGS International is owned by Ted Shackley, who was CIA Associate Deputy Director of Operations when Bush Sr. headed the Agency in 1976-77.

Jeb had another Contra connection in his involvement with Miguel Recarey, Jr., a right-wing Cuban who headed the International Medical Centers (IMC) in Miami. In 1985 and 1986, Recarey and his associates gave more than $25,000 in contributions to political action committees controlled by then Vice-President Bush.

In 1986, Recarey hired Jeb, a real estate developer, to find a new headquarters for IMC. Jeb was paid a $75,000 fee, even though he never located a new building.

In September 1984, two months after IMC's $2,000 contribution to the Dade County Republican Party, which was headed by Jeb, the vice-president's son contacted several top HHS (Department of Health and Human Services) officials on behalf of IMC. "Contrary to rumors, [Recarey] was a good community citizen and a good supporter of the Republican Party," one official of the HHS remembered Jeb telling him in late 1984. Jeb successfully sought an HHS waiver of a rule so that IMC could receive more than 50 percent of its income from Medicare.[29]

Leon Weinstein, an HHS Medicare fraud inspector, worked on an audit of IMC in 1986; he has charged that IMC used Medicare funds to treat wounded Contras at its hospital.[30] The transaction was arranged by IMC official José Basulto, a right-wing Cuban trained by the CIA, who arranged for Contras to receive treatment in Miami.

Basulto was praised for his commitment by Félix Rodríguez: "He has been active for a decade in supporting the Nicaraguan freedom fighters ever since the Sandinistas took power and is constantly organizing Contra support among Miami's Cuban community. He has even been to Contra camps in Central America, helping to dispense humanitarian aid."[31]

At the same time as Recarey was providing medical assistance to the Contras, he was embezzling Medicare funds. IMC, one of the largest health maintenance organizations in the United States, received $30 million a month for its Medicare patients, clearing $1 billion in federal monies from 1981 to 1987. While he headed IMC, Recarey's personal wealth jumped from $1 million to $100 million, U.S. investigators believe.[32]

"IMC is the classic case of embezzlement of government funds," according to Robert Teich, the head of the Drug Enforcement Administration's Office on Labor Racketeering in Miami. Teich described PAC's skimming Medicare funds as a "bust-out" where money was "drained out the back door." A Florida state investigator concluded in a 1982 report that some federal funds IMC received "are being put in banks outside the country."[33]

Recarey's links to the Mafia also raised eyebrows in Washington. "As far back as the 1960s, he had ties with reputed racketeers who had operated out of pre Castro Cuba and who later forged an anti Castro alliance with the CIA," the *Wall Street Journal* reported. The *Journal* added that the late Santos Trafficante, Jr., the Mafia boss of Florida, "helped out when Recarey needed business financing." Trafficante, a major drug trafficker, joined a failed CIA effort to assassinate Cuban President Fidel Castro in the early 1960s.[34]

Recarey's access to Republican circles was probably one reason he was able to rip off U.S. tax dollars for so long. He hired former Reagan aide Lyn Nofziger, the public relations firm Black, Manafort, Stone and Kelly, which was close to the Reagan White House and attorney John Sears, a former Reagan campaign manager, to look out for his interests in Washington.

Recarey fled the United States in 1987 to avoid a federal indictment for racketeering and defrauding the U.S. Government. The Bush Administration has made no effort to extradite him from Venezuela where he is currently living.

Jeb Linked to Smugglers and Thieves

Jeb Bush has also been linked to Leonel Martínez, a Miami-based right-wing Cuban-American drug trafficker. Martínez, who was linked to Contra dissident Eden Pastora, was involved in efforts to smuggle more than 3,000 pounds of cocaine into Miami in 1985-86. He was arrested in 1989 and later convicted for bringing 300 kilos of cocaine into the United States. He also reportedly arranged for the delivery of two helicopters, arms, ammunition and clothing to Pastora's Costa Rica-based Contras.[35]

Federal prosecutors in Miami have a photograph of Jeb and Martínez shaking hands but won't release the photo to the public. Whether Jeb was aware of Martínez's drug trafficking activities is not known, but it is known that Leonel and his wife Margarita made a $2,200 contribution to the Dade County Republican Party four months after Jeb became the chair of the local GOP.

It is also known that Martínez wrote $5,000 checks to then Vice-President Bush's Fund for America's Future in both December 1985 and July 1986 and made a $2,000 contribution to the Bush for President campaign in October 1987.

Martínez's construction company gave $6,000 in October 1986 to Bob Martínez (no relation), the GOP candidate for governor in Florida; he was governor from 1987 to 1991. At that time, Vice-President Bush was serving as head of the South Florida Drug Task Force and later as chair of the National Narcotics Interdiction System, both set up to stem the flow of drugs into the United States. While Bush was drug czar, the volume of cocaine smuggled into the United States tripled.[36]

President Bush later appointed Bob Martínez in 1991 head of the U.S. Office of National Drug Control Policy — the drug czar to succeed the controversial William Bennett.

Jeb Gets in on the BCCI Action

In 1988, Jeb was mentioned in a deposition taken by a Senate Foreign

Relations subcommittee, chaired by Sen. John Kerry (D-Mass.), which was investigating drug-money laundering operations in the United States.

"I saw Jeb Bush two or three times over there with [Abdur] Sakhia," stated Aziz Rehman, a junior BCCI Miami official in the 1980s. "This was all part of the bank's trying to cultivate public officials and prominent individuals."[37] Rehman said BCCI's practice was to "bribe" government officials in the United States.

"Jeb Bush, V.P. George Bush's son," Sakhia noted in a 1986 BCCI document, was a "name... to be remembered."[38]

Jeb's name also shows up in a September 1987 BCCI document written by Amjad Awan, then a senior BCCI-Miami official. The memorandum planned a BCCI breakfast meeting with a senior level delegation from the People's Republic of China and high Florida state government officials, including Secretary of Commerce Jeb Bush. Among the Chinese delegation was Ge Zhong Xue, Deputy Division Chief of the Ministry of Public Security, a top police official.[39]

Meanwhile, Jeb and his business partner Armando Codina profited handsomely when the Bush Administration bailed out Broward Federal Savings and Loan in Sunrise, Florida, which went belly up in 1988. The Federal Deposit Insurance Corporation (FDIC) absorbed $285 million in bad loans, including a $4.6 million loan by the Bush-Codina partnership. According to the deal struck by federal regulators, the Bush-Codina partnership wrote a check for $505,000 to the FDIC and the government paid off the remaining $4.1 million of the loan for an office building on which Jeb and Codina defaulted. As a result of the bailout, the Bush-Codina partnership retained possession of its office building at 1390 Brickell Avenue in Miami's posh financial district.[40]

Currently, Jeb is involved in a number of joint ventures with Codina, a Miami real estate developer who is also a leader of the right-wing Cuban American National Foundation (CANF). The Brickell Avenue office building is owned by IntrAmerica Investments. Jeb was listed in business documents in 1985 and in 1986 as the president of IntrAmerica Investments and the building is managed by one of Jeb's real estate companies. Codina owns 80 percent of the building, while Jeb owns the remaining 20 percent.

Jeb has acted as the Reagan and Bush administration's liaison with the politically influential Cuban exile community in South Florida. Jorge Mas Canosa, president of CANF, succinctly described Jeb's role as the ultra-right Cuban-American community's liaison with the White House: "He is one of us."[41]

Jeb Asks Dad To Free Terrorist

As a link to that powerful and wealthy South Florida community, Jeb has been a tireless supporter of some of the most reactionary Cuban-American political causes — from promoting CANF projects like Radio and TV Martí, to lobbying for the release of anti-Castro terrorist Orlando Bosch from a Miami jail. TV propaganda broadcasts into Cuba, considered by legal experts a violation of the International Telecommunications Convention, are fully subsidized by U.S. taxpayers.[42]

Anti-Castro terrorist Orlando Bosch was paroled in 1990 after Jeb lobbied the Bush Administration for his release from prison in Miami. Bosch had been jailed in 1988 for jumping bail on a 1968 conviction for shooting a bazooka at a Polish freighter in the Miami harbor. He is better known as the mastermind of the explosion of a Cuban commercial airliner over Barbados on October 5, 1976, in which 73 passengers were killed. A U.S. District Court judge revealed in 1988 that secret U.S. documents concluded Bosch was a leader of the Coordination of United Revolutionary Organizations (CORU), which was responsible for more than 50 anti-Castro bombings in Cuba and elsewhere in the Western Hemisphere.[43] The Cuban Government filed an order for his extradition in May 1992.

"Tell Him... The Vice-President's Son" Called

"There was no conflict of interest," third Bush son Neil told reporters after the Office of Thrift Supervision (OTS) in Washington issued a notice of intent in January 1990 to hold a hearing on the failure of Silverado Banking Savings and Loan. Neil had been a member of Silverado's board of directors from 1985 to 1988.[44] Federal regulators shut down Silverado shortly after George Bush was elected president in 1988. The federal bailout cost U.S. taxpayers $1 billion.

Neil was responding to charges made in an OTS report that he had "breached his fiduciary duty" to Silverado by engaging in unethical business deals while a board member of the Denver Savings and Loan. The report documented that Neil personally profited from questionable Silverado loans to his business partners, Ken Good and Bill Walters. Good and Walters later defaulted on $132 million in loans to Silverado, leaving the taxpayers to pick up the tab.[45]

The OTS report alleged that Neil failed to disclose his business connections to Good and Walters when he voted to approve a $900,000 line of credit to Good International, Inc. Neil got Silverado to write a letter of recommendation to authorities in Argentina, where Good International, in partnership with Neil's JNB Exploration Company, was exploring for gas and oil. Good also gave the President's third son a $100,000 loan to invest in the commodities market, which Bush was never required to repay.[46]

Neil failed to inform Silverado that Walters had contributed $150,000 to the initial capitalization of JNB Exploration, or that Walters' Cherry Creek National Bank in Denver extended a $1.5 million line of credit to JNB Exploration. Neil put up a paltry $100 in start-up funds in 1983 when he founded JNB Exploration, but over the next five years was paid $550,000 in salary drawn from the Cherry Creek National Bank line of credit.[47]

Neil brought few business skills to his job at JNB Exploration but he was adept at cashing in on his family name. "Tell him Neil Bush called," Neil once told the secretary of a wealthy Denver oil entrepreneur. "You know, the vice-president's son."[48]

"Neil knew people because of his name," acknowledged Evans Nash, one of Neil's partners at JNB Exploration. "He's the one that got us going. He's the one that made it happen for us."[49]

When Neil left JNB Exploration in 1989, the company had yet to discover a profitable gas or oil well.

Neil: The Sensitive One

Neil's business partners also included shady characters with ties to the world of covert operations. In 1985, Good received an $86 million loan from the Dallas Western Savings Association, which was tied to Robert Corson, a Texas developer and reputed CIA operative and Herman Beebe, Sr., a convicted Mafia associate of Louisiana mob boss Carlos Marcello.[50]

Neil profited from the Western Savings loan to Good, because the loan helped Good buy Gulfstream Land and Development, a Florida real estate company. Good made Neil a board member of one of Gulfstream's subsidiaries in 1988. Bush was paid $100,000 a year to attend occasional Gulfstream board meetings before it went out of business in 1990.[51]

Investigative reporter Pete Brewton identified Corson as a CIA operative in a long *Houston Post* series on CIA links to organized crime and failed savings and loans. "One former CIA operative told the *Post* that Corson frequently acted as 'a mule' for the Agency, meaning he would carry large sums of money from country to country," Brewton wrote.[52]

Corson's Vision Banc Savings in Kingsville, Texas, loaned millions to Mike Atkinson, a Corson associate, for a Florida land deal put together by Lawrence Freeman. Freeman, who laundered money for Santos Trafficante, Jr., was also tied to veteran CIA operative Paul Helliwell. In the Bahamas, Helliwell set up Castle Bank and Trust Ltd., which was the CIA's primary financial front in Latin America and the Caribbean during the 1960s and 1970s. Castle laundered funds for the Agency's covert operations against Cuba.[53]

Walters had ties to Richard Rossmiller, a Beebe associate. In the mid-1970s, Walters was a part owner with Rossmiller, of Peoples State Bank in Marshall, Texas, at the same time as Rossmiller was doing business with Beebe.[54]

Wayne Reeder, another Beebe associate, a big borrower from Silverado, defaulted on a $14 million loan. Reeder was involved in an unsuccessful arms deal with the Contras. Reeder accompanied his partner, John Nichols, in 1981 to a weapons demonstration attended by Contra leaders Eden Pastora and Raul Arana, both of whom were interested in buying military equipment from Nichols.

"Among the equipment were night vision goggles... and light machine guns," according to the book, *Inside Job: The Looting of America's Savings and Loans*. "Nichols... had a plan in the early 1980s to build a munitions plant on the Cabezon Indian Reservation near Palm Springs, California, in partnership with Wackenhut, the Florida security firm. [But] the plan fell through."[55]

There was another Silverado-contra connection, however, that didn't fall through. E. Trine Starnes, Jr., the third largest Silverado borrower, was a major donor to the National Endowment for the Preservation of Liberty (NEPL), directed by Carl "Spitz" Channell, which was a part of Oliver North's Contra funding and arms support network. A NEPL document, "Top 25 Contributors as of October 3, 1986," showed Starnes contributed $30,000 to NEPL's Central America Freedom Program. Starnes closed a deal with Silverado on September 30, 1986, for three business loans totaling $77.5 million, on which Starnes later defaulted.[56]

The Central America Freedom Program was a propaganda effort in conjunction with the Reagan Administration's campaign in 1986 to win congressional support for resuming arms aid to the Contras. When the administration wooed potential NEPL donors, Starnes was invited to a January 30, 1986, White House briefing, which included Reagan, National Security Adviser John Poindexter, White House Chief of Staff Donald Regan and Assistant Secretary of State Elliott Abrams. Congress resumed U.S. arms aid to the Contras in mid-1986.

Bushed Out

George Herbert Walker Bush is the first former CIA director to serve as president. The implications for U.S. politics of Bush's move from CIA headquarters to the White House are profound and chilling, but seldom the subject of mainstream political discussion. The corruption of the Bush family, however, is a good introduction.

The Bushes' shadowy business partners come straight out of the world in which the CIA thrives — the netherworld of secret wars and covert operators, drug runners, *mafiosi* and crooked entrepreneurs out to make a fast buck. What Bush family members lack in business acumen, they make up for by cashing in on their blood ties to the former Director of Central Intelligence who became president. In return for throwing business their way, the Bushes give their partners political access, legitimacy and perhaps protection. The big loser in the deal is the democratic process.

(1992)

Iraq and the Gulf Wars

Introduction
Ellen Ray and William H. Schaap

At the onset of Ariel Sharon's spring 2002 rampage through the occupied territories, Vice-President Dick Cheney shuttled from one familiar Middle Eastern potentate to another, openly attempting to barter minimal U.S. restraint on Sharon's ethnic cleansing of Palestinians for Arab acquiescence in Washington's plan to topple Saddam Hussein (and to gain a military staging base or two). Cheney's disingenuous role as horsetrader in human lives shocked and insulted very many Muslim sensibilities at a time when the existence of the Palestinian people was seriously threatened. It was denounced in the Arab press as "obscene," and on the Arab street as racist and imperialist.

In early February 2003, after more than 200,000 U.S. troops had already been deployed in the region, with tens of thousands more on the way, Cheney again offended Muslim sensibilities by demanding, just before the important Muslim family holiday of Bayram, an immediate vote in Turkey's parliament to approve the basing of some 60,000 U.S. invasion troops on the Turkish border with Iraq. But Turkey delayed and when the vote came, after the mid-February antiwar demonstrations of many millions around the world (including Turkey), the United States was in turn humiliated.

Nevertheless, war and the occupation of Iraq were preordained by an administration confident of divine support for its unilateral and preemptive war.

For many years, the destruction of Iraq through its dismemberment into three mini-states (Kurdish, *Shi'ite* and *Sunni*), has been an Israeli,

Zionist expansionist policy. In 1982, Israel Shahak, one of the most knowledgeable and passionate critics of Israeli foreign policy, analyzed a military plan presented to the World Zionist Organization by Oded Yinon, a former Israeli Foreign Ministry official. The paper, "A Strategy for Israel in the 1980s," set forth a timetable, somewhat optimistic, for the conquest of the Arab states in the region and the installation of Israel as an undisputed imperial power. It called for the dissolution of Syria, Iraq and Iran into small, ethnically or religiously unique mini-states, playing *Sunni* against *Shi'a*, Kurds against Turks and Persians and Arabs. "Every kind of inter-Arab confrontation will assist us," Yinon wrote.

During the Iran-Iraq war of the 1980s, the Israelis were critical of the United States when the Republican Administration's hostility toward Iran ran so deep that it covertly poured weapons (including chemical and biological) into Baghdad while they were also working with Israel in selling arms to Teheran. Despite their differences, however, both Israel and the United States profited handsomely by prolonging a war that killed over a million combatants and civilians on both sides.

By 1990, U.S. imperial strategy had developed a new thrust with respect to Middle East dominance. Flushed with an unexpected Cold War victory, President Bush orchestrated Iraq's invasion of Kuwait, precipitating the first Gulf War. While incredibly vicious (the largely indiscriminate carpet bombing during Operation Desert Storm killed some 200,000 Iraqis in just 42 days), it did not lead to the overthrow of the Iraqi regime. Nor did Washington's brilliantly unsuccessful fostering of an internal Kurdish rebellion. The war ended as quickly and as brutally as it had begun, with little resolved but new U.S. military footholds in the region.

For a decade afterwards, Washington's strategy was to maintain draconian sanctions on Iraq, with the support of Congress and a supine United Nations, while ordering almost daily bombing raids in the so-called "no-fly zones."

Hidden from the U.S. public was the effect of the sanctions on Iraqi civilians, which cannot be overemphasized. It is conservatively estimated that more than half a million to a million Iraqis, mostly children, have died since the Gulf War. The justification for such barbarity was Western insistence that Iraq possessed and refused to destroy, vast stockpiles of weapons of mass destruction (WMD), chemical, biological and potentially nuclear. Critics, like the former head of the UN weapons inspection teams in Iraq, Scott Ritter, said there was no proof any longer of such a threat, that the majority of Iraqi WMDs, such as they were, had been destroyed and that the first inspection teams, expelled in 1999, had become mere fronts for intelligence gathering — not just United States but also Israeli — in preparation for a future war. One director of the UN operation, Swedish diplomat Rolf Ekeus, had successfully lobbied for sharing intelligence with the Israelis.

Israel was not interested in "regime change," as has always been suggested. It wanted the dismemberment of Iraq. In 1992, Israel Shahak noted the significance of an interview in *Ma'ariv* with the then Israeli Deputy Chief of Staff, Gen. Amnon Shahak-Lipkin. In response to the question whether he believed "it was in the Israeli interest that Saddam Hussein remained in power," he said: "[I]n Iraq no change will ever be possible. Iraq will always remain the same, bent on defying the entire world. True, it was helped by the entire world to become what it became. But since the Iraqi thinking can never change, a possible removal of Saddam Hussein alone can only lead to the emergency of another dictator... If I have to choose between a boycotted Iraq with Saddam and an Iraq without Saddam again supported by the entire world, then I opt for Saddam, because Saddam will never be helped by anyone."

Because of this history, the new UN inspection operation that commenced in late 2002 was designed to limit U.S. control and manipulation, to the temporary embarrassment of Washington's hawks. With their practical emphasis on the making of progress, the inspectors strengthened the hands of those who sought a steady, diplomatic solution to the crisis. The United States was forced to seek United Nations backing for its invasion, while simultaneously stating that it would, if necessary, if it perceived a betrayal of U.S. leadership, go it alone.

This new, reaffirmed unilateralism heralds the demise of international law, the United Nations, perhaps NATO, all increasingly irrelevant as the United States pursues its hegemonic designs. At the same time, the domestic manifestations of the "war against terrorism" may spell the end of traditional U.S. democracy, such as it is.

By the time George W. Bush took office, it was clear to the world that sanctions had not weakened the Iraqi Government, that no coup would succeed in Baghdad and that opposition forces, such as they were, could never drive Saddam Hussein out. Only another U.S. invasion, Washington hawks proclaimed, would finish the job Bush senior had inexplicably halted. This became part and parcel of the evolving Bush Doctrine, which began by denouncing its former ally Iraq as a harborer of terrorists and a stockpiler of WMD, to be held accountable.

The palpable fears generated by the events of September 11 and the still unsolved, or covered-up, investigation of the anthrax scare have been manipulated over time to transfer the images of Afghanistan and Osama bin-Laden to Iraq and Saddam Hussein. The people of the United States were programed to equate "taking out" Osama, the primary goal of the war in Afghanistan, with attacking and removing from power Saddam Hussein. Now, taking Saddam out is justified as the appropriate revenge for September 11, even though there has never been a shred of evidence that Iraq had anything to do with it.

Attempts to further demonize Saddam Hussein flooded the U.S. media within days of September 11, alleging Iraqi involvement with the perpetrators of, or responsibility for, the anthrax attacks in the United States, with huge coverage, often accompanying articles about the impending invasion. Seven months later, some federal officials finally conceded there was no substance to the report, a retraction that got only a few inches at the bottom of an inside page in the *New York Times*. Yet the administration continued the disinformation, witness Secretary of State Powell holding a teaspoon of sugar before the cameras to indicate how much anthrax or smallpox could kill tens of thousands.

What was seldom examined in the media was that Iraq had consistently opposed Islamic fundamentalism and was despised by the *Shariah* fanatics. After the invasion of Kuwait, in fact, Osama Bin-Laden, claiming that Iraq would then move against Saudi Arabia, proposed a plan of defense to the Saudi leaders, under his leadership, involving Afghan *Mujahideen*.

Allegations linking Iraq to various terrorist groups and to the support of families of suicide bombers were designed to taint the Palestinians' struggle against Israeli occupation and to give Washington a further excuse to postpone curbing Sharon's stepped-up slaughter in the West Bank and Gaza until after the new Gulf War. Inside the Bush Administration, Iraq became the key to solving the "problem" for Israel. The impending war and the *danse macabre* at the Security Council allowed the president to brush aside his past assurances that the issuance of a long-awaited U.S. "road map" for a peace settlement would be announced after the January 2003 Israeli elections. Israel felt vindicated; it had insisted that the destruction of the Iraqi regime was a priority. Sharon's foreign affairs adviser warned that Israel would "pay dearly" for any lengthy deferral of war.

But Israel had been uncharacteristically silent during the Security Council debates over the question of Iraq's compliance with UN resolutions. And for good reason. Had it joined the United States in publicly decrying Iraq's flouting of 17 UN resolutions, it would only have highlighted its own cynical flouting of some 64 UN resolutions over past decades, condemning its treatment of the Palestinians. As French Foreign Minister Dominique de Villepin noted, the Israeli-Palestinian crisis is a far greater threat to world peace than Saddam Hussein's remaining illegal weapons.

Tightly controlled as the media has been, broadcast coverage of the countdown to war was not left to chance. The Pentagon vetted journalists to cover the conflict, training and briefing them, "embedding" them into the military, while CNN reminded all its reporters of the required home office "script approval." The limits of debate afford swift retaliation against breaching the wall surrounding U.S. (and Israeli) righteousness. As the London *Independent*'s Robert Fisk noted, "the Pentagon and the Department of State have nothing to worry about. Nor do the Israelis."

The hypocrisy of the administration in creating hysteria over the possible use by Iraq of chemical and biological weapons (CBW) and even of nuclear weapons, is boundless. For almost a century, the United States has been the most prolific user of CBW, in World War I, in World War II, in the Korean War, in the Vietnam War and throughout the Cold War. It has left generations of victims throughout the world, devastated the ecology of Vietnam for decades still to come. It has tested these weapons of mass destruction (WMD) on unwitting civilians and military personnel; it has subjected its own combat soldiers to horrific, debilitating and deadly disease. (See our recent book, *Bioterror*.) All the CBW agents Iraq ever had (and they have now been virtually destroyed) it got from the United States, in deals brokered by the very same people who now excoriate them.

Despite the absence of evidence of the continued presence of CBW in Iraq, the administration played on the fears the use of such weapons in war engenders. It then released studies announcing that, if CBW is used in Iraq, our fallen troops will have to be bulldozed into mass graves, burned and buried on the spot. The plan is evidently not new, just the announcing of it. "The bulldozers were all lined up and ready to go," in the 1990 Gulf War, a Pentagon official noted.

Reviewing the 1990 Gulf War in some detail is historically helpful in understanding Washington's actions today. In "Trading With the Enemy," written in 1991, Jack Colhoun documents the treachery in the United States about-face from ardent supporter of Iraq to implacable enemy.

U.S.-Iraq cooperation had been extensive ever since the fall of the Shah of Iran in 1979, when Iraq took over its role as the major U.S. proxy in the region. The political and economic ties were vast. In the year preceding the Gulf War, U.S. exports to Iraq exceeded $1.5 billion. U.S. Government credits, military and commercial contracts were plentiful, including extensive involvement of the Bechtel Corporation, to which Reagan's Secretary of State George Shultz had returned to head when Bush took office in 1989. The intricate ties between these transactions and a host of former Washington officials are fully described.

So much of Iraq's former CBW arsenal was "Made in the USA," that the United States removed 8,000 pages from the 12,000-page report the government of Iraq presented to the United Nations before anyone except the five permanent members of the Security Council could see it. The non-permanent members were outraged and Secretary General Kofi Annan later admitted that the decision to let the United States sanitize the report was "unfortunate." Details have always been hard to come by, but the *New York Times* recently reported that seven different strains of anthrax had been sent by the United States to Iraq in the 1980s, with Donald Rumsfeld's blessing.

In "The Middle East in 'Crisis'," written after the Iraqi incursion into Kuwait but before the U.S. attack, Jane Hunter analyzes an unexamined reason for the U.S. rush to Gulf War I: providing an excuse for U.S. military bases in Saudi Arabia, long desired by policy makers and the Pentagon and, as it transpired, a primary cause of the Muslim fundamentalist rage that culminated in September 11.

Finally, in "Iraq: Disinformation and Covert Operations," we review both the pre-war intelligence machinations as well as the propaganda operations during the war itself. It might seem surprising that, in the short time between the Iraqi invasion of Kuwait and the first U.S. attacks, the people of the United States were manipulated into believing that their former staunch ally and important trading partner, Saddam Hussein, was on the contrary a monster, a new Hitler. But that is the role of clandestine disinformation and propaganda operations. In a well-known exchange back in 1950, President Eisenhower complained to public relations guru Edward Bernays that the people of the United States did not support his going to war in Korea. Bernays replied, in essence, "Give me enough money and eight weeks and I guarantee they will support you."

Trading With The Enemy

Jack Colhoun

> For over the last decade, Saddam strengthened the sinews of his war machine through a sophisticated network of front companies and agents. Through it he got weapons, spare parts, machine tools and raw materials necessary to sustain his militarized state.[1]
>
> — John Robson, Deputy Secretary of the Treasury

> It's hard to believe that the U.S. intelligence community or that of our allies did not know about the application of technology being transferred to Iraq.[2]
>
> — Henry González, Chair of the House Banking Committee

United States policy in the Persian Gulf over the last decade has been a breeding ground for scandal. At the same time as Ronald Reagan was reviling Ayatollah Ruhollah Khomeini and the Iranian revolution, his administration was secretly providing arms to that country. George Bush has continued the tradition. Only shortly before condemning Saddam as "worse than Hitler," his administration was helping Iraq build its military-industrial infrastructure. In fact, right up to August 1, 1990, the day before Iraqi troops moved into Kuwait, the Bush Administration approved the export of U.S. high technology with dual — civilian or military — applications.

House Banking Committee chair Rep. Henry González (D-Texas) charges the Reagan and Bush Administrations did little to stop the export of U.S. technology to build the Iraqi war machine because of the pro-Baghdad tilt of U.S. policy in the Gulf prior to the Iraqi invasion of Kuwait.

The Bush Administration inherited its pro-Baghdad policy from the

Reagan Administration, which considered Iraq a critical geopolitical counterbalance to Iran. In both cases, support for Iraq was designed to contain the spread of Islamic fundamentalism in the Gulf in the wake of the consolidation of the Khomeini regime in Teheran. Under the rule of the Shah, Iran had been Washington's chief geopolitical ally in the Gulf.

Although it played both sides, Washington quietly allied itself with Baghdad in the bloody Iran-Iraq War (1980-88), in which as many as one million Iranians and Iraqis were killed or injured. Then CIA Director William Casey began to pass U.S. satellite intelligence to Iraq in 1984 to aid Iraqi bombing raids in Iran. The Reagan Administration reestablished diplomatic relations with Iraq in 1984. A U.S. naval armada in 1987 escorted Kuwaiti tankers carrying Iraqi oil through the Gulf to protect the ships from Iranian attacks. This policy of escorting Kuwaiti vessels reflagged with U.S. colors continued even after an Iraqi missile hit the USS Stark on May 17, 1987, killing 37 U.S. sailors.[3]

The Reagan Administration took Iraq off its list of countries alleged to sponsor terrorism in 1982. "As a result of the 1982 policy change, Iraq was treated like all other "Free World" countries and became eligible for a range of U.S. high technology items including a broad category of computer equipment generally denied to other countries remaining on the terrorist list," according to Dennis Kloske, Under Secretary of Commerce for Export Administration in the Bush Administration.[4]

Stephen Bryen, former Deputy Under-Secretary of Defense for Trade and Security Policy and director of the Defense Technology Security Administration, summed up the Reagan Administration's policy toward Iraq during the Iran-Iraq War. "The United States was eager to develop good relations with Iraq and trade was the keystone of that policy," asserted Bryen.[5] The Bush Administration continued to view Baghdad as a force for geopolitical stability in the Gulf after Iraq emerged in August 1988 as "victor."

President Bush continued Reagan's emphasis on good trade relations. In October 1989, he signed National Security Directive 26 "the thrust of [which]... was that the United States should keep trying to moderate Iraq's behavior and increase U.S. influence. Specifically, U.S. companies would be encouraged to participate in the postwar reconstruction of Iraq."[6]

As late as July 25, 1990, as Iraq was massing troops on the Kuwaiti border, April Glaspie, U.S. Ambassador to Iraq, told Saddam "I have a direct instruction from the president to seek better relations with Iraq." Glaspie added, "We have no opinion on Arab-Arab conflicts, like your border disagreement with Kuwait."

The Revolving Door

The relationship between U.S. foreign policy strategists and commercial planners was a cooperative one and the mesh of their respective goals was close. The two sets of interests intersected in the Washington-based U.S.-Iraq Business Forum. Set up by Marshall Wiley in 1985 with the encouragement of Iraqi Ambassador to the U.S. Nizar Hamdoon, the Forum became a "revolving door" for former U.S. diplomats with experience in the Middle East. It lobbied in Washington on behalf of Iraq to promote U.S. trade with Iraq. Wiley was U.S. Ambassador to Oman and served in the U.S. Interests Section in Baghdad in 1975-77.

"I started the Forum. It wasn't the Iraqis' idea. But when I put it up to the Iraqis, they said they liked the idea and said they'd cooperate with me," Wiley explained. "I went to the State Department and told them what I was planning to do and they said 'Fine. It sounds like a good idea.' It was our policy to increase our exports to Iraq."[7]

The Forum, which worked closely with the U.S. Embassy in Iraq, sponsored a trade mission for member companies and twice rented booths at the U.S. pavilion at the Baghdad International Fair. Wiley, an annual visitor to Iraq, arranged in 1989 for senior U.S. executives to meet with Saddam.[8]

U.S. companies wanting to do business with Iraq were required by the Iraqi Government to join the Forum. Member companies (including Amoco, AT&T, Caterpillar, First City Bancorporation of Texas, General Motors, Mobil Oil, Pepsi Cola International and Westinghouse) were mobilized on different occasions to lobby Congress in support of pro-Iraq policies. Member dues funded the operating budget for the Forum.

The relationship between the U.S. Government and the Forum was strengthened by close ties to the State Department. Wiley, who served as president of the Forum, was joined by former State Department officials Richard Fairbanks and James Placke, who acted as "advisers" to the Forum. Fairbanks' last assignment at the State Department was to head Operation Staunch. (Although this operation was set up during the Iran-Iraq War to enforce a U.S.-led arms embargo against Iran, with the cooperation of the Israelis, the United States began secret arms deals which led to the Iran-Contra scandal.) Placke last served as a Deputy Assistant Secretary of State for near eastern affairs. Fairbanks, who had a contract with the Iraqi Embassy, also served as an official representative of the Iraqis in Washington.[9]

The National Interest

The close relationship between private enterprise and government is being examined anew in light of an extensive pattern of sales of U.S. military technology which ended up being aimed back at U.S. troops. In a February 21, 1991 speech on the House floor, Rep. González raised questions about the role of the State Department and former Secretary of State Shultz with regard to Iraq. The Texas representative cited an interview in the *Financial Times* of London in which Shultz explained his involvement with the Bechtel Corporation's contract to manage the construction of Iraq's Petrochemical 2 (PC2) plant. Bechtel was one of many U.S. businesses which contributed to the development of Iraq's military-industrial infrastructure.

Shultz left his job as a top Bechtel executive when he became Secretary of State in the Reagan Administration and returned to Bechtel in 1989. Shultz said that he looked into the PC2 project in 1989 and was assured that it had nothing to do with chemical weapons. But Bechtel's PC2 project was built to manufacture ethylene oxide, a substance with civilian applications, which is also a chemical precursor for mustard gas. An unnamed Bechtel official in London indicated that Bechtel had received "direct encouragement" from the U.S. Commerce Department to take on the job.

"But I thought about it a little more and I gave my advice [that Bechtel] should get out," Shultz told the *Financial Times*. At a Bechtel board meeting in the spring of 1990, Shultz stated, "I really hit it very hard and I said something is going to go very wrong in Iraq and blow up and if Bechtel were there it would get blown up, too. So I told them to get out."[10] Bechtel subsequently left Iraq.

The BNL-Atlanta Connection

The Bechtel contract for the PC2 project provides a direct link to the Atlanta branch of the Banca Nazionale del Lavoro (BNL), the largest in Italy. Rep. González's House Banking Committee is now investigating the BNL-Atlanta scandal and has identified it as the hub of a clandestine Iraqi arms procurement network operating in the United States. "Our client, the Government of Iraq, told us we would be paid through letters of credit from the BNL-Atlanta branch," the Bechtel official in London noted.[11] House Banking Committee investigators have discovered Bechtel was paid $10 million by BNL-Atlanta for a "technical service agreement — PC2."[12]

Christopher Drougal, manager of BNL-Atlanta and two other officials of the Atlanta bank were indicted by a federal grand jury in Atlanta on February 28, 1991 on charges of making more than $4 billion in unauthorized loans to Iraq between 1985 and 1989. The three officials were also charged with conspiring to keep two sets of books in order to conceal the unauthorized loans from auditors of BNL in Italy and the Federal Reserve Board in the U.S. BNL was Iraq's biggest source of private credit.

BNL-Atlanta, the Matrix-Churchill Corporation in Cleveland, Ohio,[13] and Bay Industries, Inc., in Santa Monica, California, were identified by the Treasury Department on April 1, 1991, as part of an international network of front companies utilized by Iraq to procure arms and military technology. BNL-Atlanta provided $2.2 billion in loans to Iraq between February 1988 and April 1989, designated for the purchase of Western equipment and high-technology products. "Much of this technology transfer went into civilian projects. Much did not," asserted a House Banking Committee background paper on BNL. "The full truth behind the uses of this technology may never be known. One thing is sure: BNL money was the lifeblood of Iraqi efforts to establish an industrial base and to become self-sufficient in the production of various armaments."[14] The main function of the Iraqi network, which exported products to Iraq directly, was to identify businesses able to provide Iraq with needed technology. The front companies would put U.S. or European corporations in touch with key people in Iraq responsible for various projects. BNL loaned funds directly to the members of the Iraqi network, but most BNL loans were extended to companies recruited by the network to export goods and services to specific projects in Iraq.[15]

An Italian intelligence report dated September 14, 1989, shared with the Bush Administration, linked BNL-Atlanta money to Iraq's Condor 2 missile program. "It should be underlined that various domestic and foreign companies involved in the Condor 2 missile project have been helped thanks to the financial operations conducted by the BNL-Atlanta branch" concluded a September 14, 1989, report by SISMI, the Italian intelligence service, to Prime Minister Giulio Andreotti.[16]

"It's hard to believe that the U.S. intelligence community or that of our allies did not know about the application of technology being transferred to Iraq," González declared. "It is also hard to believe BNL escaped the attention of the intelligence community. These organizations monitor overseas telexes and phone conversations. Did they fail to discover the over 3,000 telexes between BNL and Iraqi Government agencies, many providing information detailing loans to companies that were building the Taji [weapons] complex and other military-related projects within Iraq." [17]

Milo Minderbinder In Charge

The commercial links between the United States and Iraq operated through both private financial and governmental networks and were extensive in both the Reagan and Bush Administrations. From January 1, 1985, through

August 2, 1990, the Commerce Department approved 771 license applications for exports of US. products to Iraq — many with possible military applications — valued at $1.5 billion.

With the end of the Iran-Iraq War, the United States was well positioned to cash in on Iraq's ambitious post-war reconstruction plans. A Commerce Department report on economic trends in Iraq, dated September 1989, encouraged U.S. businesses to do just that: "The best prospects for U.S. firms in the long term will include agricultural products, health care products and equipment, pharmaceutical, oilfield and refinery equipment, computers and other high-technology goods and services... The procurement of military hardware will continue to be a major import item as Iraq replenishes its military hardware and attempts to maintain its technical superiority through state-of-the-art weaponry and logistical supplies."[18]

U.S. exports to Iraq grew to nearly $1.5 billion a year by 1989, including about $1 billion in agricultural products underwritten by loans and credit from the Agriculture Department's Commodity Credit Corporation (CCC).[19]

An October 16, 1989, memorandum by the Federal Reserve Bank of Atlanta dramatically underscored how Iraq was using the CCC's farm export program to augment its military arsenal. "Iraq admitted that it routinely receives internal 'after sales services' such as armored trucks from suppliers," the memo warned. "These after sales services might be construed as kickbacks which the U.S. Agriculture Department warned Iraq in 1988 were in violation of the CCC program."[20]

Some trade, such as the $695,000 sale of sophisticated computer equipment approved by the Bush Administration on August 1, 1990, was dual-use technology. Other deals were overtly military. One particularly blatant example was a sale involving ballistic missiles. A.M. Doud (consignee in Iraq) was approved for an export license on March 22,1990, by the Commerce Department. "Description: photographic equipment (specified). End use: scientific research on projectile behavior and terminal ballistics. $10,368."[21]

A list of Commerce Department-approved exports to Iraq reveals that a total of $154,124,068 of U.S. products were sold to the Iraqi military. For example, U.S. exports were sold to the Ministry of Defense ($62,988,678), the Iraqi Air Force ($49,035,079) and the Government of Iraq ($8,200,000). These products included aircraft, helicopters and engines ($87,592,500), compasses, gyroscopes and accelerometers for aircraft ($1,036,530) and navigation, radar and airborne communications equipment ($516,758).

The Commerce Department list of approved U.S. exports to Iraq indicates $226,235,416 worth of U.S. technology was sold to Iraqi Airways, which was later identified by the Treasury Department as a front company for a clandestine Iraqi arms procurement network. The Commerce Department approved the sale of $178,230,073 to Iraqi Airways of aircraft, helicopters and engines, $148,199 of navigation, $28,463,241 of aircraft parts, boats, diesel engines, underwater cameras and submersible systems and $246,455 of navigation, radar and airborne communications equipment.[22]

The Commerce Department will not release the names of companies which exported goods to Iraq, but news reports shed light on the role U.S. businesses played in helping Iraq develop its military-industrial infrastructure.

Lummus Crest of Bloomfield, N.J. worked on the PC2 chemical project.[23]

Alcolac International of Baltimore sold *NuKraft Mercantile Corporation* of Brooklyn, N.Y., thiodiglycol, which it in turn sold to Iraq. Thiodiglycol is used in the production of mustard gas.[24]

Hughes Aircraft Co. of Los Angeles exported battlefield night vision devices to *Delft Instruments* of Holland, which in turn delivered the equipment to the Iraqi Government. Hughes is a division of *General Motors*.[25]

U.S. companies played a significant role in the development of Saad 16, an Iraqi complex which designed missiles and conducted nuclear weapons research. As much as 40 percent of the equipment used at Saad 16 was manufactured in the United States: computers sold by *Hewlett-Packard Co.*, oscilloscopes from *Tektronix Inc.* and microwave measuring devices from *Wiltron Co.*[26]

Among other materials now at Saddam Hussein's disposal are $200 million of helicopters supplied — ostensibly for civilian use, the company says — by the Bell Helicopter unit of Textron Inc. There's a plant that makes machine tools capable of making weapons, built by XYZ Options Inc, of Tuscaloosa, Alabama. In addition, the company last year sent Iraq a powder press that according to a confidential Customs Service document is "suitable for the compaction of nuclear fuels," the *Wall Street Journal* commented.[27]

Staying the Course

When the National Advisory Council met in the White House on November 8, 1989, Under Secretary of State Robert Kimmitt stressed the need to stay the course. Iraq was "very important to US. interests in the Middle East," Kimmitt stated, adding Baghdad was "influential in the peace process" and was "a key to maintaining stability in the region, offering great trade opportunities for U.S. companies."[28]

By that time, evidence that Iraq was using U.S. exports to build Saddam

Hussein's war machine could no longer be ignored. But on orders from the State Department and the White House, the administration maintained its trade-based tilt toward Baghdad until Iraqi troops occupied Kuwait.

(1991)

The Middle East in "Crisis"

Jane Hunter

Three months ago the United States was a falling star. Its militarized economy was embarrassingly irrelevant in the post-Cold War world. It was being evicted from its military outposts in Europe and Asia. Then that falling star snagged itself on Iraq's invasion of Kuwait. Now the Bush Administration, with its rush to war in the Persian Gulf, has hijacked the "New World Order" that was to rise from the ashes of the Cold War. No one could have invented a more convenient redemption.

Opinion makers hailed as "leadership" the alacrity with which the Bush Administration engineered an invitation from the Saudi royal family and the speed with which it moved over 208,000 troops to Saudi Arabia. In fact, what looked like decisive leadership was actually the opportune fulfillment of a long-standing U.S. desire for a base in the Persian Gulf. During the 1970s, a base in Saudi Arabia was a frequently discussed objective, according to a former congressional aide.

After the Gulf states rebuffed Carter Administration efforts to send troops to the region in 1980 when the Iran-Iraq War began, the United States opted instead for the mega-sales of weapons to Saudi Arabia and for the establishing of military facilities capable of serving U.S. troops. The Reagan Administration developed the Rapid Deployment Force, the Central Command that now sits in the Saudi desert. "We have a remarkable new outpost in the Gulf," exulted Assistant Secretary of Defense Paul Wolfowitz.[1]

The new foothold in the Gulf puts the United States well on its way to controlling the world's oil supply, the only primary commodity to have eluded its grasp. During the 1980s, Washington, with the collaboration of its Western allies, waged an enormously successful economic war against the Third World, not just by the devastating currency transfers extracted as debt servicing, but also by forcing down the prices of the primary materials on which undeveloped countries depend to earn hard currency. This economic discipline — a subtle, sanitized form of colonialism — and the collapse of the Soviet Union as an alternative source of political and economic support stifled the voices of Third World leaders who called for a reordering of economic relations.

The plummeting prices of the glutted oil market quelled the defiance of many Third World oil producers. The Western powers relied on Saudi Arabia and its Gulf neighbors to keep the price of oil low by over-production. They were not unduly discomfited by Iraq's efforts in July to secure a rise in the OPEC price of oil and to get Kuwait to stop pumping more than its OPEC quota. They knew their allies in OPEC could maneuver around Saddam Hussein.

But when Iraq invaded Kuwait and Saddam Hussein began talking about redistributing the oil wealth of the sparsely populated Gulf sheikhdoms to the poor, densely populated Arab countries, Washington responded swiftly. Saying Saddam had "broken the mold" and "forever changed the balance of power over there," a senior administration official declared that the situation "implies a permanent [U.S.] presence in the Gulf."[2] Once the embargo on Iraqi and Kuwaiti oil and the threat of a U.S.-led war pushed petroleum prices higher than Saddam Hussein's "leadership" of OPEC ever could, President George Bush's clarion call to defend "our way of life," cheap gas,[3] faded. But by then he was on to a better thing.

Just when it seemed that Bush could extract no more national wealth for the military and intelligence establishments — and might actually have to return a pittance in the form of a "peace dividend" — came the perfect solution: tax the people at the gas pump. This is not the tax long advocated by environmentalists to reduce this nation's consumption of oil — instead Saudi Arabia and its neighbor monarchies collect this revenue in the form of clear profit. They have agreed, after some jawboning, to return some of those profits to defray the costs of the U.S. military intervention. Nothing exemplifies the U.S. attitude toward this transaction so well as the administration's proposal that the money go into a "National Defense Gift Fund," for the Pentagon to spend as it sees fit.[4]

The Gulf crisis is no longer about oil, but about imposing the will of the United States on an uppity Third World leader. Never mind that they backed him against Iran, most of the time, and cultivated him as a prime U.S. export customer. Now it seems it is only a matter of time until Washington finds the pretext to unleash a horrific war on Iraq, driving oil prices to unprecedented heights.

The U.S. military presence in Saudi Arabia will certainly strengthen the CIA's close relations with the Saudi royal family. Many Saudis believe that the royal family has for years depended on the Agency to defend it against its own citizens. Since the Nixon years the House of Saud has appeased the Agency by contributing billions of dollars (often unknown to Congress) to some of its favorite projects, among them the Nicaraguan Contras, the National Front for the Salvation of Libya, UNITA, RENAMO and the Afghan *Mujahideen*.[5]

During the 1980s, at the behest of former CIA director William Casey, Saudi Arabia sold oil to South Africa through private dealers.[6] *Newsweek* recently reported that the Saudis were funneling money through their ambassador in Washington, Prince Bandar bin Sultan — who arranged for the Saudi donations to the Contras — to pay for a CIA operation to overthrow Saddam Hussein.[7]

Strikingly, each and every Saudi beneficiary (but the Afghans) has also been an Israeli client, making the two partners-once-removed, perhaps more. The two also have a shared interest in preventing the creation of a Palestinian state, whose secular, democratic structure might inspire certain elements within the tightly restricted Saudi society. "Call the Saudi Arabian leaders and ask them to whom did they give more help, the Palestinian national cause or the *mujahideen* in Afghanistan," challenged a West Bank supporter of the PLO.[8]

The coming war might well bring this tacit Saudi-Israeli alliance into the open. At summer's end, Saudi Arabia and Israel were among the tiny number of governments urging a quick war against Iraq, a call that has been repeated by Israel's supporters in the U.S. media. However, Saudi Arabia is terrified of Arab reaction to any linkage of Israel with the U.S. military presence on its soil. Thus, the Bush Administration is trying hard to keep Israel out of the picture. Among the several sins of Air Force Chief of Staff General Mike Dugan, who was fired September 17, were his disclosures that Israel had suggested attacking Saddam Hussein, his family and his mistress (the same "decapitation" strategy used in the Israeli-advised 1986 attack on Libya) and that the U.S. B-52 aircraft were equipped with Israeli-made Popeye ("have nap" or Cruise) missiles.[9]

Israeli analysts seem to adhere to the much-touted but nonetheless dubious notion that massive U.S. air strikes will "do the trick."[10] But it is not clear whether they really believe this or whether they have simply concluded that the United States would not do well in a desert war against Iraq. Israel wants the United States to destroy Iraq's unconventional weapons potential (thus implicitly endorsing Israel's own nuclear weapons and missiles); it may also hope to see the United States drawn into a new, no-end-in-sight Vietnam.

There are vast advantages for Israel if the United States gets bogged down in the Gulf. The general distraction will help Israel avoid dealing with Palestinian national claims. Meanwhile, the influx of Soviet Jews to Israel will permit the entrenchment of Jewish settlement in Palestine. The danger that the conflict might spread is likely to draw the United States closer to Israel — perhaps in a formal defense pact — and guarantee increased U.S. military aid for Israel.[11]

Even before the first shot is fired, Israel has asked for — and is likely to receive — more weapons and military aid, as well as immediate access to pictures taken by U.S. spy satellites.[12] Raw and real-time satellite intelligence has been denied Israel since it used such data to destroy Iraq's nuclear reactor in 1981.[13] (Israel subsequently began developing its own surveillance satellite — in cooperation with South Africa.[14])

And Those Other Countries

By political brute force Washington has established itself as crusade leader. "Country after country is being asked to define its role in the post-Cold War world in terms of its response to Iraq's invasion of Kuwait," wrote Middle East correspondent Daniel Williams.[15]

With the Soviet Union offering to share intelligence with Washington[16] and making tentative noises in support of a U.S. military move, many Third World countries have hastened to get on board what for them is now the only bandwagon. Although several expressed interest in Iraq's offer of free oil to Third World nations, most countries have mutely borne the pain of the embargo. Although many sent ships to enforce the UN embargo on Iraq, European nations pointedly declined to contribute directly to the U.S. military effort.[17]

The Bush Administration has already gone to war against the domestic psyche. Its almost daily threats of war serve not only to put pressure on Iraq, but to prepare the public for the body bags. The media has, if only for the sake of drama, adopted a militant terminology that casts Saddam Hussein as a monster, a Hitler. There are also the vaguely attributed headline stories that seem designed to build the case for war. A report in the *New York Times* on September 26 — that "one of the first tasks" assigned Iraqi troops entering Kuwait was to kill or capture Emir Sheikh Jaber al-Almed al-Sabah — had absolutely no attribution at all. "Iraqis Spent Years Plotting Kuwait Strategy," the *Los Angeles Times* reported on September 24 (to be echoed by ABC's *Nightline* on September 26), citing "new findings, circulated by the U.S. intelligence community."

Experts repeatedly expound on the ineptitude of the Iraqi Army. The real doubt, however, lies with the young people who enlisted in the U.S. military as the only way to finance an education. Will they, especially the disproportionate number of minorities in their ranks, have an appetite for killing and dying? Mindful of this and the public opposition to the war against Vietnam, the television pundits repeatedly warn that the large margin of support for the president's policy might dwindle once the shooting begins.

The administration won its first telling domestic victory in August when the Joint Chiefs of Staff and President Bush decided on Operations Plan 90-1002, which calls for a rapid, massive troop buildup.[18] The speed of the buildup, before any protest could be organized, has permitted some pundits to hail the end of the "Vietnam syndrome."[19]

(1990)

Iraq: Disinformation and Covert Operations

Ellen Ray and William H. Schaap

There has been considerable and convincing speculation that the U.S. sandbagged Iraq into invading Kuwait.[1] A senior CIA analyst, Charles Eugene Allen, warned his superiors — and officials of the State Department and the National Security Council — in July that such an invasion was imminent.[2] Not only was he ignored by all three organizations, but superiors angered by his unauthorized disclosures to State and the NSC cut his staff and suspended his biweekly reports. A Kuwaiti military attaché who warned his government repeatedly in July 1990, has received essentially the same treatment.[3]

There may be a question whether the CIA or the State Department wanted a tilt away from Iraq; what is absolutely certain, though, is that the Pentagon has for decades coveted a more substantial presence in the Middle East.[4] Until the Gulf War there was no country in the region that would accept the permanent presence of large numbers of U.S. armed forces. Now it appears there will be troops in Saudi Arabia and Kuwait — and perhaps Iraq itself — as well as the small contingent which has been sent to Bahrain, for years to come.

The Pre-War Disinformation Campaign

As soon as Iraq invaded Kuwait and became an instant enemy, a major disinformation campaign began. This was necessary to transmogrify a "friendly" into an "unfriendly" and on very short notice. As recently as May 1989, the *Washington Post* was referring to Saddam Hussein as "pragmatic."[5] This is a term Washington reserves for the bad guys who usually do what it wants them to. Hussein was certainly no U.S. vassal. He may well have attacked Iran with U.S. encouragement, but when arms sales to the Ayatollah became public knowledge, he was palpably angered by this "play both sides against the middle" strategy. Still, Washington studiously regarded him as "someone we can work with." Thus, after August 2, 1990, U.S. citizens had to be told a lot of horrifying tales about Iraq and Saddam Hussein.

Charges relating to the undemocratic nature of the Iraqi Government were clearly valid. However, it was rarely pointed out that many of the neighboring countries — soon to comprise the "coalition" — were considerably worse. Iraq alone among the Gulf states has made serious efforts to reduce the traditional subjection of women. Indeed, the failure to describe the shortcomings of the two staunchest U.S. allies in the region, Saudi Arabia[6] and Kuwait,[7] was embarrassing. But the most serious U.S. allegations were of very questionable substance. They were described by *Newsday*'s Washington reporter Knut Royce: "Iraq's invasion of Kuwait was unprovoked; Iraqi President Saddam Hussein also planned to invade Saudi Arabia; Iraq used chemical agents against its indigenous Kurds; Hussein may be on the verge of acquiring an atomic weapon."[8]

As Royce explained, these claims were all "based on unconfirmed, weak, or contradictory intelligence." The history of the Iraq-Kuwait dispute goes back many decades and the notion that Iraq was not provoked is ludicrous, whether or not one believes that any provocation could justify an invasion.[9] The notion that Iraq seriously considered going beyond Kuwait and invading Saudi Arabia is equally preposterous. Michael Emery interviewed King Hussein of Jordan who insisted that Saddam Hussein at no time had any intention of invading Saudi Arabia. Indeed, the King was in Saudi Arabia with King Fahd on August 7, when the Pentagon was warning that Iraq might "gobble up" the country and King Fahd was confident that there was no threat.[10]

Finally, the notion that Iraq was on the verge of having deployable nuclear weapons was sheer fantasy. As the war made perfectly clear, their air force was a mirage and their missiles had difficulty delivering conventional warheads.

The Presidential Findings

Although press accounts generally point to a presidential order of January 1991 as the authorization for CIA-coordinated aid to Iraqi rebel groups,[11] it appears that there was an earlier finding in September and that significant covert CIA funding for the Iraqi opposition began with this first presidential finding and its call for "non-lethal" support. Such support continued throughout the pre-war period, during the air war and the ground war and is still taking place. The aid has included training in propaganda and organization as well as in political leadership.

Some Covert Operations

Prior to the commencement of the air war there was a flurry of espionage operations inside Kuwait and Iraq. According to the *Los Angeles Times*, U.S. Special Forces were involved in a number of actions before and during the air war.[12] These involved intelligence gathering by Green Berets who "went into Kuwait City and Baghdad and even to some Iraqi military encampments in the guise of third-country salesmen, peddling military spare parts and food then in short supply." Also according to the article, "many of Britain's elite Special Air Service commandos were wandering the Kuwaiti and Iraqi deserts in Bedouin garb."

The same article stated that "U.S. commando team even planned and apparently executed 'snatches' — wartime kidnappings — of Iraqi soldiers... bringing vital human intelligence assets to planners in the rear." This suggests unlawful treatment of prisoners of war, to say the least. A rather different description appeared in *Newsweek* some two weeks after the *Los Angeles Times* article.[13] "Within weeks of Saddam Hussein's invasion last August," the newsweekly said, "a U.S. special-operations team crossed the border into Kuwait to observe the Iraqi buildup and conduct 'snatch operations,' stealing Iraqi electronic equipment and carrying it to Riyadh for analysis." Snatching people is rather different from snatching equipment.

Why Some Smart Bombs Were Smart

As everyone who was near a television set in January knows, a number of U.S. bombing raids in the first days of the air war seemed unbelievably accurate. Videotapes of "smart bombs" dropping down the central air shaft of the Ministry of Defense headquarters and the like were shown over and over. The impression given was that the air war was truly a surgical operation.

Actually, only a small percentage of the bombs dropped on Iraq were "smart," and only a small percentage of smart bombs hit their precise targets.[14] Indeed, given all the subsequent reporting of extensive civilian damage and casualties,[15] there is only one likely explanation for the high degree of accuracy of the very first raids, when contrasted to the imprecision of later raids: "The first bombs and missiles would have had an undisclosed advantage over those that followed; their ability to hit their targets would have been enhanced by homing devices at or near their targets, planted by U.S. agents in Iraq before the war started."[16] Britain's Prime Minister John Major boasted publicly about the role played by British parachute commandos, armed with laser homing devices, in allied targeting of Iraq's mobile Scud launchers.[17]

U.S. commando teams, particularly Navy Seals, were dropped behind enemy lines at the time the air war commenced in order to flash hand-held lasers on certain targets, on which Hellfire missiles then homed in.[18] The Seals were the subject of an inordinately flattering segment of ABC TV's *Primetime Live* on February 28, 1991.[19] These "elite commandos... were conducting remarkable undercover missions." One admiral told ABC; "They're as close to the movie Rambo as anything we have in the military."

The Helicopter Mission

There were many targeting missions. Perhaps the most bizarre was that presented to the world — albeit rather briefly — as the defecting Iraqi helicopter pilots. On January 7, a week before the U.S. air war began, the Pentagon announced that six Iraqi helicopter pilots had defected to Saudi Arabia, with their aircraft. The *New York Times* quoted "American officials" describing it as "one of the most significant defections of Iraqi military officers since Iraq's invasion of Kuwait."[20] Iraq denied that there had been any such defections and the next day the Pentagon retracted the story, confirming the Iraqi denials.[21] Pentagon spokesmen said they had been unable to confirm the incident, initially reported by a Saudi official in Dhahran.[22] The Pentagon retraction seemed puzzling, because its own intelligence digests had not only announced the defections as fact, but had also described the make of the helicopters (Soviet-built Mi-8-Hips helicopters) and unusual radio traffic at the time of the "defections." A senior official also said that U.S. electronic tracking confirmed the reports.[23] In fact, *Newsday* quoted "an informed source in Dhahran" that the defection was "very significant." Sources told *Newsday* "the Iraqis were asked to identify themselves and their purpose while still outside Saudi territory. The pilots said they wanted to defect and asked permission to land in Saudi Arabia. Authorization was given 'in a matter of minutes,' said a well-placed source."[24]

Despite such a wealth of details prior to the denials, after the Pentagon announced it had all been a mistake, the press not only accepted this explanation, but expanded upon it. *Newsday* said, "In a strange twist to an already theatrical incident, Saudi Arabia's defense minister sided with Iraq yesterday in denying reports that crews aboard Iraqi military aircraft landed in the kingdom late Monday night."[25] Michael Wines of the *New York Times* reported that his source in the Special Operations Command confided to him that apparently someone had accepted as fact a Saudi propaganda broadcast beamed at Iraq. The helicopter flights, his source assured Wines, "never happened."[26]

But, we have learned, they did happen and they involved clear-cut war crimes — only the criminals were not Iraqis but U.S. citizens. The helicopters were not imaginary; in a mission coordinated with the CIA they were flown by U.S. Special Operations pilots disguised as Iraqi pilots, in U.S.-owned, Soviet-built helicopters disguised as Iraqi aircraft.[27] They were returning from a secret mission, apparently involving, among other objectives, the installation of smart bomb homing devices. Apparently the mission was so secret that the U.S. troops who observed the helicopters returning to Saudi Arabia fired on them, causing at least one to crash and killing at least one Special Operations officer. Once news of "Iraqi" helicopters entering Saudi Arabia was out, the defector story was spread. Once the wreckage was removed and the other aircraft hidden, the story was denied.

It is a war crime for troops of one side in a conflict to disguise themselves as troops of their enemy, as it is to disguise one's military craft as equipment belonging to the other side.[28] In its eagerness to accuse Saddam Hussein of war crimes, of course, the United States has not bothered to admit that it is guilty of such acts. Newsweek, referring to a later incident, said: "Three days before the ground invasion, commandos slipped into Kuwait in helicopters painted with Iraqi Army markings to perform a final reconnaissance."[29] Here too, there was no indication that such an operation was illegal.

Other War Crimes

Evidence is accumulating regarding U.S. war crimes, including violations of the Nuremberg Principles. Some of the more vicious of these include the deliberate destruction of water supply and sewage systems, bringing on cholera and other epidemics and the destruction of bridges, power plants and similar targets far from any areas of military significance.

The U.S. conduct at the end of the war, as tens of thousands of retreating soldiers and refugees were massacred, parallels in viciousness any operation of the Germans or Japanese in World War II. Few incidents in history can equal what the allied forces did on the "road to Hell," the 38 kilometers between Kuwait City and Basra.[30] A seven-mile long, five-lane wide column of bumper-to-bumper traffic was halted in place by bombing the beginning and end of the gigantic caravan and then every vehicle and every person in between was burned to a crisp by more endless, merciless bombing. Virtually no one was allowed out alive.[31] A U.S. military spokesperson referred to the incident as a "turkey shoot."

Recruitment of Prisoners

Although the extent of the problem was only hinted at in the press,[32] the

Pentagon — along with the Saudi military — was involved in yet another war crime, the recruitment of Iraqi prisoners for rebel armies. Up until the ground war began, the allies separated prisoners whom they referred to as "deserters or defectors" from ordinary Iraqi prisoners of war. Such separation, according to American University professor Robert Goldman, is a violation of the Geneva Conventions governing treatment of POWs.[33]

Although the International Committee of the Red Cross — which is notoriously circumspect in its statements and observations — did not indicate it had proof that such segregated prisoners were being recruited, this was clear to other human rights observers, some of whom have spoken to *CAIB*. As Andrew Whitley of Middle East Watch told the *Washington Post*, such separation "is invidious to the prisoners because it opens them up to charges by the home government that they had somehow collaborated or provided private information" to the enemy. Moreover, Whitley said "the separation also makes it more likely that the disaffected soldiers will refuse repatriation for fear of reprisals and turns them into 'a potential recruitment pool' for operations against the Saddam regime."[34]

Assassination as an Option

One segment of the *Primetime Live* show noted above[35] was on the question of assassinating Saddam Hussein. ABC and presumably many other media organizations, were frequently asking U.S. citizens how they felt about assassinating the president of Iraq. On the February 28 show, Diane Sawyer noted that at the start of the war "nearly half" the people wanted the United States to try to kill Hussein, but by the end of February, "now that the war is over and tempers are cooling, only 23 percent think that would be wise." One can only wonder about such policy-making by telephone poll. It does not seem to bother ABC that the assassination of foreign leaders is, at least theoretically, still unlawful.

USA Today's lead story on April 15 was titled: "Nixon: I'd have the CIA kill Saddam." The media's favorite former president said to an audience of millions: "If I could find a way to get him out of there, even putting out a contract on him, if the CIA still did that sort of thing, assuming it ever did, I would be for it." This was a direct quote from Nixon's April 14 appearance on the CBS newsmagazine *60 Minutes*.

ABC was not content just to give the results of their latest poll. They also interviewed Henry Kissinger, Angelo Codevilla, William Kowen and William Colby. Kissinger thought the Iraqis ought to be the ones to overthrow Hussein. Codevilla, a former legislative assistant to Sen. Malcolm Wallop (R-Wyo.) and who was on the staff of the Senate Intelligence Committee, stated, cryptically, "It is far easier to deal with dead evil heroes than with live ones." Kowen, a former Special Forces operative, suggested that "a chemical agent in his socks" would do the trick; "we have those kinds of capabilities," he said. Colby, that irrepressible liberal, confessed that assassination attempts were "counterproductive." Kowen complained that no matter how fast his group assassinated local leaders, "the Viet Cong were able to replace those people on a quick basis." Wrapping up the segment, Diane Sawyer lamented that "the United States is the only major power with a policy against assassination." Other nations, she said, are not so "squeamish."

We only killed between 100,000 and 200,000 people in a few weeks' time; terribly squeamish of us.

(1991)

IV. End Game: The Fundamentalists Ascend

The Nuclear Terror Card

Introduction
Ellen Ray and William H. Schaap

In considering nuclear force, Secretary of Defense Donald Rumsfeld advised the Pentagon to "think the unthinkable."

The United States is considering military action against "40 to 50 countries," announced Vice-President Dick Cheney.

"If we... just wage a total war, our children will sing great songs about us years from now," was how the Chairman of the Defense Policy Board, Richard Perle, put it.

It is terrifying when the world's only superpower is in the hands of a cabal that seems not merely to believe in Armageddon, but to relish the thought. The links between Christian fundamentalists and the pro-Israel Zionist fundamentalists have been noted earlier. They all love the bomb.

The nuclear policy posturing of George W. Bush is chillingly transparent. The president asserted in the 2000 campaign that there was no longer any need for "a nuclear balance of terror," but after he took office, his Pentagon hawks prepared a Nuclear Policy Review, which was leaked to the press in early 2002. It appeared at first glance to call for a sharp reduction in U.S. dependence on nuclear weapons, along with an expansion of the use of conventional weapons. An initial news report quoted Deputy Secretary of Defense Paul Wolfowitz saying the policy review "includes a much reduced level of nuclear strike capability." The United

States, it appeared, was going to put two-thirds of its nuclear arsenal in storage; Russia would do the same.

But the real effect of the new policy, follow-up reports revealed, was to lower the threshold for the use of nuclear arms, to increase the likelihood of their use, not the contrary. The plan was to speed up the development and stockpiling of "lower-yield" nukes, tactical weapons for use in limited conflicts, to take out specific enemy installations, especially underground ones like the deep caves in Afghanistan or the thick walls of the underground bunkers in Iraq. Nuclear weapons are no longer seen as tools of deterrence, but as tools of warfare. The talk is of "mini-nukes," "neutron bombs," "bunker-busters," and of "enhanced radiation weapons." There is also reference to "e-bombs," high-powered microwave emissions designed to wipe out enemy equipment. The review further identifies Russia, China, North Korea, Iraq, Iran, Syria and Libya as potential nuclear targets.

As a result of the advocacy and adoption of this policy, the United States and consequently the other nuclear superpowers, have abandoned earlier commitments to the reduction of nuclear arsenals as overall policy goals. While they want to prevent new members from joining the nuclear club, the United States has withdrawn from the ABM Treaty and threatens to scrap or ignore other conventions against weapons of mass destruction, even as it bemoans their proliferation. Washington's nuclear fever has awesome repercussions in China, North Korea, Pakistan and India, any of whom might become embroiled in a nuclear conflict. Neither India nor Pakistan rejects the notion of nuclear war. And, as the Pentagon has contingency plans for using tactical nuclear weapons against North Korean nuclear sites, it and China threaten to retaliate.

The key to this development, in fact, overturning 50 years of international consensus, is not Iraq, but North Korea, a long-standing obsession of many key administration officials. J.D. Crouch, for example, the Assistant Secretary of Defense for International Security, has long called for returning nuclear weapons to South Korea and for using force to destroy the North Korean nuclear complex. The underground facilities in North Korea were the impetus for the development of bunker-busters long before the world learned of Osama bin Laden's caves. North Korea is the justification for Washington's plan to station missiles along the West Coast and in Alaska, even before they have been fully tested and why it has sent dozens of bombers to Guam.

While the United States insisted on the need for multilateral negotiations over the threat posed by North Korea's reactivation of its nuclear facilities and refused to engage in any dialog with Pyongyang, it was merely buying time to deal unilaterally with Iraq before dealing unilaterally with North Korea. The administration clearly is as prepared to "go it alone" in Korea as it is in Iraq. The president said of his efforts to convince North Korea to shut down its facilities, if they "don't work diplomatically, they'll have to work militarily."

The threat of a second Korean War is real. U.S. belligerence is escalating and it only fuels the understandable paranoia of the North Koreans. At the same time, it terrifies the South Koreans, for whom the first Korean War was incredibly destructive and whose people were the victims of U.S. war crimes during that conflict. The Defense Department commenced the redeployment of some 12,000 U.S. combat troops stationed along the demilitarized zone, allegedly because they were easy targets for North Korean retaliation in the event a provocative U.S. action. The move is seen as far more frightening by the South Koreans, who viewed these northernmost troops as limiting the likelihood of a direct U.S. attack on North Korea's nuclear facilities. The Pentagon, meantime, noted that a new conflict on the Korean peninsula could kill a million people. Yet another surreal aspect of the current administration posturing is Rumsfeld's role in North Korea's nuclear status. He was on the board of the Swiss-based technology giant ABB when, in early 2000, it entered into a $200 million nuclear power station contract with Pyongyang.

Intoxicated with the impending opportunity to field test every possible newfangled weapon, military brass are speaking with awesome acronyms of the "RMA" — the revolution in military affairs — concentrated in "NCW" — network centric warfare — to counter "asymmetric" challenges. Anything is possible with technological superiority. Our computers will zap their computers. And meanwhile tactical nuclear weapons are being integrated into NCA.

The open talk of the U.S. use of nuclear weapons in Iraq, including pre-emptive use, only increases the likelihood that Israel will avail itself of this option, as it asserts itself into the conflict, something most observers think is inevitable. And Washington's atomic warmongering does nothing to foster nuclear restraint in Russia or China, much less North Korea.

While Washington demanded that Iraq and North Korea abide by UN resolutions and international treaties and forgo nuclear capability, it steadfastly flouted such resolutions and treaties over the years, actively assisting Israel and apartheid South Africa in nuclear development. Though the apartheid regime is gone, along with its atomic weapons program (having simply been moved north to a more pro-U.S. neighbor), Israel became one of the nuclear superpowers, willing since the October 1973 war to use them on its neighbors. Since the first Gulf War, in fact, Israel has moved from number six to number five in the nuclear club, now with more thermonuclear warheads than the United Kingdom, reportedly between 200 and 500. Both Israel and the United States speak fondly of neutron bombs, miniature thermonuclear devices designed to kill as many people as possible while inflicting as little property damage as possible. They are reportedly a staple in the Israeli nuclear arsenal, a convenient weapon in future Middle East wars. Indeed, Israel's nuclear program is a source of deep resentment and fear in the Middle East and there is no likelihood it will be constrained.

Not content to be the nuclear superpower in its region, Israel insists it must be the only nation in the Middle East with any nuclear capacity. As its then Deputy Chief of Staff put it in 1992, "I believe that the State of Israel should from now on use all its power and direct all its efforts to preventing nuclear developments in any Arab state whatsoever."

Israel, as it happens, provides a little-known precedent for the frustrations currently expressed by nuclear weapons inspectors in Iraq. U.S. inspectors were sent to Israel in the 1960s to inspect the then secret reactor at Dimona, a move reluctantly approved by Prime Minister Ben-Gurion in order to prevent international inspections. Nevertheless, they were tightly controlled, lied to, shown false control panels pasted over the real ones and led past bricked up entrances to hidden rooms. The program, little more than a fig leaf, was abandoned in 1969 when Nixon and Kissinger concluded (perhaps with a sigh of relief) that Israel had irrevocably achieved nuclear capability.

The United States no longer pays even lip service to non-proliferation, having rejected the Anti-Ballistic Missile Treaty and moved ahead with a National Missile Defense program, reviving the Star Wars fantasies of the Reagan era and seriously threatening the weaponization of space. When the current U.S. administration took office, Rumsfeld announced that Washington "must have the option to deploy weapons in space"; the United States must "control space." Bush spoke of "total management of the planet."

U.S. plans for military control of space are real. Since 1985 there has been a unified Pentagon U.S. Space Command, with long-range plans for "space leadership," and there are now plans for a new, space-based branch of the armed forces, the Space Force. Hundreds of millions of dollars are already being spent on exotic space weapon systems, which, an Air Force report noted, "will enable lasers with reasonable mass and cost to effect very many kills." Many of the projects entail nuclear power plants orbiting the earth, despite past experience of devastation caused by the virtually inevitable plutonium fallout and despite the tragic proof of mechanical vulnerability demonstrated by the space shuttle disasters.

The articles below all demonstrate the powerful relevance of historical perspective. As William Blum points out, it is now generally accepted that the nuclear bombing of Hiroshima and Nagasaki was unnecessary to end World War II, that Japan was already on the brink of surrender and that the atomic bombs did not save hundreds of thousands of lives, as claimed. Instead, over the years, hundreds of thousands of Japanese civilians died from the bombings and their radioactive fallout.

Michio Kaku's analysis of the WMD propaganda of the first Gulf War could have been written a decade later. In 1990, as in 2003, the United States insisted that Iraq would have nuclear weapons within a year, something they have harped on for the ensuing 13 years. And then, as now, the real concerns — and the real need for negotiations, rather than mindless saber-rattling — should have been the nations with unquestioned nuclear capability, North Korea, Israel, India, Pakistan and others.

Finally, in a piece that articulates one of the fundamental precepts behind the current belligerency, Israel Shahak lays bare the two sides of Israel nuclear policy: Not just that Israel must be and remain a nuclear superpower, but also that none of its neighbors should ever have any nuclear capability. Thus does the United States go to war in Iraq; thus do it and Israel seek regime change not just in Iraq, but in Iran and elsewhere. Indeed, as with all major wars, Gulf War II will be the proving grounds for the new generation of weapons described above and the administration hopes that their display will frighten Iran into abandoning its nuclear program. If not, the bombardment of its nuclear facilities may well follow hard on the heels of the Iraqi invasion.

We hope the lessons to be learned from studying this history of U.S. terrorism and imperialism in the 1980s and 1990s are clear. Washington's accusations must always be viewed with a jaundiced eye, its motives with skepticism. U.S. imperialism's hypocrisy knows no bounds and its greed is unbridled. America's triumphalism is not motivated by a longing for worldwide democracy, peace and order. It is nothing but a call for worldwide, brutal exploitation and dominion, led by a cabal that has not learned the lesson of Ozymandias.

Hiroshima: Needless Slaughter, Useful Terror

William Blum

For months Japan was desperately trying to surrender. With full knowledge that the war could be ended on its terms, without a land invasion, the U.S. dropped two atomic bombs. Rather than the last act of World War II, this attack was the opening shot of the Cold War.

Rejected Overtures

After the war, the world learned what U.S. leaders had known by early 1945: Japan was militarily defeated long before Hiroshima; it had been trying for months, if not for years, to surrender; and the United States had consistently rebuffed these overtures. A May 5 [1945] cable, intercepted and decoded by the United States, dispelled any possible doubt that the Japanese were eager to sue for peace. Sent to Berlin by the German ambassador in Tokyo, after he talked to a ranking Japanese naval officer, it read: "Since the situation is clearly recognized to be hopeless, large sections of the Japanese armed forces would not regard with disfavor a U.S. request for capitulation even if the terms were hard."[1]

As far as is known, Washington did nothing to pursue this opening. Later that month, Secretary of War Henry L. Stimson almost capriciously dismissed three separate high-level recommendations from within the administration to activate peace negotiations. The proposals advocated signaling Japan that the United States was willing to consider the all-important retention of the emperor system; i.e., the United States would not insist upon "unconditional surrender."[2]

Stimson, like other high U.S. officials, did not really care in principle whether or not the emperor was retained. The term "unconditional surrender" was always a propaganda measure; wars are always ended with some kind of conditions. To some extent the insistence was a domestic consideration — not wanting to appear to "appease" the Japanese. More important, however, it reflected a desire that the Japanese not surrender before the bomb could be used. One of the few people who had been aware of the Manhattan Project from the beginning, Stimson had come to think of it as his bomb, "my secret," as he called it in his diary.[3] On June 6, he told President Truman he was "fearful" that before the A-bombs were ready to be delivered, the Air Force would have Japan so "bombed out" that the new weapon "would not have a fair background to show its strength."[4] In his later memoirs, Stimson admitted that "no effort was made and none was seriously considered, to achieve surrender merely in order not to have to use the bomb."[5]

And that effort could have been minimal. In July, before the leaders of the United States, Britain and the Soviet Union met at Potsdam, the Japanese Government sent several radio messages to its ambassador, Naotake Sato, in Moscow, asking him to request Soviet help in mediating a peace settlement. "His Majesty is extremely anxious to terminate the war as soon as possible said one communication. "Should, however, the United States and Great Britain insist on unconditional surrender, Japan would be forced to fight to the bitter end."[6]

On July 25, while the Potsdam meeting was taking place, Japan instructed Sato to keep meeting with Russian Foreign Minister Molotov to impress the Russians "with the sincerity of our desire to end the war [and] have them understand that we are trying to end hostilities by asking for very reasonable terms in order to secure and maintain our national existence and honor" (a reference to retention of the emperor).[7]

Having broken the Japanese code years earlier, Washington did not have to wait to be informed by the Soviets of these peace overtures; it knew immediately and did nothing. Indeed, the National Archives in Washington contains U.S. Government documents reporting similarly ill-fated Japanese peace overtures as far back as 1943.[8]

Thus, it was with full knowledge that Japan was frantically trying to end the war, that President Truman and his hardline Secretary of State, James Byrnes, included the term "unconditional surrender" in the July 26 Potsdam Declaration. This "final warning" and expression of surrender terms to Japan was in any case a charade. The day before it was issued, Harry Truman had already approved the order to release a 15 kiloton atomic bomb over the city of Hiroshima.[9]

Political Bombshell

Many U.S. Military officials were less than enthusiastic about the demand for unconditional surrender or use of the atomic bomb. At the time of Potsdam, Gen. Hap Arnold asserted that conventional bombing could end the war. Adm. Ernest King believed a naval blockade alone would starve the Japanese into submission. Gen. Douglas MacArthur, convinced that retaining the emperor was vital to an orderly transition to peace, was appalled at the demand for unconditional surrender. Adm. William Leahy concurred. Refusal to keep the emperor "would result only in making the Japanese desperate and thereby increase our casualty lists," he argued, adding that a nearly defeated Japan might stop fighting if unconditional surrender were dropped, as a demand. At a loss for a military explanation for use of the bomb, Leahy believed that the decision "was clearly a political one," reached perhaps "because of the vast sums that had been spent on the project."[10] Finally, we have Gen. Dwight Eisenhower's account of a conversation with Stimson in which he told the Secretary of War that:

> Japan was already defeated and that dropping the bomb was completely unnecessary... I thought our country should avoid shocking world opinion by the use of a weapon whose employment was, I thought, no longer mandatory as a measure to save U.S. lives. It was my belief that Japan was, at that very moment, seeking some way to surrender with a minimum loss of "face." The secretary was deeply perturbed by my attitude, almost angrily refuting the reasons I gave for my quick conclusions.[11]

Bomb-Slinging Diplomats

If, as appears to be the case, U.S. policy in 1945 was based on neither the pursuit of the earliest possible peace nor the desire to avoid a land invasion, we must look elsewhere to explain the dropping of the A-bombs.

It has been asserted that dropping of the atomic bombs was not so much the last military act of World War II as the first act of the Cold War. Although Japan was targeted, the weapons were aimed straight to the red heart of the Soviet Union. For three-quarters of a century the determining element of U.S. foreign policy, virtually its *sine qua non*, has been "the communist factor." World War II and a battlefield alliance with the Soviet Union did not bring about an ideological change in the anticommunists who owned and ran the United States. It merely provided a partial breather in a struggle that had begun with the U.S. invasion of the Soviet Union in 1918.[12] It is hardly surprising then, that 25 years later, as the Soviets were sustaining the highest casualties of any nation in World War II, the United

States systematically kept them in the dark about the A-bomb project — while sharing information with the British.

According to Manhattan Project scientist Leo Szilard, Secretary of State Byrnes had said that the bomb's biggest benefit was not its effect on Japan but its power to "make Russia more manageable in Europe."[13]

The United States was planning ahead. A Venezuelan diplomat reported to his government after a May 1945 meeting that Assistant Secretary of State Nelson Rockefeller "communicated to us the anxiety of the United States Government about the Russian attitude." U.S. officials, he said, were "beginning to speak of Communism as they once spoke of Nazism and are invoking continental solidarity and hemispheric defense against it."[14]

Churchill, who had known about the weapon before Truman, applauded and understood its use: "Here then was a speedy end to the Second World War," he said about the bomb and added, thinking of Russian advances into Europe, "and perhaps to much else besides... We now had something in our hands which would redress the balance with the Russians."[15]

Referring to the immediate aftermath of Nagasaki, Stimson wrote:

> In the State Department there developed a tendency to think of the bomb as a diplomatic weapon. Outraged by constant evidence of Russian perfidy, some of the men in charge of foreign policy were eager to carry the bomb for a while as their ace-in-the-hole... U.S. statesmen were eager for their country to browbeat the Russians with the bomb held rather ostentatiously on our hip.[16]

This policy, which came to be known as "atomic diplomacy" did not, of course, spring forth full-grown on the day after Nagasaki.

"The psychological effect on Stalin [of the bombs] was twofold," noted historian Charles L. Mee, Jr. "The Americans had not only used a doomsday machine; they had used it when, as Stalin knew, it was not militarily necessary. It was this last chilling fact that doubtless made the greatest impression on the Russians ."[17]

Killing Nagasaki

After the *Enola Gay* released its cargo on Hiroshima, common sense — common decency wouldn't apply here — would have dictated a pause long enough to allow Japanese officials to travel to the city, confirm the extent of the destruction and respond before the United States dropped a second bomb.

At 11 o'clock in the morning of August 9, Prime Minister Kintaro Suzuki addressed the Japanese Cabinet: "Under the present circumstances I have concluded that our only alternative is to accept the Potsdam Proclamation and terminate the war."

Moments later, the second bomb fell on Nagasaki.[18] Some hundreds of thousands of Japanese civilians died in the two attacks; many more suffered terrible injury and permanent genetic damage.

After the war, His Majesty the Emperor still sat on his throne and the gentlemen who ran the United States had absolutely no problem with this. They never had.

(1995)

Nuclear Threats and the New World

Michio Kaku

On the eve of the Gulf War, opinion polls indicated that the U.S. public was evenly split, about 45 to 45 percent, on military intervention. To tip the scales, the Bush Administration unleashed a blistering torrent of accusations, branding Saddam Hussein a threat to Middle East oil, a renegade, a trampler of international law and even a new Hitler. None of these tactics, however, proved particularly effective in rousing war fever. A sizable fraction of the U.S. people resisted administration propaganda and preferred to pursue patient negotiations, rather than to pull the trigger.

Then, the Bush Administration unleashed the unsubstantiated claim that Iraq would develop the atomic bomb within one year — even though most nuclear physicists concluded it would take about 10 years.[1] Within days, well-meaning U.S. citizens who had grave reservations about the use of bloodshed to restore a reactionary, feudal emirate, began to wave the flag and support invasion.

Given the success of the tactic, it is not surprising that the nuclear bogeyman reared its head again. Soon after the conclusion of the Gulf War, the *New York Times* raised the specter of a North Korean atomic bomb. For 40 years the situation in Korea had been relatively stable and, in fact, ignored by the media. Within weeks, however, the Bush Administration created a major international crisis by focusing world attention on the alleged atomic bomb factory at Yongbyon.[2] Similarly, it had been known for years that Cuba was building a Chernobyl-style reactor. After the Gulf War, however, the right-wing press ignited a fierce controversy by claiming that because Florida could be contaminated by a nuclear accident, a U.S. invasion of the island was justified.

Proliferation Justifies Invasion

Nuclear threats, of course, have historically been at the heart of U.S. foreign policy and have proven extremely useful for justifying U.S. actions.[3] This time around, however, there is a new twist added to the more traditional threats by the United States to unleash nuclear devastation on any nation challenging its powers.[4]

In the past, preventing nuclear proliferation had been a low priority for U.S. policymakers. Now, the United States claims the right to intervene militarily around the world to stop alleged proliferation.

Iraq, North Korea and Cuba are the first beneficiaries of this new "Bush Doctrine." As we shall see, the basis for calculating the extent of the threat these nations pose is a political judgment by U.S. policy makers, not an objective assessment by scientists and military analysts.

Now that the only other superpower, the Soviet Union, no longer exists, one might conclude there is no need to threaten the use of nuclear weapons. This is not the case.

On January 14, 1991, days before the beginning of the Gulf War, the Pentagon leaked to *Newsweek* a major study on the use of nuclear weapons against Iraq. It publicized the Pentagon's varied contingency plans to use nuclear weapons and pointedly mentioned General Norman Schwarzkopf's request for permission to use them in the Gulf. The plan called for neutron bombs to destroy enemy troops, nuclear "earth penetrators" to vaporize underground bunker positions and hydrogen bombs detonated over Baghdad to wipe out its communications systems.[5] During the war itself, there were approximately 300 U.S. hydrogen bombs in the Gulf aboard U.S. ships.

This policy was further clarified by a Pentagon paper leaked to the *New York Times*[6] in March 1992. According to the secret draft, top priority for the future will be preventing the rise of another rival to U.S. military supremacy. It listed seven possible nations or combinations of nations which may threaten U.S. military domination of the world. A careful look at these seven possibilities, however, shows that the Pentagon is shadow boxing. Iraq, one of the contenders, for example, is devastated and has a gross national product that is one percent of the U.S. GNP. Nonetheless, the report unleashed a firestorm of protest, including diplomatically tempered outrage from some U.S. allies ranked as potential rivals. The Bush Administration tried to distance itself from this report, calling it unofficial and low-level and not the basis of U.S. foreign policy.

Two and a half months later, according to the *New York Times*, the Pentagon issued its final report in which it backed away from thwarting "the emergence of a new rival to U.S. military supremacy"[7] as the primary goal for the next five years. Official policy or not, the report, which circulated among the Joint Chiefs of Staff, represents a major position within the military.

Ever eager to save the administration embarrassment, some commentators quickly labeled the report a "trial balloon" meant to test public opinion about a major defense strategy. More likely, however, it was deliberately released as a veiled warning to friends and foes alike that the United States will not tolerate threats to its military supremacy.

One of the key principles of Game Theory, developed by the mathematician John von Neumann for Pentagon nuclear war games, is that the enemy can be kept at bay by letting it know that you are prepared to unleash the "maximum level of violence" if necessary. The policy is like that of a tiger snarling in the forest; it knows that if the smaller animals ganged up, they would win. Through belligerent roaring and strutting and a few well-timed bluffs, the tiger can intimidate the other animals and keep them in line without engaging in a single fight. Likewise, the Pentagon's nuclear snarl warns the rest of the world not to tangle with the United States.

Selective Proliferation

Although adding charges of proliferation to the vocabulary of snarls and using it as a justification for intervention is a recent phenomenon, its inclusion is simply an extension of long-standing U.S. Cold War strategy. The United States has consistently dispensed support and in this case nuclear technology, to selected right-wing governments in reward for containing the Soviet Union. As Henry Kissinger once remarked, if a nation is on its way to building an atomic bomb, then why not provide certain assistance in order to influence its foreign policy.[8]

For decades, then, while publicly decrying the spread of nuclear weapons, the United States has been providing extensive covert and overt support, including selectively proliferating bomb technology to a number of its close allies. The real threat of nuclear proliferation comes not so much from Iraq and North Korea, which have only a primitive technological base, but from those countries such as Israel, South Africa, India and Pakistan, whose nuclear weapons infrastructures are quite mature and sophisticated. Interviews in 1988 with top United States intelligence experts indicated that Israel had at least 100 atomic bombs, South Africa had up to 20, India 12 to 20 and Pakistan four.[9] Since then, these countries have considerably modernized their nuclear production methods and accelerated bomb production.

Double Standard

In its secret nuclear facility at Kahuta, in the hills near Rawalpindi, Pakistan has been quietly amassing advanced nuclear technology. The United States gave its tacit blessing to the project largely in recognition of Pakistan's role as a strategic CIA-financed staging area for the fundamentalist rebel fight against the Soviet-backed government of Afghanistan. The Reagan Administration, in fact, pressured Congress to grant exceptions to laws requiring a cut-off of aid to Pakistan because of its nuclear program, arguing that it had not yet technically assembled an atomic bomb, i.e., it was "one screw turn away" from constructing a nuclear weapon. A.Q. Kahn, head of the Pakistani nuclear program, acknowledged that the United States was fully aware that it had the bomb. "America knows it," said the father of the Pakistani atomic bomb in one candid interview. "What the CIA has been saying about our possessing the bomb is correct."[10] In spring 1992, after years of adamant denial, Pakistan publicly admitted for the first time that it has the capability of building the atomic bomb.

While the United States richly rewarded Israel, South Africa and Pakistan, which all had extensive clandestine nuclear facilities, it used Iraq's primitive bomb-building efforts to justify a war. In that conflict, the United States and its allies dropped 88,500 tons of high explosives (seven times the Hiroshima bomb), killed perhaps 200,000 to 300,000 people and according to the UN reduced the country to a "preindustrial" state.

Access to Fissionable Materials

An examination of the relative strengths of nuclear programs makes the double standard clear. A first step in building an atomic bomb is obtaining or purifying from natural uranium the 20 pounds of enriched uranium, of uranium-235, necessary to fabricate one atomic bomb (less for a plutonium bomb). The two most common ways of obtaining weapons-grade uranium are manufacturing it domestically or buying it abroad on the open market. Using state-of-the-art production techniques, it takes approximately 1,000 ultracentrifuges operating for one year to purify enough enriched uranium to make a bomb. (Because U-235 is slightly lighter than U-238, the ultracentrifuge, by spinning natural uranium, can separate these two isotopes.) Pakistan is known to have about 14,000 ultracentrifuges, or enough, in principle, to make 10 to 15 atomic bombs per year.[11] Having apparently assembled its first atomic bomb in 1986, Pakistan could now have a small nuclear arsenal.

By comparison, Iraq had 26 ultracentrifuges before the war, far too few to manufacture an atomic bomb within a year.[12] Meanwhile, as far back as 1968, the United States provided South Africa with 230 pounds of enriched uranium to power its U.S.-made 20 megawatt Safari-1 nuclear reactor, which operates on weapons-grade (90 percent enriched) uranium. As early as August 1973, the South African Government publicly announced that it had purified a few tons of weapons-grade fuel for its nuclear reactor at Pelindaba-Valindaba. In 1975, the South African Minister of Mines, Dr. Pieter Koornhof, announced an ambitious $4.5 billion program to build a mammoth facility capable of producing 5,000 tons of enriched uranium a year. [13]

In addition, the South African Government also operates the huge 1,844 megawatt Koeberg I and II nuclear power plants. Theoretically, these plants are large enough to yield roughly 500 pounds of plutonium per year, which could then be extracted by chemical purification processes.

Clearly, South Africa's vast nuclear program, centered at Pelindaba-Valindaba, dwarfs the puny Iraqi program by several orders of magnitude and can generously supply both its own and Israel's need for fissionable materials.[14] The exact figures on South African plutonium refinement capability are unknown because Pretoria had refused to sign the Nuclear Non-Proliferation Treaty (NPT) until 1991.

Iraq, by contrast, was a signatory to the NPT, allowed inspections by the International Atomic Energy Agency (IAEA) every six months and only possessed about 50 pounds of enriched uranium. Legally obtained under strict IAEA controls and supervision, this material was apparently the basis of the Bush Administration's claim — widely disputed by physicists around the world — that the Iraqis could assemble an atomic bomb within one year. In fact, only one month before the Gulf War, the IAEA had conducted its periodic inspection and stated flatly that there was no threat from this uranium. Compare the unsubstantiated charges of imminent nuclear capability launched against Iraq with the solid evidence provided six years earlier by Israeli defector Mordechai Vanunu. The nuclear technician claimed that Israel possessed possibly several hundred atomic bombs, developed at the secret Dimona plant and even sent color photographs of the nuclear bomb cores to the London *Sunday Times*. According to Vanunu, Dimona produces 1.2 kilograms of pure plutonium per week, or enough to manufacture four to 12 atomic bombs per year. Despite this evidence, the United States publicly supported the convenient fiction that Israel did not possess nuclear capability.[15]

Secret Testing Revealed

Even after it is assembled, an atomic bomb is effectively useless unless the technology has been tested; no country will risk its existence on a potential dud. To prevent testing without its knowledge, the United States launched the Vela satellite in the 1970s specifically to detect unauthorized detonations of nuclear weapons around the world.

On September 22, 1979, a storm brewed off the coast of South Africa near Prince Edward Island (1,500 miles from the Cape of Good Hope). Two Israeli Navy warships plied the rough waters. Unexpectedly, the heavy cloud cover broke and the Vela satellite detected the fingerprint "double flash" (called NUCFLASHES in Pentagon jargon).[16]

Apparently the South Africans and Israelis were testing a low-yield atomic warhead that was later standardized for use by the Israeli Defense Force. Had the clouds not parted on their third test, they would have successfully evaded the Vela Satellite.[17] As one Israeli official involved with the test said, "It was a fuckup. There was a storm and we figured it would block Vela, but there was a gap in the weather, a window and Vela got blinded by the flash." This joint South African-Israeli test was the first and only known test by a country not in the Nuclear Club since India had tested its bomb in 1974.[18]

Developing Technology and a Credible Arsenal

The recent UN revelations that Iraq's nuclear program was concealed and more diverse than expected do not change this basic conclusion. The new information was interesting not because it showed how advanced the project was, but because it exposed Iraq's low level of technology and high level of desperation. Unable to legally obtain ultracentrifuge technology, the country had embarked on a costly search for various alternative and antiquated methods of uranium separation.

An Iraqi defector divulged that there were three previously undisclosed nuclear sites where the Iraqis even resurrected technologies long-abandoned by the West, such as the calutron (California cyclotron). The on-site UN team found that only six to 12 of the 30 calutrons in Tarmia were usable before the war and all were damaged by the war. Iraq's admission of one pound of low-grade uranium (unsuitable for bomb use) was consistent with the state of Iraq's unfinished calutron site. Furthermore, without high speed capacitors needed for precise electronic detonation of the enriched uranium or plutonium, an Iraqi bomb would have been quite unusable. The UN found no indications that Iraq had mastered the technology of high speed capacitors.

The Single Bomb Fallacy

Even if Iraq had been able to manufacture a bomb, a single nuclear weapon, contrary to public perception, does not constitute a credible military threat, nor does it have much military value in an armed conflict. A substantial stockpile is another matter.

Israel has perhaps the world's sixth largest nuclear arsenal, now estimated at 300 atomic bombs. During the 1973 October War, the Israelis were poised to fire their nuclear weapons at the Arabs if the battle had turned against them. After the 1973 war, the Israeli Defense Force apparently established three nuclear-capable battalions, each with 12 self-propelled 175-mm nuclear cannons. Three nuclear artillery shells were stockpiled for each weapon, making a total of 108 warheads for these nuclear cannons alone.[19]

Adding to its nuclear potency, only Israel, of all the nations not in the Nuclear Club, has mastered the more advanced thermonuclear hydrogen bomb technology. The pictures released by Vanunu and shown to nuclear physicists at U.S. weapons laboratories revealed that the Israelis have mastered the technology of neutron bombs — highly sophisticated "enhanced radiation" weapons, which are ideal for tactical or theater nuclear warfare.

Delivering The Bomb

Lastly, even after constructing, testing and consolidating a small arsenal of bombs, a nation must be able to deliver them. The Scud-B weapons launched by the Iraqis during the Gulf War had great psychological value, but almost no military value. Most of them broke up in mid-flight — a disaster in a war fought with nuclear weapons. Furthermore, crude atomic bombs are so large and bulky that they cannot be carried by conventional fighter bombers. By contrast, the Pakistani program is advanced enough to manufacture a lightweight atomic bomb, weighing no more than 400 pounds, that can be strapped onto the belly of a U.S. F-16 fighter bomber.[20] The South Africans have made their Overberg testing range available to the Israelis for tests of their Shavit (Comet) missile, which uses the Jericho-2B missile as its first two stages.[21] The Shavit missile launched an Israeli satellite into orbit in 1988 and can hurl a 2,000 pound bomb a distance of 1,700 miles. One top U.S. administration official, commenting on the close relationship between Israel and South Africa in developing these weapons, said, "We know everything, names, dates, everything. We don't have any evidence that it's a plain uranium-for-missiles deal. Think of the relationship as a whole series of deals."[22]

Divide and Conquer

Puny as Iraq's nuclear program seems in comparison to that of Pakistan, Israel and South Africa, it could not have been built in such a short time without substantial foreign assistance.

Ironically, Iraq's technological infrastructure was largely a creation of the West. In the early 20th century, British success in dominating the Middle East, controlling large parts of Africa and running a global empire, relied on a strategy of "divide and conquer." The British sliced up what is now Iraq, Syria, Jordan, Lebanon and Kuwait and much of Africa in order to pit Arabs against Arabs, Africans against Africans. The United States, which took over as the major Middle East power after World War II, learned this lesson well. The Shah of Iran, for example, was set up by the CIA as regional "policeman of the Gulf," charged with keeping the Arab nations in line. After his overthrow, the United States needed a counter-weight to the insufficiently tractable Iranian fundamentalists. In the interest of Middle East control and eager to see its enemies clobber themselves, the United States largely sustained and then brokered the long, bloody stalemate between Iraq and Iran.

In order to neutralize Iran, which it perceived as the greater threat, the Reagan Administration gave widespread military and economic support to Saddam Hussein, secretly feeding Iraq military intelligence information on Iran's forces, in the form of satellite data.[23]

As long as Iraq was neutralizing Iran, Saddam was the beneficiary of the selective proliferation policy. As long as Iraq was perceived to be carrying out United States wishes, it was rewarded, like Pakistan, with substantial aid and trade concessions. Thus, much of the high technology eventually destroyed by Desert Storm came from the United States and West Germany.[24] The U.S. Commerce Department licensed more than $1.5 billion in sensitive high technology for Iraq before the Gulf War. About 200 major companies in the West were involved in the high technology transfer. Hewlett-Packard, Honeywell, Unisys, International Computer Systems, Rockwell and Tektronix had lucrative trade agreements with the Iraqi Atomic Energy Commission and Saad 16, Iraq's missile research center. Honeywell even did a study for a power gasoline bomb warhead for the Iraqis.[25]

Nuclear Threats in Korea

Similarly, the Bush Doctrine has recast the Korean question. After three decades of relative stability and obscurity, suddenly, within weeks of the Gulf War, international attention was focused on the "nuclear threat" posed by the Yongbyon nuclear complex located 60 miles north of Pyongyang. The irony, as the North Koreans have pointed out, is that the United States maint ns thousands of tactical nuclear weapons around the world, with app ately 600 concentrated in the Korean area.[26]

The threat presented by this arsenal is real. During the Korean War, the United States had authorized the use of nuclear weapons in the appendix to its secret war plan, OPLAN 8-52. Recently declassified minutes of the National Security Council reveal the detailed plans by President Eisenhower and his secretary of State John Foster Dulles to exploit tactical nuclear weapons in Korea.[27] To pressure North Korea, President Bush vowed in September 1991 to withdraw nuclear weapons from South Korea. The pledge, as the North Koreans have again noted, is largely symbolic, since U.S. nuclear weapons based on ships, such as nuclear cruise missiles, can be fired into North Korea within minutes. An offshore nuclear missile is just as deadly as a nuclear missile based on land.

In any case, equating the U.S.-backed South Korean nuclear capabilities with those of North Korea is absurd. The North Korean nuclear program is qualitatively and quantitatively even more primitive than the Iraqi one, which in turn was quite backward by Western standards. The Iraqis, at least, had access to billions of dollars of advanced Western technology because of its war against Iran. The Soviets, by contrast, were historically much more tight-fisted about sharing this kind of advanced technology with their allies. In the late 1960s, they provided a small reactor. The North Koreans contracted with the British to build an old-fashioned, 1950s-style graphite reactor, called the Calder Hall, which was to be operated by the British Nuclear Fuels Company. This 20 to 30 megawatt reactor, tiny compared with the 1,000 megawatts common in the West, was begun in 1980 and was already obsolete when completed seven years later.

In 1985, although North Korea signed the Nuclear Non-Proliferation Treaty, it has been unwilling to allow totally unrestricted inspection of its facilities. As a consequence, the United States began to suspect that the North Koreans were converting the civilian reactor to military purposes. At present, the case against the North Koreans is based primarily on satellite photographs, the interpretation of which is the subject of intense controversy. The United States asserts the photos show that the North Koreans are completing a new reactor, possibly 50 to 200 megawatts in power and a new reprocessing plant which could extract plutonium from radioactive waste. These admittedly speculative conclusions have even created a dispute between the CIA on one side and the Pentagon and the State Department on the other.[28] Based on its claims that the North Koreans will have the atomic bomb within a few months, the CIA recommends immediate action, possibly including force. The Pentagon and State Department take a much more relaxed view, estimating that North Korea is two to five years from an atomic bomb. This appraisal allows ample time for a diplomatic solution.

There is some indication that the stalemate is breaking up. On March 14, 1992, a new agreement was signed between the two Koreas. The South Koreans agreed to drop their insistence on a rigid timetable for inspections and the North Koreans agreed to allow a formal inspection of the Yongbyon site — possibly in June or shortly thereafter. In April, the North Koreans even released a video of the interior of the reactor site. On May 3, they promised to hand over to the IAEA a list of nuclear-related sites for inspection.[29]

Part of the controversy has revolved around the often quoted U.S. position that satellite photographs of the Yongbyon facility show no electrical wires emanating from the site. Reactors for peaceful rather than bomb-producing purposes, the United States argued, would necessitate a network of transformers and cables connecting the site to the power grid. It was the North Koreans' word against the West's, until IAEA Director Hans Blix and his team reported after a May 1992 visit that they found "electric distribution grids outside two large nuclear power plants, suggesting that the plants are intended for power generation... [and] supporting North Korea's assertion that its nuclear plants are strictly for peaceful power-generation purposes."

They also turned up a "tiny quantity [of plutonium]," said Blix, "far from the amount you need for a weapon."[30] In fact, small quantities of plutonium are often extracted for reprocessing but are usually of a type not usable in weapons production. Despite exaggeration by the media about the Yongbyon site, the IAEA has been cautious in drawing any conclusions until a more complete inspection — expected soon — can be conducted.

Will the Bush Doctrine Backfire?

Ultimately, the Bush Doctrine may backfire in any number of ways, with a variety of dire consequences. The Bush Administration is playing with nuclear fire and it is easy to get burned.

For example, the United States has allowed the atomic bomb to proliferate so widely that, without anticommunism to keep these countries in line, proliferation may be out of its control. Already in the 1973 October War, the Israelis apparently threatened to unleash their atomic bomb on the Arabs unless the United States came to its aid. The United States was thus blackmailed and put on the receiving end of a nuclear threat.

Another potential nuclear flashpoint is the centuries-old feud between the Muslims in Pakistan and the Hindus in India. The recent crisis over Kashmir caused the U.S. State Department to express public alarm that the conflict would boil over into open warfare, with the distinct possibility that nuclear weapons could be used by both sides.

But perhaps most important, the reliance on nuclear threats to maintain U.S. military supremacy may backfire by weakening the domestic economic infrastructure. The clear implication of the leaked Pentagon report is that while other countries, such as Germany and Japan, may eventually pose a grave economic threat to the United States, Washington's nuclear superiority will keep them in line and keep the United States on top.

This reliance on military domination is a tacit admission that U.S. economic strength will continue to deteriorate into the next century. Since 1945, U.S. control of 50 percent of the world's wealth has declined to 25 percent, and is still falling. Most of that wealth was squandered maintaining a world-spanning network of 395 foreign military bases in 35 countries at a current cost exceeding $210 billion annually. With such a colossal military burden, this country is undergoing a remarkable de-industrialization process, which the world has not seen since turn-of-the-century Britain.

If the Pentagon is relying on nuclear might to keep its rising economic rivals in line, then this expensive "solution" will ultimately exacerbate the de-industrialization of the United States. A journalist once asked President Reagan whether the right-wing strategy of "spending Russia into a depression" might backfire; might not the United States be spent into a depression instead? In one of the few lucid moments of his presidency, Reagan answered, "Yes... but they'll bust first." For once, Ronald Reagan was correct. The Soviets indeed did bust first, but there are indications that the United States may be next.

(1992)

Israel, Iran, the United States and the Bomb

Israel Shahak

"The war in Lebanon is the first stage in our conflict with Iran."
— Efraim Shah, Knesset member[1]

For years, stonewalling in the face of mounting and eventually irrefutable evidence, Israel denied all reports that it had built a nuclear bomb. Now openly acknowledged, its substantial nuclear arsenal forms a grim backdrop to the Middle East political landscape.

While the role of these weapons is discussed in Israel, the implications of the world's fifth largest nuclear force are all but ignored in the United States. In the country whose taxpayers foot the bill for the Israeli program, the media spotlight only the "threat" of nuclearization by other states in the region. And in Israel, this threat and the national commitment to remaining the only nuclear state in the region, are touted as justifications for developing and possibly using the bomb.

On April 17, 1992, Deputy Chief of Staff, General Amnon Shahak-Lipkin indicated how far he believed Israel was prepared to go to prevent Middle East nuclear proliferation.[2] "I believe that the State of Israel should from now on use all its power and direct all its efforts to preventing nuclear developments in any Arab state whatsoever." The interviewer then asked the General: "Does this imply the need for violent means as well?" Shahak-Lipkin barely couched his answer: "In my opinion, all or most means serving that purpose are legitimate." Clearly, the Deputy Chief of Staff was not discounting an Israeli nuclear first strike.

Currently, the most likely target for a preemptive Israeli strike, either conventional or nuclear, is not Arab but Iranian. There is widespread speculation backed by some hard evidence that Israel is forming anti-Iranian coalitions and prodding the United States — either by itself or through its allies — to destabilize Iran and/or take out its developing nuclear capability. Israel's new anti-Iranian policy can only be understood in the broad context of its hegemonic aims.

Grand Strategy

The scope of the new Israeli grand strategy was set forth by General Shlomo Gazit (reserves), a former Military Intelligence commander. The area of military intelligence is regarded as the most important component of the intelligence community. It is composed of Mossad (which operates outside Israel and the areas it physically occupies), Shabak (the General Security Service which operates within Israel, in the occupied territories and in the "security zone" of South Lebanon) and Military Intelligence (which operates as a branch of the army). The Military Intelligence commander reports to the prime minister on behalf of all groups on matters of strategic importance.

After his retirement, Gazit became a member of the prestigious Yaffe Center for Strategic Studies at Tel Aviv University. His frequent articles on intelligence and strategy are remarkable for their lucidity and their highly placed sources.

"Israel's main task has not changed at all and remains of crucial importance. The geographical location of Israel at the center of the Arab-Muslim Middle East predestines Israel to be a devoted guardian of stability in all the countries surrounding it. Its [role] is to protect the existing regimes, to prevent or halt the processes of radicalization and to block the expansion of fundamentalist religious zealotry. Israel has its 'red lines' which, precisely because they are not clearly marked or explicitly defined, have a powerful deterrent effect by virtue of causing uncertainty beyond its borders. The purpose of these 'red lines' is to determine which strategic developments or other changes occurring beyond Israel's borders can be defined as threats which Israel will regard as intolerable, to the point of feeling compelled to use *all its military power* for the sake of their prevention or eradication." [Emphasis added.]

In Gazit's view, by "protecting" all or most Middle Eastern regimes, Israel performs a vital service for "the industrially advanced states, all of which are keenly concerned with guaranteeing the stability in the Middle East."

In the aftermath of the disappearance of the Soviet Union as a political power with interests of its own in the region, a number of Middle Eastern states lost a patron which guaranteed their political, military and even economic viability. A vacuum was thus created, with the effect of adding to the region's instability. Under such conditions, the Israeli role as a strategic asset in guaranteeing a modicum of stability in the entire Middle East, far from dwindling or disappearing, was elevated to the first order of magnitude. Without Israel, the West would have to perform this role by itself, when none of the existing superpowers really could perform it, because of various domestic and international constraints. For Israel, by contrast, the need to intervene is a matter of survival.[3]

An Iranian Bomb

So far, Israel has abjured the use of nuclear weapons. But that stated reluctance — like that of the United States — is tactical rather than moral or absolute. That Israel is prepared to go to war to defend its perceived interests is beyond doubt; that it has a large arsenal of nuclear weapons and a sophisticated delivery system is also well established; but the circumstances that would promote a decision to use the bomb are less clear. Some Israeli experts see the expected nuclearization of the Middle East in general and of Iran in particular as sufficient threat to justify any prophylactic action.

Although Israeli censorship on the subject is strict, the subject was discussed at a symposium held by the Yaffe Center. One of the speakers, Knesset Member Efraim Sneh (Labor), who had served in intelligence-related jobs in the army, is widely regarded as one of the best informed strategic experts. He declared:

"[I]t is still possible to prevent Iran from developing its nuclear bomb. This can be done, since Iran threatens the interests of all rational states in the Middle East. We should therefore do all we can to prevent Iran from ever reaching nuclear capability. Israel cannot possibly put up with the nuclear bomb in Iranian hands. If the Western states don't do what is their duty, Israel will find itself forced to act alone and *will* accomplish its task *by any means considered suitable* for the purpose." [Emphasis added.][4]

Israel is unlikely to overthrow the present regime, to win a military victory with conventional weapons, or to convince Iran to abandon plans for nuclearization. Given this military context, Sneh's pronouncement can be seen as a veiled threat to strike at Iran with nuclear weapons.

Nor are Israeli leaders confident that intelligence can accurately assess the progress of nuclearization programs or even know when and if a bomb and delivery system are on line. Aware of past failures of intelligence units,[5] Sneh warned:

"If, despite all our precautions, we are confronted with an Iran already in possession of nuclear installations and in mastery of launching techniques, we would be better off if the explosive charge of the Israeli-

Arab conflict is by then already neutralized through signing peace treaties with states located in our vicinity — concretely with Syria, Jordan and the Palestinians. We would also be better off if, until that time, we succeed in building alliances with Middle Eastern states interested in fighting Islamic fundamentalism. It would be good for us if all sane states of this region unite to resist all forces of radicalism."[6]

Also attending the symposium was General Avihu Ben-Nun (reserves), who served as commander of the Israeli Air Force until the end of 1992. Before and during the Gulf War, he was one of the most important advocates of Israeli intervention into that war who agreed with Sneh that preventing nuclearization of Iran might not be possible. Even if an Israeli-Iranian war broke out after Iran nuclearized, he reassured, the threat of Israeli retaliation — considered feasible by the Arab world — was a powerful deterrent against an Iranian first strike. And if that was not sufficiently discouraging, the United States would launch a nuclear retaliation. "But Iran *will* also have another reason for refraining from using its atomic bomb against Israel," Ben-Nun continued, "the fear of destroying the Islamic holy sites in Jerusalem. The holy sites are our best deterrent." This statement, considered too crass even for an Israeli general, was ridiculed by some commentators.[7]

Policy expert Shay Feldman of the Center for Strategic Studies at Tel Aviv University concurred. Although Iran is now trying to reactivate two nuclear reactors built under the Shah, "the Iranian leaders will not behave irrationally enough... [to] risk the total devastation of Iran that would result from an Israeli [nuclear] retaliation." Feldman blames Iran's current level of nuclear technology largely on Israel's short-sighted covert support — in defiance of the United States — for the Shah's nuclear program. "If not for the Khomeinist revolution," he argues, "Iran would have already been at a very advanced stage of nuclearization." Reviewing the status of other countries, Feldman presumes that Pakistan already has nuclear weapons; Egypt and Libya, despite renouncing their nuclear ambitions still retain technical potential and thus remain "a mild threat" to Israel; Syria presents an "even milder" threat; Iraq's nuclear capability has been destroyed; and Jordan and Saudi Arabia have no nuclear potential. Apart from Iran, then, Feldman asserts that only Algeria poses a "serious" nuclear threat to Israel.[8]

Israeli Army Defines New Strategy

Nuclear policymakers and political analysts such as Ben-Nun, Sneh and Feldman are cognizant of and strongly influenced by changes taking place within the Israeli Army. According to Shlomo Aharonson, a veteran expert on Israeli nuclear strategy with close establishment connections, the old and "deeply entrenched strategic doctrine" guiding the Israeli Army was developed in the early 1950s by Yigal Allon, the most distinguished commander in the 1947-49 war. It aimed at winning a smashing victory in the shortest possible time. Under this old doctrine, Aharonson contends, Israel needed nuclear weapons because "Allon conceived of the Arabs as irrational, barbarous and cutthroat characters, in contrast to us, [who are] shaped by 'humanistic traditions.' Consequently," Aharonson explains, "Israel should always be the first to attack in order to conquer territories and then to offer to cede some of them as a bargaining chip to attain peace. But the whole thing was bound to recur again and again." Although Allon — perhaps restrained by his friendship with Iranian secret police commanders — didn't define Iranian "nature," he probably joined other Israeli strategists in regarding them as no better than the Arabs.[9] The army's old strategic doctrine was overhauled in 1987 after "recommendations of a committee chaired by then Justice minister, [Dan] Meridor [Likud]."[10] Its implementation by the army, slowed first by the *intifada*, was given a boost soon after the 1991 Gulf War. The revised doctrine, as interpreted by Aharonson, ranks threats to Israeli national security largely by geographical proximity. The faraway enemies include Iran, Iraq, Libya and Algeria. Among these groups, whose threat is seen as somewhat less than that posed by bordering states, Iran — which got weapons from Israel until the Gulf War — is now considered the most threatening. Aharonson recognizes that Israel cannot — in accordance with Allon's doctrine of preemptive first strike — mobilize its entire army and dispatch it to fight a ground war in Iran. Likewise, the Israeli Air Force is not capable of seriously devastating Teheran using only conventional air raids. After all, this large, several millions-strong city withstood Iraqi air raids during the eight long years of war, without any significant anti-air defenses. It must also be remembered that Israel found no real answer to the grievous blows dealt by the Iraqi Scuds during the Gulf War.[11]

Aharonson is not alone in emphasizing the Iranian threat. Yo'av Kaspi, chief political correspondent of *Al Hamishmar*, reiterates the difficulty of expunging Iran's nuclear capability. In his article, "Iran needs to be treated just as Iraq had been," he interviews Daniel Lesham, "a retired senior officer in the [Israeli] military intelligence and currently a member of the Center for Strategic Studies at the Tel Aviv University." Lesham, who has helped form Israeli strategy, notes that the allied air raids did little in and of themselves to destroy Iraq's military and especially nuclear capabilities. Rather, the victory they secured allowed UN observers to go in and finish the job. Drawing a parallel, Lesham concludes:

"The State of Israel alone can do very little to halt the Iranians. We could raid Iran from the air, but we cannot realistically expect that our aerial operations could destroy all their capabilities. At best, some Iranian nuclear installations could in this way be destroyed. But we couldn't possibly thus reach them all, not even their major centers of nuclear development, especially since that development has proceeded along three different lines in a fairly decentralized manner, with installations and factories scattered widely across the country. It is reasonable to suppose that we will never know the locations of all their installations, just as we didn't know it in Iraq's case."[12]

Aharonson no doubt took these factors into consideration when he concluded that "against its faraway enemies, Israel will have to rely, not so much on the conventional components of the Israeli Army, as on other components of its national security: namely on nuclear deterrence, long-range missiles and improved cooperation with the United States and neighboring states, such as Egypt or Turkey." Aharonson and his peers do not limit the possible use of Israeli nuclear weapons to Iran alone, but consider Syria and Syria's allies as other potential targets. How to deal with these "close enemies" is part of a debate on whether Israel should continue to count on traditional masses of armor, increase emphasis on "smart weapons," or deploy radiation or nuclear bombs.

Building Coalitions Against Iran

Whatever military strategy it finally settles on, clearly Israel — in various degrees of coalition with the United States and Egypt — is exploring the means to destabilize Iran and neutralize the threat of its nuclear program. The Egyptian press has reported "the crystallization of a current Israeli-Egyptian plan to overthrow the Iranian regime with U.S. support."[13] According to Menashe Amir, director of Israeli Farsi-language radio broadcasts to Iran, "there is some truth in such reports." Amir, however, warns that any U.S. plans to forcibly overthrow the Iranian regime are pretty unfeasible, even if the United States is supported in this scheme by several states in the Middle East which, like Egypt and Saudi Arabia, have their reasons to feel threatened by Teheran. Nevertheless, the chance of seeing this regime overthrown in the foreseeable future by forces from within — although not particularly high either — does exist. Iran is ripe for it.[14]

"Apparently the Americans still don't have well-crystallized plans," Amir continues, but the surest way to destabilize the already shaky regime is by exacerbating economic conditions for the Iranian masses through sanctions and other trade manipulations. Oil exports — 90 percent of the Iranian economy — are the most vulnerable pressure point. Another tactic, especially effective if used in conjunction with stimulating Iranian domestic opposition, said Amir, would be to persuade "Turkey or Pakistan to let their territories be used for military operations against their neighbor."

Expanding on the need for Israel to form and exploit coalitions, Yossi Melman, *Ha'aretz's* intelligence correspondent, author of several books and expert on Israeli intelligence, also noted the importance of Israeli-Turkish cooperation "against Iranian subversion" in countries to the north of Iran.

"The Western Europeans contribute to United States efforts to help finance implementation of Turkish aims in Central Asia. According to senior Israeli officials, Israel has been helping Turkey promote those aims in its own ways... Policymakers in Israel believe that the United States, Israel and Turkey have a common interest in establishing a stable regional alignment of secular, moderate and pro-Western regimes in the Middle East. As a recently issued document puts it, 'Israel has an interest in strengthening Turkey for the sake of the common goal of curbing Islamic fundamentalism.'"[15]

The same policy goals apply in Azerbaijan where Israel has good relations and a remarkable degree of influence.[16]

Turning Nuclearization to Political Advantage

Nuclear proliferation is an important factor in the formation of coalitions around the Middle East. The fear of nuclearization, however, may actually be less important militarily and more important politically than first appears. The current Chief of Staff, Ehud Barak, advocated anti-Iran coalition building in 1984-85 when he served as the Military Intelligence commander in the final stages of the Lebanon War before it was expected that Iran would nuclearize. This early emphasis on weakening relatively strong Middle East states suggests that Israel's overarching goal was not simply to prevent nuclearization. Rather, Sneh, like Aharonson, contends that the coalition strategy was designed to enhance Israel's hegemonic control over the region and to use the "peace process" as a tool in the Israeli grand strategy of war-making. Thus, Barak shares common ground with the government doves: a commitment to cooperating closely with the United States and to advancing the peace process. Aharonson is certain that this U.S.-Israeli collaboration includes U.S. backing for the Israeli "option to threaten its faraway enemies" by nuclear means. In this he may be right, if by "Americans" he means the Pentagon, the CIA and their firmest supporters. But as he himself describes it, "a strident anti-nuclear lobby exists in the United States."[17]

Aharonson sees a symbiotic relationship between the United States and Israel. In developing their nuclear weapons, he explains, Iran, Algeria[18] and Libya are motivated only by their anti-Western ideology, which makes it reasonable to expect that those weapons may also be used against the United States and other Western states. The existence of a pro-Western power with its own nuclear capacity is going to considerably neutralize the Iranian or any other threat to the West. In view of that, Israel is in the position to convince the United States that the task of deterring our faraway enemies — which are also the enemies of the United States — by our own nuclear weapons and long-range missiles, should be reserved for ourselves.[19]

Daniel Lesham, a retired senior Military Intelligence officer and member of the Center for Strategic Studies at Tel Aviv University,[20] expands on the practical uses of the nuclear threat. There is both danger and opportunity in playing up Iranian terrorism to create a "situation which would appear similar to that with Iraq before the Gulf crisis." Decrying the world's relative indifference to Iranian "terrorism," Lesham, who has been involved in policy formulation, hopes Israel will use its public relations machine "to explain to the world at large" how urgent is the need to persuade the world to provoke Iran into war.[21]

"We should take advantage of [Iran's] involvement in the Islamic terror which already hurts the entire world. Right now, Israel has incontestable intelligence that the Iranians are about to resume kidnappings. We should take advantage by persistently explaining to the world at large that, by virtue of its involvement in terrorism, no other state is as dangerous as Iran. For example, I cannot comprehend why Libya has been hit by grievous sanctions — to the point that all sales of military equipment to it are barred simply because of its rather minor involvement in terrorism; while Iran, with its record of guiding terrorism against the entire world, remains scot-free of similar, or even stricter, sanctions."[22]

Aharonson suggests the United States can help Israel demonize and isolate Iran by blockading Iranian coasts and by "stationing their warships and especially their nuclear submarines threateningly close to Iran."[23] Along the same lines, Ya'akov Erez, editor of Ma'ariv,[24] proposes that Israel persuade the United States to enforce an embargo on exports of weaponry and other industrial goods to Iran from any state, including North Korea.

Erez justifies the blockade — which he thinks could be activated "without particular difficulties" — as a necessary safeguard to "Western oil supplies." For decades, the United States had used this scenario against the Soviets — vociferously charging that the Soviet Union was poised to close off the supply of world oil by closing the Strait of Hormuz. In the same vein, Erez asserts that a U.S.-imposed blockade of Iran is important because the Iranian threat to oil resources "is really far greater than that caused by the invasion of Kuwait." If Iran were to get the bomb, Sneh argues, "all Arab Gulf states and thereby the sources of Western oil supplies, would thus be exposed much more directly than they were at that time. It would no longer be a case of [Iraq] invading a single state

[Kuwait] and seizing its oil fields, but a direct threat to all immense spaces of the Arabian peninsula and to the freedom of sailing in the Gulf."

This scenario is intended to goad the United States and the Middle East states into joining an Israeli-dominated alliance against Iran. Without that coalition or the overthrow of the Iranian regime through economic pressures and/or armed infiltrations, Israel might act unilaterally and possibly with nuclear weapons.

Since nearly all Israeli experts routinely discuss neutralizing Iran when they address domestic audiences — rather than speechifying to gullible foreigners — it would be a gross mistake to dismiss the topic as simply rhetoric or disinformation. While there is always the possibility that the experts may be wrong in assessing the Iranian nuclear threat, their virtual consensus that there is a danger is politically significant.

Middle East Hegemony

Israel is becoming increasingly open about the possibility of exercising its nuclear option, even though public discussion is often couched in talk about deterrence. "We need not be ashamed," wrote Oded Brosh, a distinguished expert in nuclear politics, "that the nuclear option, as a deterrent to attack, is a major instrument of our defense. The three big democracies have relied on the same deterrent for decades." The Israeli bomb, he implied, was a necessary strategic option. "Generally, in long-term security planning one cannot ignore the political factors. Israel must take into account, for example, that the Saudi royal family is not going to reign forever, or that the Egyptian regime may also change."[25]

Precisely because of such political contingencies, Brosh asserts, Israel must remain free to use or threaten to use its nuclear weapons.

Brosh's analysis carries other implications as well: The very comparison of Israel's strategic aims with those of the United States, Britain and France illustrates Israel's ambition. If Israel is to become the regional superpower, it must establish its hegemony over the entire Middle East.

There is one crucial difference, however, between Israel and "the three big democracies": Israel, rather than paying for its own nuclear development, is financed by the United States. It is essential, then, that the American Israeli Political Action Committee (AIPAC), the organized segment of the American Jewish community and its various allies ensure that Congress continues to foot the bill which now approaches $3.1 billion. To that end, the U.S. public must be effectively deceived about Israel's real strategic aims.

Another impediment to Israeli ambition is the limitations inherent in U.S. support. When U.S. interests diverge from those of Israel, as they must from time to time, the United States will be less likely to pay for or support Israeli policies or propaganda.

For the present, however, the U.S.-Israeli coalition is strong. With the end of the Cold War and the demise of the Soviet Union, a vacuum was created. Israel is stepping boldly into that opening. It is preparing to establish overtly what it always coveted covertly: hegemony over the Middle East. And if the experts are right, it will not shy from any means including nuclear ones to reach that end. Contrary to Gazit's nonsense about benevolent intent, this venture is designed to benefit neither the West, nor potentially unstable Middle East states, nor any interest except that of Israel itself.

(1993)

Endnotes

I. WAR WITHOUT END

Tracking Covert Actions into the Future

1. Interview in *Time*, Apr. 20, 1992, p. 40.
2. See analysis of S.2198, The Intelligence Reorganization Act of 1992. In *Unclassified* (Journal of the Association of National Security Alumni), April-May 1992, pp 1-4.
3. "Pentagon Budget Plans Include War Scenarios," *New York Times* News Service as reported in the *Chicago Tribune*, Feb. 17, 1992, p. 2.
4. "U.S. Strategy Plan Calls For Insuring No Rivals Develop," *New York Times*, Mar. 8, 1992, p. 1.
5. "Pentagon Abandons Goal Of Thwarting U.S. Rivals," *Washington Post*, May 24, 1992. p. 1.
6. For details on post-World War II programs, see Philip Agee and Louis Wolf, *Dirty Work The CIA in Western Europe* (Secaucus, N.J.: Lyle Stuart, 1978); and William Blum, *The CIA: A Forgotten History* (London: Zed Books, 1986).
7. "Holy Alliance," *Time*, Feb. 24, 1992, pp. 14-21.
8. *New York Times* editorial, "How to Defeat Saddam," published in the *International Herald Tribune*, July 14, 1992, p 4.
9. Leonard Minsky, "Espionage 101," *CAIB*, Number 39 (Winter 1991-92), p. 19.
10. For details on the Black Caucus/Progressive Caucus budget, see John Canham-Clyne, "Black and Progressive Caucuses Trying to Change Political Debate," *In These Times*, June 24-July 7, 1992, p. 5. For an analysis of developments toward a new left party, see David Moberg, "2 Parties or Not 2 Parties," *In These Times*, July 21, 1992, p.5.

NATO and Beyond

1. *New York Times*, Aug. 23, 1998, p. 21.
2. James Risen, "Pentagon Planners Give New Meaning to 'Over the Top'," *New York Times*, Sept. 20, 1998, p. 18.

3. Robert M. Gates, "What War Looks Like Now," *New York Times*, Aug. 16, 1998, p. 15.

4. "The Pentagon After the Cold War," *Aerospace America*, Nov. 1998, p. 42.

5. *New York Times*, Jan. 21, 1999, p. A7.

6. Recall that Mobutu became a "dictator" in the press only when his overthrow was imminent; for 30 years, while he brutally raped the Congo, he was our anticommunist ally, Mr. President. And the *New York Times* always referred to the "Pinochet Government" succeeding the "Marxist Allende regime," even though Allende was elected and Pinochet took power in a coup.

7. Chris Hedges, "U.S. Envoy Meets Kosovo Rebels, Who Reject Truce Call," *New York Times*, June 25, 1998, p. A6.

8. At the upcoming NATO celebrations in April, the United States is to propose a "NATO Center for Weapons of Mass Destruction." Steven Erlanger, "U.S. to Propose NATO Take On Increased Roles," *New York Times*, Dec. 7, 1998, p. A1.

9. Most notably through Chilean arms dealer Carlos Cardoen. See Ari Ben-Menashe, *Profits of War* (New York: Sheridan Square, 1992), passim. Cardoen vigorously denied any links to the CIA until his company was indicted in the United States, when he immediately invoked the CIA-knew-all-about-it defense.

10. William J. Broad and Judith Miller, "Germs, Atoms and Poison Gas: The Iraqi Shell Game," *New York Times*, Dec. 20, 1998, p. 5.

11. See Michael Ratner, "The Pinochet Principle" in *CAQ*, Number 66 (Winter 1999) p. 46.

12. Roger Cohen, "NATO Shatters Old Limits in the Name of Preventing Evil," *New York Times*, Oct. 18, 1998, Sec. 4, p. 3.

13. *Ibid*

14. William Pfaff, "Washington's New Vision for NATO Could Be Divisive," *Los Angeles Times*, Dec. 5, 1998.

15. "New Visions for NATO," New York Times, Dec. 7, 1998, p. A24. Alexander Vershbow, the U.S. representative to NATO, immediately responded, in a letter to the editor, that there are "no such proposals." The new strategy, he said, "will not turn the alliance into a global police force, but will affirm NATO's adaptability in tackling new risks, like regional instability, weapons of mass destruction and terrorism."

16. Steven Erlanger, "U.S. to Propose NATO Take On Increased Roles," New York Times, Dec. 7, 1998, p. A12.

17. "The Holbrooke-Milosevic agreement on Kosovo in October was accurately described by Richard Holbrooke as an unprecedented event. NATO had intervened in an internal conflict inside a sovereign non-NATO state, not to defend its own members but to force that other state to halt repression of a rebellious ethnic minority." *Op. cit.*, n. 14.

18. The revelations, which first appeared in the *Washington Post* and the *Boston Globe* and then belatedly in the *New York Times*, caused a "furor." Tim Weiner, "U.S. Used UN Team to Place Spy Device in Iraq, Aides Say," *New York Times*, Jan. 8, 1999, p. A1. An unnamed "senior intelligence official" quoted in the *Times* said that the news "should not shock people." An also unnamed UN official said it would be "naive" to have thought otherwise.

19. Barbara Crosette, "Reports of Spying Dim Outlook for Inspections," *New York Times*, Jan. 8, 1999, p. A8.

20. Tim Weiner, "U.S. Long View on Iraq: Patience in Containing the Ever-Deadlier Hussein," *New York Times*, Jan. 3, 1999, p. 10.

21. Richard N. Haass, the director of foreign policy studies at the Brookings Institution, describes the concern as a "growing resentment factor." Serge Schimemann, "Attacks Breed a Complex Unease About U.S. Goals," *New York Times*, Dec. 20, 1998, p. 21.

22. BBC World Service, Dec. 21, 1998.
23. Barbara Crossette, "France, in Break With U.S., Urges end to Iraq Embargo," *New York Times*, Jan. 14, 1999, p.A6
24. Dana Priest, "U.S. Military Builds Alliances Across Europe," *Washington Post*, Dec. 14, 1998, p.Al.
25. *Ibid.*, p.A28.
26. *Ibid.*
27. *Ibid.*
28. *Ibid.*
29. *Op. cit.*, n. 2.
30. *Op. cit.*, n. 3.

Evangelicals for Nuclear War

1. Clyde H. Dyer and Angela Elwell Hunt, *The Rise of Babylon: Sign of the End Times* (Wheaton, Ill.: Tyndale House, 1991).
2. *Ibid.*, p. 165.
3. Marjorie Stevens, ed., *The Directory of Religious Broadcasting* (Morristown, N.J.: National Religious Broadcasters, l990), p. 9.
4. Pat Robertson and Bob Slosser, *The Secret Kingdom: A Promise of Hope and Freedom in a World of Turmoil* (Nashville, Tenn.: Thomas Nelson, l982), p. 214.
5. Jerry Falwell, pamphlet and tape set, *Nuclear War and the Second Coming of Jesus Christ*, (Lynchburg, Va.: Old Time Gospel Hour, 1983), introduction.
6. Jimmy Swaggart, *When God Fights Russia* (Baton Rouge, La.: Jimmy Swaggart Ministries, 1983).
7. Thomas writes a syndicated column for the *Los Angeles Times* and the *Washington Times*, both of which published his "let's go nuclear" views.

II. FROM CUBA TO AFGHANISTAN

Power and the Semantics of Terrorism

1. As I argue in *U.S. Sponsorship of International Terrorism: An Overview, CovertAction Quaterly*, Number 26, 1986, p. 27.
2. See Richard Leonard, *South Africa at War* (Westport, Conn.: Lawrence Hill, 1983).
3. Qaddafi talks big, but carries a small terrorist stick. The U.S. leadership, by contrast, talks "antiterrorism" and "counterterrorism," but carries a gigantic terrorist stick.
4. Bernard Weinraub, "President Accuses 5 'Outlaw States' of World Terror," *New York Times*, July 9, 1985, p. 1.
5. How President Reagan nevertheless refers to Nicaragua and other enemy states as "terrorist" will be discussed below under 'International terrorism' and its supporters."
6. The fifth edition of *Webster's Collegiate Dictionary*, for example, defines terrorism as "a mode of governing, or of opposing government, by intimidation." The *American Heritage Dictionary* defines it as "The use of terror, violence and intimidation to achieve an end." This does not exclude governments and the third accepted usage given is explicitly "A system of government that uses terror to rule." In the past, terrorism was assumed to refer primarily to acts of government. The identification of terrorism with government receded with the rise of organized Western state terror and modern public relations.
7. State terrorists use torture on a large scale; dissident groups rarely engage in this form of terror.
8. This usage is completely institutionalized in Western discussions of terrorism. This is

reflected, for example, in so-called "risk assessment" analyses by professionals in that new field. Thus the U.S. consulting firm Risks International, Inc., confines terrorism entirely to dissident violence and excludes state murders by, say, Pinochet's Government in Chile, by definition. In fact, in a recent assessment, it finds that the leading victim of terrorism in 1984 was the state of Chile! Executive Risk Assessment, Dec. 1985, p. 30.

9. The Tunis attack was, of course, directed at a PLO official residence. We may ask, however, whether if, immediately following the Beirut massacres of Palestinians, the PLO had successfully attacked the building of the Israeli parliament, killing dozens of Israeli officials, this would have been considered legitimate targeting and "retaliation." And if not, why not?

10. What makes this system of words especially inappropriate is that Israel has gone to great pains to designate the PLO as "terrorist" in order not to have to deal with the Palestinians, except as a group to marginalize and exterminate. The U.S. media swallowed entirely the Israeli claim to be "retaliating" to "terrorism."

11. A significant proportion of hostages who have been killed have been victims of state efforts to recover the hostages by force. Those so killed are usually attributed to the dissident terrorists.

12. Michael McClintock, *The American Connection: State Terror and Popular Resistance in El Salvador*, Vol. I (London: Zed Press, 1985), p. 52.

13. Alexander Cockburn, "Remember El Salvador?" *The Nation*, June 1, 1985; Eva Gold, "The New Face of War in El Salvador: A View of Counterinsurgency Warfare," NARMIC, American Friends Service Committee, Feb. 1986.

14. Brian Jenkins, *International Terrorism: A New Mode of Conflict* (California: Crescent Publications, 1975); Gabriel Weimann, "The Theater of Terror: Effects of Press Coverage," *Journal of Communications*, Winter 1983, pp. 38-45. See also, Gabriel Weimann, "Mass Mediated Theater of Terror: Must the Show Go On," and Edward S. Herman, "The Use and Abuse of Terrorism: A Comment," (a reply to Weimann), in *Media and Terrorism*, Discussion Document, Carleton Center for Communications, Culture and Society (Carleton University, Canada), forthcoming.

15. Another Orwellism may be noted here: State terrorists don't engage in terrorism, they violate "human rights"; only retail terrorists "terrorize."

16. For example, the PLO's status has been greatly reduced in the 1980s, because while massive Israeli attacks on its infrastructure have aroused no serious Western recriminations at Israeli terrorism, as each PLO attack is "terrorism" it suffers a steady accumulation of moral deficits.

17. In an interview with the Johannesburg *Financial Mail*, Nov. 18, 1983, Charles Lichtenstein, the Deputy U.S. Ambassador to the UN, stated that "destabilization will remain in force until Angola and Mozambique do not permit their territory to be used by terrorists [sic] to attack South Africa."

18. In 1985 the Reagan Administration requested $5 million for the Guatemalan police and security assistance as part of what it called a "counterterrorism" package.

19. See Robert Armstrong and Janet Shenk, *El Salvador: The Face of Revolution* (Boston: South End Press, 1982), Chapters 4-6; Raymond Bonner, *Weakness and Deceit: U.S. Policy and El Salvador* (New York: Times Books, 1984), Part 1; Richard Alan White, *The Morass: United States Intervention in Central America* (New York: Harper and Row, 1984), pp. 132-34.

20. There are, of course, rationalizations for the special exceptions. As Chester Crocker explained in regard to Angola, its government is illegitimate because it was put in place by a foreign (Soviet) power. (See *Namibia and Regional Destabilization in Southern Africa*, Hearings before the Subcommittee on Africa of the House Committee on Foreign Affairs,

Feb. 15, 1983, p. 43.) Only if a government is put in place by us, or meets our approval, are attacks on it by rebels "terrorism."

The Uses of Counterterrorism

1. Alexander Haig, *Caveat: Realism, Reagan and Foreign Policy* (New York: Macmillan, 1984), pp. 74-77, see John Prados, *Keepers of the Keys* (New York: Morrow, 1991), p. 452.

2. Robert Toth, "U.S. Acts to Curb Terrorism Abroad," *Los Angeles Times*, Apr. 15, 1984; David Roffman and Don Oberdorfer, "Secret Policy on Terrorism Given Airing," *Washington Post*, Apr. 18, 1984.

3. David Ignatius, "Iran Stiffens Stance Toward West; U.S. Saw Increasing Role in Gulf as Simple Extension of Policy," *Washington Post*, Aug. 23, 1987.

4. Bob Woodward, *Veil: The Secret Wars of the CIA 1981-1987* (New York: Simon & Schuster, 1987), pp. 393-98.

5. Bob Woodward and Walter Pincus, "1984 Order Gave CIA Latitude, Reagan's Secret Move to Counter Terrorists Called 'License to Kill'," *Washington Post*, Oct. 5, 1988; and Bob Woodward and Charles Babcock, "Antiterrorist Plan Rescinded After Unauthorized Bombing," *Washington Post*, May 12, 1985; Joe Pichirallo and Edward Cody, "U.S. Trains Antiterrorists," *Washington Post*, Mar. 24, 1985; Nora Boustany, "Beirut Bomb's Legacy: Suspicion and Tears," *Washington Post*, Mar. 6, 1988.

6. For a popular account of clandestine operation with Veil-level classification, see Bob Woodward, *Veil, op. cit.*

7. President's Special Review Board, *The Tower Commission Report*, pp. 114-28, quote p. 116.

8. *Ibid.*

9. Several NSC members contend that many of George Bush's public statements on his role in this meeting and the subsequent Iran-Contra affair were fabrications. See Walter Pincus, "Shultz Memoirs Say Bush Misstated Arms-for-Hostages Role," *Washington Post*, Jan. 31, 1993; Walter Pincus, "Roots of Bush's Iran Credibility Gap; Weinberger Note is Latest Challenge to '87 Statements on Arms Sales," *Washington Post*, Nov. 2, 1992.

10. Ronald Reagan, "The Terrorist Menace: Speech to the American Bar Association," (July 8, 1985), WCPD, July 15, 1985, pp. 876-82; see also David Martin and John Walcott, *The Best Laid Plans* (New York: Harper & Row, 1988), pp. 161-202.

11. George Shultz, "Preemptive or Retaliatory Actions to Combat Terrorism" (July 17, 1985), Department of State *Bulletin*, Sept 1985, p. 36.

12. "Declaration of G Philip Hughes" (executive secretary of NSC), May 12, 1989, *Center for National Security Studies v. Immigration and Naturalization Service*, Civil Action 87-2068, U.S. District Court for the District of Columbia; see also Eve Pell, "Kicking Out Palesinians," *The Nation*, Feb.5, 1990, pp.167-68.

13. The "Rewards Program for Terrorism Information" established by this provision had paid out approximately $2 million in rewards as of summer 1992. Janice Castro, "The Terrorist Bounty Hunters," *Time*, Aug. 10, 1992, p. 11.

14. This appears to have been the Terrorist Incident Working Group. See NSDD -276, p.3.

15. Woodward, *Veil, op. cit.*, pp. 474-77; John Walcott and Gerald Seib, "New Signs That Libya is Plotting Terrorism Bring Quick Response," *Wall Street Journal*, Aug. 25, 1986, Woodward, "Gadhafi Target of Secret U.S. Deception Plan," *Washington Post*, Oct. 2, 1986; David Roffman, "President Says He Intends to Keep Gadhafi, 'Off Balance,'" *Washington Post*, Oct. 3, 1986; John Walcott, "U.S. Credibility on Libya is Damaged by White House Campaign of Deception," *Wall Street Journal*, Oct, 6, 1986

16. *Ibid.*; Eleanor Randolph, "In the Dog Days of August, the Media Missed the Hottest Story," *Washington Post*, Oct. 3, 1986.

17. Douglas Frantz and Murray Waas, "Bush Secret Effort Helped Iraq Build Its War Machine" (Feb. 23, 1992), "Bush Had Long History of Support for Iraq Aid" (Feb. 24, 1992), "U.S. Loans Indirectly Financed Iraq Military" (Feb. 25, 1992), all in *Los Angeles Times,* Alan Friedman, Lionel Barber, Tom Lannery and Eric Reguly, "CIA allowed illegal export of U.S. missile secrets," *Financial Times* (London), May 24, 1991. George Lardner and Benjamin Weiser, "Senate Committee to Air Allegations of Slanted Intelligence Under Gates" (Aug, 20, 1991), George Lardner, "White House Curbed Release of Data on Prewar Support of Iraq, Hill Told" (Mar. 17, 1992), George Lardner and R. Jeffrey Smith, "CIA Shared Data With Iraq Until Kuwait Invasion" (Apr. 28, 1992), R. Jeffrey Smith and John Goshko, "Ill-Fated Iraq Policy Originated Shortly After Bush Took Office" (June 27, 1992), John Goshko, "Before the Gulf War, Iraq Was a 'Sixth-Floor Problem' [at the State Department]" (July 7, 1992), R. Jeffrey Smith, "Pentagon Sought Exchange With Iraq," (Aug. 4, 1992), "Verbatim Ion NSDD 261" (Aug. 5, 1992), wire services, "86 Iraq-Iran Initiative by Bush Alleged" (Oct. 25, 1992), all in the *Washington Post.* On human rights issues: Middle East Watch, *Human Rights in Iraq* (New Haven, Conn.: Yale University Press, 1990).
18. Brent Scowcroft, "We Didn't 'Coddle' Saddam," *Washington Post,* Oct. 10, 1992.

Libya in U.S. Demonology

1. "Origins and Fundamental Causes of International Terrorism," UN Secretariat, reprinted in M. Cherif Bassiouni, ed., *International Terrorism and Political Crimes* (Springfield, Ill.: Charles Thomas, 1975).
2. William Beecher, *Boston Globe,* Apr. 15, 1986.
3. *Amnesty International Report,* 1985 (London, 1985); *Political Killings by Governments* (AI Report, London, 1983); Chris Krueger and Kjell Enge, *Security and Development Conditions in the Guatemalan Highlands* (Washington Office on Latin America, 1985); John Haiman and Anna Meigs, "Khaddafy: Man and Myth," *Africa Events,* February 1986; Allan Nairn, "The Guatemala Connection," *Progressive,* May 1986. References not given here and below can be found in my *Turning the Tide* (Boston: South End Press, 1985).
4. Edward S. Herman and Frank Brodhead, *Demonstration Elections* (Boston: South End Press. 1984). They define this concept to refer to a device of foreign intervention in which elections are "organized and staged by a foreign power primarily to pacify a restive home population," discussing several other examples as well and showing in detail that they are no less farcical than elections held under Soviet authority. Their term "demonstration elections" was borrowed and radically misused with reference to the election in Nicaragua by Robert Leiken *(New York Review of Books,* Dec. 5, 1985), as part of his campaign in support of the terrorist proxy army established by the United States to attack Nicaragua from its Honduran and Costa Rican bases. See Brodhead and Herman's letter, published after half a year's delay along with others by British parliamentary observers (June 26. 1986) and Leiken's response, tacitly conceding the accuracy of their critique (by evasion) while claiming that they designed their concept "as a way of focusing attention on Western imperialism while diverting it from Soviet imperialism... in line with their apparent belief that there is only one superpower villain." This is the standard reflex of propagandists whose deceit is exposed, in this case, requiring the suppression of Brodhead and Herman's harsh critique of elections in Poland along with much else. The remainder of Leiken's response and his articles themselves maintain a comparable level of integrity and merit careful reading for those interested in the workings of the U.S. ideological system.
5. Council on Hemispheric Affairs, *Washington Report on the Hemisphere,* Apr. 16, 1986.

6. See my *Towards a New Cold War* (New York: Pantheon, 1982), for references and discussion and for more on the topic, Edward S. Herman, *The Real Terror Network* (Boston: South End Press, 1982).

7. *Ibid.*

8. *Washington Post,* June 30, 1985; *Time,* Oct. 11, 1982; Goodman, *New York Times,* Feb. 7, 1984. For recent discussion of the astonishing record of Israeli terrorism and the Western response, or lack of it, see my papers "International Terrorism: Image and Reality," delivered at the Frankfurt conference on International Terrorism, April 1986 and "Middle East Terrorism," forthcoming in *Race & Class.*

9. See references in note 6. And see Warren Hinckle and William Turner, *The Fish is Red* (New York: Harper & Row, 1981).

10. Editorial, *New York Times,* Apr. 20, 1985; *Washington Post*, Jan. 11, 1986; Rabin, *Boston Globe,* Jan. 25, 1986; *El Pais* (Madrid), Apr. 25, 1986.

11. *New York Times,* June 27; Bob Woodward and Charles R. Babcock, *Washington Post*, May 12; Philip Shenon, *New York Times,* May 14, 1985, for CIA denial of involvement "disputed by some administration and congressional officials who said that the Agency was working with the group at the time of the bombing."

12. Kennedy's program was limited to the second and third plank of the Reagan agenda; the first, which was enthusiastically supported by congressional Democrats under Reagan and indeed had already been proposed by Carter, in direct violation of the will of the public, reflects the decline in relative U.S. power in the intervening years. It is no longer feasible to pursue "great societies at home and grand designs abroad," in the words of Kennedy adviser Walter Heller, so the former must be abandoned. On public attitudes, see *Turning the Tide,* chapter 5 and Thomas Ferguson and Joel Rogers, *Atlantic Monthly,* May 1986.

13. *Middle East International.* Apr. 4, 1986.

14. See P. Edward Haley, *Qaddafi and the U.S. Since 1969* (New York: Praeger, 1984), pp. 271 f.

15. Larry Speakes, national TV, "7:30 PM", Apr. 14; *New York Times,* Apr. 16; AP, Apr. 14; *New York Times,* Apr. 15; Lewis, *New York Times,* Apr. 17; Bernard Weinraub, *New York Times,* Apr. 15, 1986.

16. Haley, *op. cit.,* n. 14, pp. 8, 264.

17. *New Statesman,* Aug. 16, 1985

18. See my *Fateful Triangle* (Boston: South End Press, 1983), p. 210); Haley, *op. cit.,* n. 14, makes a praiseworthy effort to take the comedy seriously.

19. "The Central Intelligence Agency, barred from providing military aid to Nicaragua rebels, secretly funneled several million dollars to the rebels for political projects over the past year, U.S. Government officials say," also allowing "the CIA to maintain a strong influence over the rebel movement, even though a Congressional ban existed from October 1984 through September 1985, prohibiting the Agency from spending money 'which would have the effect of supporting, directly or indirectly, military or paramilitary operations in Nicaragua,' the officials said." One purpose of what U.S. officials described as "a major program" was to "create the aura that [the Contras] are an actual political entity among our allies in Europe." Congressman Sam Gejdenson stated that "We suspected that the CIA had never really withdrawn from the scene, but the extent of the Agency's direct involvement in the Contra war may astound even the most jaded observer." UNO documents obtained by the AP "show much of UNO's political money going to military organizations allied with the umbrella group" established by the United States, while some of the funds were used to pay off Honduran and Costa Rican officials "to enable

the rebels to operate in those countries." Much of the money was funneled through a Bahamas branch of a London bank. AP, Apr. 14; *Boston Globe,* Apr. 14, 1986. The disclosures passed without comment. Subsequently, the *Miami Herald* reported that over $2 million of the $27 million provided by Congress for "humanitarian assistance" was used to pay Honduran officers "to turn a blind eye to illegal Contra activities on Honduran soil" (editorial, *Boston Globe,* May 13, 1986).

20. AP, Mar. 27, citing *El Pais.*
21. Richard Higgins, *Boston Globe,* Mar. 25, 1986.
22. Fred Kaplan, *Boston Globe.* Mar. 26, 1986.
23. London *Sunday Times,* Apr. 6, 1986.
24. Cockburn, *Wall Street Journal,* Apr. 17; also *The Nation,* Apr. 26, 1986. Lelyveld, *New York Times,* Apr. 18, 1986.
25. *Ibid.*
26. AP, Apr. 14, 1986.
27. James M. Markham, *New York Times,* Apr. 25, 1986.
28. *Der Spiegel,* Apr. 21, 1986; the front cover features the phrase "Terror against Terror," a well-known Gestapo slogan, presumably not selected by accident. See also Norman Birnbaum's article, same issue.
29. Text of interview provided by a journalist for *Stars and Stripes* in Germany. The bombing may, in fact, have been the result of gang warfare involving nightclub ownership; other sources in Berlin raise the possibility that a neo-Nazi group or the Ku Klux Klan (which had verbally attacked the club) may have been involved.
30. *Toronto Globe & Mail,* editorials, Mar. 28, 18, 5, 1986, referring specifically to Nicaragua.
31. See AP, *International Herald Tribune,* May 6, for extensive discussion; *New York Times,* May 6, 1986, a briefer mention and the text of the statement.
32. AP, Apr. 14; survey of world press reaction, AP, Apr. 15; survey of U.S. editorial reaction, Apr. 16; editorial, *New York Times,* Apr. 15, 1986; Peres, *New York Times,* Apr. 16.
33. AP, Apr. 21; *New York Times,* Apr. 20; survey of religious reactions, AP, Apr. 17; also Apr. 19, reporting a news conference of 14 religious and community groups in Seattle condemning the bombing in contrast to support for it by the Western Washington Rabbinic Board; Nye, *Boston Globe,* Apr. 16; Rostow, *New York Times,* Apr. 27.
34. On the actual record, very different from the fabrications that dominate U.S. discussion, see *Fateful Triangle,* chapter 3. For a detailed account of Israel's rejectionism under the Labor Party in the crucial 1967-73 period, based on the internal record, see Yossi Beilin, *Mechiro shel Ichud* (Tel Aviv, 1985); as this and other sources demonstrate, the story goes back to the early days of the founding of the state.
35. *Ha'aretz,* June 25, 1982; see *Fateful Triangle,* pp. 200 ff., for further quotes and similar analyses by other Israeli commentators and for a review of the events leading up to the invasion.
36. *New Republic,* Jan. 20, 1986.
37. The first Libyan intervention followed the dispatch of French Foreign Legion forces, advisers and aircraft (Haley, *op. cit.,* n. 14, p. 98), but French intervention in Africa is legitimate, indeed laudatory; as *Business Week* exulted, French forces help "keep West Africa safe for French, American and other foreign oilmen" (Aug. 10, 1981) and perform similar services elsewhere.
38. Julia Preston, *Boston Globe,* Feb. 9, 1986.

Destabilizing Afghanistan

1. Declassified United States Defense Intelligence Agency Summary Report, Jan. 7, 1980.

2. Declassified United States Department of State Memo, Apr. 30, 1978.
3. *Ibid.*
4. Zbigniew Brzezinski, *Power and Principles: Memoirs of the National Security Council Adviser,* 1977-1981 (New York: Farrar Straus Giroux, 1983), p. 73.
5. *Ibid.,* p. 212.
6. See Bruce Amstutz, *Afghanistan: The First Five Years* (Washington, D.C.: National Defense University, 1986), p. 40.
7. Brzezinski, *op. cit.,* n. 4, p. 426.
8. *Ibid.*
9. Classified Department of State Report, Aug. 16, 1979. This document and many others were captured in the takeover of the U.S. Embassy in Teheran in 1979 and are still being published as part of a 60-plus volume set entitled "Documents from the Den of Espionage" (sometimes simply referred to as the "spynest documents"). Few of these sets are available in the United States as they were initially considered contraband by the U.S. Government and are now difficult to obtain because of the U.S. embargo on Iranian products. Herein referred to as *Spynest Documents.*
10. Classified Department of State cable, May 14, 1979, *Spynest Documents,* vol. 29, p. 99. This cable refers to a previous meeting with a rebel leader in Islamabad on Apr. 23, 1979.
11. *New York Times,* July 1, 1978; Amstutz, *op. cit.,* n. 9, p. 92.
12. *Spynest Documents* op cit., n. 9.
13. *Washington Post,* Jan. 5, 1980; United Kingdom Foreign and Commonwealth Office Background Briefs, "Afghanistan Opposition Groups," Aug. 1980, p. 3.
14. Classified CIA Field Report, Oct. 30, 1979, *Spynest Documents,* vol. 30, *op. cit.,* n. 9.
15. *Ibid.* During this meeting the Chinese officials requested that Pakistan halt the supply of Chinese-made weapons to the rebels while China was involved in sensitive negotiations with Moscow. The Chinese reemphasized to President Zia, however, the importance of continued Pakistani assistance for the rebels.
16. Classified CIA Field Report, Oct. 31, 1979, *Spynest Documents, op. cit.,* vol. 30.
17. Classified Department of State Report, Aug. 16, 1979. *Spynest Documents,* vol. 30, *op. cit.,* n. 9.
18. Classified CIA cable, August 31, 1979, *Spynest Documents,* vol. 30, *op. cit.,* n. 9.
19. Classified CIA cables, September 28, Oct. 2 and 3, 1979. *Spynest Documents,* vol. 30, *op. cit.,* n. 9.
20. Classified State Department cables, May 14 and Aug. 9, 1979, *Spynest Documents op. cit.,* n. 9, vol. 29; Selig Harrison, "The Soviet Union in Afghanistan," in *Containment: Concept and Policy* (Washington, D.C.: National Defense University, 1986), p. 464.
21. Classified State Department cable, Aug. 16, 1979, *Spynest Documents, op. cit.,* n. 9, vol. 30.
22. From a declassified cable cited in Raymond L. Garthoff, *Détente and Confrontation: American-Soviet Relations from Nixon to Reagan* (Washington, D.C.: Brookings Institution, 1985), p. 902.
23. Classified State Department cable, July 18, 1979, *Spynest Documents, op. cit.,* n. 9, vol. 29.
24. Classified State Department cable, June 25, 1979, *Spynest Documents, op. cit.,* n. 9, vol. 29.
25. Classified State Department cable, May 24, 1979, *Spynest Documents, op. cit., n.* 9, vol. 29.
26. Classified State Department cables, Sept. 11, Sept. 22, Sept. 23, two on Sept. 27 and Oct. 28, 1979, *Spynest Documents, op. cit.,* n. 9, vol. 30.
27. Classified State Department cable, Sept. 27, 1979, *Spynest Documents, op. cit.,* n. 9, vol. 30.
28. Classified State Department cable, Sept. 29, 1979, *Spynest Documents, op. cit.,* n. 9, vol. 30.
29. Classified State Department cable, Oct. 30, 1979, *Spynest Documents, op. cit.,* n. 9, vol. 30.
30. *Indian Express* Feb. 13, 1980.
31. *Ibid.*

The Afghan Pipeline

1. *Philadelphia Inquirer*, Feb. 28, 1988.
2. *Newsweek*, Mar. 23, 1987
3. United States Department of State Special Report, no. 112, Dec. 1983.
4. See James Carter, *Keeping Faith: Memoirs of a President* (Bantam: New York, 1982), pp. 473-75.
5. *Miami Herald*, June 5, 1983.
6. *Boston Globe*, Jan. 5, 1980; *Daily Telegraph* (London), Jan. 5, 1990.
7. *Wall Street Journal*, Apr. 19, 1994.
8. *Washington Post*, Feb. 2, 1979; *Maclean's* (Toronto), Apr. 30, 1979.
9. ABC News, "20/20," June 18, 1981.
10. Sam Bamieh told of this deal during his sworn testimony before the U.S. House Foreign Affairs committee in July 1987; also see, Bruce Amstutz, *Afghanistan: The First Five Years* (Washington, D.C.: National Defense University, 1986), p. 202; the information about the Omani and Pakistani bank accounts came from several confidential sources.
11. See Bamieh testimony, *ibid.*
12. *Baltimore Sun*, Apr. 4, 1982.
13. *Ibid.*
14. Richard Cronin, "Pakistan: U.S. Foreign Assistance Facts," Congressional Research Service, July 20, 1987, p. 2.
15. This inadequate accounting process was discovered in January 1986 when, at the request of Senators Humphrey (Rep.-N.H.) and Chic Hecht (Rep.-Nev.), a group of Senate intelligence staffers visited Pakistan (Confidential Source).
16. *Philadelphia Inquirer*. Feb. 29, 1988; *The Nation* (Pakistan), Jan. 8, 1987.
17. *Philadelphia Inquirer*, Feb. 29, 1988.
18. *Ibid.*
19. *Washington Post*, Sept. 25, 1981.
20. Classified State Department Cables, May 14 and Aug. 9, 1979, *Spynest Documents, op. cit.*, n. 9 (in previous article), vol. 29; Selig Harrison, *The Soviet Union in Afghanistan in Containment: Concept and Policy* (Washington, D.C.: National Defense University, 1986), p. 464
21. *New Republic*, July 18, 1981; *Daily Telegraph*, Jan. 5, 1980.
22. *Le Monde*, in Joint Publication and Research Service (JPRS) (U.S. Gov.), Oct. 9, 1981; *Chicago Tribune*, July 23, 1981.
23. *New York Times*; May 4, 1983; *Eight Days* (London), in JPRS, Oct. 31, 1981.
24. *Philadelphia Inquirer*, Mar. 1, 1988.
25. *New York Times*, July 24, 1982.
26. *New York Times*, May 4, 1983.
27. Richard Cronin, "Afghanistan: United Nations-Sponsored Negotiations," Congressional Research Service, July 23, 1986, p. 8.
28. *New York Times*, May 4, 1983.
29. *Christian Science Monitor*, May 10, 1983.
30. *Ibid.*
31. Some of the more radical fundamentalist groups have already succeeded in carrying out cross-border attacks against the Soviets and have vowed to continue (*Arab News*, April 6, 1987). For a more thorough discussion of the goals of the resistance see Olivier Roy, *Islam and the Afghan Resistance* (Cambridge: Cambridge University Press, 1986).
32. *Washington Post*, Mar. 30, 1983.

33. This news was leaked by the Soviets to the *United News of India,* cited in *Christian Science Monitor,* May 10, 1983.
34. *New York Times,* May 4, 1983.
35. *New York Times,* May 27, 1983.
36. *Washington Post,* Dec. 29, 1983.
37. *New York Times,* July 4, 1983.
38. *Washington Post,* Jan. 13, 1985.
39. Confidential source.
40. This was the Tsongas resolution which was finally passed on October 4, 1994.
41. *Washington Post,* Jan. 13, 1987.
42. *Afghan Update* (published by the Federation for American Afghan Action), July 13, 1985.
43. *Philadelphia Inquirer,* Feb. 29, 1988.
44. Confidential source who traveled with the resistance and showed the author photographs of explosives with the name of this company on them.
45. FBIS, May 14, 1985.
46. *New York Times,* June 19, 1986.
47. *Wall Street Journal,* Feb. 16, 1988.
48. Thames Television (London), "The Missile Trail" on "This Week", Sept. 17, 1987.
49. Rumor has it that Nigeria was the third country, but it could have been Chile who sold Blowpipes to the CIA for its operation in Nicaragua.
50. Joint Senate Congressional Hearings on the Iran-Contra Affair, May 20, 1987; Exhibit JKS-6. The proposed plan would allow the CIA to acquire Soviet-bloc weapons for the Afghan rebels, the Contras, UNITA and other "freedom fighters" without congressional appropriations or approval.
51. *The Wall Street Journal* on February 16, 1988 revealed that weapons for the rebels had been purchased from Poland. A confidential source informed the author that Stettin was the port they were being shipped out of.
52. *The Nation* (Pakistan), Jan. 8, 1987.
53. Jack Anderson in the *Washington Post,* May 12, 1987.
54. *Washington Post,* Jan. 13, 1987.
55. *Philadelphia Inquirer,* Feb. 28, 1988.
56. *The Nation* (Pakistan), Jan. 8, 1988.
57. Confidential source.
58. *Columbia Journalism Review* May/June, 1987; it is also worth noting that Maitre was a senior editor for CIA-connected Axel Springer Publishing Company in Germany. He also, for no apparent reason, has military clearance. After the bombing of Libya, Maitre was one of the people who debriefed the U.S. pilots.
59. Announced at USIA conference on Afghanistan in Washington, D.C., May 5, 1987.
60. *Los Angeles Times,* Jan. 13, 1988. *CBS* contract journalist Kurt Lohbeck also has strong ties to "Behind the Lines News Service," an operation set up by arch-conservatives Hugh Newton and Antony Campaigne.
61. *New York Times,* June 6, 1986.
62. *Philadelphia Inquirer,* Feb. 28, 1988.
63. *Ibid.*
64. McMahon was the focus of attacks by rebel supporters on the CIA's Afghan program (especially by the Federation for American Afghan Action which claimed responsibility for McMahon's eventual resignation). Also see Bob Woodward, *Veil: The Secret Wars of the CIA 1981-1997* (NY: Simon and Schuster, 1987).
65. FBIS, Mar. 18, 1986.

66. Warren Carroll, "The Freedom Fighter," (Heritage Foundation), cited in *Afghan Update*, May 27, 1986.
67. Confidential source.
68. *Washington Post*, Feb. 8, 1987.
69. *Strategic Investment Newsletter*, Mar. 9, 1987; *Philadelphia Inquirer*, Mar. 1, 1988.
70. *Independent* (London), Oct. 16, 1987.
71. *Philadelphia Inquirer*, Feb. 28, 1988.

III. TERRORIST WARS IN THE MIDDLE EAST

Israel State Terror

1. From the personal diary of Moshe Sharett discussed in Livia Rokach, *Israel's Sacred Terrorism*, 3rd ed. (Belmont, Mass.: AAUG Press, 1986), pp. 28-33.
2. *Ibid.*
3. See Benny Morris, *The Birth of the Palestinian Refugee Problem* (Cambridge and New York: Cambridge University Press, 1988); Tom Segev, *The First Israelis* (New York: The Free Press, 1986); Simhat Flapan, *The Birth of Israel, Myths and Realities* (New York: Pantheon Press, 1987).
4. Erskine Childers, "The Other Exodus," The Spectator (London) May 12, 1961. Reprinted in Walid Khalidi, ed., *From Haven to Conquest* (Washington, D.C.: Institute for Palestine Studies, 1987).
5. Segev, *op. cit. n.2*, p.6
6. Lenny Brenner, *The Iron Wall* (London: Zed Press, 1994).
7. Reprinted in Al-Hamishmar, Dec. 24, 1987. See Middle East Report, No. 152 (May-June 1982), p. 55.
8. Thomas Friedman, "Israel Turns Terror Back on the Terrorists, But Finds No Political Solution," *New York Times*, Dec. 4, 1994
9. Reagan's description in a *Washington Post* article of August 15, 1979. He has adhered to this view consistently ever since.
10. Address by George Shultz, Secretary of State, "Terrorism and the Modern World," Washington: Bureau of Public Affairs, Department of State (Current Policy No. 589), Oct. 25, 1984.
11. *New York Times*, Mar. 14, 1988.
12. Robert McFadden, *New York Times*, Mar. 5, 1988.
13. Former Likud Minister of Science Professor Yuva Neeman, Knesset member Haim Druckman and former Chief of Staff Bytan, amongst others, are on the record justifying Israeli acts of terrorism in the West Bank and Gaza as far back as 1983. See *Christian Science Monitor*, May 10, 1983.

Israel Wages Chemical Warfare With American Tear Gas

John Krofcheck, a Pittsburgh-based researcher, contributed to this article.

1. Database Project on Palestinian Human Rights, "*Intifada* Martyrs: The First Five Months" (Chicago: DPPHR, May 27, 1988). The figures on fetal deaths are approximate; according to the DPPHR (May 31, 1988), physicians had reported 80 fetal deaths in Gaza alone as of the end of February.
2. "We are very proud of how we behave," Maj. Gen. Mitzna told Ted Koppel on *Nightline*, Apr. 28, 1988.
3. The chemical name for CS is orthochlorobenzylidene malononitrile and the chemical formula is $ClC_6H_4CHC(CN)_2$.

4. Quickly, the skin, sinuses, nose and throat feel as if they are on fire and rapid sneezing and coughing begin. From the respiratory system the gas permeates blood cells, fatty tissues and mucous membranes. Hyperactive, disoriented behavior is induced. Soft tissues are damaged and bronchial constriction leads to vomiting of blood, while gasping for air. The condition can escalate to violent spasms and convulsions and, in many cases, death.

5. As of May 27, according to data compiled by the Database Project on Palestinian Human Rights, the 50 confirmed tear gas-related deaths break down as follows: 20 infants one week to one year, five between one and 21 years, 12 between 22 and 59 years and 13 from 60 to 90 years. Thirty-two were males, 18 were females; 24, or nearly half, were living in refugee camps.

6. *Los Angeles Times*, May 10, 1988. "We want some breathing room," vice-president Burl Alison told the AP, not realizing the irony in her words. AP, May 6, 1988.

7. Forty-six percent in 1984; 50 percent in 1985; 49 percent in 1986; and 32 percent in 1987.

8. Congressional testimony, Mar. 23, 1965.

9. *Environmental and Molecular Mutagenesis*, Vol. 11, No. 1 (1988), pp. 91-118.

Israel-South African Collaboration

1. Benjamin Beit-Hallahmi, "Israel's Global Ambitions," *New York Times*, Jan. 6, 1983.

2. Quoted in Jack Colhoun, "South Africa buoyed by Israeli support," *Guardian Supplement*, Spring 1986.

3. James Adams, *The Unnatural Alliance: Israel and South Africa* (London, Quartet Books, 1984), p. 19.

4. Jane Hunter, *Undercutting Sanctions: Israel, the U.S. and South Africa* (Washington: Washington Middle East Associates, 1986), p. 32.

5. Aaron Klieman, *Israel's Global Reach: Arms Sales as Diplomacy* (Washington: Pergamon-Brassey's, 1985), p. 139.

6. Adams, *op. cit.* n. 3, p. 20.

7. John Mahoney in "The Link," Mar. 1986, newsletter of Americans for Middle East Understanding.

8. Hunter, *op. cit.* n. 4, p. 34. See also *New York Times*, Mar. 5, 1985.

9. *Ibid.*, pp. 34-35.

10. Steve Goldfield, *Garrison State: Israel's Role in U.S. Global Strategy* (San Francisco: Palestine Focus Publications, 1985), p. 26.

11. *Ibid.*, p. 27.

12. Hunter, *op. cit.* n. 4, p. 27.

13. Adams, *op. cit.* n. 3, p. 85.

14. *Ibid.*, p. 93; Goldfield, *op. cit.* n. 10, pp. 28,30.

15. Hunter, *op. cit.* n. 4, p. 28.

16. *Ibid.*

17. Adams, *op. cit.* n. 3, p. 170.

18. *Ibid.*, p. 182; Hunter *op. cit.* n. 4, pp. 15-16.

19. Quoted in Hunter, *op. cit.* n. 4, p. 17. See also Jack Colhoun, "Little doubt U.S. helped build an 'apartheid bomb'," *Guardian*, Feb. 16, 1983. And see, Barbara Rogers, "South Africa Gets Nuclear Weapons — Thanks to the West," in Ray, *et al.*, eds., *Dirty Work 2: The CIA in Africa* (Secaucus, N.J.: Lyle Stuart, 1979), p. 276.

20. Adams, *op. cit.* n. 3, pp. 38-71. And see, Michael Klare, "Arms for Apartheid," in Ray, *op. cit.* n. 19, p. 258.

21. Hunter, *op. cit.* n. 4, p. 24.

22. *Ibid.*, p. 44.
23. Quoted in Israel Shahak, *Israel's Global Role: Weapons for Repression* (Belmont, Mass.: Association of Arab-American University Graduates, 1982), p. 29.
24. *Ibid.*, p. 28.
25. Hunter, *op. cit.* n. 4, p. 51.

Disinformationgate

1. North worked with the Delta Force, which was involved, disastrously, in the early hours of the invasion of Grenada.
2. See, e.g., the *Washington Times* of Aug. 9, 1984.
3. *New York Times*, Dec. 11, 1987. The significance of the Israeli role was finally broached in the *Times* on Feb. 1, 1987, p. 1.
4. According to the *Los Angeles Times* (Dec. 28, 1986), in January 1985, "Kimche approaches McFarlane with a list of hundreds of Iranian 'moderates' and encourages the United States to open a dialogue with the Iranians." And according to the *Miami Herald* (Dec. 7, 1986), Kimche, "the prime mover of Israel's policy of secretly selling arms to Iran, tried as early as 1981 to get the United States to trade arms with Iranian moderates." Ledeen has been deeply embroiled in Iranian politics for some time and not, as it would seem, on the side of the "moderates." According to Diana Johnstone's recent (Jan. 21, 1987) *In These Times* interview with Abol Hassan Bani Sadr, former president of Iran, Ledeen, who accompanied McFarlane and North on his May 1986 trip, "is known in Iran as the man who sold out Sadiq Ghotbzadeh to Khomenei." In 1982, Ghotbzadeh, then foreign minister, was apparently involved in a plot to replace Khomeini and sent word only for the United States not to intervene. But Ledeen advised the U.S. Government that Khomenei was anti-Soviet, which was good enough for the United States; it therefore opposed any move against him. Two months later, Ghotbzadeh was arrested and executed.
5. See *CAIB*, Number 22 (Fall 1984), p. 5; and Number 23 (Spring 1985), pp. 16-17, 26, 31-33.
6. *Wall Street Journal*, July 26, 1979.
7. See *Los Angeles Times*, Dec. 14, 1981; and *CAIB*, Number 16 (Mar. 1982), p. 25.
8. Israel has the largest stockpile of U.S. weapons outside of the United States and as a result of the invasion of Lebanon and other actions a huge stockpile of Soviet weapons. Israel itself is a major arms manufacturer and exporter, especially to countries such as Iran, South Africa, Taiwan and Chile. Since Israel's military security is dependent on having the very latest weapons, there is a constant need to sell obsolete U. S. and Soviet weapons. Israel must devote sums for research and development closer to the budget of a superpower, out of all proportion to a country of 4.5 million. One way of paying is by selling 70 percent of Israeli manufactured weapons abroad.

Deltagate

1. *U.S. News and World Report*, Jan. 6, 1986, pp. 60-61; *Time*, Dec. 2, 1985, p.41.
2. *U.S. News and World Report*, Jan. 6, 1986, pp. 60-61.
3. AP, Sept. 19, 1985.
4. See the excellent article by Mark Perry, "The ISA Behind the NSC," *The Nation*, Jan. 17, 1987.
5. AP, Nov. 29, 1986.
6. See especially Phillip Keisling, "Desert One: The Wrong Man and the Wrong Plan," *Washington Monthly*, Dec. 1983, p.51; and cf., Murray Kempton, "The Good Soldier," *New York Review of Books*, Dec. 22, 1983.

Out of the Loop

1. Joel Brinkley, "Bush's Role in Iran Affair. Questions and Answers," *New York Times*, Jan. 29,1988.
2. For more on Harari and the Harari Network, see *Israeli Foreign Affairs*, May 1987 and Feb., Mar., Apr., May and June 1988.
3. Andrew Cockburn, "A friend in need," *Independent*, Mar. 19,1988.
4. Uri Dan, "Israeli is Power Behind Noriega," *New York Post*, July 11, 1988.
5. Stewart M. Powell and John P. Wallach, "Israeli Working For Noriega," *San Francisco Examiner*, Oct. 22, 1989.
6. Hearings of the Narcotics, Terrorism and International Operations Subcommittee of the Senate Foreign Relations Committee, Apr. 4,1988.
7. Transcript, ABC News, Apr. 7,1988.
8. Jim Redden, "Burning Bush," *Willamette Week* (Portland, OR), July 14-20, 1988; United Press International (UPI), May 15, 1988; Robert Parry and Rod Nordland, "Guns for Drugs?" *Newsweek*, May 23,1988.
9. ABC News interview, May 28,1988.
10. UPI, May 15,1988.
11. Interview with Brenneke, *Israeli Foreign Affairs*, June 1988.
12. *Newsweek*, May 23,1988.
13. "Arms, Drugs and the Contras," a *Frontline* television documentary aired on U.S. Public Television stations in May 1988, also identified Rodríguez as the contact.
14. Parry and Nordland, *op. cit.*, n. 8.
15. Steven Emerson, *Secret Warriors* (New York: G. P. Putnam's Sons, 1988), p. 129.
16. *Ibid*, pp. 125-26.
17. Doyle McManus, "Senate Panel to Probe Iran-Contra Papers," *Los Angeles Times*, Apr. 27, 1989.
18. Sara Fritz, "Hamilton Prods Bush on 2 Papers," *Los Angeles Times*, Apr. 15,1989.
19. Doyle McManus, "Details Surface of U.S. Deal to Aid Contras," Los *Angeles* Times, Apr. 16,1989; "Iran-Contra Prober Doubts Bush's Denials," UPI, *San Francisco Chronicle*, May 8, 1989.
20. Select Committee on Intelligence, United States Senate, "Were Relevant Documents Withheld from the Congressional Committees Investigating the Iran-Contra Affair?" June 1989 (Doc. No. 199-533-89-1), p. 7.
21. Stephen Engelberg, "'No Quid Pro Quo' President Insists," *New York Times*, May 5, 1989.
22. Council on Hemispheric Affairs, "Bush, Gregg, Negroponte: Was There a Quid Pro Quo Deal?" Press release, May 16, 1989.
23. Government submission to U.S. District Court for the District of Columbia, Apr. 6, 1989, Criminal No. 88-0080-02-GAG, pp. 31-2.
24. Gregg's testimony before the Senate Foreign Relations Committee, June 15, 1989.
25. Robert Parry, "Bush's Envoy on the Grill," *Newsweek*, May 29, 1989.
26. Robert Pear, "Bush Nominee Is Quizzed Over Illicit Contra Aid," *New York Times*, May 13, 1989.
27. Joseph Mianowany, "Former Bush aide tries to explain Iran-Contra role," UPI, May 13, 1989.
28. Emerson, *op. cit.*, n. 15, pp. 124-26.
29. "'Black Hole,'" *Newsweek*, Apr. 24, 1989.
30. Lee May, "Panel Probes Ex-Bush Aide on Contra Supply Scheme," *Los Angeles Times*, May 13, 1989.
31. Gregg's testimony before the Senate Foreign Relations Committee, June 15,1989.

32. Joseph Pichirallo and Walter Pincus, "Gregg: Kept Bush in Dark About North Role; Senators Greet Ex-Aides' Contra Testimony with Skepticism," *Washington Post*, May 13, 1989.

33. Mary McGrory, "The Truth According to Gregg," *Washington Post*, June 22, 1989.

34. Walter Pincus, "State Dept. Budget, 4 Nominations Advance; Iran-Contra Questions Delayed 1 Appointee," *Washington Post*, June 9, 1989.

35. McGrory, *op. cit.*, n. 38.

What Vice-President Bush Knew and Why He Knew It

1. Frank Snepp and Jonathan King, "George Bush: Spymaster General," *Penthouse*, Jan. 1991.

2. A good general synopsis of Bush's involvement can be found in Snepp and King, *op. cit.*; Howard Kahn and Vicki Monks, "The Dirty Secrets of George Bush," *Rolling Stone*, Nov. 3, 1988, pp. 42-50, 120; Scott Armstrong and Jeff Nason, "Company Man," *Mother Jones*, Oct. 1988, p. 47; Tom Blanton, "Where George Was," *Washington Post*, June 10,1990, p. C1; and George Lardner and Walter Pincus, "Notebook Reveals North-Bush Meeting," *Washington Post*, May 9,1990, p. A1.

3. Anthony L. Kimery, "In the Company of Friends," *CAIB*, No. 41 (Spring 1992), pp. 60-66.

4. Author's interviews with Reagan Administration officials in policy-level positions and congressional officials who dealt with policy issues, 1990-91.

5. Snepp and King, *op. cit.*

6. *Ibid.*

7. White House, National Security Council, State Department and other documents declassified for the Iran-Contra investigation and for the trials of Oliver North and John Poindexter. The Israeli deal was a 1985 swap for hostages in Lebanon that was first broached to the Reagan Administration by Theodore George "Ted" Shackley. A legendary former ranking CIA official with whom Bush is well acquainted, Shackley was the architect of the privatized "off the shelf" methods for arming U.S.-supported counterinsurgency forces. (Kimery, *op cit.*, pp. 65-66.)

8. George Lardner and Walter Pincus, "Phone Note Puts Bush Claim on Iran-Contra Into Dispute," *Washington Post*, Aug. 26, 1992, pp. A1, 28.

9. Snepp and King, *op. cit.*; Kohn and Monks, *op. cit.*; and from an overview of numerous books containing relevant information about Iran-Contra: The National Security Archive, *The Chronology: The Documented Day-by-Day Account of the Secret Military Assistance to Iran and the Contras* (New York: Warner Books, 1987).

10. Knut Royce and Miguel Acoca, "Contra Plane Linked to Bush," *San Francisco Examiner*, Oct. 10, 1986, back page.

11. Testimony of Félix Rodríguez, May 27,1987, Iran-Contra hearings; Cable from Gen. Paul Gorman to Ambassador Thomas Pickering and Gen. James Steele, Feb. 8, 1985, *Iran-Contra Affair*, Appendix B, Vol. 12, pp. 941-42; Ben Cramer, "Did He Know?", *Washington Post Magazine*, Aug. 6,1992, pp. 29-31; *Washington's War on Nicaragua* (Boston: South End Press, 1988), p. 343.

12. White House, CIA and National Security Council documents declassified for congressional investigation of Iran-Contra and for the trial of former CIA deputy director for operations, Clair George.

13. Doyle McManus, "Elaborate System Supplies Contras," *Los Angeles Times*, Oct. 9, 1986, p. 1.

14. Ben Bradlee, Jr., *Guts and Glory: The Rise and Fall of Oliver North*. (New York: Donald Fine, 1988), p. 446; and McManus, *op. cit.*

15. George Lardner and Walter Pincus, "Iran-Contra Prosecutors Concentrate on a Former CIA Task Force Chief," *Washington Post,* July 7, 1991, p. A4; George Lardner and Walter Pincus, "Ex-CIA Aide Admits Iran-Contra Role," *Washington Post,* July 10, 1991, p. Al.

16. Walter Pincus, "Witness Weeps About Scandal's Impact on CIA Career," *Washington Post,* July 30, 1992, p. A3.

17. George Lardner and Walter Pincus, "CIA Ex-Official Testifies He Told George Of Aid", *Washington Post,* July 29, 1992, p. A8.

18. *Ibid.*; declassified National Security Council documents; and notebooks of Oliver North, available from National Security Archive, Washington, D.C.

19. National Security Council documents declassified for the congressional investigation of Iran-Contra; notebooks of Oliver North; David Johnson, "North's Notes Show He Met Bush Soon After Lying to Congress in '86," *New York Times*, May 9, 1990, p. A14; Tom Blanton, *op. cit.*

20. George Lardner and Walter Pincus, "Ex-Aide Says CIA Delayed Correcting Hill Testimony," *Washington Post,* Aug. 8, 1992, p. Al0.

21. "Bush Ex-Aide Testifies at Contra Probe," (AP), *Washington Post,* Aug. 10, 1990.

22. Walter Pincus and George Lardner, "Covert CIA Operation Via Church Outlined," *Washington Post,* Aug. 1, 1992, p. A4.

23. James LeMoyne, "Testimony That Bush Was Told in 1986 of Contra Supply Scheme," *New York Times,* July 30, 1990.

24. Deposition by Robert Dutton, May 4, 1987.

25. "Bush Ex-Aide Testifies at the Contra Probe," *Washington Post*, Aug. 10, 1990; and Jim McGee and James Savage, "Bush Sent Doctor to North Network," *Miami Herald,* Mar. 15, 1987, pp. Al, 14.

26. Author's interview with former senior CIA official who worked under Twetten; George Lardner and Walter Pincus, "CIA Deputy Director Linked to Iran Arms, Testimony Shows," *Washington Post,* Oct. 10, 1991, p. A21; and Michael Wines, "After 30 Years in Shadows, a Spymaster Emerges," *New York Times,* Nov. 20, 1990, p. A18.

27. Author's interview with former senior CIA official who worked under Twetten; and George Lardner and Walter Pincus, "Senate Panel Questions Gates's CIA Ex-Associates," *Washington Post,* July 15, 1991, p. A4.

28. Twetten's 1987 testimony to congressional Iran-Contra committees, Tower Commission; Lardner and Pincus, "CIA Deputy Director...," *op. cit.*; and Walter Pincus, "Senate Role in More CIA Postings Urged," *Washington Post,* Oct. 11, 1991, p. A21.

29. Author's interview with former CIA officer who worked under Twetten, 1989; classified CIA information obtained by author in 1990.

30. Classified CIA information provided to author, 1989.

31. Author's interview with former CIA officer who worked under Twetten, 1989.

32. George Lardner and Walter Pincus, "Ex-Aide Says CIA Delayed Correcting Hill Testimony," Aug. 4, 1992, p. A10.

33. Walter Pincus, "Fernandez Iran-Contra Case Dismissed," *Washington Post,* Nov. 25, 1989, p. A12.

34. *Ibid.*; Joe Pichirallo, "Court Halts Iran-Contra Trial of Ex-CIA Official," *Washington Post,* July 25, 1989, p. A10.

35. Author's interviews with former senior CIA officials and sources close to Walsh's investigation, 1989; Joe Pichirallo, "Walsh Asks to Open Hearing on Secrets," *Washington Post,* Aug. 11, 1989.

36. Author's interviews with former senior CIA officials, 1989; *Costa Rican Prosecutor's Office Report on the La Penca Bombing,* San José, Costa Rica, Dec. 26, 1989; and Walter Pincus and

Joe Pichirallo, "Trial Could Expose CIA's Knowledge of Contra Resupply," *Washington Post*, Nov. 23, 1989, p. A12.

37. Author's interview with former senior CIA officials, 1990-91.

38. Formerly Top Secret memo to Secretaries of State, Treasury and Defense, Director of Central Intelligence and chair of Joint Chiefs of Staff, from William P. Clark, Reagan's national security adviser, May 14, 1982.

39. Formerly secret NSC memo from Constantine Menges to Robert McFarlane July 11, 1984; and Walter Pincus and Joe Pichirallo, "North Questions Embroil Foreign Aid," *Washington Post*, May 4, 1989, pp. Al, A8.

40. Author's interview, 1990.

Vice-President Bush

1. Associated Press, Dec. 4, 1986.

2. *Men of Zeal* (New York: Viking Press, 1988).

3. National Security Decision Directive #3, Dec. 14, 1981.

4. Robert McFarlane, *et al.*, "The National Security Council: Organization for Policy Making," *Proceedings*, Center for the Study of the Presidency, 1984.

5. New York: Doubleday, 1987, p. 241.

The Family that Preys Together

1. Toni Mack, "Fuel for Fantasy," *Forbes*, Sept. 3, 1990; for the Harken deal with Bahrain, see also Jack Colhoun, "Ex-Bush Aide Turns to Stumping for Kuwait... While Jr. Reaps Oil Windfall," (New York) *Guardian*, Dec. 12, 1990 and Jack Colhoun, "Bush Brood's Bargains With BCCI," (New York) *Guardian*, May 13, 1992.

2. Stephen Hedges, "The Color of Money — The President's Eldest Son and his Ties to a Troubled Texas Firm," *U.S. News & World Report*, Mar. 16, 1992.

3. *Ibid.*; and Jonathan Beaty and S.G. Gwynne, "A Mysterious Mover of Money and Planes," *Time*, Oct. 28, 1991.

4. Thomas Petzinger, Jr., Peter Truell and Jill Abramson, "How Oil Firm Linked to a Son of Bush Won Bahrain Drilling Pact," *Wall Street Journal*, Dec. 6, 1991.

5. *Ibid.*

6. *Ibid.*

7. David Armstrong, "Oil in the Family: George W. Bush and His Slippery Friends," *The Texas Observer*, July 12, 1991; *Wall Street Journal*, Dec. 6, 1991; and *Time*, Oct. 28, 1991.

8. Petzinger, *op. cit.*; see also Kurt Abraham, "Harken Energy Enters Bahrain," *World Oil*, Apr. 1990.

9. Petzinger, *op. cit.* and Armstrong, *op. cit.*

10. *U.S. News & World Report*, Mar. 16, 1992; Keith Bradsher, "Article Questions Sale of Stock by Bush Son," *New York Times*, Mar. 9, 1992.

11. Hedges, *op. cit.*

12. "Bush's Son Misses Deadline For Reporting 'Internal Sale'," *Wall Street Journal*, Apr. 4, 1991.

13. Petzinger, *op. cit.*; and Beaty, *op. cit.*

14. Beaty, *op. cit.*

15. *Texas Observer*, July 12, 1991; Jonathan Kwitny, *The Crimes of Patriots: A True Tale of Dope, Dirty Money and the CIA* (New York: W. W. Norton), pp. 36-7, 126-42, 358.

16. Petzinger, *op. cit.*

17. Margaret Shapiro, "Bush Brother Does Business in Asia Before President's Trip," *Washington Post*, Feb. 15, 1989.

18. Douglas Frantz and Jim Mann, "Bush's Brother Linked to Firm in Panama Deal," *Los Angeles Times*, Dec. 30,1999; Adi Ignatius, "Well Connected Americans Return to China," *Asian Wall Street Journal*, Sept. 18,1989; Masayoshi Kanabayashi and Jill Abramson, "Bush Kin, Japanese Gangster May Be Linked," *Asian Wall Street Journal*, June 10, 1991; and Kyodo News Service, May 13, 1988.

19. *Asian Wall Street Journal*, Sept. 18,1989; *Los Angeles Times* Dec. 30,1989; and Peter Gosselin and Stephen Kurkjian, "Bush Ties Scrutinized in Brother's Ventures," *Boston Globe*, Feb. 4, 1990.

20. Jim Mann and Douglas Frantz, "Firm That Employs Bush's Brother Stands to Benefit from China Deal," *Los Angeles Times*, Dec. 13, 1989; and Milton Mueller, "Don't Sanction China's Satellite," *Wall Street Journal*, Nov. 24, 1989.

21. David Hoffman and Ann Devroy, "Bush Rejects New Sanctions For China, Clears Satellites," *Washington Post*, Dec. 20, 1989; Andrew Rosenthal, "President Waives Some China Curbs," *New York Times*, Dec. 20, 1989; George Lardner, Jr., "U.S. Began Lifting Business, Military Sanctions on China Months Ago," *Washington Post*, Dec. 12, 1989; and John Burgess, "Bush Act Heats Up Feud in U.S. Space Industry," *Washington Post*, Dec. 21, 1999.

22. Jack Colhoun, "Prescott Bush and the Gangsters," *Lies Of Our Times*, Apr. 1992; and Robert J. McCartney, "Japanese Company Sues Bush Brother," *Washington Post*, June 16, 1992, p. C1.

23. "Bush's Brother Dealt With Japanese Underworld Boss," Kyodo News Service, June 7, 1991; Leslie Helm, "Bush Brother Was a Consultant to Company Under Scrutiny in Japan," *Los Angeles Times*, June 11, 1991; Kathleen Day and Paul Bluestein, "Bush Brother Said to Aid Firm Ties to Japan Mob," *Washington Post*, June 11, 1991; and Yumiko Ono and Clay Chandler, "Mobster's Death Robs Authorities of Key Witness in Japan Scandals," *Wall Street Journal*, Sept. 6, 1991.

24. Gary Sick, *October Surprise: America's Hostages in Iran and the Election of Ronald Reagan* (New York: Times Books, 1991), pp. 23-24, 26-28, 33-36, 137, 170; see also Jack Colhoun, "Hostages Push Probe of 'October Surprise'," (New York) *Guardian*, June 26, 1991.

25. Joanne Omang, "14 Million in Medical Aid Funneled to Central America," *Washington Post*, Dec. 27, 1984; Holly Sklar, *Washington's War on Nicaragua* (Boston: South End Press,1988), pp. 239-41; and Russ W. Baker, "A Thousand Points of Light: Americares, George Bush's Favorite Charity Dispenses Bitter Medicine Around the World," *Village Voice*, Jan. 8, 1991.

26. John Spicer Nichols, "La Prensa: The CIA Connection," *Columbia Journalism Review*, July-Aug, 1988.

27. George Bush's March 3 1985 letter to Castejón is reprinted in Jim McGee and James Savage, "Bush Sent Doctor to North Network," *Miami Herald*, Mar. 15,1987. Other material on Castejón is also drawn from this article.

28. *Ibid.*; see also Peter Kilborn, "Bush Referred Guatemalan to North on Contra Aid," *New York Times*, Mar. 16, 1987.

29. Carl Cannon, "Democrats Question Bush Family Deals," *Miami Herald*, Apr. 26, 1992; and Sydney Freedberg, "Paid to Treat Elderly, IMC Moved in World of Spying and Politics," *Wall Street Journal*, Aug. 9, 1988.

30. Freedberg, *op. cit.*; and Jefferson Morley, "See No Evil," *Spin Magazine*, Mar. 1991.

31. Basulto and Rodríguez — who was linked to Bush and Oliver North's Contra arms network — have been comrades-in-arms since their days in the CIA, Brigade 2506 and the clandestine U.S. war against Cuba. (Felix I. Rodríguez and John Weisman, *Shadow Warrior: The CIA Hero of a Hundred Unknown Battles* (New York: Simon and Schuster, 1989), pp. 109-11.)

32. Freedberg, *op. cit.*; and Morley, *op. cit.*

33. Freedberg, *op. cit.*

34. *Ibid*; for Trafficante's role in the CIA's assassination plots against Fidel Castro, see Arthur Schlesinger, Jr., *Robert Kennedy and His Times* (Boston: Houghton Mifflin, 1978), pp. 482-84; and Warren Hinckle and William Turner, *The Fish Is Red: The Story of the Secret War Against Castro* (New York: Harper & Row, 1981), p. 315.

35. The section on Leonel Martinez is based on Morley, *op. cit.*

36. See Joe Conason and John Kelly, "Bush As 'Drug Czar'," *Village Voice*, Oct. 11, 1988.

37. Deposition of Aziz Rehman, October 24, 1988, included in "Drugs, Law Enforcement and Foreign Policy: The Cartel, Haiti and Central America," Part 4, Hearings before the Subcommittee on Terrorism, Narcotics and International Operations, pp. 630, 644.

38. *Wall Street Journal*, Dec. 6, 1991.

39. BCCI: Latin America and Caribbean Regional Office, memorandum, Sept. 11, 1987, from Mr. A- Awan, subject: Chinese Delegation Breakfast.

40. Jeff Gerth, "A Savings and Loan Bailout and Bush's Son Jeb," *New York Times*, Oct. 14, 1990; and Sharon LaFraniere, "S and L Bailout Involved Jeb Bush Partnership," *Washington Post*, Oct. 15, 1990.

41. Julia Preston and Joe Pichirallo, "Bay of Pigs Survivors Find Common Cause With Contras," *Washington Post*, Oct. 26, 1986.

42. Jack Colhoun, "U.S. Rattles Electronic Sabre At Cuba," (New York) *Guardian*, June 27,1990.

43. Mike McQueen, "U.S. Says Bosch Has Longtime Ties to Terror Groups," *Miami Herald*, July 18, 1990; James LeMoyne, "Cuban Linked to Terror Bombings Is Freed by Government in Miami," *New York Times*, July 18, 1990; and Jack Colhoun, "Plane-Bombing Pair Tied to Bush and Heir," (New York) *Guardian*, May 20, 1992.

44. Neil Bush quoted in Steven Wilmsen, *Silverado: Neil Bush and the Savings and Loan Scandal* (Washington, D.C.: National Press Books, 1991), P. 195.

45. Office of Thrift Supervision, "Notice of Intent to Prohibit and Notice of Hearing: In The Matter of Michael Wise, James Metz, Neil Bush and Russell Murray," Jan. 1990; Stephen Pizzo, "The First Family," *Mother Jones*, March/ April 1992; and Jack Colhoun, "Bush Son Weds Mob, CIA At Silverado S&L," (New York) *Guardian*, July 4, 1990.

46. Robert Rosenblatt, "Bush's Son Defends Role at S&L, Explains Loan Ties," *Los Angeles Times*, May 24,1990.

47. Pizzo, *op. cit.*

48. Neil Bush quoted in Wilmsen, *op. cit.*, p. 70.

49. *Ibid.*

50. Pete Brewton, "The Suspicious Trail of Denver S&L Failure," *Houston Post*, Mar. 11, 1990; David Armstrong, "The Great S&L Robbery: Spookmaster Pete Brewton Tells All," *Texas Observer*, Apr. 5, 1991; and Rebecca Sims, "The CIA and Financial Institutions," *CAIB* Number 35 (Fall 1990), p. 48.

51. Pizzo, *op. cit.*; and Michael Selz, "Ken Good: What Me Worry?", *Florida Trend*, Jan. 1989.

52. Pete Brewton, "S&L Probe has Possible CIA Links," *Houston Post*, Feb. 4, 1990, p. 1.

53. Armstrong, "S&L Robbery," *op. cit.*; for Castle Bank, see Kwitny, *Crimes of Patriots: A True Tale of Dope, Dirty Money and the CIA*, pp. 46, 294-95; and "S.E.C. and I.R.S. Knuckle Under to C.I.A. Pressures," *CAIB* Number 9 (June 1980), p. 28.

54. Brewton, "Suspicious Trail," *op. cit.*; and Armstrong, "S&L Robbery," *op. cit.*

55. Stephen Pizzo, Mary Fricker and Paul Muolo, *Inside Job: The Looting of America's Savings and Loans* (New York: McGraw-Hill, 1989), p. 304.

56. Jack Colhoun, "Contra Backer Dipped Into S&L's Deep Pockets," (New York) *Guardian*, Oct. 31, 1990.

Trading with the Enemy

1. John Robson, Deputy Secretary of the Treasury, statement, Apr. 1, 1991.
2. Statement on the floor of the House of Representatives, Feb. 4, 1991.
3. Jack Colhoun, "Congress Irked as Iraq Reveals U.S. 'Kid Gloves'," *Guardian*, Oct. 3, 1990.
4. Dennis Kloske, statement, hearings before the Subcommittee on International Economic Policy and Trade of the House Committee on Foreign Affairs, Apr. 8, 1991.
5. Stephen Bryen, testimony, hearings before the House Banking Committee, Apr. 9, 1991.
6. Don Oberdorfer, "Missed Signals in the Middle East," *Washington Post Magazine*, Mar. 17, 1991.
7. Marshall Wiley, interview with author, Apr. 9, 1991.
8. Marshall Wiley, statement, hearings before the House Banking Committee, Apr. 9, 1991.
9. Marshall Wiley, statement, April 9; see also Joe Conason, "The Iraq Lobby," *New Republic*, Oct. 1, 1990; Murray Waas, "What We Gave Saddam for Christmas," *Village Voice*, Dec. 18, 1990, *Los Angeles Times*, Feb. 13, 1991; and *Wall Street Journal*, Dec. 7, 1990.
10. *Financial Times*, Feb. 21, 1991.
11. *Ibid.*
12. "Background on the BNL Loans to Iraq," House Banking Committee report, distributed at Apr. 9, 1991 hearing.
13. A House Banking Committee report cited Matrix-Churchill as an example of how the Iraq arms network functioned: "Upon gaining control of... Matrix-Churchill, a procurement division was established within the company. The procurement side of the company received its orders, mostly in Arabic, directly from Baghdad. It was apparently charged with finding other U.S. companies that would build industrial plants in Iraq. Matrix-Churchill would help find U.S. contractors to build a fiberglass plant and [a] sophisticated cutting tool plant in Iraq. The tool plant may have been used to manufacture parts with nuclear applications, while reports link the fiberglass plant with the production of missiles." (Staff Report, "The Role of Banca Nazionale Del Lavoro in Financing Iraq," House Banking Committee, Feb. 1991.)
14. "Background on the BNL Loans to Iraq," *op. cit.*
15. *Ibid.*
16. Quoted in Lionel Barber and Alan Friedman, "A Fatal Attraction: Arms to Iraq," *Financial Times*, May 3, 1991.
17. Rep. Henry González (D-Tex.), chair of the House Banking Committee, in a statement on the floor of the House of Representatives, Feb. 4, 1991; see also Jack Colhoun, "Secret U.S. Arms Network Built Iraqi Arsenal," *Guardian*, Mar. 20, 1991 and Jack Colhoun, "U.S.-Iraq Scandal: Will Victory Flag Cover Bush?", *Guardian*, Mar. 27, 1991.
18. "Foreign Economic Trends and Their Implications for the United States," Department of Commerce, International Trade Administration, Sept. 1989.
19. "Approved Licenses to Iraq," Mar. 11, 1991, Department of Commerce, Bureau of Export Administration.
20. *Financial Times, op. cit.*, May 3, 1991.
21. A Commerce Department list of export licenses approved to Iraq, released Mar. 11, 1991. An asterisk notes: "State Department determined that no foreign policy controls applied; returned without action."
22. Approved Licenses to Iraq, *op. cit.*
23. *Washington Times*, Apr. 27, 1990; see also Jack Colhoun, "Before War, Iraq Was 'Irresistible'," *Guardian*, Mar. 13, 1991.
24. *New York Times*, Jan. 31, 1989.
25. Associated Press, Feb. 21, 1991.

26. *Wall Street Journal*, Dec. 7, 1990; see also *Wall Street Journal*, Feb. 28, 1995.

27. *Ibid.*

28. *Ibid.*

The Middle East in "Crisis"

1. ABC, *Nightline*, as quoted in *In These Times*, Aug. 29-Sept. 11, 1990.

2. David Hoffman, "White House Counts on Military Buildup to Force Saddam's Hand," *Washington Post*, Aug. 15, 1990.

3. AP, Aug. 15, 1990; R.W. Apple, Jr., "Bush Says Iraqi Aggression Threatens 'Our Way of Life'," *New York Times*, Aug. 16, 1990; Thomas L. Friedman, "U.S. Gulf Policy — Vague 'Vital Interest'," *New York Times*, Aug. 12, 1990.

4. AP, Sept. 19, 1990.

5. Steven V. Roberts, *et al.*, "Prop for U.S. Policy: Secret Saudi Funds," *New York Times*, June 21, 1987; "USA/Chad Target Gadaffi," *Africa Confidential*, Jan. 6, 1989.

6. Louis Freedberg, "Irangate's South Africa Connection," Pacific News Service, Mar. 21, 1987, *USA Today*, Oct. 22, 1986, cited by (Amsterdam) *Newsletter on the Oil Embargo Against South Africa*, Jan. 1987.

7. Reuters, Sept. 3, 1990.

8. Jacob Wirtschafter, "Arabs in Areas Put Best Face on Kuwait Crunch," *Jerusalem Post*, Aug. 23, 1990.

9. Rick Atkinson, "U.S. to Rely on Air Strikes if War Erupts," *Washington Post*, Sept. 16, 1990; John D. Morrocco, "Have Nap Offers Stand-Off Capability for B-52s in Mideast," *Aviation Week and Space Technology*, Sept. 3, 1990.

10. "U.S. Goal: Destroy Hussein's Regime," *Forward*, Aug. 31, 1990.

11. Eric Rozenman, "Arens tells Americans: Huge Sale of Arms to Arabs Upsets Balance," *Jerusalem Post*, Sept. 18, 1990.

12. Joshua Brilliant, "Arens to Seek Access to U.S. Spy Photos," *Jerusalem Post*, Sept. 16, 1990.

13. Bob Woodward, *Veil* (New York: Simon and Schuster, 1987), pp. 160-61.

14. *Israeli Foreign Affairs*, June, July and Nov. 1989.

15. Daniel Williams, "Jordan Walks a Tightrope on the Edge of the Perilous Gulf Whirlpool," *Los Angeles Times*, Sept. 27, 1990.

16. AP, Sept. 19, 1990.

17. AP, Sept. 7, 1990.

18. Bob Woodward and Rick Atkinson, "Mideast Decision: Uncertainty Over a Daunting Move," *Washington Post*, Aug. 26, 1990.

19. Michael Barone, "The end of the Vietnam Syndrome," *U.S. News and World Report*, Aug. 20, 1990.

Iraq: Disinformation and Covert Operations

1. The most comprehensive analysis is Michael Emery's "How Mr. Bush Got His War: Deceptions, Double-Standards and Disinformation," *Village Voice*, Mar. 5, 1991. Algerian Foreign Minister Sid Ahmed Ghozali charged that Iraq has been under escalating U.S. attack for two years. (Algiers Domestic Service in French, 1800 GMT, Feb. 14, 1991, FBIS-NES)

2. Michael Wines, "CIA Sidelines Its Gulf Cassandra," *New York Times*, Jan. 24, 1991, p. D22.

3. William Claiborne "Envoy Recounts Warning in July of Invasion; Kuwaitis Cut Him Off," *Washington Post*, Mar. 18, 1991, p. A26.

4. See, for example, Eric Rassi, "All the Slaughter That Money Can Buy," *Downtown* (New York), Mar. 13, 1991, p. 1.

5. Patrick E. Tyler, "Iraq Pursues Politics of Pragmatism," *Washington Post*, May 13, 1989, p. A13.
6. In Saudi Arabia, slavery was formally abolished in 1962, but the practice remains common. See Robert Lacey, *The Kingdom: Arabia and the House of Sa'ud*, (New York: Harcourt Brace, 1991).
7. Germaine Greer, "Our Allies the Slaveholders?", *New York Times*, Nov. 14, 1990, p. A29.
8. Knut Royce, "A Trail of Distortion Against Iraq," *Newsday*, Jan. 21, 1991, p. 21.
9. See Michael Emery, *op. cit*
10. *Ibid.*
11. See, for example, Susan Page and Knut Royce, "Bush Again Urges Coup To Overthrow Hussein," *Newsday*, Apr. 4, 1991.
12. Melissa Healy, "Special Forces: U.S. 'Eyes' Deep in Enemy Territory," *Los Angeles Times*, Feb. 28, 1991, p. Al.
13. Joshua Hammer, "'Special Ops': The Top Secret War," *Newsweek*, Mar. 18, 1991, p. 32.
14. See Edward S. Herman, "Smart Bombs and Dumb Bombs," *Lies Of Our Times*, Mar. 1991, p. 4. The *Philadelphia Inquirer* suggested that perhaps 60 percent of smart bombs hit their targets (Earl Lane, "Smart Bombs May Be Dumb About 40 Percent of the Time," *Philadelphia Inquirer*, Feb. 11, 1991, p. 12A).
15. The scale of Iraqi civilian casualties is the subject of intense debate as we go to press. The U.S. refuses to comment. Infant mortality, already up sharply, is projected to rise by 170,000 this year due to the demolition of Iraq's civilian infrastructure.
16. *Antiwar Briefing Week Four*, Feb. 16, 1991, p. 1, from AWB, Box 122, Jackson, MS 39205-0122.
17. Michael Evans, "How the SAS took out the Scuds... by Major," *London Times*, May 15, 1991, p. 1.
18. See Michael R. Gordon, "Desert Missions By Commandos Aided in Victory," *New York Times*, Mar. 1, 1991, p. Al.
19. All quotations from transcript, "Primetime Live," Feb. 28, 1991.
20. Michael R. Gordon, "Six Iraqi Pilots Defect and U.S. Claims a Psychological-War Gain," *New York Times*, Jan. 8, 1991, p. Al.
21. *New York Times*, Jan. 9, 1991, p. A9.
22. Barton Gellman, "U.S. Denies Iraqi Copter Defections," *Washington Post*, Jan. 11, 1991, p. A13.
23. *Ibid.*
24. Susan Sachs, "Iraqi Pilots Defect to Saudi Arabia," *Newsday*, Jan. 8, 1991, p. 7.
25. Susan Sachs, "Saudis Deny Pilot Incident," *Newsday*, Jan. 9, 1991, p. 29.
26. Michael Wines, "CIA Joins Military Move to Sap Iraqi Confidence," Jan. 19, 1991, p. 9.
27. Ellen Ray and William H. Schaap, "Minefields of Disinformation," *Lies Of Our Times*, Mar. 1991, p. 7.
28. See Geneva Conventions.
29. Hammer, *op. cit.*
30. See Ellen Ray, "The Killing Deserts," *Lies Of Our Times*, Apr. 1991.
31. The road was littered with charred bodies and scattered limbs, but few U.S. citizens saw anything of this. *CAIB* learned that salespeople at several major photo services, from which the vast majority of newspapers get their international pictures, were told by their supervisors to remove from sale all the most gruesome photos. Photos of destroyed vehicles were plentiful; photos of the human remains in those vehicles were virtually impossible to find. In the last few days of the land war, the offices of one leading photo house in New York City were crowded with researchers asking, unsuccessfully, for pictures "with bodies in them."

32. See George Lardner, Jr. and Steve Coll, "Some Iraqi POWs May Be Recruited by Saddam Foes," *Washington Post*, Mar. 12, 1991.

33. *Ibid.*

34. *Ibid.*

35. "Primetime Live," *op. cit.*

IV. END GAME: THE FUNDAMENTALISTS ASCEND

Hiroshima: Needless Slaughter, Useful Terror

1. Tim Weiner, "U.S. Spied on Its World War II Allies," *New York Times*, Aug. 11, 1993, p. 9.

2. Stewart Udall, *The Myths of August* (New York: Pantheon Books, 1994), pp. 73-79.

3. *Ibid.*, p. 73. Vice-President Truman was never informed about the bomb. After Roosevelt's death, when he assumed office, it was Secretary of State James R. Byrnes who briefed him on the project. (Henry L. Stimson and McGeorge Bundy, *On Active Service in Peace and War* [New York: Harper, 1947]). Bundy is recognized as the principal author of these Stimson memoirs.

4. Udall, *op. cit.*, p. 76.

5. Stimson, *op. cit.*, p. 629.

6. Charles L. Mee, Jr., *Meeting at Potsdam* (New York: M. Evans, 1975), p. 23.

7. *Ibid.*, pp. 235-36. See also: Hearings Before the Committee on Armed Services and the Committee on Foreign Relations (U.S. Senate), June 25, 1951, p. 3113, for reference to another peace overture message.

8. Stanley Meisler, "Unburied Treasures Lure Researchers to National Archives," *Los Angeles Times*, Jan. 9, 1995, p. 5.

9. Mee, *op. cit.*, p. 239.

10. *Ibid.*, pp. 75, 78-79; and William Manchester, *American Caesar: Douglas MacArthur 1880-1964* (Boston: Little Brown, 1978), p. 437.

11. Dwight Eisenhower, *The White House Years: Mandate for Change, 1953-1956* (New York: Doubleday, 1963), pp. 312-13.

12. In an attempt to, as Churchill said, "strangle at its birth" the infant Bolshevik state, the United States launched tens of thousands of troops and sustained 5,000 casualties.

13. Mee, *op. cit.*, p. 22.

14. The 1945 National Security Agency document containing this report was declassified in 1993 after a three year-long FOIA process by investigator Sanho Tree.

15. Mee, *op. cit.*, pp. 89 and 206; the first is from Churchill's diary; in the second, Churchill's aide is paraphrasing him.

16. Bernstein, Diplomatic History, *op. cit.*, pp. 66-8. This citation, actually written by Bundy for *On Active Service*, was deleted from that book because of pressure from State Department official George F. Kennan.

17. Mee, *op. cit.*, p. 239.

18. *Ibid.*, pp. 288-89.

Nuclear Threats and the New World

1. "Unless Stopped, Iraq Could Have A-Arms in 10 Years, Experts Say," *New York Times*, Nov. 18, 1990, p. 1.

2. "U.S. Officials Step Up Warnings to North Korea on Nuclear Arms," *New York Times*, Nov. 21, 1991.

3. Michio Kaku and Daniel Axelrod, To *Win a Nuclear War: The Pentagon's Secret War Plans* (Boston: South End Press, 1987).

4. As early as 1948, during the Berlin Crisis, President Truman authorized Operation Broiler, which included plans to drop 34 atomic bombs on 24 cities in the Soviet Union in a first strike by B-29 bombers. During the 1954 Vietnam crisis, President Eisenhower authorized Operation Vulture, which included using two to six 31-kiloton atomic bombs to vaporize Vietnamese troops at Dien Bien Phu. (Kaku and Axelrod, *op. cit.*)
5. *Newsweek*, Jan. 14, 1991.
6. Patrick F. Tyler, "U.S. Strategy Plans Call for Insuring No Rivals Develop," New York Times, Mar. 8, 1992, p. Al.
7. Barton Gellman "Pentagon Abandons Goal of Thwarting U.S. Rivals," *Washington Post* May 24, 1992, p. Al.
8. Seymour Hersh, *The Price of Power: Kissinger in the Nixon White House* (New York: Summit Books, 1983), p. 148.
9. "Bombs in the Basement," *Newsweek*, July 11, 1988, pp. 4245.
10. *Ibid.*
11. *Ibid.* Because of breakdowns, the Pakistani ultracentrifuges most likely operate at much less efficiency, perhaps producing only enough fissionable material for one to five atomic bombs per year.
12. *New York Times*, "Unless Stopped…," *op. cit.*
13. Ronald Waters, *South Africa and the Bomb* (Lexington, Mass.: Lexington Books, 1987).
14. Seymour Hersh, *The Samson Option: Israel's Nuclear Arsenal and American Foreign Policy* (New York: Random House, 1992).
15. "Revealed: The Secrets of Israel's Nuclear Arsenal," London *Sunday Times*, Oct. 5, 1986. See also Frank Barnaby, *The Invisible Bomb* (London: I.B. Tauris, 1989); *CAIB*, "Israel's Nuclear Arsenal," No. 30, Summer 1988, p. 45; and Louis Toscano, *Triple Cross* (New York: Birch Lane Press, 1990).
16. The "double flash" is the fingerprint of a nuclear detonation. Only an atomic (not a chemical) bomb can generate this rapid sequence of flashes.
17. Hersh, *op. cit.*, pp. 217-72.
18. *Ibid.*, p. 267.
19. *Ibid.*, p. 276.
20. *Newsweek*, "Bombs in the Basement…," *op. cit.*
21. "Israel's Deal with the Devil?" *Newsweek*, Nov. 6, 1989, p. 52.
22. *Newsweek*, "Bombs in the Basement…," *op. cit.*
23. "Bush's Iraqi Blunder York Times, May 14, 1992, p. A17.
24. "Building Saddam Hussein's Bomb," *New York Times Magazine*, Mar. 8, 1992, p. 30.
25. *Ibid.*
26. *Op. cit.*, n. 2.
27. *Op. cit.*, n. 3.
28. "Koreas Agree to A-Inspection by June," *New York Times*, Mar. 15, 1992, p.3
29. "North Korea to Drop First Veil," *New York Times*, May 4, 1992, p. A7.
30. T. R. Reid, "N. Korean Plutonium Plant Cited," *Washington Post*, May 17, 1992, p. A25.

Israel, Iran, the U.S. and the Bomb

1. *Yediot Ahronot*, July 30, 1993
2. Yaakov Erez and Immanuel Rozen, *Ma'ariv*, Apr. 17, 1992.
3. Shlomo Gazit, *Yediot Ahronot*, Apr. 27, 1992.
4. Way Kaspi, "Hotam," *Al Hamishmar* (Friday Supplement), May 21, 1993.
5. The inability of intelligence to predict accurately Saddam Hussein's incursion into Kuwait is often cited as one of the numerous failures of Israeli intelligence.

6. Yo'av Kaspi, *op. cit.*

7. *Ibid.*

8. *Ibid.*

9. Shlomo Aharonson, "Ha'olam Haze," *Ha'aretz,* Apr. 21, 1993; and Aluf Ben, *Ha'aretz,* Apr. 25, 1993.

10. Aluf Ben, *op. cit.*

11. *Ibid.*

12. Yo'av Kaspi, *Al Hamishmar,* Feb. 19, 1993.

13. Interview by Yom Melman, *Ha'aretz,* May 13, 1993.

14. *Ibid.*

15. Yossi Mel*man, Ha'aretz,* Mar. 12 1993.

16. Pazit Ravina, *Davar* (Friday Supplement), May 28, 1993.

17. Yo'av Kaspi, *Al Hamishmar,* Feb. 19, 1993.

18. Although Algeria is not "anti-Western" in the same way that Iran and Libya are, the present regime is hostile to Israel and supportive of the Palestinian cause. Algeria, for example hosts meetings of the Palestinian National Council including the last one in 1988. Given this alliance, the Israeli "party line" (Hasbara) seeks to persuade the West that Algeria is anti-Western.

19. Kaspi, *op. cit.*

20. *Ibid.*

21. *Ibid*

22. Lesham quoted by Kaspi, *op. cit.,* Feb. 19, 1993. This analysis was written before the World Trade Center bombing and before the Libyan "pilgrims" arrived in Jerusalem

23. Gazit, *op. cit.*

24. *Ma'ariv* is a newspaper currently owned by Ofer Nimrodi, the son of Ya'akov Nimrodi. Before the fall of the Shah, Ya'akov had been an Israeli military attaché in Tehran and was very friendly with the Shah and some of his high-ranking officials. He later was implicated in Irangate for supplying weapons to Khomeini. (*Erez,* Feb. 12, 1993.)

25. *Ha'aretz,* Apr. 17, 1992.

Index

Contributors

Philip Agee author of three books, international public speaker and out-spoken critic of the CIA, was a CIA operations officer (1957-68) in Ecuador, Uruguay, Mexico and at CIA Headquarters. His U.S. passport was revoked in 1979.

Eqbal Ahmad was Professor Emeritus of Politics and Middle East Studies at Hampshire College. He was a prolific and well-respected lecturer and writer on Middle Eastern affairs until his death in 1999.

Naseer Aruri is Chancellor Professor Emeritus of Political Science at the University of Massachusetts at Dartmouth and a former member of the Palestinian National Council. He is the author of *Occupation Israel over Palestine* and *The Obstruction of Peace: The U.S., Israel and the Palestinians.*

William Blum is the author of *Killing Hope: U.S. Military and CIA Interventions Since World War II*; *Rogue State: A Guide to the World's Only Superpower*; and *West-Bloc Dissident: A Cold War Political Memoir* (www.killinghope.org).

Karen Branan is a free-lance reporter based in Washington, D.C. She has also served as the coordinator for the Public Policy Institute of the Planned Parenthood Federation of America and has written for Front Line Research.

Noam Chomsky is Professor Emeritus of Linguistics at the Massachusetts Institute of Technology and an internationally renowned critic of U.S. foreign policy. He is the author of numerous books, most recently the best selling *9/11.*

Ramsey Clark is a former Attorney General of the United States and a practicing attorney, an outspoken critic of recent U.S. administrations, particularly their foreign policy.

Jack Colhoun is a free-lance writer in Washington, D.C. and the former Washington correspondent for the (New York) *Guardian* newsweekly. He has a Ph.D. in U.S. history, specializing in post-World War II foreign and military policy.

Steve Galster is a Washington-based writer who has done extensive research on U.S. policy toward Afghanistan. He was the Project Director for the National Security Archives Afghanistan collection and has written for numerous periodicals.

Edward S. Herman is Professor Emeritus at the Wharton School of the University of Pennsylvania and the author of numerous books and articles on U.S. foreign policy.

Jane Hunter is the author of several books and contributor to several foreign newspapers. From 1985 to 1993, she edited and published the independent monthly report *Israeli Foreign Affairs*.

Larry Jones is a freelance writer in New York. His interest in evangelical politics dates from graduate studies in religion at Columbia University during the 1980s.

Michio Kaku is Professor of Theoretical Physics at the City College of the City University of New York and co-author of *To Win a Nuclear War: The Pentagon's Secret Plans* and numerous scientific works. He has hosted a weekly radio program on science for more than 10 years.

Anthony L. Kimery is managing editor of *Sources*, the Security Intelligence News Service. He has worked at the American Banker Newsletters, specializing in banking regulations and supervision and was the Washington Bureau Chief of *Money Laundering Alert*. His investigative work has appeared in many newspapers and magazines.

Fred Landis was a consultant to the Church Committee that investigated U.S. intelligence abuses in the 1970s. He was also in Chile during the Allende Administration and has written extensively on the CIA destabilization of that government and on propaganda and psycho-logical operations.

Clarence Lusane is a professor at American University's School of International Service, specializing in African and Caribbean politics and Black political theory. He is the author of *Race in the Global Era* and numerous other books and articles.

Ellen Ray is a journalist and film maker, president of the Institute for Media Analysis, Inc. and a cofounder of *CovertAction*.

William H. Schaap is an attorney in New York City, a journalist and a cofounder of *CovertAction*.

Israel Shahak was Emeritus Professor of Chemistry at the Hebrew University in Jerusalem until his death in 2001. A Holocaust survivor, he was one of the most articulate and erudite analysts and critics of Israeli foreign policy, author of numerous books and articles on the subject.

Christopher Simpson is professor in the School of Communications at American University and author *of Blowback, The Splendid Blond Beast, Science of Coercion and National Security Directives of the Reagan and Bush Administrations* from which his article in this book was adapted.

Louis Wolf is an investigative journalist and researcher in Washington, D.C., one of the co-founders of *CovertAction* and its current publisher.

Also from Ocean Press

BIOTERROR
Manufacturing Wars The American Way
Edited by Ellen Ray and William H. Schaap
While Washington contemplates "first strikes" against those nations unilaterally identified as the "Axis of Evil" and said to be stockpiling weapons of mass destruction, this controversial, well-documented book proves that the United States itself has been a notorious practitioner of chemical and biological warfare.
ISBN 1-876175-64-8

LATIN AMERICA
From Colonization to Globalization
By Noam Chomsky
An indispensable book for those interested in Latin America and the politics and history of the region.
ISBN 1-876175-13-3

CHILE: THE OTHER SEPTEMBER 11
An Anthology of Reflections on the 1973 Coup in Chile
Edited by Pilar Aguilera and Ricardo Fredes
Amidst the flood of books on 9/11, the editors remind us that September 11 is the anniversary of another horrendous event — General Pinochet's coup in 1973 against the democratically elected government of President Salvador Allende. Includes articles, essays, speeches and poems by Ariel Dorfman, Joan Jara, Salvador Allende, Pablo Neruda, Beatriz Allende, Víctor Jara and Fidel Castro.
ISBN 1-876175-50-8

DEADLY DECEITS
My 25 Years in the CIA
By Ralph McGehee
Deadly Deceits is a classic account of the deeds and deceptions of the CIA by one of the Agency's most prized recruits. Ralph McGehee spent 25 years in the CIA, from 1952–1977. He entered a super-patriot at the height of the Cold War; he left disillusioned and shattered by what he had seen and learned, especially in Vietnam where he saw a tragic and sense- less war develop.
ISBN 1-876175-19-2